"All descriptions agree that hell's half acre formed an exceedingly lively . . . portion of the city."

—B. B. Paddock, 1922

NUMBER 9, CHISHOLM TRAIL SERIES

HELL'S HALF ACRE

The Life and Legend of a Red-Light District

Richard F. Selcer

Fort Worth: Texas Christian University Press

Second Printing

10 9 8 7 6 5 4 3

Library of Congress Cataloging-in-Publication Data

Selcer, Richard F.
Hell's half acre: life and legend of a red-light district / by Richard F. Selcer.
p. cm.—(Chisholm Trail series: no. 9)
Includes bibliographical references and index.
ISBN 0-87565-086-4: $24.95.—ISBN 0-87565-088-0 (pbk.): $15.95
1. Fort Worth (Tex.)—History. 2. Fort Worth (Tex.)—Social conditions. 3. Prostitution—Texas—Fort Worth—History. 4. Violence—Texas—Fort Worth—History. I. Title. II. Series.
F394.F7S45 1991
976.4'5315—dc20 91-6380
CIP

Cover illustration and map on pg. x–xi are by James R. Spurlock.

Contents

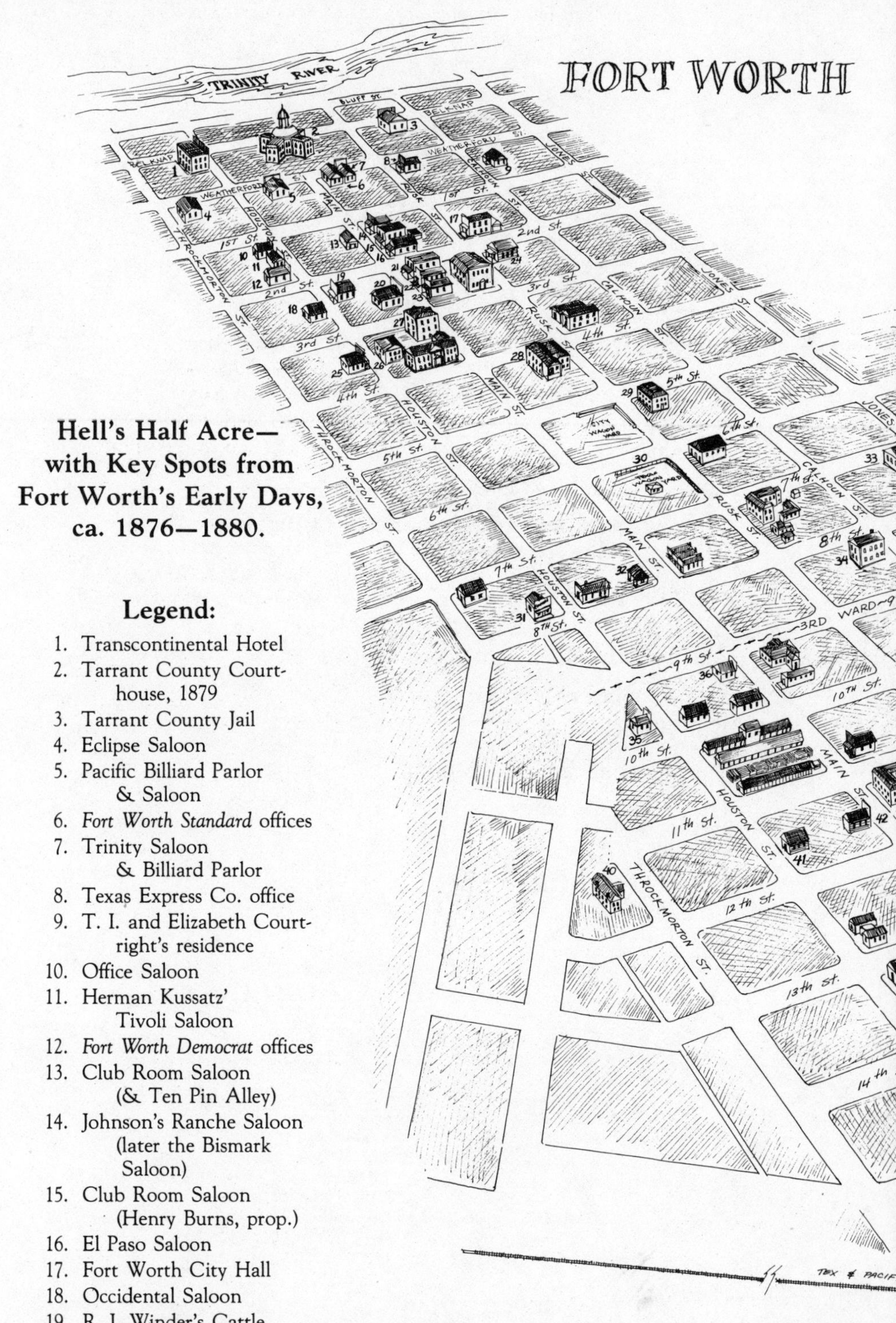

Hell's Half Acre—with Key Spots from Fort Worth's Early Days, ca. 1876–1880.

Legend:

1. Transcontinental Hotel
2. Tarrant County Courthouse, 1879
3. Tarrant County Jail
4. Eclipse Saloon
5. Pacific Billiard Parlor & Saloon
6. *Fort Worth Standard* offices
7. Trinity Saloon & Billiard Parlor
8. Texas Express Co. office
9. T. I. and Elizabeth Courtright's residence
10. Office Saloon
11. Herman Kussatz' Tivoli Saloon
12. *Fort Worth Democrat* offices
13. Club Room Saloon (& Ten Pin Alley)
14. Johnson's Ranche Saloon (later the Bismark Saloon)
15. Club Room Saloon (Henry Burns, prop.)
16. El Paso Saloon
17. Fort Worth City Hall
18. Occidental Saloon
19. R. J. Winder's Cattle Exchange Saloon

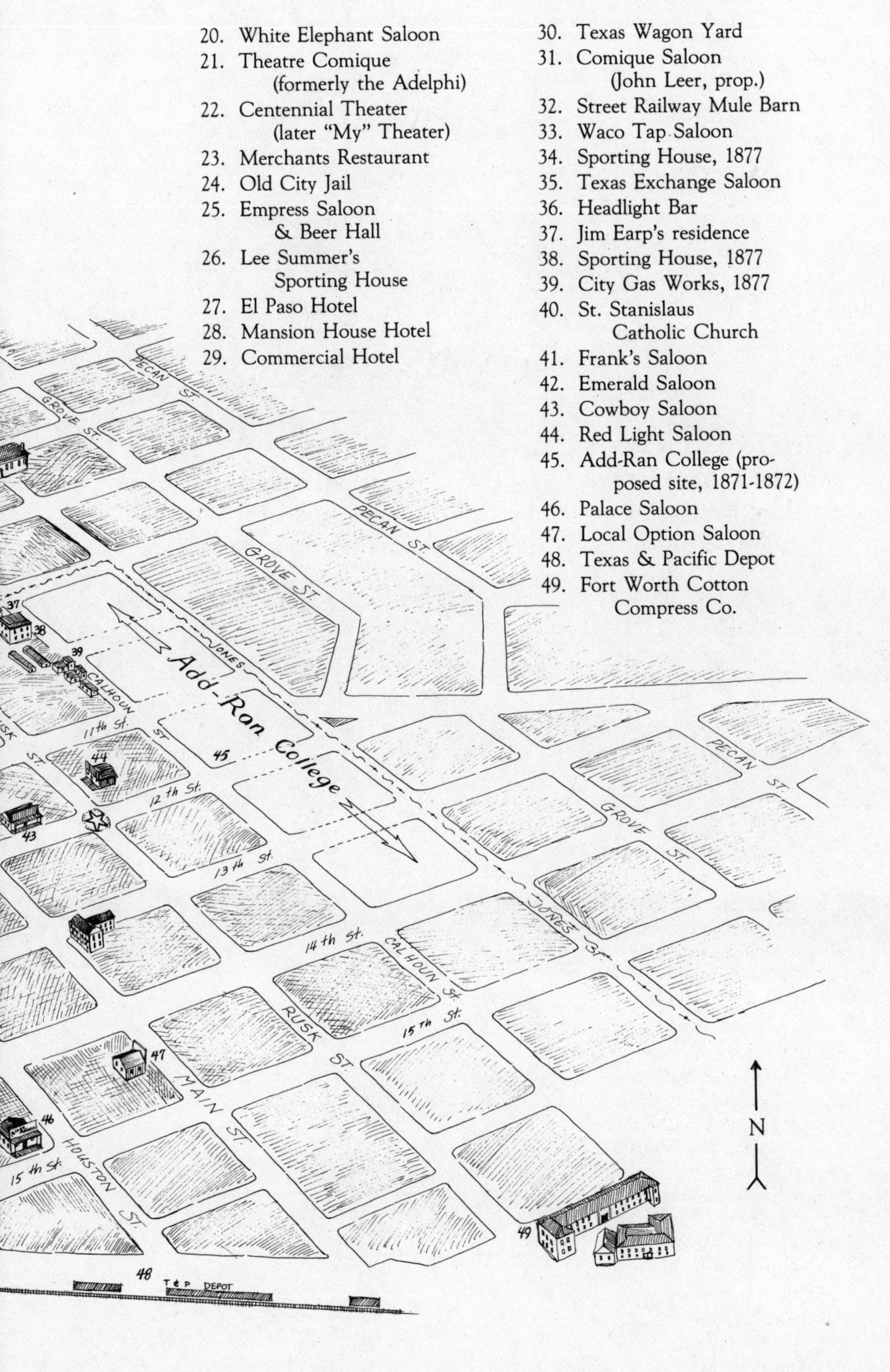
20. White Elephant Saloon
21. Theatre Comique (formerly the Adelphi)
22. Centennial Theater (later "My" Theater)
23. Merchants Restaurant
24. Old City Jail
25. Empress Saloon & Beer Hall
26. Lee Summer's Sporting House
27. El Paso Hotel
28. Mansion House Hotel
29. Commercial Hotel
30. Texas Wagon Yard
31. Comique Saloon (John Leer, prop.)
32. Street Railway Mule Barn
33. Waco Tap Saloon
34. Sporting House, 1877
35. Texas Exchange Saloon
36. Headlight Bar
37. Jim Earp's residence
38. Sporting House, 1877
39. City Gas Works, 1877
40. St. Stanislaus Catholic Church
41. Frank's Saloon
42. Emerald Saloon
43. Cowboy Saloon
44. Red Light Saloon
45. Add-Ran College (proposed site, 1871-1872)
46. Palace Saloon
47. Local Option Saloon
48. Texas & Pacific Depot
49. Fort Worth Cotton Compress Co.
PECAN ST.
GROVE ST.
JONES ST.
CALHOUN ST.
RUSK ST.
MAIN ST.
HOUSTON ST.
11th St.
12th St.
13th St.
14th St.
15th St.
Add-Ran College
T&P DEPOT
N

To Julia, Alice, and Molly, each of whom helped and encouraged me
in different ways and at different times, and especially
to my mother, who has labored over this project from the beginning.

Introduction

IN 1915 THE DISTINGUISHED CHICAGO SOCIOLOGIST Robert Park declared that it was in the very nature of urbanization for a city to develop vice districts, or what he called "moral regions." He explained that "A moral region is not necessarily a place of abode. It may be a mere rendezvous, a place of resort."[1] There was nothing particularly shocking in this observation, but Park went far beyond mere observation by urging that society "accept these moral regions and the more or less eccentric . . . people who inhabit them . . . as part of the normal life of a city." While this viewpoint was shocking to progressive-minded Americans with their lingering Victorian sensibilities, it was nothing new on the frontier where vice districts had been an accepted part of the local scene for decades. A certain amount of prostitution, drunkenness, gambling and fighting was acceptable, even desirable in a growing frontier town. But how much? Every town drew the line at a different place, some using more tolerant standards than others.

Fort Worth, like most other western towns built on the cattle trade, had to wrestle with this problem in its early days. What kind of town did the citizens want? How much of a trade-off were they willing to accept between prosperity and morality? How much were they willing to pay for law enforcement? The answers to these questions did not come easily. City fathers had to weigh their moral and legal responsibilities against their desire to see the struggling settlement grow and prosper. Inevitably, some were also guided by baser motives that had nothing to do with civic-mindedness. It is easy now to condemn their decisions. Modern standards of law and order a century after the frontier closed are considerably higher.

Law and order in early Fort Worth were conspicuously absent if we use Hell's Half Acre as a reference point. Whenever there was a violent crime, a suicide or a fight, it usually took place in the Acre, or at least that is the way it was remembered in the public consciousness. The truth, of course, is easy to verify — all one has to do is check addresses of crime scenes to see if the acts took place within the bounds of the Acre. A remarkable number, it turns out, did.

Hell's Half Acre was definitely a real place on the map, but separating the myth from the reality is difficult. What is "known" today about the district is about two-thirds myth, including many oft-repeated stories about its location, the number of violent crimes that took place there, when it began and when it was finally "shut down." In 1990, for example, on the centennial anniversary of the founding of the Fort Worth Young Men's Christian Association, a spokesman for the organization told a reporter that YMCA founders saw the town as "overrun with a bad influence" when they began their mission here. He singled out "the proliferation of saloons and that sort of thing in Hell's Half Acre *in the stockyards* [emphasis added].[2] The truth of the matter is that the Acre was nowhere near the stockyards; they were on opposite ends of town. But the popular perception of Hell's Half Acre is rooted in mythology, not fact. The precise location of the Acre is less important than what it represented. The same applies to when it began. Ask a present-day Fort Worther when it began and the answers range from "before the Civil War" to "sometime during the Depression." The problem with getting to the historic roots is that the historical viewpoint languishes while the mythology is self-perpetuating. Over the years a succession of journalists, amateur historians and local characters have all contributed to the mythology. Their contributions have filled in and smoothed over the gaps in the historic record until it has become almost impossible to tell where the historic record stops and the mythology begins.

Death has claimed everyone who knew Hell's Half Acre in its glory days of the late nineteenth century, and their descendants are hardly flattered by being asked about Granddaddy's (or Grandma's) connections to Fort Worth's tenderloin. To suggest that the dearly departed might have been a regular visitor to the Acre's hot spots will earn the researcher a quick good-bye every time. The response is only slightly less frustrating when dealing with living memory. Anyone old enough to have first-hand knowledge of events around World War I (when the Acre was still going strong) shows one of two reactions when asked to describe the area. They either disclaim any knowledge of it because "nice people" did not know about such places, or they are among the folks who "never had any dealings there myself but I heard stories about it. . . ." When pressed for details they fall back on the familiar store of anecdotes about cowboys riding their horses right through saloon doors, shooting out streetlights and accosting decent ladies on public streets. These hand-me-down stories and twice-told tales are the stuff of folklore, and while folklore is fascinating, the historian must always regard such tales with healthy skepticism and use them with caution.

In the absence of living witnesses we would expect to turn next to primary-source literature in the form of diaries, reminiscences, correspondence and perhaps an autobiography or two. But such sources are either non-existent or locked away among forgotten family papers with the former being the more likely case. For the most part the cowboys, railroad hands, tinhorns and prostitutes who came through the Acre were neither articulate nor literary-minded enough to chronicle their adventures. They simply left no record of their daily lives. The prize find is the occasional, though extremely rare, first-person account which survives in print, usually in the form of newspaper stories, sometimes oral history interviews such as those to be found in the "Federal Writers Project" sponsored by the WPA in the 1930s.

Similar problems arise from other primary sources: public documents, newspaper accounts, photographs and artistic representations. Public documents, including tax records, property rolls, criminal court dockets, city directories, census records, birth and death certificates, marriage records, and the like are scanty for the frontier period. Fire, poor record keeping and the ravages of time have all done their part to pull a curtain across the past. Fortunately, the complete minutes of the Fort Worth City Council from 1873 onward exist on both microfilm and in original form. They were an invaluable source for this study, as were the logs of city ordinances beginning with No. 1 in 1873 and extending into the hundreds by the end of the century. (Handling the originals and reading the pioneer city fathers' handwriting was almost a mystical experience for this researcher.) The records of the county courts from this time, which might likewise have provided crucial information, exist only in fragmentary form, yet they add detail to an emerging picture. What they do not tell only tantalizes the historian and researcher.

There are few artistic and photographic representations as well. Nineteenth-century Victorian moral standards generally prohibited respectable artists and photographers from portraying the underside of society. The Acre was not a proper "artistic" subject. The most famous photograph connected with the Acre is the well-known studio portrait of the Wild Bunch, and it hardly gives a taste of life on the streets. Instead, it looks more like a Hollywood movie still, which is how it has come to be best known. The first photographs clearly identified as the Acre were made in 1906 by a social reformer hoping to arouse public indignation against the immoral conditions to be found there. Even his pictures conformed to late Victorian tastes, showing only stark exteriors of buildings — no people.

What we are left with are newspaper accounts, a fascinating but often distorted and one-sided view of contemporary life. The problems, attitudes, family backgrounds and ordinary lives of people in the Acre did not make news, however, so one has to read between the lines to fill in the picture. When crime and vice were recorded in the local papers, the reporting was lurid and sensational. News reporting, then as now, focused almost obsessively on the sensational, the violent and the sordid, and reporters in that day were even less bound by the strictures of professional journalism than are today's supermarket-tabloid writers. The late nineteenth century was the heyday of yellow journalism. What mattered was the story, not the facts. The result is a chronicle that is unashamedly biased but remarkably candid and colorful. Printed stories speak of "colored viragos," "black bucks," and even, on occasion, "niggers," while women are portrayed as poor creatures, callously taken advantage of by men, their purity ruined, leaving them to face a life of sin and degradation, or loneliness and vain regret. These were the usual stereotypes. Tinhorn gamblers and con men were regularly named, tried and even convicted in the newspapers for their crimes. Criminals had colorful names and their deeds had a dash of roguishness that often invited sympathy rather than outrage. Such was newspaper reporting in the glory days of the Wild West. And the most remarkable fact may be that not one libel suit was ever filed in Fort Worth by the subjects of such stories.

As time passed, attitudes changed. Fort Worth's chief chronicler in the early days was a newsman — Buckley B. Paddock, editor, lawyer, mayor and self-appointed civic booster — and the pages of his papers, the *Democrat* and the *Gazette,* are a rich source of information on local events, as are several volumes of history published toward the end of his lifetime. Ironically, while editor Paddock regularly lambasted the Acre in the pages of his papers, he had considerably fonder memories of Fort Worth's wild and woolly days when he sat down to write his historical account. "Oh! The fun we had," he recalled in *Early Days in Fort Worth.*[3] It seems that even the veteran newsman was not immune to the mythology that had grown up around the Acre.

Later, Hell's Half Acre was considered such a blot on the city's past that no city leader liked to even talk about it. One Fort Worther who was involved in the newspaper business for years says that Amon Carter, founder and owner of the *Fort Worth Star-Telegram*, maintained a long-time policy that practically banned the name "Hell's Half Acre" from the pages of his paper because, like the descriptive term "West Texas desert," it was bad for the city's image.

At best, therefore, an incomplete picture of the Acre can be constructed from original local sources. The historian must fill in the rest of the picture using his knowledge of the times, a little scholarly imagination and the more complete accounts of similar red-light districts in cities like Denver, New Orleans, San Francisco and Dodge City. The red-light districts in all these cities have been chronicled in much greater detail thanks to an abundance of first-hand sources to draw upon. Their stories in many ways parallel Fort Worth's and can therefore be used to fill in some of the gaps in the local picture. For instance, the system of "fees and fines" that supported local government in Fort Worth for years and guaranteed a tolerant official attitude toward vice operators was virtually the same all over the West. The explanation of how fees and fines worked in the Kansas cow towns proved applicable to Fort Worth and filled in an important part of the puzzle for which there were no contemporary explanations in Fort Worth literature.

Finally, the historian must hope that a book like this will bring additional diaries, correspondence and photograph albums out of fam-

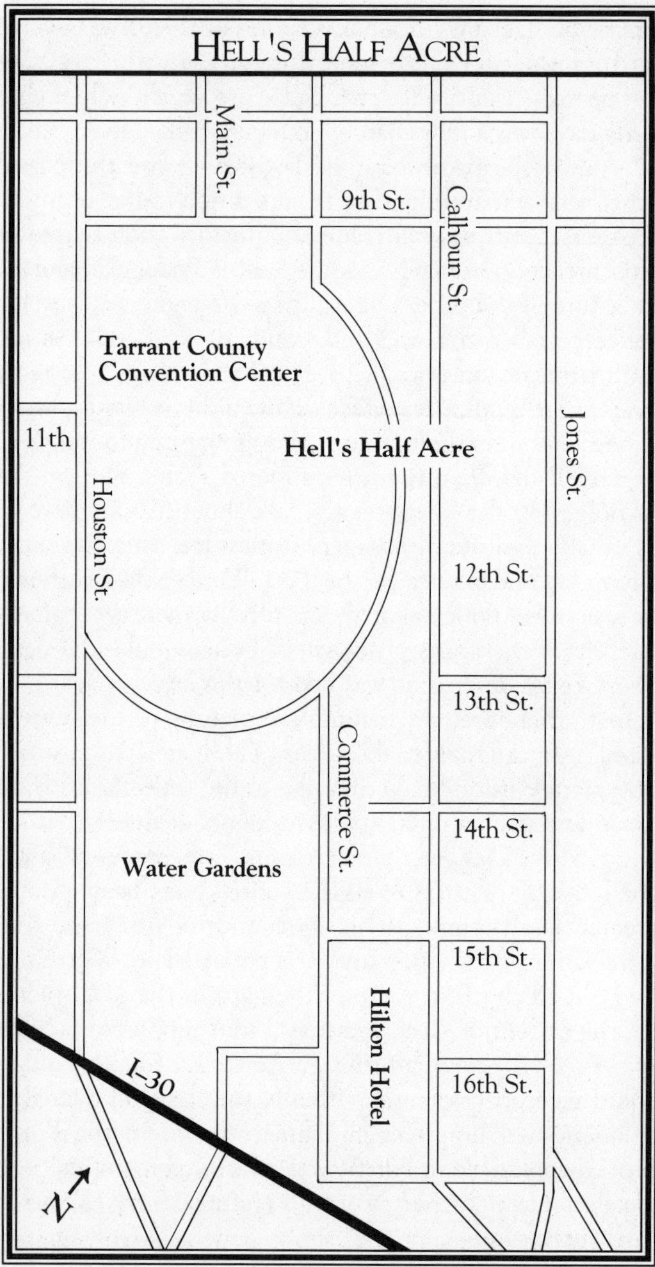

What was once Hell's Half Acre is now the eminently respectable Tarrant County Convention Center: a new image but the land is still devoted to the entertainment dollar (*Fort Worth Star-Telegram*).

ily trunks for the next edition. Surely, there are more first-hand accounts of the old days out there somewhere than what we have now. They are waiting like the legendary Lost Dutchman gold mine for some historical prospector to stumble across them.

Was all the digging worth it? Most certainly. Four important historical points became clear in the course of this research. First, the permanent residents of the district were primarily black by the end of the nineteenth century. Hell's Half Acre was their neighborhood for better or for worse, although whites might come and go as businessmen, policemen and customers. Whether the district was ever lily-white is a matter of some doubt. Second, the Acre was never as wild and woolly as its reputation or legend would have us believe. Many people lived out their lives there without getting shot, stabbed or mugged. Third, the chief method of dying in the Acre was suicide, and the chief victims were not cold-blooded killers but lonely, down-and-out prostitutes. Finally, the Acre was never formally demarcated as a red-light district. No signs read: "Caution, you are entering Hell's Half Acre. Proceed at your own risk." The boundaries of the Acre always existed more in the minds of Fort Worth citizens than on any map or city plat. Every vice establishment on the south end of town (the "Acre") had its counterpart in some other portion of the city, but public attention was always on the Acre.

These facts begin to put a different light on the Acre. In the new light it does not look any better, but it is more believable and has more to say to us today. "Crime," as one authority has said, "is a subject which helps illuminate the broader history of past societies."[4] Hell's Half Acre is an important part of Fort Worth's past that needs illuminating.

• •

Many friends helped with this book. Ruby Schmidt, past president of the Tarrant County Historical Society, graciously allowed me to rifle through her files and camp out for long periods on her living room floor when I first started. Brian Perkins, owner of Barber's Book Store, always said he wanted to "give back something to Fort Worth" for all the years it has supported him, and his involvement at the beginning of the project is what got it off dead center. Along the way he directed interesting books and people my way that helped tell the story. With this book he is giving something back to Fort Worth.

Mack Williams, who may be Fort Worth's greatest collector and purveyor of old-time stories, shared his files unselfishly. Don Worcester, of Texas Christian University, gave this project a kick start when it badly needed one. Judy Alter, director of TCU Press, along with her staff took the manuscript when it was an unwanted orphan and let me have more freedom than any first-time author has a right to expect. And Bill Morris, a.k.a. Bill Day, whose musical and historical interests and unflagging enthusiasm were a late source of inspiration, got caught up in the excitement of the chase and was inspired to write "The Ballad of Hell's Half Acre."

Thank you all.

ONE

Cowboy Capers or "Dress and Delight Days"

CRIME AND VICE IN EARLY FORT WORTH WERE VIRTUally synonymous with Hell's Half Acre. The night of April 9, 1877, represents a typical example. The cattle season had not really gotten underway, so there were few cowboys on the street and things were a little slow in the popular night spots. But homesteaders, section hands and drummers were looking for action. At the Blue Light Saloon and Dance House on Rusk Street, the girls leaned up against the bar, sharing a drink with anyone who was buying. The man at the piano played absently, wishing the cowboys would hit town so things would pick up.

Then Ben Tutt walked in. A small-time gambler, more often minnow than shark when he sat down at the table, Ben had a sour look on his face and more than a few drinks under his belt this night. Tutt made a beeline for the bar and demanded that the bartender set up drinks on the house. Startled, the bartender looked warily at the obviously drunk and agitated gambler and decided not to argue. He poured a shot of the cheap stuff, and Tutt downed it in one swallow.

Without another word, the gambler reached for his six-shooter and let fly three rounds in the general direction of the bartender, who prudently ducked behind the bar. The few patrons in the saloon dived for cover. Having made his point, Tutt backed unsteadily out the swinging doors, keeping the room covered with his gun. Outside, he fired three more shots into the saloon, grazing the bartender with one. Then he hotfooted it down the street.

Before the echoes of the second volley had died, the bartender grabbed his own pistol from under the bar and fired several shots out the door. They all missed. Folks inside rushed to the door to see which way Tutt went, but he had already disappeared. Figuring that the excitement was over, they went back to their dancing and drinking, but the pace had definitely picked up a little.

Someone sent for the town marshal who listened to the story, then took out after Tutt. Later that evening, the object of the manhunt turned himself in, but nobody filed charges, so he was released with only a stern warning from the lawman.

That was not the end of the story, however. On Sunday, April 15, Ben Tutt was again the talk of the town. It seems he was in the Theater Comique watching the girlie show when he began fooling around with his six-shooter, probably trying to impress the girls. He didn't make much of an impression, however, when he shot himself in the hand.

Tutt was hustled over to Doc Burts, who took the bullet out with the skill of one who had treated more than a few gunshot wounds in his day. A few days later, the *Fort Worth Daily Democrat* reported that Tutt was "doing well." He'd be dealing cards again soon.[1]

• •

Fort Worth in the late nineteenth century was no different than dozens of other western towns built on cattle and railroads. They all had their Ben Tutts and Blue Light Saloons and Theater Comiques. In fact, every frontier community — from Deadwood to Denver and San Francisco to San Antonio — had its own red-light district. They were as ubiquitous in the West as "boot hills" but much more fun and profitable for everyone involved. In Texas the chief rivals to Fort Worth for "Sin Capital of the State" were Austin, San Antonio, El Paso and Galveston — in all, two cattle towns, a railroad town and a seaport. Austin had an unfair advantage because, some said, politics are the worst sin of all and that was the main business in Austin. Dallas, some Fort Worthers were proud to point out, was not even in the running.[2]

In the typical red-light district, prostitution went hand-in-hand with gambling, drinking and general hell-raising. One just naturally led to another. The amount of sinning and hell-raising that went on in these districts largely explains a curious sameness in the names of the most notorious examples. From Devil's Addition in Abilene to Hell's Half Acre in Fort Worth, most paid homage to Satan, the devil or hell somewhere in their names. Neither creative originality nor any desire to come up with mellifluous-sounding monikers entered into the picture; nor did anyone ever hold a contest to "Name that red-light district." Instead, the same names appear again and again in the local histories of western towns. San Antonio called its red-light district "Hell's Half Acre"; so did Tascosa, Texas, and Perry, Oklahoma. Even Dallas, only thirty miles away, had a smaller, less notorious district that went under the same name as Fort Worth's.[3] Hell's Half Acre was such a common name on the frontier, it acquired an almost generic status. A cowboy could ride into practically any trail town and ask the first citizen he met, "Where's the Acre?" and the locals would know exactly what he was talking about.[4]

Several theories can be advanced to explain the origin of the name Hell's Half Acre. One of the numberless mining camps in California during the 1849 gold rush was named Hell's Half Acre. Like so many of those camps built out of canvas and false hopes, it soon disappeared when the local claims played out, and no record of Hell's Half Acre, California, exists today. The earliest known use of the name in Texas was also well before the Civil War when the tiny community of Webberville, near Austin, was known as "Hell's Half Acre" because of its notorious lawlessness and immorality.[5] But the name really came into vogue in trail towns after the Civil War. Texans may have brought it back with them from the bloody battlefield of Stones River in Tennessee where it was applied to a different type of hellhole for a few brief hours.[6]

In Texas and Kansas a number of such red-light districts sprang up after the Civil War to serve cowboys who traveled up and down the trails between cow towns. Many, like Abilene, scarcely existed before the cattle boom era, while others, like Fort Worth, were small villages at a crossroads or a river crossing. All of that changed after 1866 when the first successful cattle drive traveled up the Chisholm Trail from south Texas to Kansas.[7] The vast unclaimed herds of longhorns in south Texas and the highly profitable beef market in the East made cattle driving the most lucrative business on the frontier. As one historian expressed it: "No event since San Jacinto . . . meant as much to Texas as the cattle drives."[8]

Fort Worth's location on the Trinity River, on a direct line between San Antonio and the Indian Territory, placed it in a unique position, both economically and geographically, to cash in on the cattle boom. It was the last major stop between the broad, unfenced ranges to the south and the rail centers of the Great Plains. The journey north took up to two months, and even under the best of conditions, it was six weeks of eating dust, living in the saddle, and keeping one eye open for hostile Indians and the other for potential stampedes. Fort Worth was also the first rest stop for thirsty and lonely cowboys after they left the Indian Territory on the return trip.

The first herd of cattle moved through Fort Worth in 1866, when the town consisted of one dusty street and a handful of one-story, wooden shanties on the site of the old military post for which it was named. In the next eighteen years, during the height of the cattle-driving era, three and a half million beeves were trailed northward, including more than 600,000 in the peak year of 1871. But the best news for places like Fort Worth, San Antonio and Abilene was that these herds required a cowboy escort, which some authorities estimate numbered as many as 35,000 over the course of two and a half decades.[9] Although a cowboy might earn only $30 a month, he was quite likely to spend the entire amount on one night's fun in town. Multiplied by the thousands of drovers who might pass through a major cow town during a season, this translated into big profits for local businesses.

To the cowboy, towns like Fort Worth meant the same as shore leave for the sailor — money in his pocket and plenty of opportunity to spend it. He tended to measure a town by two simple criteria: the pleasures it offered and how well he was treated by the local constabulary. Cowboys were not interested in church socials, bingo parties or shopping sprees when they hit town. Their needs were more basic: a bath and a haircut, then a drink, fun and female companionship. They found all these in Fort Worth, and dubbed it "the Paris of the Plains." Excitement, like beauty, is in the eye of the beholder. The semi-annual visits of cowboys to Fort Worth were occasions to "light up" and take in the city sights. The drovers called these times "dress and delight days."[10]

How and when Fort Worth's district acquired the name Hell's Half Acre is impossible to determine. The name must have been in common currency by 1881, however, when the *Fort Worth Democrat* described the district as lying "midway between the [courthouse] square and the [Texas & Pacific] depot," and commented on how rapidly it was growing.[11] This reference in the *Democrat* is the first known use of the name in public print. The use of the full name rather than the abbreviated form, "the Acre," suggests that the designation was still fairly new. The fact that the writer felt obliged to describe the location for his readers also supports this conclusion.

In most cow towns the "Acre" was not hard to find even without directions. It usually was located on the end of town that the cowboys first entered. This was true of Fort Worth. Coming into town by way of the Chisholm Trail, herds entered from the south and went north on what is now Commerce Street. For the first few years the street did not even have a name; it was considered more an extension of the trail than a city street proper. Later, as businesses grew up along either side of this thoroughfare, it was named Rusk Street after one of the heroes of the Texas Revolution.[12]

Once the cattle were through town and across the Trinity River north of the bluff, the trail drivers made camp and then rode back into Fort Worth for a little fun before making the long drive through Indian Territory to the Kansas railhead. They rode hurriedly past the nice homes on the bluff overlooking the river and past the courthouse square with its offices and outfitting stores. They were only interested in the saloons, cat houses and gaming tables — places either remembered from earlier visits or described in detail around the evening campfire on the long journey from South Texas. The drovers did not get off their horses until they came to one of these "comfort stations." The hour didn't matter; it was hell-raising time.

Throughout the 1870s, Hell's Half Acre hardly had an exclusive license on local vice, despite its later legendary status. The truth is, vice was not concentrated in any one section of the city yet. Rather, saloons, pool parlors, dance halls, theaters and gambling dens were scattered all over on every major street and on both ends of town. There were as yet no boundaries between residential and commercial, nor rich and poor, nor moral and immoral neighborhoods. A liquored-up cowboy, a tinhorn gambler, or a dance-hall floozie out for a stroll would have felt comfortable in any part of town. Such unsavory characters would hardly have drawn a second glance on any of Fort Worth's streets. The city was a jumble of people living together in a frontier town that had hardly more plan to it than if a giant hand had dropped a set of building blocks on the ground. To be sure, streets

Fanciful picture of "Cowboys Capturing a Texas Town" (detail) as a *Leslie's Illustrated Newspaper* artist envisioned it in 1882. According to *Leslie's*, cowboy joy parties were "a common diversion in the early '80s," although most trail and rail towns like Fort Worth had long since outgrown such shenanigans (courtesy Library of Congress, Washington, D.C.)

were laid out nice and neat, but their dimensions and sharp angles looked much better on official maps than they did in reality. Fort Worth was not even big enough to rate a city directory before 1877. Prior to that time, everyone knew everyone by name, and there were simply not enough businesses to make the job of putting out a directory anything more than a pretentious waste of time and money. Things were so quiet in those days that a visitor once reported seeing a panther asleep in the middle of Main Street, and before the end of the decade a dozing, twelve-foot alligator was pulled out of the Trinity River near the city.[13] It would be another decade before all the rough edges were smoothed off, and vestiges of this wide-open, boom-town atmosphere would linger long after that. During all those years, Fort Worth remained pretty much a "hiyu" community.

In the 1870s, the town and its nascent red-light district grew apace, their growth marked by the successive creation of new numbered streets — Fifth, Sixth, Seventh, and so on, down to Fourteenth Street and finally to the railroad reservation, which marked the southern boundary of the city by the end of the decade. Many of these streets were quickly populated by characters who believed that the farther they were from the courthouse and city hall, the better off they were. They had no interest in contributing to the growth of a decent city though they did so unwittingly.

In the absence of photographs, city maps and detailed descriptions, one has to use a little imagination today to visualize how the Acre looked in the 1870s. The casual visitor would not have noticed much difference between uptown and downtown judging by the style and construction of those early buildings. Most were one-story, wooden-frame structures made of unseasoned yellow pine and held together with a few nails. Some had false fronts to make them look grander than they really were. Others leaned at crazy angles because they had no foundations. Gray was the dominant color scheme as rain and sun took their inevitable toll on the unpainted lumber. Public buildings had the classic hitching post out front; a few also had boardwalks, although there was no uniformity in height or width. Most folks walked in the streets, keeping an eye out for horse and wagon traffic, not to mention other surprises beneath their feet. Interspersed among the public buildings were private homes, boarding houses and numerous outbuildings.

All Fort Worth in the 1870s reflected the rapid evolution of frontier architecture; wooden-frame buildings stood beside simple log structures dating from the first building boom. More than a few tents dotted the landscape, reflecting both the population boom and the chronic shortage of lumber in most frontier villages. In 1877 the first brick buildings began to go up, beginning with the El Paso Hotel, the city's first three-story structure and genuine first-class hotel. The El Paso boasted eighty rooms, each with solid walnut furniture and Brussels carpet.[14] The rest of the city's buildings fell far short of such lofty standards, and in 1879 the city council ordered all ramshackle buildings torn down, a directive that covered any "structure liable to fall down and injure persons or property."[15] Paved streets and a metropolitan skyline were visions of the future.

The buildings were not crowded together cheek-to-jowl like on a Hollywood set, and fences were a rarity because they cost money and were unnecessary in a town that still considered itself "wide-open." Only much later would come paved streets, multi-storied buildings, continuous sidewalks and fenced lots. The impression one gets from comparing Fort Worth with photographs and descriptions of other cow towns is that all western cow towns of a couple of thousand people looked pretty much alike, just like all modern metropolises of several hundred thousand do today.

In Hell's Half Acre, the cracker-box house and the one-story, wooden shanty remained the principal form of architecture almost to the end of the century. Residential dwellings continued to outnumber businesses for many years, in the form of "shotgun shacks," tenements and boarding houses. The big landmarks on the south end of town for years were not the saloons, theaters, and dance halls of legendary fame, but Battle's Cotton Yard at Fourteenth and Main, the Fort Worth Gas Works at Tenth and Rusk, and Elliott and Roe's Lumber Yard between Tenth and Eleventh on Main.

Contributing to the feeling of openness were block-sized areas designated as lumber yards, coal yards, cotton yards and stockyards, reminders that Fort Worth was still very much a frontier community and collecting point. Other open areas were the public square on the north end of town, and several wagonyards scattered about the town. In the days before automobiles and parking lots, wagonyards were an absolute necessity. Anybody who had to travel more than ten miles to get into town probably stayed overnight and made the return trip the next day.[16] They needed some place to park their wagons

Hugh Dugan's Wagon Yard about 1880—one of several early-day "parking lots" for visitors to Fort Worth. Dugan's was located in the 200 block of West Weatherford Street, convenient to merchants on the north end of town. At that time, this particular yard was described as "a thriving business enterprise" (courtesy Fort Worth Public Library and Amon Carter Museum, Fort Worth).

and corral their horses while they were in town. Wagonyards filled that need. The Texas Wagon Yard, between Seventh and Eighth on Main, and the City Wagon Yard, between Fifth and Sixth on Rusk, served businesses on the north end of town. Another large yard between Tenth and Eleventh on Throckmorton was ideally situated to serve those with business in the Acre. Eventually, as land values went up and developers filled in the empty spaces, almost all the wagonyards would be converted to more profitable use and they would disappear from the scene and from memory.

At first there was only one major street going uptown — Main Street, an eighty-foot-wide disaster most of the time. Dusty in the summer, it turned into a mud track when the fall and winter rains came. The slightest sprinkle was sufficient to produce an impassable mire of black, waxy mud that clung to everything as if it possessed a will of its own. After a heavy rain it was customary to see wagons bogged down in the middle of Main Street, creating the forerunner of the modern urban traffic jam. One man recalled some seventy years later: "My most vivid impression was the muddy streets when I saw Fort Worth for the first time in 1878."[17] His recollections were probably shared by many visitors in those years.

Local residents were similarly disgusted by the muck and mire that passed for thoroughfares. B. B. Paddock took his fellow citizens to task on the front page of his newspaper in 1877 for the deplorable state of their streets. "Some people dam up water, and others dump gravel and refuse. Ladies are seen with gaiters, stockings, and skirts bedraggled with muck from the puddles."[18] When the weather dried out, the situation did not improve much; the wagon tracks turned to deep ruts and a haze of dust constantly filled the air. Street sprinkling in the summer alleviated the problem somewhat.

During the trail driving season, all traffic stepped aside for the cattle herds. Drovers knew to keep their steers off Main Street if they wanted to be welcome in the city, but this consideration did not extend to Rusk Street for several years. Residents on Rusk continued to watch the herds move past their homes until the late 1870s.

After Christmas day, 1876, a mule-drawn streetcar hauled passengers up and down Main Street from the north, or courthouse, square to the railroad depot at the south end. Right in front of the depot, the streetcar let off its last passengers and picked up another load for the return trip. There was a lot of respectable public traffic on the south end of town, fed by the streetcars and trains until 1880 when the passenger depot was moved five blocks east to serve both the T&P and the Missouri Pacific lines. Between Grove and Pecan streets, where the east-west T&P tracks intersected the north-south Missouri Pacific tracks, the city built Union Depot in 1880. The new station boasted not only expanded facilities, but a hotel on the platform right next to the passenger depot. The old location at the foot of Main was then used by the T&P as a freight depot. The respectable traffic of the early days had little reason to frequent this area now. Railroad passengers had to walk or get a carriage to the business district but could now bypass the worst parts of Hell's Half Acre. These developments contributed to the transformation of the south end of town into a district given over completely to vice, slums, and industrial property.

Fort Worth lacked many of the amenities of more civilized cities in the 1870s, principal among these being decent travelers' accommodations, churches, and what we call today family entertainment. In February, 1873, B. B. Paddock complained in his newspaper that Fort Worth needed a proper church building "to accommodate its church-going people."[19] On other occasions he noted that the town also lacked a town hall for business meetings or a legitimate theater as an alternative to the saloons and dance halls. In the next few years, the city built a city hall, an opera house (Greenwall's) and a natatorium. They were the brick-and-mortar symbols of a respectable town, but none had any effect whatsoever on Hell's Half Acre.

A visitor's first impression of Fort Worth upon arriving on the south end of town was of a very unsanitary place. There was no municipal garbage collection, nor was there any municipal water system. In the early years citizens carried their own water up from the Trinity River. Later a water wagon made the rounds, carrying water from a public well at Second and Grove streets to paying customers. When W. J. Gilvin drove the wagon, he charged a nickel to fill the customer's water barrel.[20]

The generally unsanitary condition of lower Main Street was added to by a meat market that did business in the Acre for many years. This nameless market offered fresh game such as rabbits, squirrels and prairie chickens, hanging them up for display over the public sidewalk. In warm weather flies and odor were almost unbearable.[21]

Main Street, Fort Worth, about 1876 looking north toward the courthouse. Note the clean, graded street and the number of substantial buildings, including the Clark House Hotel (right foreground). The mule-drawn trolley began service in 1876 (courtesy *Fort Worth Star-Telegram*).

Until the 1880s, hogs roamed free in the streets rooting for garbage. When an ordinance was finally passed getting the hogs off the streets, this was seen symbolically as a long step forward in the city's growth.[22]

Flies were an ever-present problem in hotels, restaurants and bars, all of which lacked even simple screens to keep out the pests. What they did use to cover the windows were wooden shutters, but in the Acre the shutters were never closed, and the doors were only closed when it was necessary to keep out bad weather.[23]

On the main business streets running north and south, crudely lettered and usually faded signs rather than distinctive architecture indicated what kind of establishment occupied a building. The chief exception to this rule were the traditional swinging doors that indicated a saloon. Since lumber was scarce and skilled contractors were more scarce, many buildings were occupied by more than one enterprise. For instance, B. B. Paddock's *Fort Worth Democrat* started publishing from the second floor over Moore & Company's General Store and the Banking House of Tidball and Wilson.[24] When R. E. Beckham arrived in Fort Worth in 1873 he further added to the crowded conditions by opening his law practice in Paddock's editorial office. A number of establishments in the Acre offered gambling, drinking, dancing and prostitution all under the same roof, a sort of one-stop entertainment emporium. Most businesses were of the hole-in-the-wall variety since glass-paned windows, raised ceilings and cross ventilation were eastern luxuries. The typical saloon or gambling joint was usually dark and smelly, a fact that did not seem to matter to boisterous cowboys upon arrival and mattered even less after a few drinks.

Since saloons tended to be the cowboy's home-away-from-home, they did more than just serve drinks. Most frontier saloons also offered a limited menu displayed in white-washed letters on the mirror behind the bar. The selection seldom if ever varied, and the quality was uniformly poor, but it kept hungry cowboys from wandering off the premises in search of a meal. The standard price of a meal in 1878 was twenty-five cents. The Tivoli Hall Saloon offered the best deal: a hot lunch served all day to bar customers. It was said that cowboys who could not read always ordered ham and beans. Management did not care what a man ordered, however — the real business was selling liquor, and bartenders sold plenty of it.

Whiskey and beer were the chief refreshments dispensed in such places. Most of the whiskey, like the food, was of indifferent quality and went by any number of colorful names according to its lethal properties or potency. Among the favorites for frontier whiskey were "rotgut," "red-eye," "tarantula juice" and "who-hit-John." A load of this stuff could make a man feel ten feet tall and strong enough to whip a den of wildcats. The effects the next morning were considerably different. Some of the legitimate stuff was as dangerous as Mickey Finns. Beer was usually served at room temperature until refrigeration arrived late in the decade. Herman Kussatz had the first refrigerated storeroom in Fort Worth. The preferred beers included lagers, strong ales, and a local brew called W. J. Lemp's.

A handful of uptown establishments catered to more sophisticated tastes, serving Kentucky whiskeys and imported ales and port. One place even bragged that it stocked "pure grape wine direct from California."[25] Such affectations did not much impress the usual run of cowboy customers.

Both the city and the state attempted to regulate the saloons using taxes and licenses but with mixed results. Barkeeps were supposed to keep a record of sales with one of James Ritty's recently invented "bell registers," which were in the process of revolutionizing the retail sales business in the 1870s.[26] These primitive cash registers, sometimes known as "Ritty's Incorruptible Cashiers," recorded all transactions on a paper roll, but had to be cranked every time a sale was rung up. The bell rang every time the cash drawer was opened. The paper roll on which receipts were recorded was used by authorities to determine how much the establishment owed in liquor taxes.[27] Sometimes the barkeeps "forgot" to turn the crank on sales, which could earn them a trip to court and a fine if discovered by the authorities. Other ordinances regulating saloons prohibited them from "selling spiritous [sic] and intoxicating liquors in quantities less than one quart without a license," and from selling on Sundays or election days.[28]

Drinking and gambling went hand in hand on the male-dominated frontier, and most saloons offered a wide range of gambling opportunities. Cards were the preferred game of chance, and all the experts agree that faro was the cowboy's favorite because it offered the best odds for winning.[29] The main challenger to faro's pre-eminence at the gambling table was monte (not the old carnival and street swindle called "three-card monte"), a game whose origins could be traced to the days when the Spanish ruled the Southwest. Neither draw nor stud poker ever came close to displacing faro among the booted and spurred working class. Poker rules were still evolving and might vary greatly from city to city or even from game to game, and stakes tended to run high. These facts alone made poker the private preserve of the professional gamblers, a class of men with no roots who traveled the gamblers' circuit across the West.

Before the end of the Acre's first decade, Fort Worth would become a regular stop on the circuit for men like Bat Masterson, Wyatt Earp and Luke Short. Other stops included Denver, San Antonio, Abilene and Dodge City. These men might make their bankrolls off the cowboys in the Acre, but they lived for the "Big Game" — an invitation-only, high-stakes showdown in the clubroom of one of the larger establishments. Participation was limited to professional gamblers and a short list of local men with lots of money and influence. Poker was the official game at these get-togethers, and stud was preferred over draw. Some Big Games became legendary in the West for the celebrities who participated, the amount of money that changed hands or just their length. Stories are told of games that lasted twenty-four and thirty-six hours non-stop with the pot reaching thousands of dollars. Fort Worth's White Elephant played host to some Big Games in its day, but the run-of-the-mill saloons and joints in the Acre never saw this kind of action.

Most ramshackle saloons in Fort Worth also had a pool table in one corner that did a steady if uneventful business. In addition, some places operated purely as billiard halls. The city directory lists three of these for 1878 and '79, including one in the El Paso Hotel.[30] The El Paso's pool room was a major gathering place for local gents for years. Shooting pool was a popular pastime and also the great forgotten sport of the frontier West — one that has largely been overlooked by the mythmakers and the historians alike because it generally attracted a quieter clientele than faro or poker. Pool-shooting and people-shooting generally did not go together. There were a few notable exceptions to be sure, like the time a Dodge City gambler named James G. Burke shot a Texas cattleman named Morris Weil in a Fort Worth saloon after a quarrel over a pool game, but those who knew him agreed that Weil deserved it because he was "overbearing and disagreeable."[31] More publicity attended the murder of Morgan Earp while playing billiards with the owner of Hatch's Saloon in Tombstone, Arizona. The killers had no interest in the game; they were gunning for the Earp brothers in the aftermath of the O.K. Corral shootout.[32] On yet a third bloody occasion, the violence was directly related to the billiard contest. Harvey Logan of the Wild Bunch cleared out a bar in Knoxville, Tennessee, and shot two policemen who were trying to arrest him in a dispute over a game.[33] These, however, were exceptions.

Some saloons in the Acre were designated as pool parlors, but most catered to pool players and card players both. Like other activities where the outcome was in doubt and money was at stake, pool attracted its share of sharps and gamblers. The elements of skill and coordination involved in playing billiards discouraged most uncivilized types from trying their luck, but there were always enough suckers even in a town like Fort Worth to keep a small fraternity of "crack billiardists" profitably employed. These men could be seen making the rounds of the local establishments like so many sharks, looking for a "soft snap" as suckers were known in the business.[34] Besides their cool professionalism, they were readily identifiable by their fancy dress and personal pool cues, the uniform and the tools of the trade respectively.

Shooting pool sometimes was taken quite literally by inebriated cowboys in the Acre. What they called "pistol pool" was played by shooting the balls into the pockets with bullets fired from their six-shooters instead of using a pool cue. Since most cowboys were only slightly better with a gun than with a pool cue, this game could be hard on both the balls and the tables. However, the pool table keepers did not mind much because there was a considerable surcharge added to the bill for pistol pool. Most of the boys cheerfully anted up the extra amount.[35]

Occasionally, the "pool table keepers" were pulled in by Fort Worth police during their infrequent raids on the gambling joints.[36] On those occasions, they paid their fines and were back in business the next day. Fort Worth citizens would have been truly shocked to see the saloons, gambling parlors, pool halls and the like shut down for any length of time.

Fancy Dan gamblers who came in from Denver, Kansas City or one of the other big cities were often surprised to find that Fort Worth offered the more sophisticated pleasures of roulette gambling. While the prohibitive odds of the roulette wheel tended to scare away most cowboys, there were still enough takers to make the click of the roulette wheel and the rattle of poker chips familiar sounds to anyone walking down Main Street in the late 1870s.[37]

Keno, an early-day form of bingo, appeared in Fort Worth in the early 1870s and soon acquired a small but highly partisan following. An undated *Fort Worth Democrat* from this era noted, "The disciples of keno now have three shrines at which to worship and yet 'tis said they are not happy."[38] Keno had to wait until the next decade to catch on locally, and even then it was always the timid man's game, usually played in the tonier uptown establishments that could afford separate facilities for the keno clientele. Like bingo, keno required no particular skill with cards or dice. In a typical game, the operator's set-up consisted of a device for holding the numbered balls and a master board for keeping track of the numbers that had already been called. The entire set-up was known as a "keno bank." The players marked their own cards, sometimes using grains of corn, and when a player got three grains in a row he hollered "Keno!"

Keno never seriously threatened faro and poker as the professional gamblers' favorites because it relied too much on luck over skill. For the average player, the problem with keno was its well-known reputation as the easiest of all games to rig for cheating.[39] As soon as the novelty wore off and losses to the house began mounting, it faded from the local scene. Keno's place in local lore, however, is firmly fixed. Despite evidence to the contrary, there is a popular local legend that it was first brought to Fort Worth by Luke Short.[40] In actuality, keno games were already being run illegally by local gamblers long before Short arrived, but he popularized it and his name will forever be associated with it.[41]

Keno, roulette and other fairly sophisticated casino games were never the bread and butter of the Acre's gambling fraternity. Anything that required more equipment than a table and a deck of cards, or more skill than luck, had little chance in the seedy dives and joints along Main and Rusk. Cowboys, buffalo hunters and railroad workers were happiest when they had a handful of cards and a stack of chips in front of them.

In Hell's Half Acre any man with money in his pocket was welcome to take the first empty seat at a gaming table. Fort Worth had a reputation as a wide-open town for good reason: the stakes were unlimited, the operating hours unrestricted. At any hour of the day or

Keno was a more genteel game than poker or monte—also more egalitarian. A woman keno player attracts an admiring crowd in a gambling joint while the "roller" spins the "goose" (courtesy Denver Public Library, Western History Department).

night a game could be found in the Acre. If the liquor flowed too freely and the action occasionally ran to violence, nobody complained much. Sheriffs and city marshals looked benignly on the twin activities of drinking and gambling. "Rare was the western peace officer who was not also a familiar figure at the gaming tables."[42] Easy access to the best games in town was considered one of the perks that went along with the job of sheriff or marshal. Even judges and city councilmen were usually on a first-name basis with the gambling fraternity.

Like every other frontier town, Fort Worth had ordinances against gambling almost from the beginning. In 1873, after setting regular meeting times, creating a corporate seal, setting up a system of bookkeeping and establishing officials' salaries, members of the first city council turned to the matter of "gambling and gambling houses." Ordinance No. 6 passed on April 8, 1873, was the first attempt to regulate gamblers' operations, but like similar laws that followed in later years, it suffered from lack of enforcement.[43] Cowtown gambling ordinances were generally enforced only against sharpers whose activities tended to encourage violence and give the games a bad image. Cowboys and local citizens were always welcome in gambling joints. City fathers and chamber-of-commerce types drew a fine line between bad gambling and what they called "legitimate and honorable gambling."[44] The latter variety was also known in western vernacular as "square games."

As frontier towns like Fort Worth became more civilized, gambling gradually put on two faces: organized gambling which migrated uptown and was in the hands of a well-heeled fraternity, and unorganized gambling, which tended to stay downtown and was constantly under threat of an official crackdown. In the 1870s, however, there was no such thing as genteel distinctions between uptown and downtown. As one old-timer recalled many years later, "At that time there were no select residence districts, no 'reservation'; the good and the vile were mixed promiscuously."[45]

There is no doubt that Fort Worth's saloons were rough places, unfit for the fairer sex or for the faint-hearted. Even the pets that some owners kept on the premises were as tough as the customers. One saloon kept a half-wild wolf in a cage. The panther kept by the Keg Saloon was also mostly wild and had a reputation for meanness. On January 25, 1873, the *Democrat* reported this bloody encounter without comment: "The panther at the Keg Saloon scalped another man yesterday evening." A man could not be too cautious with his money or his scalp when he entered one of the local saloons.

Being "scalped" by the gamblers or the resident house pet was not the worst thing that could happen to a man. Being shot or carved up was a more serious possibility. The typical saloon might look like a conclave of heavily armed desperados when the place was busy. Few men were brave enough or foolish enough to enter a bar unarmed. Never mind the ordinances against carrying guns; those were widely ignored anyway. Many men carried, in addition to their six-shooter, a knife of some sort for close-in fighting. Even if a man checked his gun at the door, he hung onto his knife. The result of having so many well-armed men in such a confined space is best described by a small-town Kansas newspaper of the era as "more like an arsenal than a bar room." And it was not just the customers who were well-armed. The same newspaper said the barkeeps were often more heavily armed than the customers.[46]

The preoccupation with gambling was not limited to indoor sports like cards and dice. Horse racing was the favorite outdoor sport that brought men together, whether it was cow ponies up and down Main Street or purebreds on the little race track at Cold Spring just north of town. It was likely that more money changed hands over a single horse race at the track than in an all-night card game in the Acre, and sometimes with the same heated results. Again, local law-enforcement officers were just as active as anyone when it came to backing their favorite horse. On Saturday afternoon, August 11, 1877, an inebriated Marshal T. I. Courtright got into "a regular fist-fight" with one O. F. Cheney over the results of the last race. The fight took place on Fort Worth's main square and a mob estimated at 300 quickly gathered "to see the fun." Pistols were flourished, although no shots were fired, and Sheriff John M. Henderson eventually had to be summoned to break up the commotion. In the course of events both Anderson and Courtright were bloodied. Marshal Courtright was charged with public fighting and forced to appear in court five days later, but a jury of sympathetic gentlemen, which probably included more than a few fellow gamblers, failed to reach a verdict.[47]

Prostitution was the third leg of the three great frontier pleasures upholding the local economy. Next to gamblers and barkeepers, the bawds were probably the most numerous members of the working class in the Acre. For the most part, saloons were male preserves that were considered off-limits to women, but the women set up shop not far away. In its own way, prostitution contributed significantly to the building boom in Fort Worth during the trail-driving days. Just as in many frontier towns, the first two-story structures to go up were saloons with rooms to rent upstairs, where cowboys could spend a few exciting hours with the local ladies of the evening. For sleeping purposes, the cowboys saved their money and rode back to camp.

The girls were called "soiled doves" as the preferred euphemism of the day because it conveyed a sense of lost innocence that was appealing to Victorian sensibilities. A profile of typical soiled doves in a cow town like Fort Worth shows them to be white and under twenty, with some as young as fourteen.[48] Later reports of the large number of black girls working in Fort Worth highlight the significant differences between this city and the major Kansas cow towns. The usual stories from Dodge City, Abilene and Ellsworth among others, make no mention of black prostitutes, while Fort Worth newspapers talk about them constantly. The difference may be that Fort Worth newspapers were more biased than their Kansas counterparts in focusing on the perceived "debauchery of the dark-skinned race"; or perhaps the explanation was simply the result of demographics: Texas had a larger black population than any other state west of the Mississippi before the end of the century.[49] Regardless of whether biased reporting helped distort the picture or not, Fort Worth had a significant number of black Cyprians by the 1880s, so there must have been enough demand to give them regular work.

The typical cow-town bawd described in contemporary accounts and depicted in a handful of surviving photographs appears to have been a pretty hardened and unattractive member of her sex, even when she was just in her twenties or younger. Nicknames like Big-Nose Kate and Squirrel-Tooth Alice, two of the better-known residents of Dodge City in its heyday, support the assertion that beauty was greatly discounted among the sex-starved men of the West. Among Fort Worth's working girls, the nicknames included Irish Kate, Kansas City, Monkey and Pokey Negro. Some were arrested so often that after a while they were just listed on the jail records by their familiar nicknames, such as "Birdie" or "Monk," two of the regular occupants of the city lock-up a few years later.[50]

A persistent myth of the West is that these girl-women eventually married respectable citizens and settled down to lives of domestic tranquility. However, this myth cannot be supported by any statistical evidence. Most lived short and unpleasant lives.

It is impossible to say just how many soiled doves worked Fort Worth in the wild 'n' woolly frontier years. The number — which fluctuated with the season — may have run into the dozens, but the record indicates that the number of *full-time* bawds was far fewer. In 1881 an article in the *Democrat* reported seventeen prostitutes with the notation: "Several drunks and *all the girls* [emphasis added] were up [yesterday] to pay their 'occupation tax' [in the Mayor's Court]." They were: Birdie Parks, Corine Levy, Lilly Lynn, Nellie Fitus, Nellie Ferns, Ella Marks, Belle Marks, Stella Clements, Lizzie Jones, Annie Smith, Fannie Gordon, Cora Phillips, Annie Porter, Fannie Allen, Mattie Allen, Ida Allen, and S. Briggs. All were slapped with vagrancy charges, fifteen being fined $13.10, while two paid lesser fines of $9.10.[51] (No explanation is given for the difference in penalties.) One must assume these were notorious full-timers whose names and working addresses were well-known to authorities. The amateurs and part-timers were probably not subject to the monthly "call-up." Even allowing for a few who escaped the round-up, this number is still surprisingly small for a town the size of Fort Worth.[52]

The needs of the local demimondes were sometimes served by back rooms, more often by one-room apartments known as cribs, or the handful of sporting houses which could be found in every town. The cribs provided the cheapest and quickest service. They were usually relegated to one or two side streets where a half-dozen or more of the cramped shacks, each identical to the next, occupied the length of the block. Such a row of shacks, sometimes on both sides of the street, was known as "the line," and girls who worked there as "girls of the line." The exact location of Fort Worth's cribs is revealed by the Sanborn Fire Maps from the mid-1880s: on Tenth and Twelfth streets between Main and Rusk.[53] This placed them between Main Street's saloons and Rusk Street's sporting houses, which was about as shrewd a business location as one could have asked for.

There was a depressing sameness to the cribs in every red-light district. One historian has described Denver's line as "a succession of wooden cubicles standing shoulder to shoulder, each barely wide enough for a door and a front window, and ten to twelve feet deep, the standard rental of which was twenty-five dollars per week, paid in

"Home for the Boys" is the caption for this *Harper's* illustration of June, 1865. It is a busy night in the Cozy Home Saloon, location unspecified. Many western saloons tried to portray themselves as a "home away from home for the boys"; it was good for business (courtesy Library of Congress).

advance."[54] Landlords were prompt in collecting payment because girls of the line were not reliable renters. They tended to move often and without warning. They might work for months in a town, and then be gone overnight at the first hint of trouble with the law.

For the customer who was not too picky, a deal could be struck with a crib girl for what amounted to little more than pocket change — even in that day and age — depending on whether the girl was white or black. (The difference reflected the racial prejudice of the day and was accepted by all parties without complaint.) When the color line was crossed, however, proper citizens responded. A Dallas newspaper complained in 1877 of "white prostitutes living in negro dens," and called them a "disgrace" to the city. "The police are respectfully requested to pay attention to them, and not let them offend the neighborhood by their disgusting actions."[55] Racist sentiments like these did not stop at the Trinity River, and one can be sure Fort Worth policemen were always on the alert to keep the city's vice segregated by color, at least in public view.

Dance hall girls (unidentified) in a western saloon, some time during the late nineteenth century—probably not in Texas or the Deep South because of the mixture of races pictured (Fred Mazulla Collection, Amon Carter Museum).

While some of the larger cities like Denver and San Francisco provided work for several classes of prostitutes, Fort Worth had just two categories of full-timers — crib girls and sporting-house girls. (Dance-hall girls operated in a gray area between full-time prostitutes and legitimate working girls, although they are usually lumped together with the former.) By tradition, sporting houses, also known as bawdy houses, cat houses, parlor houses and "female boarding houses," provided the most elegant surroundings and fetched the highest prices. In the early days, before all forms of vice tended to cluster together in the Acre, such houses could be found in any part of town including the residential area near the bluffs. In 1874, J. G. Bishop and a group of irate residents of Belknap Street petitioned the city council to remove a "bawdy house" from their street. The council accepted their petition but took no action[56] — the city was still too young to begin erecting moral boundaries. In 1878 and '79, Lee Summers ran her house on Houston Street near Fourth. It was not only in the heart of the business district and close to the courthouse, but it was directly behind the posh El Paso Hotel, where guests on the second floor got a free show every night put on by Lee's girls and their customers.[57] Lee's awkward location caused her more trouble with city authorities than that had by madams on the south end of town, whose operations were beyond the pale. By the early '80s, public opinion would force the bawdy houses out of the north end of town, and the madams would settle on the lower end of Rusk where a tacit agreement with city authorities allowed them to operate unmolested by the law.

After more than a century, the number and location of Fort Worth's early sporting houses can no longer be determined. There probably were not more than a handful where as many as three or four girls lived, and in appearance these places were probably indistinguishable from the other wooden, box-type houses that made up the city's unimposing skyline. Aside from newspapers, city directories provide the only clues to who these women were and where they lived. Any woman designated "Miss," who lived alone, had no given occupation, and was not designated "widow," is a suspect for the oldest profession. "Nice girls" were listed with their fathers, husbands or guardians. If they lived alone, their place of work was included beside their address. If none of the above applied, they were classified "widow." In 1877 and 1878 Miss Mary Blair, Miss Emma Burns, Kitty Brown, Miss

Christy Eubanks, and Belle Lillard are listed in the city directory and fail the three tests of respectability. Sure enough, the names of Misses Blair, Burns and Brown all turn up in the newspapers for being arrested as prostitutes several times during those two years. Mary (a.k.a. Molly) Blair's house was located on the corner of Eighth and Calhoun, and she shared it with Emma Burns.[58] Kitty Brown kept a house on Ninth between Calhoun and Jones where the lights burned all night and the police occasionally raided.

The big boarding houses that appear on the Sanborn Fire Maps of the 1880s were several cuts above the early cat houses, like Lee Summer's or Kitty Brown's. But they never rivaled the legendary parlor houses of New Orleans, Denver and San Francisco that served as both home and working quarters for six or more girls. These houses had amenities like a genuine parlor where the customer selected his girl, bought drinks and chatted with the madam. In addition to a selection of girls for every taste, furnishings might include mirrors decorated with gold leaf, chandeliers of fine crystal, bearskin rugs, player pianos and the legendary brass beds. In contrast, Fort Worth's three or four well-known sporting houses are better described as "boarding houses," which is how they were usually described in public print.

Between the crib girls and their younger, more attractive sisters in the boarding houses was an unbridgeable gulf of economics and social convention. No self-respecting madam permitted her "boarders" to associate with the crib girls. This enforced segregation was a matter of economics: madams had to convince patrons of sporting houses that the quality of merchandise justified higher prices.

While everything else might be a matter of taste, the price charged was the one hard line between the sporting girls and the crib girls. In Texas sporting houses of the late nineteenth century, the going rate for a visit was one to three dollars.[59] For crib girls, the price started at twenty-five cents for the oldest, ugliest or non-whites and escalated to $2 in the bigger cities where the traffic would bear it.[60] Since Fort Worth was not one of those bigger cities, the local crib girls were probably in the two-bit to six-bit range found in some of the Kansas cow towns.

Western prostitutes were an itinerant lot who drifted from town to town, always looking for more profitable markets. They tended to travel light and move often, which was whenever they wore out their welcome in one town or just got a hankering for a change of scenery.

The madams tended to move on periodically also, but less often than their girls because they had a lot more baggage to carry and because it sometimes took years to cultivate a good working relationship with the local authorities. Once this relationship went sour, however, a madam almost always had to move on. In the spring of 1879, Lee Summers got crossways with Fort Worth officials when she fell behind in her payments (or fines) to the city. Threatened with a stretch in the disgusting confines of the county jail, she packed up all her valuables and furnishings and announced she was headed for Austin's "more congenial climes."[61] There are no reports that the city mourned her going. She had only been in business about a year, and there were plenty more establishments of a similar nature in town.

The move to Austin was a step up for Lee. The state's capital city had almost twice the population of Fort Worth at this date with the usual majority of men over women. The male population of Austin was served by only 177 regular bawds or about one girl for every forty men.[62] There was plenty of opportunity for an aggressive entrepreneur like Lee Summers to set up housekeeping on a profitable basis.

When a girl or madam made the move from one town to another, she found things tended to run the same whether it was Fort Worth, Austin, San Antonio or dozens of other towns. Variations in sales pitch, methods and prices were insignificant. Costume distinguished the girl in one of the big cities from her small-town sister. In Denver, dress was more ornate and provocative, usually consisting of a brightly colored, low-neck, knee-length dress covered with spangles. Black silk stockings completed the outfit. By contrast, Fort Worth, despite its extravagant claims to the contrary, was a prairie town struggling to become a big city. The local bawds favored the simpler Mother Hubbard dress of wool or cotton that covered everything from shoulders to ankles.[63] Feathers, spangles and beads — which might grace a sporting girl — were never seen on the Acre's side streets where the crib girls plied their trade. Whether such finery was even part of the Fort Worth boarding-house girls' costume is questionable. If their appearance was less refined than their sisters in bigger cities, it may have been because the taste of their customers was also less refined.

One factor united all bawds whatever their background or professional status: once they entered the profession, they found it impossible to get out. Rare indeed are stories like that of the farmer's daughter who came to Fort Worth looking for the fast life and found it in one of the sporting houses on Rusk Street. In the summer of 1877, her father came to town to sell watermelons off the back of his wagon. As he made his way down Rusk, he passed one of the more notorious bordellos on the south end of town. Spying a man sitting in a second-story window, he "halloed" up to him and asked if he wanted to buy a melon for his girl. The man said no, but then a woman came to the window. To the farmer's shock, he recognized his daughter. He pleaded with her to "abandon her life of sin and shame and go home with him." The girl finally agreed and father and daughter were reunited.[64] Rusk Street had one less prostitute that night, but it is doubtful anyone noticed.

The farmer might have gone to the marshal to help get his daughter back. Prostitution was clearly illegal by statute and ordinance but was treated with benign neglect by local authorities. The first city council in 1873 passed ordinances "regulating houses of ill-fame and the inmates thereof," also "suppressing disorderly houses." These ordinances, numbered eleven and fifteen, respectively, on the city books, indicate a relatively high priority attached to this age-old problem.[65] But like early ordinances regulating gambling houses, shooting galleries and deadly weapons, they were observed mostly in the breach.

In 1877, four years and several ordinances after the city council had first taken up the problem of prostitution, the *Fort Worth Democrat* was making frequent complaints about the still-unresolved problem. "The dens of vice and immorality are open night after night, contrary to the law, and sworn officers wink at and permit them to go on, knowingly and willfully."[66] A few months later the *Democrat* castigated the mayor in its pages for not fining "the demi-monde and their pimps the maximum sum allowed by law."[67] Mayor G. H. Day was gone in the next election but the problem remained to plague succeeding administrations.

The difficulty in suppressing so-called "disorderly houses" began with a definition of the term. The original city charter offered a helpful explanation to guide the courts and law enforcement officials, defining disorderly houses as "houses wherein indecent, lewd, or immodest dramatic or theatrical representations are given, [also] houses of prostitution." The term served as a legal catch-all that could be hung on any place which offended public decency. In practice, most cases hauled before the courts under this ordinance involved prosti-

More functional than fancy: one of the latter-day parlor houses on Rusk Street. This particular house closed off one end of Eleventh Street and faced St. Patrick's Catholic Church on the other end of Eleventh. Reverend J. T. Upchurch took the photograph in 1906 for his series of articles condemning Hell's Half Acre. Below, an elevated view of Hell's Half Acre from *The Purity Journal* (1906), showing a parlor house and several cribs on Rusk Street. The intersection is probably Eleventh Street, with the Texas Brewing Company in the background (both photos courtesy Dallas Historical Society).

tution, usually blatant and highly organized. Unlike other vice ordinances against gambling, horse racing, prize fighting, carrying guns, and the like, those governing prostitution were laxly enforced for practical reasons that had nothing to do with more urgent law-enforcement problems. The real reason for the great disparity between local law and its enforcement can be expressed in a simple mathematical ratio: according to the 1870 census, there were two men to every woman in Fort Worth.[68] That meant business was always good for the professional bawd.

The preferred customer, however, was not from the local population. He was the itinerant cowboy — plain, half-naïve, usually flat broke. The name itself was a badge of pride for most of the drovers, giving them membership in an exclusive male fraternity and a license to raise hell in any number of towns. Still some men, particularly Texans, resented the term "cowboy." Jim Shaw, a successful cattleman who spent several years driving steers up the trails, expressed strong objections to having his horses called "ponies" and his crews called "boys." "Hell, man!" he fumed, "they were 'horses' and 'men.'"[69] But the good citizens of Fort Worth played host for six months each year to visitors who smelled like ponies and whooped it up like boys.

All the town's activities were geared toward serving the visitors during their brief stay. What local historian Oliver Knight called "cowboy joy parties" of twelve to fifteen men would descend on the town in waves, determined to spend a month's wages in a single, wild session. One cattle season could be pretty much like another from year to year, but there were exceptions. Fort Worthers, for instance, had good reason to remember the year that unusually heavy rains caused the Trinity River to flood over its banks, washing out the usual crossings. Fifteen herds, averaging some 3000 head, were backed up on the south side of the river unable to continue their journey. It was a banner season for the local merchants, and the city's vice emporia were the biggest beneficiaries of having several hundred restive cowboys stuck in the area with time on their hands.[70] Times like these went a long way toward creating the legend of the Acre.

While the cowboy was only one of several types who helped put the Acre on the map, his name is most closely associated with the legendary district. Today the cowboy enjoys a mythic image, but a century ago he was not nearly so popular a character. In his heyday he was more liable to be a petty hoodlum or a misfit than the noble type seen in Hollywood films. In the 1870s Fort Worth citizens tolerated the cowboy for his economic contribution. They did not idealize him.

On the other hand, the cowboy probably had a much higher opinion of Fort Worth than the town deserved, and many drovers who visited Hell's Half Acre on a regular basis probably took away a wealth of pleasant memories. Most, however, never bothered to record their thoughts for posterity. One who did was Tom Blevins, an old cowpuncher who still had a vivid memory when he sat down to tell his story to an interviewer in 1925. At that time Tom was eighty years old, but he remembered his days riding the trails in the 1870s. He also remembered Hell's Half Acre quite well: "Back in 1873 when I got back from driving a herd up the Chisholm Trail, my boss said — 'Tom, take a rest. You've been working steady for two years, here's four month's pay, ride into Fort Worth and get frolickly for a spell.'"

The place Tom picked to "get frolickly" was one of the saloon-bordellos in Hell's Half Acre, this one known as "The Two Minnies." Tom recalled that the Two Minnies "looked like any other buildin' on the outside, and I just walked in, and seen a fine room with cushion chairs and tables to drink off of. I'd been riding for three days, and made bee-line for the bar, but a big negro, as polite as a basket of chips, stopped me and took my chaps and gun and hung them up."

What Tom Blevins did not realize was that the Two Minnies was not the run-of-the-mill saloon. The legend has it that he had strolled into one of the tonier establishments in the Acre. He described his discovery in vivid detail:

> I asked fer whiskey and wanted to set 'em up fer the house, but the bartender frowned and drawed himself up. The Two Minnies has the dudiest men; pins in their neckties and their hair was combed.
>
> So I poured out a drink and says to myself — "Don't look like we're going to have much fun here, and I throwed my head back fer to swallow — but I NEVER GOT THAT DRINK." No one ever got their first drink in the Two Minnies. When I throwed my head back to dreen the poison I seen the ceiling was glass, and there was anyways Forty girls walking around up their — NAKID as a jaybird, playing ten pins.[71]

Other drinking establishments of the period, such as Tom Prindle's Saloon and Steele's Tavern, never achieved the notoriety of the Two Minnies but did serve thousands of drinks across their bars to customers no different from Tom Blevins.

The overwhelming majority of customers who came through the Acre were nameless workingmen: cowboys, buffalo hunters and railroad hands. But there were a handful of other, more famous characters, who came through and were honest enough, or just plain ornery enough, to admit they had been there. Among the most famous was Shanghai Pierce.

Born Abel Head Pierce but nicknamed "Shanghai" early in his career, he was one of the numerous cattle barons who carved out enormously successful range empires in Texas in the nineteenth century. At six-feet-four with a booming voice, Pierce was as big as his legend, too big to let a little thing like being associated with Hell's Half Acre bother him. Pierce delighted in making a mockery out of the traditional "Code of the West," whether it was refusing to wear a sidearm or cheerfully owning up in his respectable old age to youthful peccadilloes that shocked a more genteel generation.

In the 1870s, Pierce regularly drove his herds up the Chisholm Trail, stopping in Fort Worth for provisions on the way north and for the usual rest and relaxation on the way home. Determined to place as much distance as possible between himself and a strict Presbyterian upbringing, he found Hell's Half Acre ideally suited to his personal reform campaign. He became a regular customer in the Acre during the cattle season. Years later, a local historian claimed that long after Pierce had become wealthy and respectable, "his heart was [still] in Hell's Half Acre."[72]

Pierce probably would not have disputed that epitaph.

TWO

"The Wages of Sin Are A Damned Sight Better Than the Wages of Virtue"

IF ALL THE COWBOYS WERE NOT AS LEGENDARY AS Shanghai Pierce, their exploits at least tended to be remembered that way. Stories of gunplay in the streets, of cowboys riding their horses up to the bars and demanding service, of those same cowboys shooting out the lights or the mirrors behind the bars are all part of the reputation of Hell's Half Acre in the late 1870s. Being wild 'n' woolly was a reputation that Fort Worth was rather proud of. And why not? It was certainly lucrative. In just three short years, Fort Worth had gone from what the 1873 *Centennial Gazetteer of the United States* described as a "postal village and the county seat of Tarrant County, Texas" to being promoted in T&P Railroad literature as the "Queen City of the Prairies," a "farmer's paradise," and "a beautiful city of heights . . . offering unusual inducements to the banker, the merchant and the mechanic, with work for all."[1] In 1873 the population was 850. After the railroad arrived it had swollen to 5000, numbers any business man could appreciate. More importantly, business receipts had gone up commensurately, a fact reflected in the city's take. In November, 1876, it was reported that Fort Worth was receiving $4000 annually from saloon licenses alone — the most profitable of the various occupation taxes imposed by city government.[2]

It is no wonder that Fort Worth citizens did not want to endanger their economic success by administering too stiff a dose of morality. That would be bad for business. Even the Bible thumpers tailored their message to local conditions. The relationship between the churches and the vice establishments (which outnumbered churches two to one) could best be described as "live-and-let-live." "The drinking places didn't bother the churches," one veteran reporter recalled, "and the churches didn't bother the saloons."[3]

The Reverend J. Morgan Wells was the first in a long line of flamboyant preachers to leave his mark on Fort Worth. Like some of his equally distinguished successors, Wells was Baptist. He came to town in 1876, a dapper figure customarily attired in top hat and frock coat and swinging a cane. The year before his arrival, local Baptists had built their first church on a south side lot facing the spot where the cattle trail entered town. As soon as Wells settled into his new parish, he began making regular calls on every saloon, business house and hotel in town, inviting one and all to attend Sunday services. He filled the pews but was unhappy with the location of the church. It was "too far from town" and dense clouds of dust caused by herds of passing cattle choked Sunday morning worshippers until "all thoughts of religion vanished." On his own initiative, he launched a campaign to build another house of worship at Third and Taylor streets. When his parishioners failed to fulfill their pledges, the good reverend, decked out in his finest, made the rounds soliciting money from gamblers, saloon keepers and others of ill repute until he had raised the incredible sum of $65,000. With that funding he was able to build an English Gothic structure uptown completely free and clear of debt.[4] There was a lesson in the episode for Fort Worth's other holy rollers — even the Lord's work could prosper if his ambassadors were not too proud to make an accommodation with the wicked and impious.

Fort Worthers made their accommodation with Hell's Half Acre, producing some strange, even downright amusing tales. One of the strangest was covered by the *Democrat* in 1878 after a full solar eclipse. In a column titled "Eclipse Postscript," the reporter related that a crowd of cowboys had been out on the range watching the phenomenon. When the eclipse was full and the sun totally blocked out, the drovers, supposing that night had set in, mounted their ponies and rode off at full gallop for the pleasures of Hell's Half Acre.[5]

All the cowboys who came to town to liven things up were not fresh off the trail. The country around Fort Worth was dotted with ranches, some of them sizeable spreads employing thirty-five or forty cowboys. It was not unusual for ranch owners to bring their men into town for a "merry time," excursions that helped to keep Fort Worth alive when the cattle season was not in full swing. Local or transient, cowboys were always welcome in the Acre.

Besides the cowboys, many others made a beeline for the Acre as soon as they hit town. Prominent among these were buffalo hunters who came in off the West Texas plains. They were just as tough, independent-minded, and uncivilized as the cowboys, if not more so. Only in terms of sheer numbers and in the popular fancy do the buffalo hunters take a back seat to the cowboys. Buffalo hunting was very nearly as important to the early Fort Worth economy as trail driving. In fact, one longtime resident recalled the business generated by buffalo hunters as "the city's biggest industry before the railroad came."[6] In 1876 there were more than 1500 buffalo hunters operating in West Texas. When the railroad arrived in Fort Worth that same year, the city became the principal shipping center for buffalo hides. In 1877 alone, over 100,000 skins were sent to points east and north.[7] It was not unusual to see caravans of ten or more wagons loaded down with hides arriving in Fort Worth accompanied by a complement of hardy, grime-covered buffalo hunters just itching to bust loose.

Stacks of strong-smelling hides taller than a man's head covered several acres around the railroad depot, which helps explain why the city eventually separated the freight depot from the passenger depot, moving the latter several blocks eastward and upwind. The skins sat for days in the broiling sun waiting to be shipped out. Hunters sold their loads for a dollar per hide and immediately set off to spend their profits in the vice dens of the Acre, leaving their empty wagons in the Acre's largest yard. The hunters were easily distinguished not only by their rough, unkempt appearance or even the size of their heavy-caliber rifles, but by their strong aroma which soap and water could not entirely remove. But in the Acre their money was as good as the cowboy's or the gentleman's.

As an economic and social force, the buffalo hunters' day was over by the end of the 1870s. They were soon almost forgotten, but for a few years they contributed just as much to the color — and the stench — of the Acre as their first cousins, the cowboys.

Fort Worth grew like every other cow town in the 1870s by placing a discount on respectability and law and order and a premium on money-making and hell-raising. There was plenty of opportunity for the latter during the cattle season every year. The chief problem was not the behavior of the cowboys while they were in town, but that the cattle drives only came through half the year from late spring to early fall, leaving businesses to struggle the rest of the time when the town reverted to little more than a quiet village on the Trinity. In 1870, the official population was only 300 souls, less than the population in 1860, and Fort Worth was described by one observer as a "dirty, dreary, cold, mean, little place."[8] The next year when more than 600,000 cattle came through, the population took a healthy upswing.

Big changes were in the winds that blew off the North Texas prairie after 1871. The cattle drives went into steady decline as new routes took business away from the Chisholm Trail and new railheads sprang up on the plains. But there was good news, too, in the form of rumors that Fort Worth would soon get its own railhead. The bright outlook for the future boosted the population within three years to more than 3000 — most coming from the vast transient population of the West, men and women who followed the promise of instant opportunity and easy money.

In 1873, anticipating the arrival of the first railroad, Fort Worth's leaders filed for incorporation as a city with the legislature in Austin. The charter was granted and optimism was so high that a fanciful map was circulated showing Fort Worth as the hub of not one but nine railroads. Texas & Pacific Railroad track had already been laid to within twenty-four miles of town when a nationwide financial panic brought everything to a grinding halt. The population shrank to 600 as businessmen and settlers alike pulled up stakes and took off for greener pastures. But three years later the railroad did finally arrive. On June 27, 1876, the *Dallas Herald* reported the end of the track was only nine miles from Fort Worth. In a sarcastic gibe at Fort Worth's biggest booster and leading newspaperman, the *Herald* predicted, "When that blessed road does get to Fort Worth, it will be hard work holding [B. B.] Paddock to the ground."[9] Indeed, the whole town was waiting to take off.

But making the last few miles would not be easy. Workers were racing against a deadline imposed by the Texas legislature, which had promised a land grant to the T&P only if the railhead reached Fort Worth by the adjournment date of the first legislature meeting under the revised Texas constitution. Tarrant County Representative Nicholas Henry Darnell managed to keep the House in session long enough to delay the meeting's end, while Fort Worthers pitched in with the T&P crew and worked feverishly to finish the road. On July 6, they reached Johnson's Station, site of present-day Arlington. Despite the hot summer sun and a shortage of timber, they were laying track at the rate of a mile per day.[10] By common agreement, local businesses closed their doors so that their employees could join the work force pushing the rails toward the city. The heavily sweating laborers included brawny teamsters who parked their wagons in town so they could lend a hand. Men worked through the night by torchlight, snatching a few hours' sleep in shifts, while the town's women organized to carry food out to them.

Fort Worth's saloons had never been so empty. To make up for lost business, saloon keepers like Herman Kussatz hauled beer out to the workmen. Their civic gesture would pay off many times over after the railroad reached its goal. On July 15, B. B. Paddock reported that work on the tracks was visible with the naked eye from his second-story newspaper office on Main Street.[11] Fort Worth beat the deadline and completed its railroad. On July 19 the first Texas & Pacific train pulled into town, stopping in an open field devoid of platform or station. Someone looked at his watch and noticed it was 11:23 A.M. Paddock jumped into the locomotive and pulled the steam whistle cord to punctuate the historic occasion.

While Fort Worth patted itself on the back, Dallas took a more condescending view of its neighbor's accomplishment. During the final flurry of construction, the *Dallas Herald* had suggested that "for a first-class bore in hot weather," Dallas citizens should take an excursion to Fort Worth as soon as the last rail was tied down. The day before the last rail was tied down and the last spike hammered home, the Dallas headlines proclaimed "All Aboard for Pantherville" and "Pantherville Ablaze."[12]

The celebration outshone anything previously staged in Fort Worth. An assembled crowd numbering in the thousands gathered to greet the arrival of Engine No. 20 on the site of the future T&P station. A grand barbecue, which had been postponed repeatedly, was rescheduled one more time. Mint juleps flowed freely and an invitation was even extended to Dallasites to come over and join the party. The laborers, who had been working eighteen-hour days, laid down their picks and shovels and took off for the saloons to repay the kindness of the barkeepers who had shuttled liquid refreshment to them on the job. The festivities continued long into the night. When money ran out, credit was extended to the celebrants who thronged the saloons, gambling houses and rented rooms all over town.

This may have been the night Hell's Half Acre was truly born, with all that came before merely prologue. Now it burst into life. City officials did their part, looking the other way while the extended celebration went on. Newspaper editor Paddock counseled his readers: "D.D.'s [drunk and disorderlies] must be treated with leniency for a few days."[13] This laissez-faire attitude set a precedent that would plague municipal government for the next thirty years.

July 19, 1876, was also the date of Fort Worth's rebirth. When the railroad arrived, Fort Worth was transformed from a "howling wilderness" into a boom town, and from then on it was only a matter of time until it became "the wildest town in western Texas."[14] The first order of business was building a railroad station. The first station was a small wooden structure almost a quarter-mile from the center of the business district. It was constructed on a 320-acre parcel of prime land on the south end of town, most of it donated by Captain E. B. Daggett, one of Fort Worth's founding fathers.[15] The property remained the "railroad reservation" for many years. Meanwhile the other holdings that Daggett hung onto adjoining the reservation increased significantly in value, explaining in part why Daggett was one of the city's most successful businessmen.

Soon after the Texas & Pacific arrived, stage lines were established to neighboring areas, pulling visitors, settlers and all sorts of small-time entrepreneurs into town. Regularly scheduled stage service arrived at and departed from the major hotels, especially the El Paso, serving as an important transportation link between Fort Worth and the surrounding countryside. On July 7, 1876, the *Democrat* reported that two coaches daily were coming in "loaded to the guards," and departing empty. "This constant flow of people in one direction will build the city after awhile."[16]

Long-distance stage service carried mail and passengers beyond the end of the rail line in Fort Worth to West Texas and New Mexico and Arizona territories. The Fort Worth-Fort Concho line was the first of these overland routes and provided daily service to present-day San Angelo. Late in 1877 the U.S. Post Office let a contract for regular service between Fort Worth and Yuma, Arizona. The 1560-mile journey took seventeen days one way. The time was later cut to thirteen days.[17]

Passengers and mail left Fort Worth in the familiar Concord coach pulled by six horses, changed to a surrey pulled by two horses at Thorp Spring, and finally to "a buckboard and two bronchos" at Brownwood for the longest part of the trip. There was no way such a journey could have been enjoyable; it was barely tolerable, traveling straight through day and night, "if they were not interrupted."[18] Those interruptions might take the form of robbers, hostile Indians, bad weather and breakdowns. Robbers were the most feared.

The stage companies and the railroads were the twin transportation pillars on which Fort Worth growth rested. Only gradually did railroads supplant horse-drawn coaches as the principal mode of mass transportation in the West. In the seventeen years after the coming of the Texas & Pacific, five more rail lines were built into Fort Worth ending both long- and short-haul stage service. During those years the stage lines and the railroads made an impact on Fort Worth that went far beyond transportation development and economic growth. They attracted a new class of criminals — full-time professional train and stage robbers who styled themselves "holdup artists." They never flaunted their profession like the gamblers and prostitutes but nonetheless swelled the population of the saloons and gambling rooms of Hell's Half Acre, where they spent their ill-gotten loot or planned their next move. Fort Worth was not only a regional transportation hub, but the liveliest city for several days' ride in any direction if one did not count Dallas. Fort Worth, however, had the reputation over Dallas as a "wide-open" town so it was preferred by most of the shady characters passing through North Texas, among them Sam Bass and his gang. Bass was the first famous outlaw to operate in this area, and during his heyday as a stage and train robber in 1877 and '78, he brought his gang to Fort Worth on several occasions between jobs.[19]

The fact is, it was the railroad, not the Chisholm Trail that really put Hell's Half Acre on the map. The railroad brought the stagecoaches, and the two together brought the large numbers of people necessary to create a boom town.

The community outpouring that brought the first iron rails to Fort Worth was a once-in-a-lifetime effort. It had saved the city, but Fort Worth's future growth would depend on the course charted by elected officials. Under the 1873 charter, city government consisted of a mayor and four alderman elected at large. Each April, yearly elections produced a rapid turnover in city government and allowed

In the late 1870s stages arrived and departed regularly from the city's better hotels like the Waverly House (Fifteenth and Main) and the El Paso (Fourth and Main), "carrying passengers to and from all points southwest and northwest." After 1877 the Fort Worth-Fort Yuma stage made the El Paso Hotel famous far and wide as Fort Worth's finest. Westbound stages left from there three days a week and took seventeen days to cover "the longest stage route in the world." It is doubtful if many sombrero-adorned citizens saw the coaches off as this fanciful depiction shows (courtesy Bettmann Archives, New York City).

for little long-range planning. For the first three years of its existence, city government had little to do, a fact supported by the chronic absenteeism at city council meetings, as well as by some of the responsibilities heaped on committees appointed by the council: the committee on "hitching places," the committee to investigate hogs running loose, and the "Negro burial ground" committee. After 1876, however, the council had a real city to look after. From that time on, the annual municipal elections became a barometer of the public attitude toward crime and vice in general, and the Acre in particular.

A fateful development that occurred after incorporation was allowing Hell's Half Acre to establish itself within the four square miles of the city limits. It was inevitable since Hell's Half Acre was the south end of the city proper. Until the railroad depot was built in 1876, there were no buildings on Main Street below Fourth, and the depot stood in lonely isolation until construction beginning about 1879 began to fill in the intervening space.[20] Not surprisingly the first buildings to go up were saloons. Tom Whitten opened one of the first not far from the courthouse between Houston and Main, calling it simply "Tom Whitten's Saloon."[21] The drinking parlors were followed by gambling joints, cribs and dance halls. By the beginning of the 1880s, Hell's Half Acre had assumed its distinctive character, and by that time it was too late to segregate it legally.

In its early years, Hell's Half Acre was not commonly recognized as a blight on the city's public image. It was just a jumble of shacks, houses and commercial establishments, indistinguishable from the rest of town. During its first decade, it grew up to become a troublesome stepchild living under the roof of the city charter and impossible to ignore or disown. In those early years it might have been moved, lock, stock and beer barrels outside the city limits. This was done in several Kansas cow towns, which kept their red-light districts outside the town proper at arm's length from the business area and seat of city government. But Fort Worth citizens got used to the idea that the Acre was an integral part of their town. They extended town services, streetcar lines and municipal government to the Acre and made a sometimes uncomfortable accommodation with its nefarious activities.

Hell's Half Acre was in every sense a part of Fort Worth from the beginning. In fact, it was located on land properly and legally known as the Daggett Addition. The Daggett Addition, named for E. M.

Daggett, and the Jennings Addition, named for Hyde Jennings, were the two earliest subdivisions, dating to 1873 when the township was incorporated. Ephraim Merrill Daggett had been a Texan since 1840 and a resident of Fort Worth since 1854. He was one of the largest landowners in the county when Fort Worth was incorporated and was committed to seeing the little hamlet grow into a thriving business community. Growth would hardly hurt the value of his property holdings. Hyde Jennings came to Fort Worth the same year the town incorporated and set up a successful law practice. His extensive land holdings came to him through his mother's side of the family, and it was she who suggested the names for the major streets in the Jennings Addition (Monroe, Taylor, Throckmorton, Jackson and so on) based on men she admired in the nation's history. Both Ephraim Daggett and Hyde Jennings were large, rotund men who enjoyed eating well and making money.

The Daggett and Jennings Additions were privately owned by the two pioneer founders in 1873 but "dedicated to public use" as soon as the charter of incorporation was approved. Both additions show on the oldest known map of the city made in March 1877 and signed by twenty-five property owners including Daggett, Jennings and John Peter Smith, another giant in the city's early history. The legal borders of the subdivision for all practical purposes defined the rough, unofficial boundaries of the Acre: Ninth Street east to Jones, Jones Street south to Front Street (later Lancaster), Front Street west to Throckmorton, Throckmorton north to Ninth. Only Throckmorton, the boundary between the Daggett and Jennings Additions, remained relatively free of vice establishments. Otherwise, E. M. Daggett's subdivision, with most of its lots platted and sold by the owner to private individuals, was the home of the vice district that came to be known as Hell's Half Acre.[22]

Both the Daggett and Jennings Additions were soon absorbed by the expanding town and lost their original identities, but the similarity stopped there. The former Jennings Addition maintained an aura of respectability in later years while the Daggett Addition became the "wicked district," in the words of its detractors. The Daggetts were probably just as glad not to have their proud family name associated with the area after it acquired the more colorful appellation Hell's Half Acre. As Hell's Half Acre it took on some of the airs of a modern-day amusement park, according to one scholar.[23] The analogy is not as far-fetched as it might seem. The Acre was a public "amusement park," a major local attraction and an important source of municipal income. It also depended on a steady flow of out-of-town visitors to keep the doors open.

The railroad put the district on the map and ensured its long-term survival because the railroad brought a new class of visitors to the Acre to spend their money and rub elbows with the cowboys and buffalo hunters who were already there. These newcomers were described by the *Dallas Herald* as an "accumulation of adventurers and disreputable characters."[24] Dallasites knew this from their own experience. Before Fort Worth, Dallas had been a "terminal town" on the Texas & Pacific line. The experience of Dallas and other terminal towns in the West had shown that the worst human flotsam and jetsam accumulated at the end of the line. The *Herald* warned that the rails "will be to Fort Worth what the Red River raft is to that river. They will block up there and make the place a social pandemonium until the road goes on. Good Lord deliver us from a terminal town."[25] Proprietors in Hell's Half Acre, however, were licking their lips in anticipation of the influx. It was not long in coming.

By the end of 1876 there were fifty-nine businesses in town, most of them run by newcomers intent on cashing in on the boom times that followed the railroad. One was the Adelphi, the city's first genuine theater. Although the Adelphi was the first, it soon lost the distinction of being the only theater in town when the Theater Comique opened for business at Third and Main. The Adelphi always enjoyed the more colorful reputation, not for its stage shows, which hardly anyone remembered, but for its boisterous customers. The toughest guys in town would sit in the balcony and shoot the keys off the piano, the sort of high jinks shrugged off by fellow customers. The boys were just having a little fun.

The many trains and stages that came through kept a steady supply of customers lined up at Acre doors. Among them were a host of characters which a Dallas newspaper described this way:

> Emigrants "green from the States," young men reeking from college, going west, prospecting land speculators with corner lots in their eyes, fledgling lawyers and doctors, looking for a soft spot to fall on; old sports going out

to start a little game, cattle men going after that bunch of cattle out west, and, in fact, all kinds and classes from here and everywhere.[26]

What the greenhorns, emigrants and sodbusters found waiting for them in the Acre were the crooks, gamblers and confidence men who had arrived in the first wave after the railroad, among them men with names like Pony Bill and Three-card Johnny. Bill was a small-time gambler who ran a profitable monte game until authorities finally ran him out of town. Three-card Johnny was a much more interesting character whose other professional names included "Chuck-luck Johnny" and "C — — H — - Johnny." (One is forced to rely on imagination to fill in the blanks since newspapers of the day refused to print scatological nicknames.) His real name was either John or Johnson Gallagher, and he had made a formidable name for himself in the Kansas cow towns in the early 1870s before coming to Fort Worth. The *Topeka Daily Commonwealth* described Gallagher's standing among his fellow gamblers as "a Gulliver in a world of Lilliputians," and historian Ed Bartholomew describes Gallagher's upbringing this way: "He took to cards as soon as he could discriminate between the spots."[27]

Sometime between 1876 and 1879, Johnny spent considerable time plying his trade in Fort Worth. Like every successful gambler he had developed his own special tricks. Johnny's method was to play his suckers carefully, allowing them to win the first pot or two. Once they had acquired a taste for winning and were feeling cocky, he was able to take them for everything they owned. As he once modestly described his technique, "I not only get his money, but his watch and revolver besides, if he has any."[28]

Johnny was only in his late twenties when he was working Fort Worth, but his reputation and his obvious talents made him a respected member of the gambling fraternity. After leaving Fort Worth, Gallagher worked his way north to Dodge City. Newspapers there took note of his arrival in July, 1879. During a long stay in Dodge, he crossed paths with Luke Short, Wyatt Earp, Bat Masterson and Rowdy Joe Lowe. It may even have been Gallagher who told Luke Short about the lucrative opportunities for a sharp gambler down Fort Worth way. Just how close these two men were was demonstrated in May 1883 when they were both ordered out of Dodge at the same time by rival gambling interests; the difference on that occasion was that Luke chose to call in reinforcements and return for a showdown whereas Gallagher preferred to keep going.

While few of the gamblers who swarmed into Hell's Half Acre in the wake of the railroad could match skills with the likes of Gallagher and Short, there was still no lack of what Bartholomew calls "floaters, hucksters, thimble-riggers, spielers, cappers, auctioneers, shandies, and others whose callings are not even recognizable today."[29]

Fort Worth's economy at this time was based mostly on service-oriented businesses, with all the gamblers, prostitutes and con men serving the emigrants, sodbusters, cowboys and greenhorns who poured into the town. The customers were fairly easy to please; whatever their differing backgrounds or their motives for coming to Fort Worth, they all shared the same urges once they hit town. Men feeling thirsty, lucky, lonely, or all three, headed for the Acre first. There was no place like it either to the west or the north, which is why the city was soon dubbed the "Paris of the Plains," and the "Queen City of the Prairies."[30]

And for those visitors who might need a little persuading before venturing into the Acre, there were always "drummers" on hand at the railroad station and stage stops to greet new arrivals and entice them to try the Acre's charms. These drummers, mostly young boys who were paid by the saloon and gambling hall owners, could be persuasive agents for their employers. Next to word of mouth, they were the principal advertising medium for the Acre. They were so ubiquitous and persistent in their solicitations that in October, 1877, Ordinance No. 129 was passed "regulating and licensing street drummers or runners."[31]

It was partly due to the seductive appeals of hard-working drummers that respectable family men were often enticed into the Acre for a few hours of illicit pleasure, there to be seen rubbing elbows at the bar or on the dance floors with the less savory elements of society. When queried about their presence in such shady surroundings, these respectable gentlemen invariably explained that they were waiting for the next train or else just looking for a little "harmless fun." Frequently after a night of harmless fun, they woke up the next morning lying in the dirt behind some saloon with their wallets gone and a terrific headache. The police were called and a newspaper reporter usually showed up, too, but there were seldom any arrests, nor much sympathy for the victim. In the end, the gentleman went home to his family a little wiser and a lot poorer. When a common cowboy woke up in the street the next morning with a splitting headache and empty pockets, local authorities showed even less concern. The drover was a transient with no social standing and precious little economic clout — less so after he was rolled. He had paid his money and taken his chances in Hell's Half Acre. This attitude was so pervasive and so familiar in western trail towns that "even the victims themselves accepted the cleaning philosophically."[32]

Sometimes relieving a greenhorn of his money went beyond mere Mickey Finns and a heave-ho out of the back door. On October 13, 1877, W. P. Barton strolled into Arch B. Johnson's Ranche Saloon at 45 Main about noontime. Accompanying him was a new acquaintance — local gambler Michael Tooney, better known among his pals as English Tom. What the two had in mind was a little gambling in the back room of Johnson's saloon, but what Barton did not know was that English Tom and the saloon proprietor were in cahoots and had something more in mind than a friendly game. During the card game in a closed room at the rear of the saloon, they secretly sent out for a dose of morphine, which was slipped to Barton, and when that did not work, they sent out for some laudanum which they also slipped to him. That lethal combination did the trick. Barton had bet his last stack.

Johnson and Tooney were subsequently arrested, and a week later a jury of inquest charged them with murder. Three other men, presumably present at the game, were charged as accessories to the crime. The entire city was abuzz over what had happened. The newspapers called Barton's murder, "one of the most diabolical and heinous that has ever disgraced and blackened the criminal records of our county and city."[33] There were "whispers" of short-circuiting the judicial process with "a rope and lamp post." In a few days such wild talk died down, but the effect on Hell's Half Acre was more lasting. This sort of publicity hurt business because it gave potential customers pause before venturing into any of the Acre's seedy establishments. There was even talk of a general crackdown on all the gambling houses in the Acre. Such talk was sufficient to cause some of the less savory characters to pack up and move out of town, but others took their places as soon as business picked up. And inevitably business did pick up again.

The economic boom that followed the coming of the railroad in 1876 saw the number of businesses in town increase to some 460 in just four years with much of the increase catering to manly pleasures. Most of the saloons and gambling parlors settled on Main Street, while one block over on Rusk was where many of the low dives and bawdy houses were to be found. The better class of saloons kept to Main Street in the years to come, and half a century later old-timers still remembered the "many famous bars [that] flourished here."[34] Both Rusk and Main were anchored on the south end of town by the Texas & Pacific Railroad depot, which served both passenger and freight trains. When it was hastily thrown up in 1876, the station was the only building on Railroad Avenue, to which it gave its name, but before long the Palace Saloon opened its doors across the street from the depot as Hell's Half Acre extended its reach. The terminal and the T&P tracks served as the town's unofficial southern boundary for years to come. It was one measured mile straight down Main or Rusk from the public square to the depot, with morality tending to decline rapidly as one walked south. Rusk's reputation was no worse than Main Street's in these early years; they just represented different tastes in sin — Main for drinking and gambling, Rusk for whoring.

Eventually Rusk beat out Main for the title of "Sin Street"; curiously, Front Street — at the southern edge of the Acre — was never in the running. Front, which began as Fifteenth Street and later became Lancaster, got its name when the railroad reservation was created. It marked the boundary between the business district and the reservation. On the south side of the thoroughfare were the T&P tracks; on the north, facing the tracks, was an eclectic mix of saloons, residences, barns and warehouses — all rather tame by the standards of the day. By contrast, many Kansas cow towns also had a Front Street, the most notorious of them in Dodge City.[35] These streets usually faced the railroad tracks and had a reputation for being the most wicked in town — a strip where pleasure palaces and gambling halls reigned supreme. In Fort Worth, however, Front Street enjoyed a quiet reputation and a peaceful history.

From its humble beginnings, Hell's Half Acre spread in all directions like a coffee stain on a white linen tablecloth. By the early 1880s, the Acre had outgrown its original, unofficial boundaries two and a half times. For unknown reasons, Houston and Throckmorton streets to the west seemed to hang onto their virtue in these years, while Calhoun and Jones to the east were pulled into the Acre's orbit almost as soon as they were populated.

The southern ends of Calhoun and Jones could easily have developed differently and become a good influence on the Acre if a certain landowner in the district had not moved out. In the early 1870s, Joseph Addison Clark bought land on the south end of Jones and Calhoun between Ninth and Fourteenth streets with the idea of building a private academy for educating the young men of Fort Worth's better families. The city had no public school system at the time and its several private institutions were doing an indifferent job of teaching even the basics of reading and writing. The nearest institution of higher learning was Mansfield College (eighteen miles to the southeast), which opened in 1872 but was too far away by either stage or horseback to attract Fort Worth students.

With assistance from his wife Ida and his two sons, Addison and Randolph, Clark envisioned a family-run school. By 1873, however, he became alarmed at the non-stop pandemonium going on just to the west of his property: the twenty-four-hour saloons, gunfire, loud music and whooping cowboys were too nearby. Such a neighborhood was no setting for the quiet life of scholarly pursuits that the Clarks were planning. The location might even discourage respectable families from enrolling their children in the school.

The Clarks decided to leave Fort Worth and establish their school at Thorp Spring in nearby Hood County. That school was named Add-Ran College in honor of the two sons; eventually it returned to Fort Worth in 1910 as Texas Christian University, settling on fifty acres of prime land far from the center of town and from the bad influences of the Acre.[36]

The continual expansion of the Acre in these early years might have been checked if the Clarks had succeeded in establishing their school. As it was, the land that would have been home to Joseph Addison Clark's college instead was occupied by a collection of saloons, cribs and poor housing for the city's ethnic minorities, namely the Irish, the Chinese and the blacks. Instead of the school's uplifting Hell's Half Acre and the surrounding neighborhood, the Acre managed to drag down the entire Daggett Addition.

In these early years neither the law, nor the weather, nor even normal business hours could place a damper on the Acre. Sporting events were carried on outdoors as well as in, at all hours of the day and night. A man could always find a horse race or a cock fight somewhere up and down Main or Rusk. The *Democrat* reported in

1878 that cock fighting had become "quite popular among the city's sporting fraternity."[37] There was a two-bit admission charge to most fights and spectators were always welcome. Betting was optional but strongly encouraged. One of the most popular locations for cock fighting in the Third Ward was on the second floor of an establishment known as the English Kitchen.[38] Farther uptown on Main Street, Henry Burns' saloon had a cock pit out back, as well as a pit for dog fighting and a prize-fighting ring — all seeing regular, though illegal, use by Henry's customers.[39]

Horse racing on the frontier was as natural as guns and cards and about as prone to violence and excitement. In the early days in Fort Worth, all that was needed were a couple of horses and riders and a straight, level stretch of ground. Impromptu wagers soon became major sporting events with too many spectators and too many contestants to be held on the city streets. Fort Worth's first race track and grandstand was built in 1877 on the Cold Spring Road two miles north of town. On race day, carriages and saddle horses jammed the area formerly used by picnickers. The betting was hot and heavy because everyone generally knew the horses and riders. After the races, winners and losers alike adjourned back to the Acre to celebrate their good fortune or drown their sorrows. Taking horse racing off the main streets of Fort Worth and putting it on a track took away some of the spontaneity but changed nothing else about it.

• •

The chief landmarks in Hell's Half Acre were the big saloons like the Comique, the Palace, the Local Option, the Emerald and the Waco Tap, each of which enjoyed a large and loyal clientele. All except the Waco Tap were located near the railroad station to take advantage of travelers who wanted a drink first thing when they got off incoming trains or last thing before they boarded outgoing trains. Either way, these saloons enjoyed an advantage over those farther uptown. The Waco Tap, on the far eastern edge of the city, was next to a ravine "that ran down off Seventh Street" between Grove and Calhoun streets.[40] It did not catch much traffic from the trains, but its location made it a favorite of the cowboy crowd who could park their herds across the river and come back to the Waco Tap without riding through the center of town. With no close neighbors to speak of, the cowboys felt free to let off steam with less fear of disturbing the peace.

Fort Worth was no stranger to cock-fighting in the 1870s, despite the fact that it was against the law. Behind Henry Burns' Saloon on Main Street was a cockpit probably just like this one; also a pit for dog fighting and a prize ring. "Many were the battles pulled off in this resort," recalled Howard W. Peak (Schuchard Collection, Daughters of the Republic of Texas Library at the Alamo, San Antonio).

The Local Option opposite the T&P station was one of numerous saloons that opened for business in 1876. The owner may or may not have been making a political statement when he named it. The question of prohibition was heating up in Texas in the 1870s and public opinion was deeply divided. Politics aside, the Local Option proprietor was either incredibly stupid or remarkably shrewd: In the city's first commercial directory, he advertised that he offered the "worst liquors, poorest cigars, and miserable billiard tables."[41] He must have attracted attention, and the curious probably tried the place to see if his products were as bad as advertised.

A higher class of saloon was to be found nearer the courthouse square. The Pacific Saloon, the Cattle Exchange, the Merchant's Exchange and the Star Saloon all advertised fine imported liquors and Havana cigars for the discriminating patron. They discouraged cowboys and drifters from coming in, and the prices they got for their liquors and cigars underscored the point. They also offered billiards and gambling tables for faro, keno and monte players.

Fort Worth had a variety of saloons for every taste and pocketbook, with some twenty-six listings in the *City Directory* of 1877 and thirty-one listings two years later. But even the *City Directory* was not the last word because some places sold liquor and beer by the drink but did not bother to solicit a listing in the *Directory*. The true number of saloons and bars in Fort Worth was probably much higher than these records show.[42]

The names of the saloons were as varied as the clientele and the house rules. The Last Chance Saloon at one time placed a one-pint limit on all customers. Since one thing leads to another, the Last Chance Saloon led to the First and Last Chance Saloon where anybody could come in and drink as much as they wanted. The house rules at the First and Last Chance Saloon were also liberal when it came to things like expectorating on the floor or curling up in a corner. For customers who passed out in the middle of the floor there was a back room where they could sleep it off or sober up. The management of the saloon provided another popular service for its predominantly cowboy clientele: they would take charge of his bankroll when he first walked in the door and keep a running tab for him the rest of the evening. When his roll ran out, they would close the bar to him and send him back to camp. The cowboys had more faith in the saloon keepers than they did in themselves or any of the congenial characters a man might meet in a night of serious drinking. Such trusting relationships, operating on many levels, were the norm in the early days when every face had a name and genuine strangers were rare.

While hospitality at many bars included the back room where men could sleep it off, the inebriated customer with no friends to take him home was more likely to be unceremoniously shown the door by the "porter." (Contrary to popular myth, in most saloons the bartender did not perform this function, the porter — or bouncer as he is known today — did.) The practice of bouncing drunken customers contributed to the generally unsanitary street conditions because the porter would dump the unconscious drunks in the nearest gutter where they lay until sober enough to stagger off. Nothing was ever done about the drunks or the gutters by the local authorities. The gutter population was just part of the local scenery.[43]

The Headlight Bar, the Silver Dollar, the Cotton Bowl and the Dixie Bar were all holes-in-the-wall that also catered to cowboys. The owner of the Dixie Bar may have hoped his choice of a name would corner the business of all the unreconstructed Johnny Rebs in town, but there is no indication that such subtle advertising played any part in determining customers' drinking habits. On the other hand, the proprietor of the Headlight Bar attracted more than his share of business by advertising for customers to "Ride right in, boys, and get bar service in the saddle," a gimmick which may have made it the first drive-through establishment in history.[44] The big cattlemen with more money to spend were said to favor the Maverick or the Buckhorn, where they could cut deals over whiskey and cigars. In 1876, when Burk Burnett, Joseph McCoy, W. K. Shaefer, James Hickey and D. R. Fant brought their herds through Fort Worth, they probably stopped off at the Maverick or the Buckhorn.

There were also bars for Fort Worth's ethnic minorities. Germans were always welcome at J. Bohart's Bismarck Saloon and Herman Kussatz's Tivoli Hall, although neither place depended solely on ethnic clientele to keep the doors open. Kussatz offered a free lunch all day and "fresh beer always on tap." His was the first bar in the city to install one of "Gurley's patented refrigerators" which kept the beer "cold as ice itself." The refrigerator could hold 150 kegs of beer according to reports, or enough for any run on the bar. Bohart's establishment was named for Germany's Chancellor Otto von Bismarck, although most of Bohart's customers probably did not know the Iron Chancellor from an iron skillet. Both places served local German beer, made at a little brewery "back of Samuels Avenue."[45]

Burly farmers with German accents and wiry cowboys with southern drawls mixed freely at places like the Bismarck, the Headlight and most of the other working-man's bars, but the lines were more strictly drawn when it came to blacks. Although still an insignificant part of Fort Worth's population in the 1870s, they nevertheless had their own bars because Jim Crow laws operated on the frontier as much as they did in the eastern part of the nation after Reconstruction. Drinking establishments catering exclusively — or primarily — to black patrons were not listed in the standard city directory and there was no "colored directory" until after the turn of the century.

Some saloons stood out from the crowd for unusual reasons. The Empress Saloon and Beer Hall at 44 Houston was owned and operated for more than half a dozen years by N. H. Wilson.[46] Wilson was a pugnacious character and self-appointed champion of the town's morality at a time when there was not much to champion. His outspokenness won him some bitter enemies among town officials and fellow barkeepers. The Bank Exchange Saloon on Main was another "popular resort in the Third Ward" for more than a decade.[47] This record of longevity under the same name is remarkable in itself as the tenure of most saloons tended to be considerably shorter: ownership moved on, ran afoul of the law, or lost their regular clientele to a rival establishment; and names were changed according to whim or fad. The Bank Exchange was a pretty ordinary place until it became the focal point of the long-running conflict between uptown and downtown interests. The ownership had pretensions of being classed with the uptown places like the Pacific, the Cattle Exchange and the White Elephant. The challenge did not go unmet. The Empress and the Bank Exchange Saloon were both associated with violent events which assured their lasting fame.[48]

Barroom art was a fairly late addition to Fort Worth's saloons, coming at the end of the century. The city's better saloons added a touch of ersatz class by putting up a few paintings on the wall, or sometimes just one big oil painting looking down from behind the bar. The subject matter tended toward voluptuous nudes in sylvan settings. A modern description of Fort Worth's barroom art mentions several memorable works. One saloon in the 1600 block of Main displayed a huge oil painting of chubby misses romping playfully and dressed only in gossamer scarves that hid their most private parts. This work hung over a big black, ornately carved bar that was described as "out of this world."[49] Such surroundings, however, were far from typical for the usual class of workingman's bars in the Acre.

The bar in the old Seibold Hotel at Eighth and Rusk streets had several pictures hanging on its walls, some depicting western campfire scenes. They were later moved into the hotel's dining room where diners could gaze upon the cowboy at work while partaking of the product of that work, a thick beefsteak that had probably been on the hoof only a few hours earlier.

Another saloon at the corner of Ninth and Main also had a number of paintings adorning its dark, smoke-stained walls. The most popular featured several semi-nudes reclining in a pose known to artists as "odalesque." Another featured a group of high-kicking girls who may or may not have been doing the French-imported can-can. The propriety of such paintings was never questioned since those most likely to complain, the womenfolk, were by custom excluded from saloons.

Like the cheap Currier and Ives prints of the nineteenth century, barroom art eventually acquired an aura of highbrow respectability. Some artists whose works first graced common saloons — men like William Adolphe Bougereau and Charles M. Russell — eventually found their way into fine museums and galleries. A hoary legend about Amon Carter, Sr.'s, fabulous art collection says it started with the purchase of a Russell out of a northern bar for $125. When Carter was offered $2500 for the same work a year later, he began to look at so-called western art with a more appreciative eye.[50]

Art on the walls and a piano to one side, sawdust on the floor and spittoons in every corner — though this image does not describe all saloons (no two were alike) it captures the essence of a typical drinking parlor. All possessed a rough-hewn frontier ambience with swinging front doors, open bar and continuous hours of operation. With a clientele divided strictly along racial and sexual lines, the public saloon represented both the clannish and egalitarian instincts of Americans.

When K. M. Van Zandt first arrived in Fort Worth in 1865, the little village on the Trinity did not have a single saloon (the business district consisted of a blacksmith shop and a shoe shop), but by the late 1870s Fort Worth had more than enough barrooms; at least it seemed that way to many early residents. Ida Van Zandt Jarvis distinctly recalled "a saloon on every corner and the cowboys always stopped to . . . shoot off their pistols and give the cowboy yell."[51] Dewitt Reddick told an interviewer virtually the same thing: "Barrooms were on every corner."[52] And when the saloons were full, just being on the street could be life-threatening.

Cowboy Mythology: "In Without Knocking," a painting by Charles M. Russell, 1909. This is the way most present-day Fort Worthers picture a band of cowboys paying a visit to Hell's Half Acre. Truth is, Russell never saw Fort Worth and painted his picture after descriptions of a night in town by Montana cowboys (courtesy Amon Carter Museum).

THREE

"Better Undressed Than Unarmed"

HISTORIAN AND NOVELIST WILLIAM MacLEOD RAINE described Texas in the 1870s, with only slight exaggeration, as "the most lawless spot on earth."[1] As the state's premier cow town, Fort Worth was responsible for more than a little of that reputation. Closer to home, Reverend Addison Clark compared Fort Worth to Chicago — then considered a Babylon unequaled on the national level — "A lad living here then," he recalled many years later, "and retaining anything of moral character could stomach two trips to Chicago."[2] Mrs. Ida Van Zandt Jarvis, another long-lived early resident who retained a vivid memory, told an interviewer in 1938, "after the railroad came in 1876 and this became its terminus as well as the point where it met the Chisholm Trail, the town became lawless and colorful."[3]

The memories of genteel citizens and reform-minded clergymen do not tell the whole story. They must be judged against the equally valid recollections of men who served on the police force during the city's wild and woolly days. Jim Wood and Joe P. Witcher, both longtime law-enforcement veterans, tended to be more philosophical about what they observed on their daily beats. Wood told the *Star-Telegram* in 1921, "although the means of murder swung on the hips of the majority of the male population of Fort Worth, killings were less thirty years ago than they are today."[4] Witcher, who ultimately became captain of the police force in 1901, recalled that "the majority of arrests were made for intoxication," not violent crime.[5]

To understand how these perceptions could be so different, one must turn to a more objective contemporary observer. Rudyard Kipling never visited Texas but he saw numerous other western towns like Fort Worth during a lengthy tour of the United States in 1889 and 1890. Kipling thereafter distinguished between violence in America's East and West. From his cultured British perspective, America was a lawless place to begin with, but he found that society in the West held its citizens to a different set of standards. He spoke approvingly of the "energy and high spirits of the West," but characterized lawlessness in eastern cities like New York as "squalid barbarism and reckless extravagance."[6] Perhaps what Reverend Clark and Mrs. Jarvis recalled was "squalid barbarism," whereas Officers Wood and Witcher saw it simply as "high spirits."

The simple truth is, polite people who expected the West to be wild and woolly were seldom disappointed, while those of a more adventurous bent who took the West on its own terms found less to be shocked by. The reputation of a place like Hell's Half Acre might be half myth but the other half was plenty rough and tumble. Law and order came late to the "Paris of the Plains," and even then it was the unique, frontier variety that could easily be confused with lawlessness.

• •

Local wisdom at one time said that a man would rather be caught without his pants than without his six-shooter.[7] In the early 1870s carrying a six-gun was not only legal, it was expected. Shooting galleries were licensed within city limits, allowing a man to sharpen his aim or test his skills against other men without leaving town. Even after a law was passed by the state legislature ordering all men east of Parker County to stop wearing sidearms in town, it was widely ignored. Two city ordinances regulating the carrying of pistols and other deadly weapons had little effect when it came to changing the unwritten "Code of the West." Ordinance No. 13, passed in 1873, contained a loophole that allowed a man to carry a gun for the purpose of self-defense "if he could show reasonable grounds to anticipate an immediate attack upon his person."[8] Ordinance No. 164, passed in 1878, zeroed in on the problem of concealed weapons, including slingshots, knives and brass knuckles.[9] Neither ordinance was an effective deterrent because they were not strictly enforced. But having them on the books allowed the city in 1878 to boast that it had the most stringent laws against carrying weapons of any town in Texas, and it was probably true that not many men were guilty of carrying concealed slingshots or bowie knives. Moreover, violators could be fined in both the Mayor's Court and the County Recorder's Court, but not even the threat of double jeopardy could overrule the "higher law" represented by the "Code."[10] Fort Worth was an armed and dangerous city.

Still, just how much of the city's violent reputation was strictly fact and how much was exaggeration, legend or the product of municipal feuding between Fort Worth and Dallas is another matter. There is more than a little difference between common brawling — a favorite activity in the Acre — and deadly homicide, for example. There is not a single recorded instance of a shootout on a Fort Worth street before 1886. Fort Worth was never as bad as Abilene, Dodge City or some of the other cow towns during the period.[11]

Most lawbreaking tended to be harmless, like the incident on the night of April 9, 1878, two days after the first herd of the season coming up the Chisholm Trail arrived in town. After a night of revelry and carousing, a dozen or more inebriated cowboys mounted their horses outside the Red Light Saloon, drew their six-shooters, and fired off twenty or thirty shots into the air. They then put spurs to horses and galloped down Main Street to the railroad station where they reloaded and filled the air full of holes again. Apparently, they saw no harm in what they had done; instead of hightailing it out of town before the law could be summoned, they adjourned to the Waco Tap. Here the marshal and his deputies caught up with the merrymakers and took them off to jail.[12] The entire episode got scant mention in the newspaper the next day.

There are numerous stories like this in local lore whose point is not that Fort Worth was a hopelessly violent town, but that a certain level of mayhem was tolerated. Oliver Knight reported that one of the cowboys' favorite tricks as they rode out of town after a hard night in Hell's Half Acre was to shoot at a big coffee pot hanging over Jim Bradner's tin shop. The only harm done was filling Bradner's sign full of .45 slugs since apparently no one was ever arrested for this little bit of foofaraw.[13]

Bradner's sign was not the only prominent object to provide target practice for frolicsome drovers if we can believe another local legend. For years it was said that the face of the big clock on the tower of the Tarrant County Courthouse displayed bullet holes left by rois-

"Shooting up the Town," by Frederic Remington, 1902: a heroic-sized sculpture (originally entitled "Coming Through the Rye"), it depicts a typical Saturday night frolic by cowboys confined to the ranch all week—but not necessarily in Fort Worth (courtesy Amon Carter Museum).

tering cowboys.[14] A similar story long circulated about a suit of armor that occupied a fourth-story niche on the Knights of Pythias building on Main Street. Soon after the red-brick castle was completed in 1881, somebody shot the right hand off "St. George," as he was called fondly by locals. The mailed fist was still missing several years later, and cowboys headed the list of suspects.[15]

Whether it was street lights, Bradner's much-abused sign, the courthouse clock or St. George of Cowtown, the excuse for assorted damages was always the same: no real harm was done. A few bullet holes were part of the cost of doing business in a boisterous cow town. Besides, somebody usually came around and settled up later. After a particularly busy night of revelry in the Acre, it was not unusual to see a local ranchman or a trail boss making the rounds, "their pockets bulging with bills." They would go from saloon to saloon paying off the damage done the night before. Veteran bartenders always knew who belonged to which outfit and remembered who did what. When the boss showed up, they would quietly point to bullet-shattered mirrors or wrecked bars and receive compensation.[16] Matters could usually be settled without the involvement of the law, both the saloon keepers and the cowboys preferring it that way.

In those days, according to Oliver Knight, "the cowboy was king," which helps to explain his cavalier disregard for the law.[17] Although cowboys could hardly be mistaken for choirboys, there were few hardened criminals in the fraternity. According to Joe Witcher, cowboys could be rough and reckless, but were seldom dangerous if treated fairly. Witcher recalled his own experiences with the boys this way: "They were more clannish than sailors on shore leave in a foreign port and would fight a policeman or anyone else at the drop of a hat if they believed a friend had been mistreated."[18] The sentimental recollection ignores the fact that cowboys fought for a lot of other, less admirable reasons, both with the townspeople and among themselves. Usually the scraps were harmless, just like the gunfire as they left town, but sometimes things turned lethal before it was over. After a visit to the Acre, many a cowboy could identify with the lament of "The Dying Cowboy," a song sung by drovers on the Chisholm Trail:

> It was once in the saddle I used to go dashing,
> It was once in the saddle I used to look gay;
> But then I took to drink and then to card playing.
> Got into a fight and now to my grave.[19]

Hell's Half Acre sent plenty of men to their graves, as illustrated by a comment in the *Gazette* a few years later: "It's a cold day when the 'Half Acre' doesn't pan out a cutting or shooting scrape among its male denizens."[20] Such comments, which became familiar in local newspapers, were sufficient warning to decent folks. If one wanted to avoid trouble in Fort Worth, he stayed off the streets on the south end of town at night and out of the saloons and gambling joints during any hour of day or night.

B. B. Paddock, editor, lawyer and sage observer of early Fort Worth, identified two categories of local crime: violations of ordinances against drinking, gambling and prostitution; and violent crimes among persons involved in those activities. This generalization squares with reports of other frontier towns from Kansas to California. The modern litany of crimes, beginning with burglary and petty thievery and escalating to mass murder, did not become a problem until the end of the century. In the early days, citizens commonly left their doors unlocked, their possessions unguarded. The county tax collector even made his rounds alone, carrying his collections in saddle bags and spending the night on the road wherever he happened to be when night began to fall.[21]

Captain J. C. Terrell, Civil War veteran and pioneer resident, adds that two crimes were "never condoned" by Fort Worth citizens: theft of horses and disturbance of religious worship. When those two articles of the "Code of the West" were violated, punishment was swift and severe, sometimes "without the benefit of clergy."[22] Apparently, all other misdeeds were tolerable or at least justifiable.

Some Fort Worthers actually lamented the absence of excitement on occasion. One man wrote to the newspaper in the summer of 1876 with the following complaint:

> Why don't somebody kill a man, or get hashed up in a saw mill or something of that sort? It would be a terrible relief to newspapermen just now. If somebody could manage to get up a first-class scandal it would grease the wheels of local journalism wonderfully.[23]

It must have been an unusually peaceful time in the Acre that summer. Peaceful perhaps, but not unique. The same wistful sentiments were expressed by some pioneer residents in later years as they watched the city grow up.[24] Such comments were always noted in the newspapers in the best tradition of "man bites dog" reporting. When the town was *too* tame — that was news.

Some of Fort Worth's violent image was little more than yellow journalism, the product of a long-running municipal feud between Dallas and Fort Worth. The major newspapers of the two cities delighted in gigging each other at every opportunity. Whenever Dallas papers printed anything negative about Fort Worth, the Fort Worth newspapers retaliated in kind and vice versa. In the 1870s, Dallas editors mostly accused Fort Worth of being a boring and sleepy town. In April, 1876, for example, the *Herald* quoted an English traveler recently arrived from Fort Worth who reported that "the only persons he saw doing anything in that village were the brothers Paddock and Carb playing checkers and a distinguished member of the bar asleep with his pipe in his mouth."[25] The often-told panther-in-the-street story was a favorite. Fort Worth newspapers, on the other hand, scorned Dallas for its violence and lawlessness. In June of 1873, the *Democrat* remarked that "Dallas must be a delightful place to live in. Every day or two they have a murder or two to enliven the times. . . . Truly, they are a peace-loving people."[26] In November, 1875, the *Democrat* scored again with this comment: "Matters seem to be growing desperate at Dallas. Murders and robberies are so frequent that the daily papers are little more than reporters of desperate and daring crimes." In reporting that comment, the *Herald* sniffed, "The *Democrat* is still throwing dirt at Dallas."[27] In a few short years, however, the Dallas newspaper would begin carrying a regular column devoted to the latest sins and crimes of Fort Worth, and some of the most lurid tales of Fort Worth lawlessness come from Dallas newspapers. Dallas reporters added to but did not create Fort Worth's reputation as a lawless town. Fort Worth newspapers, with Paddock's *Democrat* at the forefront, reported plenty of local misdeeds over the years. Of course, criticism from a family member is always better received than criticism from outsiders, so Fort Worthers turned their violent image into a badge of pride when it was pointed out from the other side of the Trinity River.

In their own councils, Fort Worthers realized something had to be done to curtail the unregulated mayhem that plagued their city. The business boom that followed the coming of the railroad in 1876 outran both politics and law enforcement in Fort Worth. In 1877, city fathers took several steps to put teeth in local law enforcement and to manage political growth. Altogether, the city council had passed nearly one hundred ordinances before 1877 to curb the worst excesses of vice and disorder, but many languished on the books unenforced. Hell's Half Acre was the greatest affront to law and order, a fact that the townspeople themselves recognized. In April 1877, twenty-five concerned citizens petitioned the city council for additional police protection. The outgoing council referred the matter to the incoming councilmen, who discussed it but finally voted it down because of budgetary constraints.[28] While the petitioners were not successful on this occasion, they were now being heard in increasing numbers.

The year 1877 was a turning point in the transformation of Fort Worth. In a calculated step to help manage growth, the city was carved into political districts, or wards, a sure sign of an expanding population and its differing constituencies. Equally significant, municipal elections that year took on a different tone as reform issues came to the fore; although city government was only four years old, charges of corruption and criminal collusion were already being leveled at elected officials. Finally, the 1877 elections saw an incumbent marshal reelected for the first time. All these developments had major consequences for the future of Hell's Half Acre.

The year's significant events began on February 6, when the city was officially divided into three political districts: the First Ward, lying east of Main and north of Ninth Street; the Second Ward, lying west of Main and north of Ninth Street; and the soon-to-be-infamous Third Ward, encompassing everything south of Ninth Street down to Railroad Avenue. Henceforth, two aldermen would be elected from each ward instead of all the aldermen running at large. This change allowed more neighborhood involvement in city government, but also encouraged more influence for special-interest groups. With its thriving liquor and gambling rackets, no neighborhood had more special interests than the Third Ward. In the years that followed, the Third Ward would be synonymous in the public mind and in local print with Hell's Half Acre.

Charged with the daunting task of trying to keep the peace in Fort Worth were several levels of courts, the town marshal and the county sheriff. At the top of the local judicial system was the Tenth District Court, which held session at the county courthouse only twice a year to hear the most serious crimes and appeals. Below that, a county criminal court sat on the first Monday of every month. Below that was the County Commissioners Court, which met four times a year (February, May, August and November); and a Justice of the Peace for Precinct No. 1, who held court on the fourth Monday of every month. The queerest judicial duck was the Mayor's Court, which was at the bottom of the judicial hierarchy, but for that very reason was the court that often had first contact with the petty criminals of the Acre. This court was created by action of the first city council on April 12, 1873 (Ordinance No. 26), to sit in continuous session with jurisdiction over all misdemeanor cases in violation of city ordinances. It was not a court of record — a double pity from a historical standpoint because its transcripts would have provided an invaluable record of crime and punishment in the city — but its charter included provision for jury trials of six men upon request. Drunks, disturbers of the peace, gamblers, vagrants and whores were hauled before this court for speedy disposition of their cases — usually after a single night in jail. They entered their pleas, paid their fines and walked out the door as soon as the gavel was hammered down. Lawyers were seldom present; the mayor dispensed justice according to his own lights and the city's financial exigencies. Justice was not always sure, but it was definitely swift.[29]

The two chief officers of these different courts were the marshal and the sheriff, who in theory were the right and left fist of the legal system. Responsibility for enforcing the law within the city limits rested squarely on the shoulders of the city marshal (sometimes misspelled "marshall" in contemporary accounts), who was forced to serve two masters in the normal performance of his duties: the city council and the voters. He received a report card each April when the citizens went to the polls. Although the office was elective — the marshal had to campaign, make promises and defend his record like any other public official — the city council confirmed the voters' choice by appointing the winner head of the police force, usually an automatic endorsement. The council appointed all policemen and retained the power to fire the marshal for good cause. When the public's expectations and the council's directives diverged, the marshal's job security became precarious.

In the hierarchy of city officers, the marshal was the lowest of the lowly. Despite the similarity of titles, his job did not have the pay or the glamour of a United States marshal. The latter was the primary symbol of law and order in the unsettled West, and his image has become legendary as a man tall in the saddle, fast on the draw and tough as nails. Not so the city marshal. Experience was not a prerequisite for his job, nor was strict honesty or close familiarity with the law. Aided by council-appointed policemen, his task was to enforce whatever ordinances the city fathers passed and to run their errands. Being handy with fists, a six-gun and common workingman's tools were definite assets, as were stoicism and a strong stomach when it came to doing the council's dirty work — cleaning the streets of garbage and dead animals, filling fire barrels or swabbing down filthy jail cells after a busy weekend. It was not a profession for the squeamish or the timid since the marshal spent as much time on sanitation duties as law enforcement. Fort Worth's marshal was automatically appointed to the Board of Health upon election and during the course of his term in office served on numerous ad hoc committees.

Working almost the same beat — though on a higher professional scale — was the local sheriff. He too was elected annually and was a familiar figure on Fort Worth streets, enforcing county and state laws and patrolling the area outside city limits. The sheriff enjoyed a much higher level of public respect, not having to kowtow to the council's whims. Any time city and county jurisdictions conflicted, the marshal deferred to the sheriff, and the professional relationship between the men was always an uneasy one.

The first city marshal was Ed S. Terrell, elected in April 1873. The inaugural city council, elected at the same time, gave him four deputies to assist in the performance of his duties, but before the month was out he was already back asking for another policeman. The council took the matter up for discussion but turned him down.[30] They did authorize Terrell to buy a tin star for himself and each of his officers at city expense. The stars were to be worn in plain sight whenever the officers were on duty.[31]

The new marshal soon got crossways with the council over money. The marshal, and each of his officers, were paid a salary of $37.50 per month which they could supplement by performing extra duties, described as *ex officio* services.[32] In May 1873, for instance, the council paid Terrell $25 for cleaning the streets. Problems arose, however, because of the method of payment and because the terms for extra-duty pay were vague and depended on the generosity of the council. Payment was in scrip because the city was financially strapped most of the time. The practice of issuing municipal scrip was not unusual, but that did not make it any the less irksome to a workingman. The scrip could be redeemed only from the city treasurer and only when funds were available, which was a chronic problem. When Terrell submitted a bill for $75 in June, 1873, the council first tabled it, then referred the matter to the finance committee. Five months later, the lawman still had not been paid. He resigned in disgust and one of his policemen was appointed to fill the rest of his term.[33]

In the next city election on April 2, 1874, T. M. Ewing was voted in; Fort Worth had its third marshal in a year. The weeks following the election saw Ed Terrell still trying to get his money out of the city council, but as an ex-marshal he had no more success than when he had been in office. His account was referred to the new finance committee as soon as it took over, but municipal finances were in no better shape in 1874 than they had been the previous year. On April 28 the council passed a resolution thanking the policemen for agreeing to relinquish their salaries for the previous year. That apparently included ex-officers. Adding insult to injury, the council also ordered Terrell to "make an immediate settlement and turn over any and all papers pertaining to the office of Marshall [sic] to T. M. Ewing."[34] Fort Worth's financial problems explain why keeping the peace was a part-time occupation for men like Terrell, T. M. "Doc" Ewing and T. P. Redding. During Ewing's brief tenure, for example, he split his time between doctoring and arresting criminals.

Law enforcement was, in fact, a casual affair. There was never any hurry in making arrests; sometimes a man who had been running wild would not be collared by the law for a week or more. Furthermore, some did not take kindly to being arrested and put in the city jail. One inmate locked up by Doc Ewing stayed put about five minutes before kicking down the door and heading straight for the saloon where the marshal was taking a drink.

"How did you get out of the calaboose?" demanded the astonished marshal.

"Kicked the door down and walked out. I am not going to stay in that infernal hole," he answered.

"All right," said the marshal, "I have done my duty in the case and I don't propose to have another blamed thing to do with it." And he didn't.[35]

On November 10, 1874, seven months after taking office, Doc

Ewing submitted his resignation to the city council. They accepted it without argument. Perhaps Ewing had learned a lesson from Ed Terrell's problems. He made sure he was paid $100 for six months *ex officio* services before he quit. He had submitted his accounts in October and was paid the same month. He was gone the next month.

T. P. Redding, better known as "Uncle Tom" Redding, took over as city marshal on October 27, 1875. Most of the time Uncle Tom was the town barber. His title of marshal was best described by one resident as "more of an appellation than a de facto carrying out of the requirements of an executor of the peace and dignity of the hilarious town of that day." Many years later, this same old-timer remembered that "the boys did rather as they pleased, regardless of this peace officer."[36] In fact, they did more than just ignore him. One of the boys' favorite diversions was "buffaloing" the marshal. This popular frontier sport ranked just below drinking, gambling and horse racing, but probably about equal to "hurrahing" the town. "Many's the time," recalled another early resident, "I've seen cowboys run Tom Redding into a saloon by twirling their ropes after him or shooting under him."[37]

It may have been this sort of disrespectful treatment that got Uncle Tom suspended before his term was up. The council would not tolerate a lawman who was a laughingstock. They appointed John Stocker to fill out the balance of Redding's term, forcing Stocker to put up a bond of $1000 as insurance that he would discharge his duties in a professional and honest manner.[38] Stocker would serve from February 8, 1876, until city elections came around in April.

One of Uncle Tom's hirelings who outlasted the marshal was a young man named Timothy Isaiah Courtright, then employed as a jailer at the city's tumbledown lockup.[39] Observing the turmoil at the top of the city's law-enforcement ranks, Courtright began planning how he could use the situation to promote himself.

• •

The casual attitude evidenced by the behavior of the first men who wore the marshal's badge reflected the mixed feelings of those who elected them. For a long time, the good citizens of Fort Worth were not absolutely convinced of the need for a city marshal, at least not a full-time marshal. In 1874, there had been a public debate on the need for year-round city government of any sort. Some citizens believed that, as an economy measure during the "dull season," the affairs of city government "should jog along as best they could." The *Democrat* agreed to a point but drew the line when it came to the city marshal. His services were needed full-time, the *Democrat* argued "in preserving order and cleanliness on our streets, and in removing obstacles from the pavements, and for various other matters."[40] Presumably the "other matters" included crime prevention and detection. But many citizens continued to see no year-round need for a city marshal. With such a relaxed attitude about law and order, it was inevitable that Fort Worth would soon acquire the reputation of being a wide-open town. The election of Timothy Courtright, the former jailer, to three consecutive terms starting in 1876 was the first step toward solving some of the problems that came with that reputation. Continuity and stability in the marshal's office was one necessary reform, but only one.

City officials were joyous at the town's growth, and Hell's Half Acre represented a substantial part of that growth. To nurture the boom, lawmakers adopted an approach aimed at regulating rather than eliminating the Acre. Ordinances were enacted which were paradigms of law and order on paper, even if they were often unenforceable. One of the most bizarre was Ordinance No. 92, passed by the city council on December 26, 1876. It prohibited "male persons" from "riding, walking or promenading" the public thoroughfares with any "prostitute or woman of ill fame, commonly denominated whores." Fines for such activity were set at $10 to $25. The outcry that followed this enactment, however, led to an amendment two months later that covered only riding or driving with such women, and then only between the hours of 4:00 A.M. and 9:00 P.M.[41] Presumably, walking with a prostitute was now legal, and getting around in any manner with such femmes fatales was okay after nine o'clock at night. Although it remained on the books, even this watered-down ordinance became virtually a dead letter for the next fifteen years. The troubling legal question of who was a "prostitute" under this ordinance was determined by the "general reputation" of the accused or by "prima facie evidence."[42]

Quite often, the fines that were assessed under the anti-vice ordinances were applied selectively, mostly against the vagrants who made up a large proportion of every cow town's population. This faceless, nameless "class of citizens," as B. B. Paddock called them, lacked the influence and the money of the well-heeled gamblers and madams who also plagued Fort Worth. They were a symptom, not a cause of Hell's Half Acre, but that fact did not protect them against the zealous defenders of law and order. City Ordinance No. 9 passed in April, 1873, defined a vagrant as "any person without visible means of support" and provided a fine of $5 to $50 for persons arrested under this act. The city's vagrant population that was hauled before the courts for summary justice included both men and women, whose chief crime was being a public nuisance. There was a certain smug sense of accomplishment among city officials from clearing their likes off the streets. Vagrant laws, which never touched the big operators, were a popular measure for dealing with petty crime and vice and a favorite reform measure at election time. They were also practical. Many of the prisoners who could not pay their fines were employed in the back-breaking work of grading and cleaning up city streets. Apparently the work details were not watched too closely, however, because in February, 1877, the marshal was ordered to post a guard to prevent men from "walking off" the job.[43]

The same summer that the T&P arrived in town, the marshal and his minions worked overtime rounding up vagrants under Ordinance No. 9. Quite a few who appeared in the Mayor's Court were fined or ordered out of town, according to the mayor's judgement. B. B. Paddock reassured citizens, "The law is strict and idlers, etc., must obtain employment or skip town."[44] Some no doubt did find employment other than street maintenance for the city, but an unknown number were pointed out of town. Unfortunately, those leaving did not come close to offsetting the numbers pouring into town on daily stagecoaches and trains.

Vagrancy laws were enforced because they did not hurt the city's economy, but similar ordinances against gambling and prostitution were another matter. Here city officials maintained a truce with the Acre's business interests. As long as businessmen (or women) of the Acre kept the lid on violence and confined their activities to their end of town, lawmakers were tolerant. It was the job of the marshal and other elected officials to oversee this truce, keeping all involved parties happy. Most citizens went along, but there was the occasional voice in the wilderness. In 1876, N. H. Wilson took out a paid advertisement in the *Democrat* accusing the mayor and the town marshal of having a hand in running the very establishments they were supposed to be prosecuting.[45] This was the first, but hardly the last, time such a charge would be trumpeted in Fort Worth. Mr. Wilson's accusations, however, may have been based on some other emotion than moral outrage. Wilson was the proprietor of the Empress Saloon and Beer Hall at 44 Houston Street on the north end of town. As Wilson watched most of the customers flock to the downtown bars he fired what may well have been the first salvo in the long-running rivalry between uptown and downtown vice interests.

Wilson's charges also produced another result. The town marshal at the time was Timothy Courtright. Courtright took exception to the accusations and decided to do something about them. He went looking for Wilson and put a bullet in him the same day the paper came out. Fortunately for the saloon keeper, the gunshot was only a flesh wound in the thigh, but it had the desired effect. He voiced no more complaints in public print about Marshal Courtright's "official conduct."[46] As for Courtright, his career suffered no immediate ill effects from this encounter. He was efficient and well-liked, even if he was a little on the flamboyant side.

While moral indignity sometimes depended on one's point of view, there was plenty of justification for all the outrage that could be mustered against the Acre. Contrary to legend, the ordinary saloons and gambling houses were not the worst offenders of the public order — dance halls were. Perhaps this is not so curious when one considers that dancing was one of the tamer activities that went on inside the dance halls. To the usual mixture of drunken and belligerent men who were found in any gambling room or saloon, dance halls added a volatile catalyst in the form of unattached women. Such a mixture was never far from the exploding point, which is why many saloons and gambling halls took the precaution of barring women from their premises. The city council addressed this problem in its very first session by ordering that, "Any person who shall keep a . . . dance house . . . shall be deemed guilty of a misdemeanor."[47] Fines ranged from $1 to $50. The order was suspended six months later.

The problem was the same in all cow towns. As one customer in a Kansas cow town described his experience, "The girls get drunk, shout, swear, and make exhibitions too indecent for description. A staid man would think hell had broken loose to witness one of these disgusting dances."[48] Joseph McCoy, the man who put Abilene on the map as the "Queen of the Cow Towns," commented that "few more wild, reckless scenes of abandoned debauchery can be seen on the civilized earth than a dance house in full blast in one of the frontier towns."[49] Fort Worth residents early on had to get used to the "screeching of fiddlers and the foghorn voice of dance figure callers" resonating up and down Main Street at all hours of the day and night.[50] Sometimes the very buildings themselves shook to the stomping and clapping.

The privilege of dancing in such establishments was either free or ridiculously cheap. Shy cowboys were introduced to available girls by men known as "rustlers" — the same men who served as dance callers once the music started. A cowboy was encouraged to purchase tokens for a particular number of dances, but dance-hall owners made their big money from requiring the patrons to buy drinks for themselves and their dance partners at exorbitant prices. Buying fifty-cent drinks two at a time could soon eat up a cowboy's bankroll. Out of that dollar, the girl usually got a quarter's tip from the house, credited to her account and paid at the end of the evening.

The girls — who were most likely *not* full-time prostitutes — also paid a fee to the proprietor for the right of arranging their extracurricular business deals on the premises. Most dance halls had small, private rooms either upstairs or attached on the ground level to facilitate those arrangements. The dancing merely served as an introduction to the next event on the evening's program.

Why the dance-hall girls went into prostitution is not hard to understand. They realized little in the way of profit from an evening's work on the dance floor, despite dancing as many as fifty or sixty sets. They were nothing more than middlemen in separating the customers from their money. Ultimately, the proprietors pocketed the biggest profits. Girls who did not accept this fact were soon bounced out onto the streets and reduced to working out of the cribs. It was a very short fall from a dance-hall girl to a girl of the line. Naturally, none of this was on the mind of the cowboy looking for a good time. When cowboys confused professional friendliness with genuine affection, however, emotions sometimes got ugly. Violence frequently resulted, sometimes involving cowboys, girls and onlookers in one big free-for-all.

The low repute of the dance-hall girls was often deserved, but at least one voice was raised in their defense by one who had occasion to know many of them well. Eddie Foy, the famous vaudevillian, worked

"A 'Texian,' as he calls himself, must not be expected to do much out of the saddle. When his feet leave his wooden stirrups, it is generally to thread the dance on the light fantastic toe," wrote Mary Jacques in 1893 (*Texas Ranch Life*).

This particular dance hall, with its kerosene lighting, "St. Louis Beer" and fiddle players, was located in Denison, Texas, in 1873 when this picture was drawn (courtesy Denver Public Library, Western History Department).

the honky-tonk and saloon circuit in the 1870s before he made it big on the legitimate musical stage. He played in some of the best and some of the worst places in Dodge City, Tombstone, Leadville, Denver and other towns all over the West. In the course of his own performing, he was in a position to observe the girls night after night. While he did not approve of their line of work, he felt obliged to say that "some of those dance hall girls were personally as straight as a deaconess. Their job was to dance with the men, talk to them, perhaps flirt with them a bit and induce them to buy drinks — no more."[51] Despite Foy's honest effort to defend their virtue, most of the girls who worked the dance halls would never be confused with deaconesses. And judging by the newspaper reports and criminal court records, their conditions of employment often went beyond simple terpsichorean skills on the dance floor.

The two most notorious dance halls in the Acre were the Waco Tap and the Red Light. They also happened to be two of the most popular drinking establishments. The Waco Tap, after starting out as a cowboy saloon, was owned in the mid-1870s by a local courtesan named Lou Brown. She ran an establishment that was as profitable and immoral as any of those operated by her male counterparts — and just as violent. Even the musicians were not safe when the action got underway. After one particularly rowdy Friday night, the newspapers reported that one musician "had his nose demolished" by a cowboy.[52] There were probably more laws broken on a regular basis in the Waco Tap than any other place in Fort Worth until the honky-tonk burned to the ground in 1879. No one knew how the place burned, but it was a fitting end to what had long been known as one of the hottest spots in town.

The Red Light was located on Rusk Street, even before that dusty track was officially designated by name. In the early days it was a rather unimposing structure, sitting in the middle of a large empty lot on the south end of town. The exterior was unpainted clapboards, but this humble appearance belied the fact that it was the largest and busiest place in town. Inside were two large public rooms — the dance hall and saloon — and a number of smaller private rooms — the apartments where customers could enjoy a few moments of intimate privacy with the dance-hall girls. According to a tally by the *Democrat*, there were between ten and twenty-five of these apartments that could only be entered from the outside, preserving a modicum of propriety. The whole operation — dance hall, saloon and private rooms — was located on ground level. Those interested only in drinking or dancing entered through the main entrance on Rusk Street, passing through the saloon to reach the dance hall. The dance floor was thirty by fifty feet with a row of benches all around "for the ease and comfort of those who want to sit down and chat with the girls." On a typical evening, however, the noise level and crowded conditions prevented much chatting. That did not matter much because chatting was an inefficient use of the girls' time when they could be earning fifty cents per dance. After whirling around the floor a couple of times, the women steered their partners to the bar for a round of drinks. The barroom was known as the "White House," and did a booming business between dance sets.

The Red Light violated every principle of decency and morality known to man. The *Democrat* described it as a "repository of crime, where vice, recklessness, dissipation and wickedness abound."[53] The clientele included all types from young scions of respectable town fathers to ordinary cowboys and out-of-town cattle dealers. The *Democrat* reported that "hundreds of cowboys, frontiersmen and grangers" frequented the Red Light nightly.[54] An assortment of thieves and pickpockets also mingled with the crowd, looking for a chance to score. The smell of cheap whiskey and a haze of dust hung over the place and helped cover up the stench of sweaty, tightly packed bodies.

Overseeing all of this boisterous activity was a proprietor who had to be equal parts businessman, diplomat, host and enforcer. He was probably also a gambler on the side. The first proprietor of the Red Light was an unsavory character named John Leer who turned the keys over to Joe Lowe in 1876 or '77. Leer then moved over a couple of streets and opened the Comique Saloon at Eighth and Houston. He spent the next decade fencing with the law over charges of keeping a disorderly house, running a gambling parlor and libel.[55]

Despite Leer's aggressive pursuit of the criminal life, his reputation never did measure up to Joe Lowe's. Lowe became the Acre's first vice king and one of Fort Worth's most colorful figures in its cow-town days. Bat Masterson, who knew Lowe well as a gambler and saloon keeper in several Kansas cow towns, counted him among the legendary gunfighters of the West.[56] Coming from a man who knew many of the legendary gunfighters personally, that was high praise indeed.

Joe came to Fort Worth from San Antonio where for the better part of three years he had run an unpretentious joint called the Clipper. As one historian has noted, this was an appropriate name for a place that was a "notorious skinning house."[57] Before San Antonio, Lowe's address had been Wichita, Kansas, and his move to Texas in 1873 was strongly influenced by a murder charge against him in Wichita. It was not the first time he had been in trouble with the law. He was known in all the cow towns as "Rowdy Joe" due to his penchant for gunfighting and brawling with all comers. His equally colorful wife was known as "Rowdy Kate." Historian Ed Bartholomew describes the feisty couple: "He was a strange sort of badman, and she was a strange sort of female desperado."[58] The two of them left Wichita in 1873 after Joe was involved in a bloody feud with a man named Ed Beard, better known to the townspeople as "Red Beard." The two men ran rival saloons-cum-dance-halls next door to each other, and the rivalry erupted into gunfire on two occasions. Both times innocent bystanders were shot, and in the second shoot-out, Rowdy Joe and Red Beard were also wounded in what the *Wichita Eagle* described as a "dance house row."[59]

When Red Beard died of his wounds, Lowe was charged with murder plus attempted murder of the wounded bystanders. In his first trial on the charge of murder he was acquitted. But he still had to face the indictment for attempted murder. Unwilling to trust his fate to the hands of another fickle Wichita jury, he slipped out of town on a quiet Sunday morning when most of Wichita's citizens were sleeping off the effects of the previous Saturday night. The *Wichita Eagle* reported his departure a few days later: "At this writing nothing has been heard of him."[60] They failed to add that Kate was also gone. Unbeknownst to the citizens of Wichita, the Lowes were headed for Texas. By the fall of 1876 they had settled in Fort Worth; in October of that year the *Democrat* announced that Joe Lowe was taking over the Centennial Hotel and planning to operate it as the Centennial Theater.[61] Since Fort Worth was a wide-open town in 1876 there was no absence of opportunity for a sharp, aggressive operator like Rowdy Joe to carve out a niche for himself in the new, booming gambling district. These were good times, and Joe Lowe was in on the ground floor. His experience and reputation in the Kansas cow towns could be put to good use in Fort Worth. Many of the cowboys who passed through the doors of the Red Light had been regular customers in his establishments on the other end of the Chisholm Trail. He could call them by name and probably even knew what kind of whiskey many of them drank.

His relations with the city council got off to a rockier start, however. When Joe refused to pay his taxes, the council drafted an ordinance to prohibit "the sale of intoxicating liquors in houses where shows of any kind are carried on."[62] This would have struck directly at Joe's Centennial Theater, probably putting him out of business. But the council did not intend to enact the ordinance, just use it as a threat to force him to pay his taxes. The proposed ordinance was tabled until the city secretary could show it to Lowe "and notify him that unless he pays his taxes regular, the same will be approved."[63] Lowe anted up and the council tabled the ordinance permanently.

Soon after they settled in Fort Worth, Joe and Kate came to a parting of the ways, and Kate left the city. She did not move too far away, however, for in May, 1877, the *Weatherford Exponent* reported that she ran "a den of infamy in the business portion" of that town. The *Exponent* was most indignant about her presence in "the most moral town in Northwest Texas."[64] If they hoped such public criticism would persuade her to move on, they were wrong. In 1881 the record shows that Kate was still living in Weatherford because she was brought up before the local court on unspecified charges.[65]

Meanwhile, Joe was in Fort Worth making money hand over fist with his dance hall and saloon properties. In addition to the Red Light and Centennial, he had an interest in several other Fort Worth bars, theaters and brothels during the late 1870s and early 1880s.[66] In 1878 he was charged with "keeping a disorderly house" but a jury acquitted him on the technicality that it could not be proven that he was anything more than the "proprietor" of said establishment.[67] The real owner or owners were not charged with anything. This may have been the first time such a problem reared its head in local legal proceedings, but it was hardly the last. Some of the worst places in the Acre operated in buildings or on land owned by some of the best people of Fort Worth, but the owners' names never appeared in court records. Some prominent names did appear in newsprint, however. In 1879 the *Democrat* named S. H. Holmes, respected alderman from the First Ward, as the owner of "five houses in this city which he rents to prostitutes." The *Democrat* was forced to admit, however, that "there is no law by which he can be held responsible as a landlord to such characters."[68] While absentee owners dealt in real estate, the proprietors on the scene like Rowdy Joe made their money on the shadier side of the law and paid for it when the police cracked down.

Joe Lowe's advantage in such an arrangement was his carefully cultivated public image as a genteel scoundrel. Despite his bad temper, Joe was neither crude nor unlettered. He habitually wore the top hat and black frock coat of a gentleman gambler and went clean-shaven except for a small mustache. He could be charming, even gallant when the occasion demanded. As he walked around town, he tipped his hat to ladies and exchanged pleasantries with businessmen. He held benefit balls in the Centennial to help raise money for the volunteer fire department, for the needy and for victims of an 1878 yellow-fever outbreak.[69] But there was no denying that he also had a quick temper and could be a very dangerous man when aroused, which was too often for his own good. He was also hard on women, which may be why only a woman like Rowdy Kate would stay with him for long.

Sometime in the early 1880s, Joe sold out his interests in Fort Worth and moved on. He made stops in several other cow towns and possibly went up to the Black Hills where the gold rush was creating a different sort of boomtown. He ended his days in Denver, Colorado, in 1899, face-down on a barroom floor with a bullet in him after a gunfight with a younger and faster opponent.[70] He made his living in saloons and dance halls, so it was only appropriate that he should die there, too.

Joe Lowe was a genuine frontier character, but it is doubtful if many mourned his passing. No monuments reminded Fort Worth of him, unless one counts the Red Light saloon, which he made into a local legend during his reign as Fort Worth's first vice king. It was the standard by which all other wide-open establishments in the city were measured, and for that reason it always attracted the most public attention and press notoriety. Its reputation was earned the hard way and fully deserved. At one time the Red Light produced one-third of the city's major arrests.[71]

The problem with the dance halls was not that Fort Worth citizens objected to dancing as an activity. In fact, dancing was a "principal form of recreation" in the early days.[72] B. B. Paddock in his reminiscences had fond memories of "dances in the court room, in a hall over a livery stable and at private residences [where] they danced the cotillion, lancers and Virginia Reel."[73] Fort Worth citizens were

Both of these pictures purport to be of Rowdy Joe Lowe, another import to Fort Worth's gambling fraternity from the Kansas cow towns. One is obviously retouched (left) but is believed to have been made in Fort Worth about 1876 or '77 (N. H. Rose Collection, Western History Collections, University of Oklahoma Library). The picture at right is courtesy Kansas State Historical Society, Topeka.

not prudes when it came to dancing. What they objected to was the setting in the midst of a combination saloon-bordello like the Red Light or the Waco Tap. Acceptable dancing was the kind that was done in some settler's home, never in one of the downtown, public dance halls.[74] The two styles were as different as homemade elderberry wine and rotgut whiskey.

Other dance halls in the Acre, smaller and less notorious than the Red Light and the Waco Tap, caught the overflow from the larger establishments. There was always plenty of business to go around, and all the dance halls had the same prurient atmosphere that decent folks found shocking. The prurient atmosphere was not the main problem, however; violence was the main problem.

The campaign against the dance halls might be said to have begun on January 16, 1877, when the *Democrat* editorialized, "Blood has been shed at the dance houses. Close them out." But this was easier said than done. From its vantage point thirty miles away, the Dallas newspaper was amused by Paddock's one-man crusade against the dance houses. The *Herald* commented, "Dance houses are the bugbear of the Democrat."[75] Soon the *Fort Worth Standard* added its voice to that of the *Democrat*, lambasting the dance houses in practically every issue. This late convert to the crusade prompted another wry comment from the *Dallas Herald:* "The Fort Worth papers are rivals as to which can condemn the dance houses most severely. Perhaps neither would consent to having them closed if it was known that the other was the cause of having them closed."[76] It was not that the city council was unconcerned with the problem; they had tried for years to bring them under control. An ordinance against dance halls was always on the books in some form or another, but under pressure from the owners it was usually ignored. The Paddock-initiated campaign finally paid off in June, 1877, when all the dance houses were closed without exception and the proprietors fined $10 each in the Mayor's Court "for their revelry"[77] They were open again a month later, however, and five local citizens were arrested at one popular place for "exhibiting themselves in a public or indecent manner."[78] The city council retreated again in September when it legalized the dance halls but tried to regulate their operation through licensing. The fact that licensing brought in more money than fines no doubt played a part in their thinking. Even this concession by the city did not significantly reduce the level of saturnalia at the worst dance houses, and the relatively mild licensing ordinance was soon repealed.

The fragile truce between elected officials and vice operators was broken with alarming regularity. The city's tolerance, whether driven by greed or by higher motives, was repaid by the dance-house owners with open defiance. Another ordinance passed in August, 1878, did not even last long enough to get a fair trial. The council was forced to act because dance halls had "become such a problem that the City Council is tired of passing ordinances prohibiting them, then repealing those same ordinances." The new law was another attempt at licensing the establishments, this time at "a hundred dollars a quarter, payable in advance." When Mayor R. E. Beckham vetoed the ordinance at the next meeting, the council meekly repealed it. The *Democrat* informed its readers, "Dance halls are unrestricted again."[79] Mayor Beckham's reputation as a "reformist mayor" survived the episode: voters rewarded him with another term the next spring after he campaigned on the same promise to clean up the city. But his craven retreat from his campaign promises on the subject of dance halls was still a blow to reformers, and they began looking for a new champion to carry their banner.

The *Democrat* and *Standard* had already found a new, powerful ally for their cause, the Reverend Francis Grant, formerly a Baptist minister in Dallas who had decided that Fort Worth was closer to the front lines in the war against sin. Grant came to Fort Worth in the summer of 1877 and promptly launched an evangelical crusade against the dance houses from his pulpit. On September 30, 1877, he preached a hellfire-and-brimstone sermon on "The Three Crosses." The major newspaper of his former town wondered if he would nail the editors of the *Democrat* and the *Standard* to the outside crosses "in a characteristic sense of the word as it were."[80] Like John the Baptist preaching in the wilderness, Francis the Baptist did not save many sinners in this cow town.

The question of who would close out the dance halls was complicated by the fact that those charged with enforcing the ordinances were themselves patrons of the establishments. The *Dallas Herald* charged that "the city council and the dance houses stand in with one another."[81] A Fort Worth resident recalled "It was no uncommon thing to see a policeman at the head of a [dance] set, while the chief of police might be upstairs betting a stack of reds on the high card."[82] Finding a man with the courage and the reputation to go up against the dance halls, dives and dens of iniquity in Hell's Half Acre was a tall order. And that unusual man would also have to satisfy both the business-minded city fathers and the high-minded puritans.

"Old Ed" Terrell, as he was affectionately known to Fort Worthers in his later years, celebrating his ninety-third birthday, 1905. Before serving (unhappily) as Fort Worth's first marshal (April-October, 1873), Ed tried farming, fur trapping, horse trading, cattle shipping and shopkeeping—all with notable lack of success. He also was the owner of the First and Last Chance Saloon for several years. Pictured here with his granddaughter Fannie Vardy in front of the county courthouse (courtesy Ruby Schmidt, Fort Worth).

FOUR

"Lord Make Us Good But Not Right Now": The Timothy Courtright Years, 1876–1886

T. I. COURTRIGHT WAS THE MAN BUSINESS-MINDED CITY fathers could count on to protect their interests and provide law and order.[1] Courtright — a gunfighter who dabbled at gambling — cast a long, sometimes violent shadow over the Acre for a decade during its glory years.

Courtright came from a typical western background. Born on the Iowa frontier in 1848, he served on the Union side in the Civil War under General John "Blackjack" Logan. After the War he drifted around the West, working as army scout, sharpshooter, buffalo hunter — whatever did not require regular hours or hard physical labor. Along the way he married a farmer's daughter named Sarah Elizabeth Weeks, eight years his junior. When he moved on, she went with him and quickly adapted to his lifestyle. He taught her how to shoot and she became a crack marksman in her own right. They even performed together for money, a fact which led some later chroniclers to say that they toured for a time with Buffalo Bill's Wild West Show.[2] While this story seems unlikely, it is just one of many question marks in Timothy Courtright's relatively short but exciting life.

Apart from his lightning-fast draw, Courtright's chief claim to fame was his hair, which he wore longer than most (leading to his famous nickname "Longhair Jim"), and his penchant for wearing two six-guns, butts forward. This unusual rig marked him instantly as a professional. His long, lanky figure completed the picture, and the net result was a man who commanded attention wherever he went. He was good with guns, not so good with cards, and mean-spirited, altogether a dangerous combination in the West.

Timothy Isaiah Courtright won his first race for city marshal of Fort Worth in 1876, beating out four well-known local citizens for the office.[3] Such a large field was not unusual in the rough-and-tumble politics of the frontier before party machinery took control of the local electoral process, but there were still extenuating circumstances in the 1876 marshal's race. The regularly elected marshal, Uncle Tom Redding, had been dismissed from office a couple of months earlier in a dispute with the city council. The caretaker marshal, John Stocker, was one of Courtright's opponents in the race, but none of the candidates could truly be considered a local favorite, which helped Courtright's chances as a dark horse.

Timothy Courtright was still a relative newcomer to Fort Worth in 1876, having come to the area some three years earlier as an unemployed drifter with a wife and a strong desire to settle down. He leased a bit of property on the north side of the Trinity River and tried his hand at farming. But Courtright did not have the temperament for farming. He preferred town to farm, and the companionship of good friends to the lonely life of the sodbuster. He finally gave up on that field of endeavor, but his failure at farming and his relative newcomer status did not count against him too much with the voters. The West was full of busted homesteaders, and on the frontier no one held it against a man who was new in town. Most Fort Worthers, in fact, were newcomers. The *Dallas Herald* expressed the prevailing sentiments when it said, "As a rule Texans don't care a straw what a man had been or where he came from — they judge him entirely by his own ability in sustaining himself. . . . Every tub stands upon its own bottom here, and will stand in no other way." The *Democrat* quoted that assessment and added its own endorsement: "In Texas, more than in any other state, a man is judged solely on his merits, and has no use for commendatory letters or pedigrees."[4]

When he ran for city marshal in 1876, Timothy Courtright lacked most of the necessary qualifications for elected office. A political novice who had never run for office before, he also lacked the natural advantages of having good family connections, strong political identification, and a solid record of civic accomplishments. On the plus side, he had served as city marshal of Omaha, Nebraska, for a time, apparently "to the perfect satisfaction of its citizens."[5] He also had worked as the city's jailer, an inconsequential post but nonetheless a cog in the machinery of local law enforcement. Finally, he belonged to a select group who enjoyed a certain celebrity status in small communities all over America, the local volunteer fire brigade. Hook and ladder companies like the M. T. Johnson Company, to which Courtright belonged, were commonly recognized as stepping stones to politics on the local level in the nineteenth century. "The station house, like the saloon, was a poor man's club where the boys got together for a smoke, small talk, and an occasional game of cards," and the boys could always be counted on to vote for one of their own.[6]

His experience as marshal of Omaha and his membership in the hook and ladder company were definite assets, but Courtright's strongest qualification was his nonpareil reputation as "the best pistoleer in Texas."[7] He was one of the few men anywhere who could use two guns simultaneously with equal speed and accuracy — qualifications that outweighed all others. On the negative side, he was also known to be moody, restless and overbearing. As long as things went his way he was pleasant enough, but he was not one to be crossed, nor to forget a slight. Timothy Courtright was a man who carried a grudge. He was far from being a model lawman, even by the rough standards of the frontier, but he was better with a gun than any of his opponents in the marshal's race or anybody else in town for that matter. In short, he was just what a half-tamed cow town needed. The *Fort Worth Standard* recognized this when it described Courtright's qualifications, starting with the fact that he did not drink intoxicating liquors and was always "at his post," then coming to the main point that he was "not afraid to take on any man who walks the earth."[8] He was in the same category with his contemporaries Wild Bill Hickok and Wyatt Earp; they were not nice men, but they could deal with armed and dangerous lawbreakers on equal terms.

Courtright's election was hardly a foregone conclusion.[9] Of the five men running for city marshal in 1876, Courtright won by a razor-thin margin of three votes. His 106-vote total constituted less than one-third of all the ballots cast. In a shrewd political move that acknowledged the divided loyalties of the voters, the new city council immediately appointed the runner-up, C. C. Fitzgerald, to the deputy marshal's job. This made him second-in-command in the law enforcement hierarchy, more than a mere policeman, but still in an appointive post occupied at the pleasure of the marshal and council. The narrowness of Courtright's victory would cause him problems with a disgruntled constituency long before his job was finished.

One has to wonder why any of the five men who ran for marshal wanted that particular job in a small town like Fort Worth. Leaving aside explanations of psychological motivation such as the thrill of power or the excitement of living on the edge, one looks for concrete reasons to explain the appeal of the job. It could not have been the prestige that came along with the badge, since facing down desperados ranked near the bottom of the job description. In fact, Bat Masterson always believed the job of city marshal was "degrading to a certain extent." In Masterson's opinion (he was in a position to know, having served in law enforcement on the frontier for much of his life), the job of sheriff was "a true lawman's work."[10]

Besides the degrading duties, there was the tedium of official paperwork, another aspect of marshaling never mentioned by the mythmakers of the West. H. P. Shiel was the first Fort Worth marshal required to file reports of his official activities. In February, 1875, Marshal Shiel was ordered by the city council to file a "general report" at the first regular meeting of every month beginning in March. The council also ordered his four officers to do the same.[11] It was a sad day when paperwork arrived in frontier law enforcement. Some of the officers were barely literate, and their reports must have been more puzzling than enlightening to their bosses. But it was part of the job.

If not the prestige or excitement, what then was the attraction? It was certainly not the size of the salary since the city marshal drew pay best described as subsistence level. Until 1877 Fort Worth marshals were paid $37.50 per month, the same as city policemen. According to Ordinance No. 27, which dealt with hiring and paying the police force, the salaries of the marshal and policemen were to be paid out of "any funds in the City Treasury."[12] Quite often that meant payment in scrip or no pay at all.

When Timothy Courtright first became marshal in April, 1876, he received only $25 per month thanks to an austerity drive launched at the beginning of the year (a cut of $12.50 a month from what his predecessors were making). That summer, with the railroad finally nearing completion, the amount was boosted to the munificent level of $50 per month. The city council made the marshal's raise permanent eighteen months later when it formally approved an annual salary of $600 per year. Coming on December 25, the council's action was no doubt a welcome Christmas gift.[13]

By contrast, an ordinary cowboy could make $25 to $35 each month for baby-sitting longhorns up the Chisholm Trail.[14] More to the point, Abilene, Kansas, paid Bill Hickok $150 monthly when he first put on the badge in 1871.[15] Not many cow towns paid such princely salaries to their law officers, but on the other hand, wearing a badge could be downright unhealthy in Abilene. Hickok's immediate predecessor, "Bear River Tom" Smith, was killed while serving a warrant on a homesteader.[16] Courtright's six immediate predecessors were all living to a ripe old age long after he became marshal.

If not the salary, the working conditions or the prestige that came with the marshal's badge, there must have been some less obvious enticement not included in the job description that attracted men of vigor and ambition. Indeed there was: an extralegal arrangement between the city and the marshal that had the potential to increase an officer's salary several times over. The marshal, in effect, worked for the city on commission, surviving not on his meager salary alone but on a system of fines and fees set up by the city council.

At the heart of the system were the fines collected from lawbreakers for a standard list of offenses ranging from being drunk and disorderly to prostitution, fighting, carrying a gun and so on. For non-violent crimes, the typical fine handed down by the local courts was either $5 or $10. In a wide-open town like Fort Worth, fines against prostitutes, dance houses and gambling dens were collected so routinely that the practice amounted to virtual licensing. Sometimes the city enjoyed the best of both worlds by collecting licensing fees and criminal fines on the same activities. For instance, after the city ordered the dance houses closed down in May, 1877, city revenues dropped and the public howled about lost cowboy business when the next cattle season rolled around. After a summer of slow business and pinched budgets, the dance houses were permitted to re-open but only after being licensed, and the city collected money from every establishment twice: first, in licensing fees; second, in fines. Since a night did not pass that the dance houses did not break some law or another, this was a very profitable set-up.

Even enforcement of relatively mild laws was something of a joke. Fines on the operators of dance houses and bawdy houses were set low enough that they constituted little more than a minor inconvenience to the violators. Court records show that nobody ever served time for gambling or running a "disorderly house." During periodic drives against the Acre's well-known operators, gamblers and madams were picked up in bunches like grapes and tried the same way: a bunch of gamblers one day, a bunch of madams the next day. The local judicial system processed them through with nary a hitch. The standard operating procedure for the shady characters brought in by such roundups was to plead guilty, pay their fines and be back at their place of business in a few hours. Some of the worst offenders, who were also the biggest operators, seemed to spend more time in court than they did running their businesses, but operations apparently did not suffer any from their periodic absences. It was not that the legal proceedings in every case were long and drawn out, just that the same people made frequent appearances in court. Occasionally, a fine of $100 or $200 would be handed down against one of the gamblers or madams, but the defendant would always appeal. The case would then drag on for months with continuances and delays, but the accused always posted bond and went back to work while his or her lawyer handled the legal details.

Some of the defendants who appeared before the courts enjoyed the protection of more powerful local figures. When Luke Short operated a gambling room in Fort Worth, he always took care of any of his dealers arrested for illegal gambling. When they appeared in court he promptly posted their bond, whereupon they just as promptly skipped town by an agreement that was probably made when they were hired. Luke never had any trouble finding new dealers to take their places. Notorious madam Mary Porter also enjoyed the protection of her own guardian angels in the persons of respected businessmen E. B. Daggett and W. H. Ward who posted bond for her on occasion.[17] The bigger fish, like Porter and Luke Short, paid proportionately larger fines which reflected their exalted status in the city's vice operations. But large fines or small, they were all paid with a wink and a smile before being divvied up by the city.

The "fees" constituted the marshal's cut of those fines plus whatever additional payments he received for performing unpleasant or dangerous services. Much as professional athletes have performance bonuses written into their contracts today, the marshal could improve his base salary considerably by aggressive enforcement of laws on the books. Until the summer of 1877 this whole fee business was a casual agreement between the marshal and the city council. In July of that year an ordinance was finally passed officially recognizing the practice; Ordinance No. 117 created a special fund "from fines, penalties, and forfeitures" plus one-quarter of all license and occupation taxes, to be used in paying the city's law officers.[18] The system was finally becoming institutionalized.

The fees and fines together were known in western parlance as a "taxation on disorderly elements" and were commonly split between the city council and the marshal all over the West.[19] Made famous by Joseph McCoy in Abilene, Kansas, they were a cost-efficient method of supporting local law enforcement.[20] The practice proved such a success there that it was eventually adopted by almost every other cow town in the West, and invariably proved to be the largest source of municipal income for those tax-starved towns dependent upon the cattle trade.[21]

Fort Worth's marshals were not as generously provided for as Abilene's, who received twenty-five percent of the fines they collected.[22] In the first four years of the city's existence, Fort Worth officers received a straight fee of a dollar for every arrest and subsequent conviction. In December, 1877, the fee schedule was revised: a dollar for each arrest, fifty cents for each case successfully tried, a dollar for each search warrant executed, and a lengthy list of special fees for other duties.[23]

There was one notable exception to the straight fee schedule used in Fort Worth. In July, 1878, the council passed a new ordinance prohibiting concealed weapons and regulating the possession of a variety of other weapons in addition to guns. To encourage vigorous enforcement — potentially a very dangerous job for the man with the badge — the council ordered that fifteen percent of the fine go to the arresting officer. The council got more than it bargained for. The ordinance was apparently abused by over-eager policemen hoping to cash in, because a howl of public outrage forced city fathers to eliminate that provision a few months later.[24] The fee system itself remained intact.

The practice of fee-splitting in Fort Worth persisted for many years, as pernicious as it was profitable. The dividing line between licensing fees for legitimate business operations and fines for lawbreaking was thin and often blurred in the practical application. In August,

1878, the city council voted unanimously to license dance houses at $100 every three months (payable in advance), thus giving them the stamp of legitimacy despite their shameless record of lawbreaking. Nearly twenty years later, in 1897, the *Morning Register* still found cause to complain about the "regular monthly fines," which amounted to the same as fees, imposed for violating the city's ordinance against "vagrancy," a catch-all category for prostitutes and other undesirables.[25] All of the money from fees and fines helped fill city coffers and keep down general taxes, explaining why the system was so popular among respectable citizens.

It was even more popular among the city's law officers. An aggressive, hard-worker like Timothy Courtright could pull down a nice supplemental salary for *ex officio* services every month. In July, 1876, just his third month in office, Courtright turned in a bill for $59.33 to the council in addition to his regular salary. The total put the marshal in a higher income bracket than the mayor, who only drew $75 monthly.[26]

Unfortunately for Courtright, authorities did not always approve the full amount of his expense account. There were also the slow months between cattle seasons, when a marshal made fewer arrests and therefore received a commensurately lower income. The whole system was inefficient, capricious and susceptible to abuse. A shrewd operator with a gun and a badge could collect fees by making arrests, or he could collect payoffs for *not* making arrests. In the balance, it was those who could not afford to pay their "fees" up front who were usually arrested.

Timothy Courtright was the sort of man who felt right at home in a system where fee-splitting was the normal way of doing business. The only problems from his point of view were that the city determined the cut and the marshal got the smallest share. This is why one of the city's first marshals ("Doc" Ewing) maintained his dental practice after he was elected and did his marshaling on the side. The fees and fines collected in the normal course of the marshal's duties were not enough to keep Courtright in the kind of lifestyle he preferred, so he branched out, using his badge as an entrée into the city's gambling rooms and saloons. That badge, backed by his reputation with a gun, gave him all the authority he needed to pocket a larger percentage of the proceeds than he got from fee-splitting alone. On one occasion, for instance, he broke up an illegal prize fight by declaring one combatant the winner, then collecting on the bet he had placed on that man. After he had made his point and pocketed his winnings, he showed the genial side of Jim Courtright by buying everybody present a drink at the bar.[27] Big operators were willing to give Courtright his share of the profits. Business in the Acre could be good to everybody, and entrepreneurs of the Acre were in no position to protest what amounted to a shake-down. Eventually, Courtright's high-handed, violent and greedy methods would get him in trouble with the voting populace, as evidenced by the ugly accusations of graft and corruption that dogged him in later years, but in his first year such problems were only whispered on the streets.

Marshal T. I. Courtright and the T&P Railroad both made their local debut in 1876. Both left a permanent imprint on the city, but they were not the only local newsmakers. It was a landmark year in several respects. Fort Worth built its first street railway, which ran the length of Main Street connecting the brand new railroad station on the south end of town to the courthouse on the north end. Fare for the ride was a nickel, and the mule-drawn cars would remain the only form of public transportation in the city for the next thirteen years. The courthouse burned to the ground in 1876, but plans were immediately made to build an even bigger and better one. The first telegraph line reached the city in 1876 also, a connection to the outside world second only to the railroad in importance. The building boom in Fort Worth got a substantial addition the same year with the completion of the first Catholic parish church. The inaugural high Mass was celebrated in St. Stanislaus Church at 10:00 A.M. on October 29, 1876, by Father Thomas Loughrey, who had been in town just a few months.[28] Representatives of the diocese paid $300 to E. M. Daggett for a parcel of land on the western edge of Hell's Half Acre where the church was built.[29] The site selected was unusual but Daggett offered them a good price for the property.

Before the year was out, Fort Worth was being referred to, with some justifiable hyperbole, as "the most progressive town in all of Texas."[30] The new railroad and telegraph and the building boom had more to do with the self-proclaimed title than any outstanding commitment to reform among the citizenry. Morality, it seemed, was still on hold.

On the national level, 1876 was also filled with headline-making events. The United States celebrated its first hundred years as a nation. In the midst of the Centennial celebration that summer, Colonel George Custer and a large part of the Seventh Calvary were massacred at the Little Big Horn in the worst defeat suffered by the U.S. Army in the Indian wars. Alexander Graham Bell first demonstrated the use of the telephone, and by the next year this modern marvel had reached Fort Worth. Late in 1876 Americans trooped to the polls for the most disputed presidential election in United States history. Fort Worth, like most of Texas, voted for Democrat Samuel J. Tilden, but his Republican opponent Rutherford B. Hayes won anyway. Most Texans did not mind too much if only Hayes would follow through on his promises to withdraw the last federal troops from the South, ending the twelve-year ordeal known as Reconstruction, and to build a new transcontinental railroad across Texas. On September 7, 1876, the Jesse James gang staged an ill-considered raid on Northfield, Minnesota, which brought an end to their bank-robbing days when the town's citizens filled the desperados full of lead. On August 2, 1876, James B. Hickok, better known to an adoring public as "Wild Bill," was gunned down from behind by a tinhorn gambler in a saloon in Deadwood, Dakota Territory. Bill was sitting at a card game and never knew what hit him. The townspeople later executed the murderer.

Fort Worth had its own problems with crime in 1876, some of which could be solved by Marshal Courtright, and some of which he created. For better or for worse he was the man charged with keeping the peace in Hell's Half Acre. That meant enforcing various "blue laws" against gambling, drinking and prostitution. These were well-intended laws, passed in the sober light of day, then ignored as soon as the sun went down. City Ordinance No. 6 made it unlawful, for instance, for any person within the city to "set up, exhibit, or keep any gaming table or bank . . . used for gaming," such activities being designated a misdemeanor punishable by a $50 fine. The ordinance further stated that it was the duty of the city marshal to arrest any person found in violation.[31] But Courtright preferred to enforce a personal rather than statutory form of law. In his dealings with visiting cowboys, who were more unruly than dangerous, Courtright preferred tolerance and persuasion over coercion as the best way to keep a lid on things. In his own unique view of what a town marshal should do, he saw his job as being "to prevent the flow of blood, not liquor."[32] If his methods were not entirely by the book, they were appropriate for an 1870s cow town. He rarely dealt with violent "desperados" or "bad actors" (as they were often called) like murderers and horse thieves. They were usually handled by the county sheriff.

Drunks and rowdies were customarily confined in the log jail at the corner of Rusk and Second streets to sleep it off or reflect overnight on their unseemly behavior.[33] Courtright usually filled the jail up on Friday and Saturday nights. By Monday morning the place was empty again and everything was back to normal until the next rush of guests came through. During cattle season even weeknights could be busy, leading to a joke that made the rounds in the city: "What's the difference between the moon and the Fort Worth jail?" Answer: "The moon is full only once a month. The Fort Worth jail is full every night."[34]

Jokes such as this only told half the story of the city lockup. The little log jail on Rusk was a public disgrace of the first order. There was no running water and no toilets, and a single barred window provided light and ventilation. Built for the bargain sum of just $497.83 in 1873 after the city incorporated, it was outgrown several times over in the next four years, but no funds were available to replace it. Even after county commissioners, in a separate move, built a county lockup in 1877, the city still required its own facility and awarded a contract in the summer of 1877 to Thomas S. Levy and Sons to build it for $839.75.[35] A series of financial and construction delays dragged the project out for the next year.

In the meantime, the marshal and his officers had to continue using the old log jail despite its dilapidated condition and inadequate size. When the neighbors around Second and Rusk complained about the terrible stench emanating from the place and the constant clamor raised by its drunken inmates, Courtright was ordered to clean it up and, if necessary, to gag the most clamorous prisoners.[36] This stopgap was too little and too late, however, to mollify irate citizens whose homes and businesses were nearby; a group of them were already threatening to sue the city if the jail was not moved.[37] As the official representative of law and order, Courtright was forced to bear more than his share of the public's wrath.

Drunk and disorderlies as they were tagged were the principal but not the only inhabitants of the city jail. On his own initiative Courtright also opened the building during slow times to sick and diseased indigents because the city had no public hospital.[38]

Dangerous criminals were locked up in the county jail to await

Above, the earliest panoramic view of Fort Worth (1879), showing the business district looking south down Main Street from the courthouse—a wishful view that owes more to boosterism than to reality at this date (courtesy W. D. Smith Commercial Photography, Fort Worth). Right, the Fort Worth courthouse in 1879, built to replace the one that burned in 1877. The *Democrat* quoted "a stranger who saw it for the first time . . . [as saying] it looked like a huge vegetable run to seed" (courtesy Bettmann Archive).

their turn before the bar of justice. Nearly seven months after the disastrous fire of 1876 that destroyed the original courthouse and lockup, the county awarded a contract to the Fort Worth firm of Thomas and Werner for $65,000 to build new structures.[39] The jail part of that project was turned over to county commissioners at the end of May, 1877. County and city officials, newspaper reporters from Dallas and Fort Worth, and the just plain curious inspected the building and pronounced it acceptable. Some city fathers even allowed themselves to be locked in one of the cells "that they might see how it is themselves."[40]

Three weeks after the county took title to the new calaboose, the first jail break occurred. Six men escaped by picking the locks to their cells and walking out the front door. They left a seventh prisoner behind who was not desperate enough or quick enough to join the party. Ironically, Thomas and Werner had recently patented a new, heavy-duty lock mechanism that they wanted to install when they built the place, but the county, in a cost-cutting measure, settled for standard locks on the cells.[41] The escape of six hardened criminals — murders, horse thieves and robbers all — from the brand new jail

BILLIARD SALOON

became a major news item in Fort Worth and Dallas papers. When further breaks followed in rapid succession, questions were raised around town whether the contractor had cut corners on construction and pocketed the difference.[42] Thomas and Werner blamed lack of adequate supervision by the sheriff's men for the escapes. J. R. Thomas even put his money where his mouth was by offering a $1000 reward to anyone who could break out of the jail within twenty-four hours after they were locked up.[43] No one stepped forward to take him up on his offer, but the county jail's revolving door kept turning out as many prisoners as it took in. In the most bizarre case, an inmate named William Jones got away while another prisoner was being locked up. Jones was recaptured, but a month later he pulled the same trick as another new arrival was being put in his cell.[44] By autumn of 1877, the newspapers were reporting the latest jail breaks matter-of-factly: "A lot of prisoners escaped from the calaboose in Fort Worth last night," read one report in the *Dallas Herald*.[45]

While the sheriff had his hands full chasing down escapees, Courtright went about his business of trying to preserve a modicum of law and order within the city limits. That job would not have been easy under any conditions, but Courtright's tolerance in running his city went beyond what most other frontier lawmen allowed. For instance, he hardly helped himself by allowing men to carry their side-arms in town, something neither Wyatt Earp nor Bill Tilghman stood for when they wore the badge in Dodge City.[46] On the other hand, he kept the peace in his own inimitable way, and Fort Worth never had any celebrated events like the Dodge City War or the shootout at the O.K. Corral in Tombstone, Arizona Territory.

By the summer of 1876 there were 2000 people living in Fort Worth, making it larger than Dodge City, but of course not nearly so famous. Like Dodge City, however, its population swelled by hundreds of visitors during the big spring and summer cattle drives. During those times Courtright needed all four deputies provided by the city. Two patrolled by day and two by night. Sometimes the marshal and all four deputies had to be on duty, and even that was not enough to keep the peace when the Acre was really jumping.

Although policemen were appointed by the city authorities, not by the marshal, the councilmen allowed Courtright a free hand with his officers. For a while in the summer of 1876, Courtright's force was reduced to two policemen, but it was raised to four again in September. The force was reduced again in January 1877, this time to three, reflecting the slower season and the city's continuing budgetary problems. That same month a committee was formed, composed of Marshal Courtright and Mayor G. H. Day, to select an official uniform for the force. Up to this time, policemen had dressed pretty much as they pleased and at their own expense, except for the required star. The uniform suggested by Courtright and Day and approved by the council consisted of a gray coat and a hat or cap.[47] Officers were allowed to choose between the cap or the hat but a black slouch hat became the preferred headgear, giving the force something of a raffish appearance. Later that year, at Courtright's urging, the uniform was changed to a blue coat, which for unrepentant rebels was an unpleasant reminder of Yankee bluebellies who had ruled Texas under Reconstruction until recently.[48] For this reason the men never took to the new uniforms. As soon as Courtright departed in 1879, they went back to the more acceptable Confederate gray, but for the better part of two years, while it was his police force, he enforced his will.[49]

The casual methods and more casual attire of Courtright's police force would appall modern law-enforcement officials. There was no patrol wagon to make the officers' job easier. When they had to carry "a lump [sic] and helpless two hundred pound cowboy . . . to lock-up," they had to depend on brute force.[50] Policemen were not equipped with nightsticks either, and their cheap tin badges looked like carnival prizes. Some officers preferred to provide their own badges and absorb the additional expense. When Joe P. Witcher first joined the force he took a Mexican silver peso to a local jeweler and had it made into a badge the shape of a star with the word "POLICE" engraved on it. Even with his fancy, customized badge, he preferred to wear the symbol of office pinned to the vest he wore underneath his coat where it was out of sight, despite city orders to the contrary.[51]

Like their leader, Courtright's policemen drew a meager salary, depending on the same system of fees and fines to supplement their income. Quite often the fines were collected even before the wheels of justice were allowed to turn. This happened when the policemen collected a fine from the accused in advance of any trial or even instead of a trial. Such short-order justice saved everybody a lot of time and trouble and it was unofficially approved by more than one city marshal. Only once in all the years that fees and fines served as the standard operating procedure was a murmur of protest raised, and that occurred right before the city elections in 1879. Officer W. P. Thomas arrested a gambler and collected the fine on the spot. Unfortunately, Thomas was also a candidate for the marshal's job that year and somebody complained. The newspapers publicized it, the city council hastily scheduled a hearing and everybody claimed to be shocked. At his hearing Thomas claimed the system had been working that way for years and he had received the official blessing of Marshal Courtright. Courtright testified that the officer was acting under his instructions when he collected the fine, but noted that "it was customary to turn the fines over when collected." Thomas, it seems, had neglected to do that. The council let him off with a reprimand. Two weeks later Thomas came in second in the marshal's race — ahead of the incumbent, however, his boss Marshal Courtright.[52]

Most of the policemen were single and to save money they boarded with other officers in one of the numerous cheap rooming houses that dotted the city. S. M. Farmer and Joe Witcher lived together in the early 1880s. Many of the officers also held down other jobs that probably provided a bigger percentage of their income than police work. It was not hard for a man with a badge to find additional work, particularly where ethics and standards were not considerations. Joe Witcher was a good example. When not patrolling his beat as a policeman, he ran a little saloon. He would have been amazed if anyone had questioned him about conflict of interest. On the contrary, his two lines of work complemented each other. The generally poor working conditions resulted in a high turnover rate among city policemen and a chronic problem for the city council. Finding replacements was not difficult in a community where most of the population was male and most of those were well-armed already, but keeping them was another story. At this early date police work was not so much a profession as an adventure or a second job.

Moonlighting officers and the penurious system of fees and fines may have saved the city money but it did not encourage the highest morals among members of the police force. There was no code of conduct governing the police until September, 1877, when the council belatedly adopted one.[53] The lack of such a code was reflected in some of the dicier episodes involving the "boys in gray" before that date. In June of 1877 one of the officers eloped with a prostitute, leaving behind a wife and two small children.[54] As a group, the police had to be as tough as the criminals they dealt with, but several of them also crossed over the thin line between law-breaking and law-enforcing. Policeman H. P. Shiel ran an illegal game and for years tried to sell liquor without paying any taxes. Several years after taking off his badge, he also dabbled in prostitution, running a disorderly house in the Acre. Joe Witcher was convicted of "aggravated assault and battery" while he was on the force. Officers Bony Tucker and J. J. Fulford were also charged on different occasions with "assault" and "aggravated assault" respectively for dealing too roughly with some of the local citizenry. Neither was convicted, but their arrest and indictment contributed to a definite image problem among Fort Worth's early policemen.[55] Such men were not the fearless champions of law and order that mythology has made them out to be, conscientiously going about their job of keeping the peace and making Fort Worth a safe place to live. Arrest records of some of the most respected officers indicate that they were busier following their true professions — usually gambling — and were on call when emergencies arose.

On a busy Saturday night, however, the officers earned every penny they were paid. Besides the cowboys who came to town in groups of twelve to fifteen from their camps across the river or from nearby ranches, the Acre was populated by rough characters who came in on the freighting wagons from Fort Sill, Oklahoma, and off the frontier to the west. T&P workers also came into Fort Worth at the end of each month, from wherever the end of the line happened to be as the railroad pushed across the prairie toward El Paso. If these groups all hit town at the same time, then Lord help the peace-loving citizens. On those occasions all four officers plus Courtright had to be pressed into service around the clock in an effort to keep some semblance of law and order. This was good enough reason for Courtright to complain bitterly when his force was cut to fewer than four officers.

The standard operating procedure any time the odds became too great for one officer to handle was to call for help, perhaps even calling the jailer. This happened one memorable night when a band of cowboys, estimated at a dozen or more, set out to "raise merry cain" at one of the Acre bars. The two officers on duty had to draft a third and finally the city's jailer before they could subdue the rowdies. Without the reinforcements, one of the officers later said he would have had to shoot one of the cowboys to arrest the others. The newspaper reported the incident the next morning without mentioning where Marshal Courtright was while all this was going on. It did report, however, that "the officers were very much exercised over the treatment they received at [the cowboys'] hands."[56] The increased demands on the police force caused city councilmen to raise the force from four to seven during Courtright's second year in office. Even this number was hard-pressed on some wild Saturday nights when hell was in session in the Acre.

In his last two years in office, Courtright spent a lot of time away from town chasing stagecoach and train robbers who were preying on Tarrant and surrounding counties. A series of stage robberies near Fort Worth between December, 1877, and March, 1879 were part of a larger epidemic all over Texas. The situation got so bad in 1877 that Governor Richard B. Hubbard offered a $250 reward for every bandit caught.[57] But the robberies went on. The targets around Fort Worth were both the local and long-distance stages, including coaches on the 1500-mile route from Fort Worth to Yuma, Arizona. Though that stage route was the longest in the world at the time, the thieves always seemed to strike just a few miles outside of the city.[58]

Besides the Yuma route and another long-distance line to Fort Concho, local coaches ran to Granbury, Weatherford and Cleburne on a daily basis. They left from several locations in the city, among them the Waverly House at Fifteenth and Main and the El Paso Hotel at Main and Fourth. A mile outside the city limits, the country turned wild and open. The solitary coach, with its bouncing passengers, was the only man-made thing as far as the eye could see. The road followed the contours of the land, providing numerous spots for robbers to lie in wait. The lack of regular traffic on the stage roads also made the robbers' job easier.

On December 21, 1877, the rash of local robberies began when the Fort Worth to Cleburne stage was hit just ten minutes out of town where scrub oak crowded close to the road and the Concord coaches had to slow down to cross a creek bed. The gang of robbers got a return of only $11 for their efforts. Undeterred, they were back at the same spot on January 28, 1878, hitting the Weatherford stage. Five passengers were relieved of their money and valuables by an equal number of masked bandits. The take this time was $500 and two gold watches. One of those watches plus $35 belonged to passenger Valentine Werner, architect of the new Fort Worth courthouse and jail, completed only three months before.[59] As he handed over his money and his watch, he must have hoped the masked men holding guns on him would find themselves guests in the new facility at an early date. But the only thing he said as he scrambled out of the stage and raised his hands above his head was, "For God's sake, don't shoot."[60] No one was arrested for either robbery, and newspapermen could only guess at the identities of the outlaws.

Robberies by local gangs, styled the "Bold Banditti" or the "Knights of the Road" by news editors, continued with depressing regularity throughout the year. In the fall of 1878 one gang struck twice in a three-day span near Mary's Creek, just thirteen miles from downtown Fort Worth and the site of earlier robberies. The *modus operandi* was the same in both cases: two masked gunmen halted the stage, ordered the passengers out of the coach, then took their money and valuables. They also rifled the contents of the mail pouches. In the second robbery one outlaw was shot and killed, but none of the loot from either job was ever recovered.

The rash of holdups continued into the early months of 1879. On February 24 the Yuma stage was hit by three men just a mile and a half outside of Fort Worth. Less than a week later the westbound stage was hit again by the same trio, this time at 6:00 A.M. on the Granbury Road. Then on March 11, 1879, the Fort Concho stage was robbed by a pair of masked desperados who got away scot-free. Bandits were literally threatening to take over the roads around Fort Worth and close them to all stagecoach traffic.

Popular opinion held that most if not at all the robberies were the work of a local gang.[61] The fact that only outgoing stages were being robbed, and always within a few miles of Fort Worth, seemed to point to this conclusion. When some gang members were finally caught, they did indeed prove to be familiar faces among the denizens of the Acre — a surprise to no one.[62] Courtright himself arrested Charlie Freeman, a well-known dealer at both the Waco Tap and Red Light saloons, following a stage holdup on March 19, 1879.[63]

Later on, some of the robberies were pinned on one of the most famous outlaw bands in the West, the Sam Bass gang. Bass was a choirboy-looking outlaw who wore a moustache to make himself appear older. He was born in Indiana in 1851, but like many of the young men of his day, spent a lot of time wandering the West. He lived in Denton, Texas, in the early 1870s under the sheltering wing of the sheriff and his wife. They provided him with regular work and good role models, but Bass soon turned his back on both. As a wrangler and teamster for Sheriff W. F. Egan, known to his friends and constituents as "Uncle Bill," young Bass made frequent trips to Fort Worth, so he knew both the town and its citizens. In 1874, just twenty-three years old and leaning more to the life of a gambler than a blue-collar worker, he left Denton to make his mark on the world. Bass came to Fort Worth on several occasions in 1875 with a fast little mare named Jenny and a black jockey named Dick to try his luck at the local race track. According to reports, Jenny and Dick beat every challenger and Bass left with a pocketful of winnings that he soon spent gambling and drinking.[64] When horse racing could no longer support either his lifestyle or his taste for excitement, he headed north to embark on a life of crime. In the fall of 1877 he helped rob a Union Pacific train at Big Springs, Nebraska, getting away with some $60,000 in gold dollars. Some of those dollars — identifiable as California double eagles with an 1877 date mark — later turned up in Fort Worth.[65]

Bass returned to North Texas after the Big Springs job and showed up in Fort Worth at the beginning of November, 1877, with Jack Davis, one of his partners in that robbery. They spent a few weeks enjoying the local hospitality, then split up, Davis catching an eastbound T&P train for New Orleans and Bass hitting the trail for his old haunts around Denton.[66]

Soon thereafter Bass organized a gang consisting of Frank Jackson, "Arkansaw" Johnson, Henry Underwood and Seaborn Barnes. Barnes was the only one with Fort Worth connections, having grown up in nearby Handley. At seventeen he shot a man and spent a year in the Fort Worth jail awaiting trial. Finally acquitted, he continued his criminal ways by hooking up with Bass.[67] The gang established their headquarters in the Cross Timbers section of Denton County, then began hitting local stages. Bass and his men were blamed for both the December 21 Cleburne robbery and the January 28 Weatherford stage robbery. After the first stickup, Bass, Underwood and Jackson spent the night at the recently opened El Paso Hotel, comforting themselves for the meager $11 take by luxuriating in the plush accommodations. At daybreak on the 22nd, they checked out as quietly as they had checked in and returned to their Cove Hollow hideout.[68]

Bass called the Weatherford stage robbery, "the best haul I ever made out of a stage." He got $500 and two gold watches out of it, but is still said to have quipped, "There's mighty poor pay in stages generally, though."[69] Soon after, Sam Bass switched to robbing trains, and he is best remembered in outlaw history for this second career.[70] It was based on a simple economic principle: as more and more of the West's wealth was transported in express cars rather than strong boxes, train robbing provided a bigger return for the risk involved. A successful outlaw had to be able to change with the times.

The Bass gang was next heard from when it held up a train at Allen, Texas, on February 22, 1878. They got away with $1280 in silver coins and valuables. The Fort Worth office of the Texas Express Company, which was responsible for most of the loss, announced a reward of $1500 for the capture of Sam Bass and friends. In the next two months, they hit three more trains in the Fort Worth area. The lightly guarded trains were a logical target, and Fort Worth was an attractive center of operations because local cattle traders frequently received large sums of money by express shipment to use in their transactions.[71]

In none of the four robberies did the gang get away with much loot, but their brazen activities provoked local authorities from four counties to organize a massive manhunt. When the Texas Rangers, the Pinkertons and Wells Fargo detectives also joined in the chase, the press dubbed it the "Bass War."[72] James B. Gillett, a veteran Texas Ranger who participated in the chase, later estimated, "Counting the 30 rangers and the different sheriffs' parties, there were probably a hundred men in pursuit of the Bass gang."[73]

Meanwhile, Bass had been a frequent visitor to Fort Worth since setting up his hideout in the Cross Timbers during the fall of 1877. After his brief visit to the elegant El Paso Hotel, his comings and goings remain something of a mystery but it seems likely that he enjoyed the irony of knowing that some of the same stagecoaches he watched departing from the front doors of the city's hotels were future targets of his gang. On other visits to the city, he bought six-guns and a change of clothes at a downtown store and exchanged some stolen gold coins at one of the city's banks. Local legend has it that he and his friends walked into A. J. Anderson's gun shop on Courthouse Square on one occasion and bought out the entire supply of guns. This was unusual enough to attract attention by itself, but not nearly as much attention as when they paid for everything in gold dollars. Since he was not much of a drinker, Bass probably avoided the sleazy dives of the Acre, but as a man who loved to gamble, he must have visited

Sam Bass and two members of his gang posed for the camera in this undated Austin studio portrait before the law finally caught up with them. Camaraderie and six-guns were on proud display. Ironically, Jim Murphy (left) would betray Bass (center) to the Texas Rangers, setting up a final shootout at Round Rock, Texas, on July 19, 1878. The man on the right is unidentified but is probably Seaborn Barnes, Bass' chief lieutenant and closest friend who was gunned down on the same day as Bass (courtesy Denver Public Library, Western History Department).

some of the gaming rooms. As he strolled up and down the city's gas-lit Main Street, carefully stepping around the rooting hogs that still ran free, he may have felt a certain sense of complacency because most of the folks he passed did not recognize the slightly built drifter; neither were they too concerned with where he came from or what business brought him to Fort Worth. He generally kept to himself unless he brought his companions with him, always making it a point to stay out of trouble when he was in Fort Worth, and Fort Worth authorities did not trouble Sam Bass.

This frontier live-and-let-live attitude began to change as one depredation followed another. Although the epidemic of stage and train robberies took place outside the city marshal's jurisdiction, Courtright and his officers were pressed into service to look for the bandits, joining a host of lawmen from Dallas and Denton in the chase. One source reported that Denton was almost deserted as every able-bodied man was employed scouring the countryside.[74] Some Fort Worth citizens grumbled that while the city's police force were out beating the bushes, the robbers were probably having a high old time in the Acre celebrating their success.

In June, 1878, Courtright and policeman A. N. "Ab" Woody joined the chase after the city council approved a ten-day leave of absence for them to participate in the "biggest manhunt in North Texas history."[75] It seems doubtful they went willingly, particularly since they had to serve with a posse under the authority of County Sheriff John M. Henderson's office. They did not have to take their riding orders directly from Henderson, but as long as they were outside the city limits they were under his authority, and Henderson was no friend of Courtright's. Their rivalry was both personal and official based on a number of incidents in their past dealings. At least temporarily their differences had to be buried. Pressure from the Texas Express Company's office in Fort Worth had forced city fathers to take some action to end the crime wave. The company was incensed enough about the situation to fire two of its employees after the Eagle Ford holdup, express manager J. H. Hickock and a guard who had opened the door of the express car to the bandits without so much as firing a shot in defense of their employer. An official announcement bluntly stated the cause for the dismissal: "They let their guns freeze in the holsters."[76]

Added to the clamor for law and order were voices of local

merchants who complained that the crime wave was bad for business and for the city's image. If the big cattlemen took their transactions elsewhere, they argued, the city would dry up and blow away. The council responded by sending Courtright — who had experience as a scout during the Civil War — to join Deputy Sheriff John Stocker, a former city marshal himself, and other law enforcement officers who were already in the Cross Timbers trying to pick up Bass' trail. For the first two days Courtright and Woody stayed in the saddle almost continuously. They were part of a group that caught sight of the gang at one point and chased them into the Elm Fork river bottoms but lost them in the gathering evening darkness.[77]

Most of the posses never even got close enough to sight the outlaws. As one writer described it, "More men were employed in this campaign, more powder burned, more bullets buried in post oaks and green hillsides, more horses rode to death, more ground galloped over, more false alarms given, more prophecies blown into thin air, more expectations blasted and fewer men captured than ever before occurred in any similar campaign in human history."[78]

After a few weeks of eating dust, riding through the underbrush, and sleeping in the saddle, Courtright returned to Fort Worth in disgust.

The law finally caught up with Sam Bass at Round Rock, Texas, on Sunday July 21, 1878, the famous outlaw's twenty-seventh birthday. Before he died, Bass boasted, "I have never stolen a horse nor robbed a widow," but that did not prevent Texas Rangers from gunning him down when they cornered him.[79] Although his criminal career lasted only four years, no Texas outlaw ever captured the fancy of as many people as did Sam Bass.[80] His successful string of stagecoach robberies, which ran to nine, helped put the western lines out of business, an event that he did not live to see.[81] His foray into train robbing was not so significant. His gang was neither highly efficient nor tightly knit. As either stagecoach or train robbers, in fact, they were "highly amateurish," which helps explain their remarkably brief career.[82]

A postscript to Bass' outlaw career is that it might have ended in Fort Worth. With the law closing in, Bass and his last three confederates hoped to pull off a big bank or train job and score enough money to get out of the country. When they rode out of Denton County for the last time in July, 1878, they had settled on a Fort Worth bank.

Unknown to the other three, one of the gang, Jim Murphy, had betrayed them to the Texas Rangers and had arranged to finger them when they hit Fort Worth. As things turned out, the Fort Worth plans fell apart because the other gang members grew suspicious of Murphy. Fort Worth was also too busy and too close to their favorite stomping grounds, so they changed their destination and rode on to Round Rock.[83] But for fate, Fort Worth might have been the scene of one of the great outlaw shootouts in western history.[84]

Courtright was not present when Sam Bass met his inglorious end. He was back in Fort Worth taking care of his marshal's duties. His part in the long chase had only been a footnote, but the memories of it remained for a long time. There were those in Fort Worth who always wondered why Bass had not been arrested during any of his visits to the city. Rumor had it that the outlaw and the marshal had crossed paths more than once in the city's gambling rooms while Bass was a wanted man. The answer offered by the pragmatic marshal as to why he did not do his duty was simple: "The Texas Rangers would claim him, the city council would collect the reward and I'd be left holding the bag."[85] This sour attitude was hardly the stuff of which legends are made.

Although all the historical attention has naturally focused on Sam Bass, there were other robberies taking place all around Fort Worth in these same years. Before the fall of 1877 and after the summer of '78 the region was plagued by highwaymen who were just as active if not as notorious as Mr. Bass. Hell's Half Acre's part in all these robberies came before and after the actual crimes. Passengers waiting to board one of the T&P trains or Concord coaches were likely to spend a few hours gambling and drinking in the Acre. The size of a man's bankroll was quickly sniffed out by the con artists and bartenders, and if the passenger won anything at gambling, that fact was just as quickly spread over the grapevine. Even if the visitor could escape the clutches of Hell's Half Acre with his bankroll intact, he was still not safe after he boarded his stage going out of town. Armed highwaymen knew the timetables followed by the stages and could lie in wait just outside the city limits. They may even have checked out prosperous-looking travelers at the hotels before setting an ambush in the place of their choosing. At least the *Democrat* thought so when it harrumphed to its readers, "Those dare devils are beyond a doubt in this city sailing under false colors, and even now may be considering another plan to waylay the next stage that leaves the city."[86] Among the unsavory types who hung out in the Acre, there is no doubt that any number were robbers or potential robbers just looking for the right opportunity. B. B. Paddock always believed that many of the stage robbers actually ran their operations out of Hell's Half Acre "and probably spent some of their loot in its pleasure palaces."[87]

Despite his fearsome reputation, Marshal Courtright did not seriously disrupt criminal activity in the Acre. An early newspaper reporter who covered the police beat for many years recalled that there was not much discipline in the police department in those days, which suited everyone just fine. "While Long Hair Jim was a game man, he didn't believe much in discipline, and for that reason he got along well with the boys."[88] He spent a lot of his time gambling in the same saloons he was supposed to be policing, mostly those in the Acre, including the Waco Tap and the Red Light. Everybody in town knew that these places, and dozens more like them, operated in open defiance of the law, "while sworn officers wink[ed] at and permit[ted] them to go on, knowingly and willfully."[89]

Little is known of Courtright's home life, except that he and Betty had a growing family after 1872, when their first child — a son named James — was born. In subsequent years Betty gave birth to three more children, two daughters and another son. While they lived in Fort Worth, Betty also found time to work in a shooting gallery at 300 Main Street owned by one Ella Blackwell. This honorable enterprise placed the two women in the exclusive company of liberated frontier females who were more than housewives and homemakers. In Betty's case, it also allowed her to keep an eye on her free-spirited husband, though indications are that he was faithful to his wife, unlike his equally free-spirited contemporaries Wyatt Earp and Wild Bill Hickok. Betty was eight years younger than Jim, a girl-woman at twenty-four when he was first elected city marshal. For the rest of their time in Fort Worth she remained far in the background of her husband's intemperate activities.

Courtright, like most western gunmen, loved to gamble, but he was not known to be very good at the tables. What he was good at was keeping Fort Worth gambling peaceful and profitable. In frontier towns like Fort Worth and Dodge, gambling was an organized enterprise, operating in the gray area between legitimate business and illegal vice. Frontier lawmen like Timothy Courtright made that arrangement work, but they were also constantly at risk of being sacrificed when public morality caught up with urban growth. A few months after Courtright was elected city marshal, the *Democrat* observed, "The sporting fraternity are becoming quite numerous in the Fort, and all manner of games are thrown out to lure the 'festive greener' who presumes he has struck a soft thing, and consequently invests only to come out 'busted.'"[90] Courtright could hardly be held solely responsible for throwing Fort Worth open to the gamblers, but he certainly shared the responsibility for providing a congenial environment for them to set up shop.

Courtright was not only the representative of law and order, he was also the main protection that Fort Worth gamblers had against that same law and order. An ordinance prohibited open gambling within the city limits, and although it was flouted at will, its very existence threatened the comfortable operations of the gamblers. Courtright offered to ease some of their concern as a sideline to his regular duties, exercising immense power in this dual role. Whether that power went to his head or he simply differed with the town fathers over how best to enforce the law, he came to a bitter parting of the ways with his superiors in 1879.

For three years Courtright had maintained a good working relationship with town fathers, at the same time keeping enough public respect to be reelected twice. But from the first there had been criticism of Courtright's professional ethics.

N. H. Wilson's paid advertisement in the *Democrat*, which succeeded only in getting its author shot, was just the first finger pointed at the new marshal. Many others agreed but did not take up the pen to write inflammatory letters to the newspaper. Gradually, the complaints grew louder as Courtright's behavior grew more erratic. His name started appearing on court dockets as "Defendant." On March 20, 1877, a case was pending against him in District Court for "assault to murder." In August of that year another case was filed against him for "malfeasance in office." Both were subsequently dismissed or no action taken, but the memories lingered in the public mind long after the law was satisfied.[91]

Problems between Courtright and city authorities also arose for different reasons. In the past, his voucher to the city council for *ex officio* services was frequently held up, and on at least one occasion, it was turned down.[92] He also requested that he receive a cut of the fines worked off on city labor details by indigent prisoners; this, too, was denied. He had asked for additional policemen for the force only to have his requests denied or tabled. Then there was the matter of being paid in scrip and the demeaning duty of looking after hogs impounded by the city: all these things stuck in the marshal's craw.[93]

But the biggest difference between the marshal and the council was over the question of how strictly to enforce ordinances against gambling, prostitution and drunkenness. If the laws were enforced too rigidly, cowboys would stay away and business would suffer. On the other hand, if not enforced strictly enough, the city could quickly become totally lawless. In simplest terms, the question was "What price law and order?" The thorny question of economics versus morality grew more complicated in the late 1870s. A new element entered the picture the same year that Courtright put on his marshal's badge when large numbers of cattle began moving up the Western Trail to Dodge City in 1876. This new route took the herds through Fort Griffin, then northward to Dodge City — some fifty to sixty miles west of the old Chisholm Trail — bypassing both Fort Worth and Abilene, Kansas, the two towns which had dominated the cattle trade for several years. In Fort Worth this economic challenge did not go unanswered. In 1877, Paddock berated Fort Worth merchants and officials for letting much of the cattle business "slip out of their hands."[94] The crisis united mayor, council and businessmen more than any issue since they joined together to bring the railroad to Fort Worth.

Immediate concern over the competition from Fort Griffin was at least partly behind the following letter to the *Democrat* at the beginning of the 1879 cattle season:

> The cattle season beginning, we think more freedom ought to be allowed, as everyone is aware of the amount of money spent in this city by the cattle men and cowboys, this making every business and trade prosper.
>
> We notice especially this year that, contrary to their usual custom, almost all of them remain in their camps a few miles from the city, and give as the cause, the too stringent enforcement of the laws closing all the places of amusement that attract them, and thus their principal pleasures being closed and forbidden, they remain away from the city, paralyzing a large number of business houses and diverting from this city an immense amount of money which this city has always been the recipient of and benefited by.

We hope the honorable mayor and city council, who have always been foremost in the ranks when the city's prosperity has been concerned will see this in the same light and urge an enlightened view of the situation.[95]

The letter was signed simply, "Many Citizens and Businessmen."

Six days later, the *Democrat* chided city officials again. "We have a model and moral town . . . and no merchant in the city is doing enough business to pay his expenses."[96] Hell's Half Acre was both the problem and the cure. While Fort Griffin was a convenient stopping place on the trail north, it lacked one thing that Fort Worth had in abundance thanks to the Acre — rip-snortin' entertainment. With a six-year head start, the Acre had much more to offer in both the variety and quantity of vice. By 1879 thanks to an aggressive solicitation campaign the previous two years, Fort Worth won back much of the cattle business it had lost to Fort Griffin. The advantages of better grazing and fewer fences along the Western Trail were more than offset as far as the cowboys were concerned by the attractions Fort Worth offered as the "entertainment capital of the prairies."[97]

The issue of reform came up annually in every election in the late 1870s. In 1877, the incumbent mayor, G. H. Day, was blamed by his opponent, J. F. Beall, and both major newspapers for the lawless nature of the city. However, the specter of Fort Griffin hung over the election and Beall overdid it with his strident reform rhetoric. Mayor Day won another year in office by the old political solution of simply standing on his record.[98] Courtright managed to ride out the storm in his first reelection campaign. There were eleven candidates in the race for the marshal's job that year but Courtright got 337 votes, leading his nearest opponent by 169 ballots. There seemed to be no doubt that Fort Worth preferred Timothy Courtright this second time around, but the fact that he had ten challengers left some unanswered questions about how secure his hold was on the office. If all the votes for the other ten candidates had been rallied behind one man, Courtright would have been out of a job.

The following April, 1878, reform was again the principal issue in the election, and R. E. Beckham, the challenger, managed to appeal to both the businessmen and the churchgoers. He blamed the depressed state of the city's finances on his opponent and vowed to improve both finances and morality if elected. Despite his campaign promises of reform, candidate Beckham said nothing against Hell's Half Acre directly. On election day, the lion and the lamb trooped to the polls together and made Beckham the new mayor of Fort Worth. Timothy Courtright displayed a growing popularity by winning his third term in office.

The new "reform" administration tried an odd twist at fulfilling its campaign promises. In December, 1879, the city council cut the police force to three officers under Courtright. Earlier they had passed the first Sunday closing law in the city's history along with new zoning ordinances covering variety theaters, dance halls and other vice establishments.[99] By passing new city ordinances while at the same time cutting back on the city's police force, officials were trying to work both sides of the street.

Since most of the elected officers were also Fort Worth's principal businessmen, it was clear that they preferred the most liberal interpretation of city ordinances against vice. Courtright once complained to Heck Thomas, later to become a famous frontier lawman in his own right:

> They have their own ideas about what constitutes law and order. They think I should do nothing more than protect women against insults and arrest drunks who shoot off their pistols in the streets, gambling dens, and whore houses. They actually believe this town would die if regulations were enforced to shut down or hamper the tavern proprietor.[100]

Courtright's tone of wounded innocence was probably more calculating than sincere. In truth, his ideas about law enforcement were closer to those of his good friend, saddle buddy and fellow lawman, Jim McIntire (sometimes spelled McIntyre). McIntire, who served from 1880 to 1882 as town marshal of Las Vegas, New Mexico, before being reunited with Courtright, cheerfully admitted his laissez faire approach in his memoirs:

> There were all kinds of people here and they were mostly a rough lot. I threw the town wide open and allowed all kinds of gambling. The streets were crowded with monte men, sluice games, shell men and fakers of all kinds and descriptions. . . . I permitted them to "whoop it up" so long as they submitted to being arrested and fined regularly for the support of the marshal and the Justice of the Peace. The fakers and gamblers were so plentiful and prosperous that it was an exceedingly profitable job for me.[101]

Courtright never got around to recording his memories as McIntire did, but there is every reason to believe that he tried to run Fort Worth the same way his buddy ran Las Vegas. Both men were products of the frontier, more comfortable with the lawbreakers than the lawmakers. Their escapades together as later described in the newspapers and in McIntire's memoirs clearly indicate this.

Whatever the cause of the dissatisfaction between Courtright and city fathers, it ultimately proved his downfall. His reign as city marshal and godfather of Fort Worth gambling came to an unexpected end in 1879. In April of that year he ran for reelection for the third time. He might have gotten a hint of his declining popularity when there were five other candidates for his job, including one of his own officers, W. P. Thomas, and a former marshal, H. P. Shiel.

The campaign took a surprising turn when, shortly before the election, a scandal in the police department drew public attention to city law-enforcement procedures. It also made the marshal's race the hottest one on the ballot. The scandal was the one involving Officer W. P. Thomas, who had arrested a man in the Acre and collected a fine from him before official charges were filed, much less a trial held. A police board investigated and charged Thomas with "corruption and malfeasance in office." Thomas defended himself by saying he was only operating under orders from Marshal Courtright, adding "the same thing has been done before among the policemen." The matter was referred to the council, which spent several hours in heated debate before finally vindicating both Thomas and Courtright.[102]

The *Democrat* reported the whole affair in breathless detail, but surprisingly, B. B. Paddock, the outspoken editor, dismissed the allegations against Courtright and endorsed the marshal's reelection. "It is generally acknowledged that T. I. Courtright has performed the duties of his office fearlessly, efficiently, and devotedly. He has used discretion in making arrests, not annoying persons for frivolous misdeeds for the sake of making a fee. . . . No braver man than Jim Courtright exists. He would arrest a circular saw if necessary."[103]

Fortunately, Courtright was not called on to face down any circular saws. Nor was his oratory, or lack of same, an issue in the campaign. In an appearance on Tuesday night, the week before the election, Courtright and the other candidates took turns addressing a large crowd at Joe Lowe's Centennial Theater. Courtright's brief speech, said observers, proved "he was no speech-maker." Despite this fact he sat down "amidst tremendous applause."[104]

Courtright's campaign strategy apparently was to stand on his record and rely on the good citizens of the Third Ward to provide the margin of victory. He had a special affinity for the people who called the neighborhood around Hell's Half Acre home, and he expected that they felt the same sentiments for him.

On election day, rumors circulated that Courtright had withdrawn from the race. He had not, but the damage was done. What effect this rumor had on the outcome is impossible to gauge, but Courtright came in a very poor third in the preferences of the voters — even behind two of his erstwhile deputies, W. P. Thomas and S. M. Farmer. The voters had spoken loud and clear about whom they wanted to wear the badge for the next year. The new city marshal was S. M. Farmer.

The council could be included among those who were most surprised by the outcome of the election. For a while they threatened to withhold their appointment of Thomas as chief of police, thus leaving him a marshal without a police force. Reluctantly, they recognized the will of the voters, and Fort Worth had a new city marshal for the first time in three years.

A bitter and disgusted Timothy Courtright hung around Fort Worth for three more years, although just how he earned a living is unclear. Possibly he lived off his wife's income from the shooting gallery, but it is hard to believe that source alone could support a man with a wife and children. One later authority claims that the lanky gunman worked as a bouncer around town after he took off his badge.[105] His most likely source of income is indicated by his lengthy arrest record during these years. On November 3, 1880, he was arrested and charged with "exhibiting a keno bank," a violation of the city's anti-gambling ordinance. He pleaded guilty and paid a $25 fine. Less than a month later he was back before the court, charged with "unlawfully keeping a [keno] bank for gaming." Again he pleaded guilty and paid the fine.[106]

He had never been a naturally skilled gambler and even devoting full time to his previous avocation apparently did not improve his skills. Some men could support themselves in style with a deck of cards or a pair of dice, but Courtright was not among them. That may explain his arrest in 1881 on a "minor theft" charge. Fortunately for him, the case was dismissed before it came to trial, leading one to wonder if the victim had second thoughts about prosecuting the bad-tempered, gun-toting ex-marshal.[107] In fact, Courtright found himself more and more on the opposite side of the law, the law breaker rather than the law enforcer. In 1880 he was charged with "unlawfully accepting a challenge to a duel," another charge which was dismissed before it could be tried.[108]

He might have heard the whisperings around town about how low the once-mighty marshal had fallen. His troubles with the law and with finances must have been galling to a man who was used to people stepping aside when he walked down the narrow sidewalks with his twin six-shooters and his marshal's badge. He still had the guns but no longer enjoyed the protection of the badge.

There was another problem, too, that ate away at Courtright. Life in Fort Worth was becoming too tame with all the laws against gambling, carrying guns, disturbing the peace and selling liquor on Sundays. He started drinking heavily, and a new side of Timothy Courtright was revealed for the first time — Longhair Jim, the mean drunk. Drinking not only eroded the skills he depended on for a living, it increased his living expenses. He had to find remunerative employment. It is no wonder when the first good offer came along to go where the pay was attractive and his talents were appreciated, he leaped at it. He moved to New Mexico, which was still a battleground between ranchers and nesters, between big ranchers and small ranchers, and between Anglos and *Mexicanos*. He had been approached by Colonel A. J. Fountain of the New Mexico territorial militia to come to Lake Valley and take on the job of cleaning up the mining camp there. Courtright packed his guns, kissed his wife and kids goodbye and headed west. After a few months as town marshal, he quit to become a guard for the Sierra Mining Company of Lake Valley; then he changed jobs one more time, signing on as a ranch foreman for his old friend and former commanding officer, John Logan.

Courtright earned his pay from Logan not by bossing cowhands but by intimidating squatters and rustlers who ventured onto the Logan spread. In this he was aided by his long-time friend and fellow gunman Jim McIntire. When two squatters refused to be intimidated, Courtright and McIntire shot them to death on May 5, 1883. Such shootings were not an uncommon occurrence in the bloody New Mexico range wars of this era, but authorities still frowned on them, especially when carried out by Texans, and a warrant was issued for the arrest of Courtright and McIntire. Unwilling to face a lengthy court trial and possible imprisonment, they fled the territory. Courtright came home to Fort Worth while McIntire headed up to Wichita Falls where he had friends and good connections.

In Fort Worth, Courtright considered himself safe enough to walk the streets in broad daylight and visit his usual haunts. He even went so far as to open his own private detective agency and was making some money. Friends noticed, however, that he did not say much about the time he had spent in New Mexico. It was almost as if he were trying to hide something. Folks shrugged it off because he had never been much of a talker. It was known he went there on business, so it was assumed he had finished his business and had come home. Gun-toting types never stayed in one place too long anyway. Whatever the story, nobody pressed him when he did not seem inclined to talk about it.

Courtright had good reason for not talking about it; he had a price on his head in New Mexico, and he knew authorities there would love to get their hands on him. As a Texan and a hired gun, he would not fare too well with a New Mexico judge and jury. For a time after he returned he was careful to check out any newcomers who came to town and to scan the room when he first walked into one of his favorite hangouts. There was always the chance some hotshot bounty hunter might try to collect the $500 reward. What he did not expect was any sort of official extradition action cooked up between Texas and New Mexico authorities. But that is exactly what happened. On October 18, 1884, a special New Mexico officer, Sheriff Harry Richmond of Albuquerque, showed up in town with two Texas Rangers and extradition papers signed by Texas Governor John Ireland.[109] What followed was one of the strangest episodes in Fort Worth history. Naturally, it began in Hell's Half Acre.

The peace officers did not immediately announce their purpose in being in Fort Worth. After all, they were in Courtright country and unsure of the reception they would get from the ex-marshal's friends and neighbors. Instead, they casually inquired around the town about Courtright, and when they found him at the Cattle Exchange Saloon, invited him up to their hotel room to "look over some photographs of suspects believed to be hiding in Fort Worth."[110] Courtright, the old lawman, was flattered by their attention and accompanied them ap-

Saddle buddies: T. I. Courtright (top) and Jim McIntire (bottom). They rode the trail together and probably committed murder together. Rumor even had them going to Central America together when they were on the run from New Mexico lawmen. Both also wore a lawman's star at different times (N. H. Rose Collection of "Old Time Photographs of the Frontier," Amon Carter Museum).

parently without suspicion. When the men arrived at the room, however, Courtright was quickly disarmed, handcuffed and chained. Then they settled down to wait, the lawmen occasionally peering out the second-story window to look up Grove and Pecan streets toward the north end of town. About all they could see from their limited vantage point were the nearby Southern Hotel and Diamond Flour Mill, but what they saw reassured them somewhat. Everything was quiet on this Saturday afternoon in Fort Worth.

The hotel where they waited was the Ginocchio, one of the nicer public accommodations that had sprung up in the building boom of the 1880s to take advantage of the new railroad lines coming into town. Unlike other hotels, the Ginocchio enjoyed the advantage of being right next door to the Union Depot, on the station platform in fact. It was the first public accommodation visitors saw when they got off the Missouri & Pacific or Texas & Pacific trains. Although Charley Ginocchio was later described by one of the town's early residents as being "as genial a host and as fine a gentleman as one would care to meet," he was actually an absentee proprietor who lived in Marshall, Texas, and left the day-to-day running of the hotel and its restaurant and saloon to local managers.[111]

In 1884 the resident manager was John Laneri who had lived in the city since 1865 after immigrating from Italy sometime before. Laneri might have been hired to bring a little Old World charm and hospitality to a frontier hotel that boasted of its first-class accommodations and "rooms unsurpassed for comfort."[112]

The Ginocchio's advertising belied its modest appearance and its location beyond the southern edge of downtown. The nearest neighbors were the railroad reservation and Hell's Half Acre. It was a carriage ride or a good ten-minute walk to the main part of town. The Ginocchio was not the cheapest hotel in town, but it offered the most convenient accommodations for a party of nervous lawmen hoping to make a quiet and speedy business stopover. The imported liquors, fine cigars and "choice confectioneries" offered by Charley Ginocchio were all well and good, but they had come to Fort Worth for one purpose: to arrest Timothy Courtright and hustle him out of town as fast as possible. They planned to slip their captive out on the 9:00 P.M. westbound train. A short walk out the hotel lobby and down the platform would get them to the station waiting room just before 9:00, then they could be on the train and gone before the good citizens of

Fort Worth knew their local hero was missing. It was an excellent plan. Unfortunately, the nervous lawmen did not figure on how fast news travels in a small town, particularly when that news involves one of the town's most prominent citizens. Long before 9:00 P.M. a mob of angry citizens gathered in the street outside the hotel and demanded Courtright's release. When that did not happen, they threatened to take him back forcibly. Some sources report there were as many as 2000 guns in the crowd.[113]

Finally, Courtright was slipped out the back door of the hotel onto the station platform, then across the T&P tracks and into a carriage which made a dash for the jail. With Courtright behind bars, the Rangers could breathe easier and plan their next move. The prisoner was guarded by half a dozen policemen — some of them Courtright's old cronies — besides the two Rangers. Because of his local status, Timothy Courtright was not kept locked up in a cell but allowed the run of the jail. His special privileges included eating his meals across the street in the Merchant's Restaurant at 41 Main Street. C. C. Lawson, the proprietor, was a personal friend who had served Courtright many a meal during his marshaling days.[114] On Sunday, October 19, Courtright took breakfast and noon dinner at the restaurant, telling his friends there he would be back for supper. Such shenanigans did not sit well with the two Rangers, but Sheriff Richmond did not seem worried. He should have been.

It did not take the prisoner's many friends long to concoct a daring escape plan based on the relaxed circumstances of Courtright's incarceration. Somehow, they got details of the plan to Courtright, possibly through one of the policemen assigned to watch him. In any event, when Courtright and his three guards came over to Merchant's for supper that evening there were two revolvers concealed underneath the table where they were seated. According to the prearranged plan, the restaurant was also full of Courtright's friends.

With almost comical ease, Courtright retrieved the two guns and got the drop on his three guards. Then, in true Wild West fashion, he backed out the door into the street, leaped on a horse conveniently waiting for him, and galloped off down Main Street. Accounts differ as to just who arranged the daring escape. One historian claims unequivocally that it was Courtright's old friend and fellow officer Ab Woody, with his son William A. Woody, who arranged for the pistols to be under the table. Another historian suggests that it was another old friend, Heck Thomas, who had the most important role in the affair.[115] Whether it was the Woodys or Thomas or some other unknown conspirator, nothing was ever proved and no one was even arrested following the successful getaway. It was one of the slickest escapes in western history. County Attorney W. S. Pendleton was incensed over the prisoner's escape and took his wrath out on the arresting officers for treating Courtright like a celebrity rather than a felon. According to Pendleton's classic description of the escape, Courtright was escorted to a public restaurant where he was served "quail on toast and pistols under the table for dessert."[116] Governor Ireland, the Texas Rangers, and the territorial officials in New Mexico did not find anything amusing in the affair.

Courtright disappeared, not to be seen again in Fort Worth for nearly two years. During that time, his whereabouts remain something of a mystery. It is known that he traveled quite a bit, but there is not a single piece of extant correspondence with his wife or friends during that time to trace his travels. Courtright's biographer believes that he caught a train to Galveston, then went by ship to New York City, and from there across the border into Canada. Rumors placed him in Washington Territory and even in Central and South America.[117] He was a frequent subject of editorial speculation in the Fort Worth and Dallas newspapers, which reported every rumor regarding his latest whereabouts. When Tom Wilson, a well-known friend, came through town in August, 1885, the newspapers hurriedly sent reporters to interview him. When queried about his good friend's whereabouts he responded in a conspiratorial tone, "In South America; perhaps in the Chilean Army. He is safe."[118] Whether this was the truth or a fish story intended to throw the law off Courtright's trail is a matter of conjecture. A Dallas newspaper that was following the story claimed there were only three men who knew of his true whereabouts, "but there is not money enough in the country to induce them to give him away."[119]

Wherever Courtright was, before long he grew homesick and early in 1886 decided to give himself up. He came to Fort Worth first before going back to New Mexico and a date with the courts. During his brief stay in the city, he arranged to be placed in the custody of George Holland, an old friend and prominent pioneer businessman, who, over the years, was also a saloon owner and proprietor of some of the city's sleaziest variety theaters.[120] If a man is known by his friends, then Courtright and Holland belonged together. About the latter and his business enterprises, one resident said, "If there was anything ever invented by man to attract the base instinct of the human which was not put on at Holland's, it was an oversight on the part of the management."[121]

On January 20, 1886, Holland was with Timothy Courtright when the fugitive stepped off the Missouri & Pacific train coming down from Oklahoma. The two men waded through snow and slush on the way to Holland's theater in the Acre. There, in a private upstairs office, Courtright was the guest of honor at a "welcome back" party.[122] Because of Holland's influence, Courtright did not suffer the indignity of being confined in jail while waiting for New Mexico authorities to come and take him into custody. The next time he left Fort Worth it was under considerably different circumstances than his previous hasty departure. But he was not gone nearly so long this time. By March 6 he was back in Fort Worth acquitted of all criminal charges because of lack of evidence and failure of New Mexico prosecutors to produce the witnesses they had counted on.

Settled down in Fort Worth, this time for good, Courtright could have lived the life of a populist hero, easing into middle age as a quiet and law-abiding citizen. But this was not Timothy Courtright's style. He preferred the fast life of gambling and danger. Fort Worth in general, and Hell's Half Acre in particular, still offered plenty of action for a man addicted to excitement. He soon had the Commercial Detective Agency open for business again.

In all of his comings and goings during the past four years, however, Courtright had failed to note the profound changes taking place in Fort Worth. There was a new power structure in the city's gambling fraternity, new arrangements which did not include him. He found himself in the position of a man in a card game who gets up and leaves his chair for a few minutes, and when he comes back to reclaim it, finds a new hand has been dealt and the rules have been changed.

FIVE

"The Gamblers Must Go!"

THE 1880s — HELL'S HALF ACRE'S SECOND DECADE — was a time of growth and of growing lawlessness. The increasing importance of the cattle trade to the Fort Worth economy was matched by the increase in businesses catering to the cowboy's pleasure. There were more saloons, more dance halls, more gambling houses and more prostitutes at the beginning of the 1880s. The clientele grew as well, including some of the most famous gunmen and gamblers of the era who were drawn by the same opportunities that attracted the nameless cowboys and con men of the 1870s.

Wyatt Earp, for example, was a familiar visitor to Fort Worth in the late 1870s and 1880s, as was his brother James. In fact, the three Earp brothers, Wyatt, Virgil and Morgan, who took part in the O.K. Corral fracas, were described as "Texas men" in one contemporary account despite their more famous association with Kansas cow towns.[1] They came down from Dodge City in the summer of 1877 following the gambler's circuit, which included stops in Mobeetie (in the Texas Panhandle), Jacksboro, Fort Griffin, Fort Davis and Fort Clark. Wyatt, with his lady love Mattie Blaylock, whom he met at Fort Griffin, was in and out of Fort Worth for the next two years, putting up in hotels and trying his luck at the gaming tables.[2]

James, the second of the six Earp brothers, was older than Wyatt. He had a milder case of the wanderlust than the other boys, although he followed Wyatt from Wichita to Dodge City to Fort Worth, and when Wyatt left Fort Worth, Jim followed him on to New Mexico and

A distinguised looking James Earp, whose only marketable skills (compared to his better-known, gun-slinging brothers) were keeping bar and dealing faro, as he appeared at age forty-four (Denver Public Library, Western History Collection).

Arizona. Jim had a gimpy arm, the result of a Civil War wound, which kept him from being as active or as belligerent as Wyatt and the others. He lived on his disability pension and the income from a succession of jobs as a bartender, hack or stage driver and card dealer. Despite an itinerant lifestyle and lack of steady employment, Jim found time to marry and father at least two children. But his responsibilities as a husband and father never got in the way of his attachment to his brothers. When they got to Fort Worth, Jim took a house at Ninth and Calhoun, but there is no indication that his wife or his children lived there with him. He found a comfortable job working for G. G. Haswell as a bartender and dealer at the Cattle Exchange Saloon. Since faro was the favorite game at the Cattle Exchange, he probably dealt faro.[3]

Wyatt never had a Fort Worth address, though he was probably a frequent visitor while James was in town since the family's history shows that James never let too much time or space separate him from his younger brother.[4] Fort Worth's attraction for Wyatt Earp had to be more than just gambling. In fact, in the summer of 1879 he probably found the gambling pickings pretty lean because recent municipal elections that brought in the first reform administration had been followed by a much ballyhooed move against the Acre. For a time, before the reform mania passed, no gambler was making a decent living. But the Earps also had friends in Fort Worth, including a rancher named John Behrens. When the local gambling dried up, Wyatt and Jim briefly considered going into the sheep ranching business with Behrens, but came to their senses before any deal could be closed.[5]

Wyatt's presence in Fort Worth is rather shadowy. Besides gambling, he also claimed to be chasing down outlaws as a bounty hunter or private detective while he crisscrossed Texas. This was probably a cover story or maybe just a conceited self-delusion, for there is no record of his catching any outlaws, nor of Earp's being commissioned to chase any. His success, or lack of it, at the gambling tables is unknown before a notable visit in the spring of 1884. When he moved on to Las Vegas, New Mexico Territory, in September of 1879, the *Las Vegas Optic* noted his arrival with the cryptic comment that he "had something to do with Fort Worth" before he arrived.[6] Between the summer of 1877, when he first came to North Texas, and September of 1879, when he showed up in Las Vegas, Wyatt went back to Dodge City where he served for a time as assistant marshal.[7] Apparently, law enforcement ran in Wyatt's blood as strongly as gambling because he always had his hand in one or the other — usually in both at the same time. He never put on a badge during his time in Fort Worth, perhaps because Timothy Courtright had the marshal's office firmly in his pocket between 1876 and 1879. If Courtright's skill with a gun was even half of what his legend says it was, and if he was already shaking down the local gamblers and saloon owners as his critics have charged, then Wyatt may have preferred to look for greener pastures to practice his brand of law enforcement. On the other hand, he never got in trouble with local lawmen either, as he did in Mobeetie, where Deputy Sheriff James McIntire ran him out of town for trying to run a "gold brick" swindle with fellow gunman and Dodge City alumnus Dave Mather. The two were conspicuous failures as con artists, peddling phony gold ingots said to have been recovered from a "long lost Spanish mine."[8] When Wyatt subsequently came to Fort Worth he confined his efforts to gambling.

Wyatt eventually dropped Mattie Blaylock and took up with

Josephine Sarah Marcus, although the precise nature of this relationship is as unclear as the earlier connection with Mattie. They continued to wander across the West, never putting down roots but living out of hotels and boarding houses. Wyatt's only permanent ties were to his brothers and a handful of close friends like Doc Holliday and Luke Short. In June, 1883, Wyatt returned to Dodge City long enough to help Short triumph in the famous "Dodge City War." Wyatt, with Josephine in tow, came through Fort Worth several times in the 1880s, still following the gambler's circuit. In Josephine's memoirs, she recalled these visits as some of the happiest times in their relationship.[9] None of the other Earp brothers were with the happy couple on these occasions.

In 1884, Wyatt and Josie, accompanied by Jim Earp, turned up in Eagle City, Idaho, where the boys opened a saloon that they called the White Elephant. They were soon happily at work relieving local miners of their excess gold.[10] Did they perhaps recall their days in Fort Worth and another White Elephant Saloon when they named their Eagle City establishment? There is no way to tell.

Another family destined for fame of sorts — the McLaury brothers, William, Tom and Frank — also lived in Fort Worth at the same time the Earps were in town. William practiced law out of a Main Street office, while Tom and Frank cowboyed, drifted and sometimes rustled cows. Whether the Earps and McLaurys crossed paths in Fort Worth is unknown, but Tom and Frank McLaury and Wyatt Earp would meet face-to-face with fatal consequences in Tombstone in 1881. William went to Tombstone to claim the bodies of his two brothers after the fight at the O.K. Corral. He returned to Fort Worth and lived in the city for several years thereafter. Like the Earps, the McLaurys may have found violence second nature. William also got in a scrape with the law in 1887 and had to defend himself against a charge of aggravated assault.[11]

Doc Holliday, another participant in that Tombstone fracas, may also have spent some time in Fort Worth. Historians are vague on the matter. One, Paula Marks, describes him as a "former Fort Worth resident" in her definitive book on the O.K. Corral.[12] Another places him in the city after 1873, where supposedly Holliday had moved because of his failing health and the economic depression that hit the country in 1873.[13] This was the same devastating depression that delayed the T&P's arrival in Fort Worth for three years. Its effects in the East were even harsher, causing thousands of young men to lose their jobs, leave their families and head west to make a fresh start. Holliday was one of those who decided to make a fresh start out West. Until 1873, young John Holliday lived in Griffin, Georgia, as a respectable dentist and upstanding citizen.[14] When he was diagnosed with tuberculosis, an untreatable disease at that time, he chose Texas to start his new life.

There is no local record of Holliday spending any time in Fort Worth, but this is not surprising since he was not yet a celebrity who would have attracted attention like Luke Short or Wyatt Earp when they came to town a few years later. He is known to have lived in Dallas between 1873 and 1875, where he divided his time between gambling and dentistry, spending considerably more time at the former than the latter. Dallas was a good spot for gamblers at the time, much better than Fort Worth, which was still struggling to overcome its "drinkwater" reputation while waiting for the railroad to come. In the meantime, the newspapers reproached Dallas for gambling activities. When another Texas paper remarked innocently that "game abounds in Dallas [County]," the *Democrat* chimed in, "yes and plenty of it, such as keno, faro and rondo."[15] Still, for a change of scenery, or perhaps just to clean out the suckers, Dallas gamblers made frequent excursions to Fort Worth in these years. It is not unreasonable to assume that Doc ventured westward across the Trinity to try his luck at the local tables.

Holliday may have had good reason to prefer the Fort Worth tables after New Year's Day 1875, when he got into a shootout with the owner of a Dallas saloon. Holliday had been working as a dealer at Austin's saloon for some time, losing the house's money during the busy Christmas season. When Mr. Austin said some uncomplimentary things about Doc's skills as a faro dealer, Doc got liquored up and, armed with a sawed-off 1875 Colt revolver, came looking for him. The two men exchanged shots across the saloon without doing any damage. A policeman disarmed and arrested both men, but they were later released. Doc's days of dealing faro — or any other game — in Austin's saloon were over. Other saloon proprietors may also have been leery of hiring the hot-tempered, gun-toting dentist, particularly if he had a penchant for losing the house's money.[16] The truth is, Holliday was an indifferent gambler who was said to put away two quarts of whiskey a day. But if he could find his way to Fort Worth in that state, he had a clean slate and a chance for a fresh start on the other side of the Trinity. Gamblers, con artists and men on the run from the law quite often used the Trinity River to put a comfortable distance between themselves and their pursuers in either Dallas or Fort Worth.

Bat Masterson, who had more than a nodding acquaintance with the Earps and Holliday, was a visitor to Fort Worth on several occasions in the 1880s. Those who knew William Barclay Masterson called him "personable and debonair," a man who never took his own reputation too seriously.[17] Bat kept company with some of the most feared men in the West, but he was never a violent or vindictive man himself. He was literate, well-spoken and usually easygoing. When Bat was run out of Dodge in 1881 by city authorities, for example, he described his hasty departure this way: "I looked down a double barrel that was about right for a narrow gauge railroad tunnel and decided to keep right on going while I still had a whole skin."[18] Bat was always a staunch friend to men like Luke Short and Wyatt Earp.

Bat's visits to Fort Worth were infrequent and unpredictable. He divided most of his time between Dodge City and Denver during the decade. Denver he considered his home in these years, but he nonetheless found time to visit his good friend Luke Short in Texas and to try his hand at the Acre's gaming tables. Like the true sport he was, Bat would bet on anything, from a hand of cards or a roll of the dice to a horse race or a prizefight. Dallas horse racing and Fort Worth gambling would have appealed to his sporting nature. On top of that, he could never turn down a request from Short to come for a visit. Bat practically made a second career out of getting Luke out of trouble when the feisty gambler antagonized powerful people, which he did quite often. For his part, Short was never averse to calling in reinforcements when he needed them.

Another gun-toting visitor to Hell's Half Acre was a man known as "Mysterious Dave" Mather. Mather's reputation was that of "a very wicked man, a killer of killers," who, if he "promised a man he would kill him . . . was sure to do it."[19] At various times he was a horse thief, a train robber and a law officer. Long, lean Dave, who bore more than a passing resemblance to Wyatt Earp, first appears in the historical record as a Dodge City gambler in the mid-1870s. He received a serious knife wound in a gambling argument but recovered in time to go to Mobeetie with Wyatt Earp. In the late 1870s, Mather and Earp were just two among many in the exodus of gamblers from Dodge City, forced out by rival interests or by reformers, depending on one's point of view. The "Dodge City Gang" fanned out over the West, descending like a plague of locusts on other gambling towns and maintaining their fraternal ties wherever they went. Other members of this loose fraternity included Luke Short, Wyatt Earp, Johnson Gallagher and Joe Lowe. Towns like Fort Worth and Las Vegas, New Mexico, benefitted when the boys hit town because the caliber of gambling went up after their arrival. They also raised the level of general crime and violence wherever they went. Working both sides of the law, they often filled the ranks of the local police force, collecting both regular salaries and protection money from local merchants, a practice they had first perfected in Dodge.[20]

Before coming to Fort Worth, Mather had spent some time in San Antonio, El Paso and Dallas. In San Antonio, he had been charged with passing counterfeit money — something he was no more successful at than passing phony gold bricks. As in his previous failed con game, he was not prosecuted but "invited" to leave town. That kind of consideration may have been extended because of the influences and long reach of the Dodge City Gang. He went from San Antonio to El Paso, where he put on a badge again as an assistant town marshal. Growing bored with that occupation, he lit out again. A gambler on the Texas leg of the circuit had to hit Fort Worth and Dallas sooner or later, and sure enough, Dave turned up in Dallas late in 1881. For the first and only time on record, he became intimately involved with a woman. Her name was Georgia Morgan and, according to reports, she was either black or mulatto. She was also the madam at one of Dallas' most popular sporting houses.[21]

In January 1882, Mather jilted his ladylove, stealing a gold chain and ring from her on the way out of town. Dave came to Fort Worth, probably figuring he had seen the last of Georgia. But, armed with a butcher knife and a pistol, the enraged madam followed and started her own search for him through the Acre. She was disarmed by Fort Worth lawmen before she could catch up with Dave, and he was taken into custody while trying to leave town on a train. Fort Worth authorities returned him and his accuser to Dallas to let that city sort out the mess.[22]

There is no record of the case's resolution, which leads one to believe that Dave was probably invited to leave yet another town. Disagreements between members of the gambling and sporting house fraternities were usually settled this way. The outcome could not have bothered Dave too much, as he was used to arriving in towns one step ahead of the law and leaving in a big hurry the same way.

Like Luke Short, Mather ran a saloon for a while, and like Rowdy Joe Lowe, he operated a dance hall in Dodge City. Also like Luke and Joe, he riled the local authorities and wore out his welcome in Dodge. Any man in his line of work acquired enemies, and Dave was not one to back down from a fight. Still in Dodge and still following the same pattern as Short and Lowe, Dave Mather started a deadly feud for obscure reasons that quickly escalated to gunfighting and then to murder. Dave made a bitter enemy of the assistant town marshal, Tom Nixon. The two men exchanged hot words more than once. Then Nixon took a potshot at Mather one night. Both men claimed to have a legitimate complaint against the other, but neither was willing to take it to the law for adjudication. On July 21, 1884, Mather shot Nixon from ambush on a darkened public street, continuing to pump bullets into him even after Nixon hit the ground. "Oh," gasped Nixon, "I'm killed."[23] Mather was acquitted despite the evidence of several witnesses and a "smoking gun" taken from him at the scene of the crime by the sheriff. It was a scenario that was repeated with surprising regularity in other gunfights: a smoldering feud fueled by hot words, an ambush on a darkened street, then a corpse filled with enough lead to kill two or three men. Less than three years later a similar affair would focus national attention on Fort Worth.

Notorious gunfighter and gambler Ben Thompson was said to be a frequent visitor to Fort Worth, according to B. B. Paddock's memoirs.[24] Paddock does not give dates or details for the visits, but they were probably after 1880 when Thompson gave up the itinerant lifestyle of hired gun and gambler and settled down in Austin. There he established his permanent gambling headquarters in the Iron Front Saloon. In the next four years, before his death in a shootout at a San Antonio variety theater, Thompson rode the rails between Austin, San Antonio and Fort Worth, making the rounds of the roughest saloons, gambling rooms and variety houses. Thompson was not a member of the gambling fraternity who particularly enjoyed his work, nor was he a very pleasant fellow to be around whether winning or losing. Thompson was the kind of parent who did not necessarily believe that dad's line of work was good enough for his son. Ben once vowed that he would rather see his son dead than working as a gambler.[25] His own troubled and violent life underscored that fatherly concern.

Besides gambling, drinking and fighting, Thompson shared another fondness with other famous gunmen of his day: he liked to pose for the camera. Western gunmen, being basically flamboyant types, welcomed the new photographic technology as soon as it arrived in the West. This interest in posing for posterity was especially strong after a run of good luck at the gaming tables. Thompson's personal love affair with the camera started in 1864, while he was stationed at Laredo, Texas, with elements of the Confederate States Army. He got into a monte game with a group of Mexican soldiers, cleaning them out, guns and all. The next morning, feeling on top of the world, he bought an elegant stovepipe hat, a suit of broadcloth and a gentleman's walking stick. He was so impressed with his dapper appearance, he headed directly for a nearby photographer's studio and had his picture taken in his new duds to send to his wife and mother back in San Antonio. Later that same day, still dressed in his finery, he got into a gunfight in which he killed two men and wounded a third.[26]

Because of his unpredictable temperament, his fondness for the bottle and his proven reputation with a six-gun, Ben Thompson was usually given a wide berth by everybody who knew him. On the night of March 11, 1884, however, a group of his enemies ambushed him inside the Vaudeville Theater and Gambling Saloon, generally acknowledged as the toughest night spot in San Antonio at the time. Thus ended the career of one of the West's most colorful figures.

None of these desperate characters, with the exception of William McLaury, ever put down roots in Fort Worth. They came looking for excitement or easy money or were on the run from the law. Tracing their steps is an impossibility today, but an educated guess says they were not strangers in the Acre. They are remembered as part of the class of transient westerners or "floaters" that swelled the population of Fort Worth in the 1880s without adding anything to the long-term growth of the city.

Not counting the drifters, the population of the city nearly tripled during the 1880s. At the start of the decade the population stood at 6,663 citizens. By the middle of the decade, it had grown to some 22,000, giving it a more legitimate claim to the title it had asserted for a decade, "Queen City of the Prairies."[27]

An 1887 editorial in the *Gazette* noted the bittersweet nature of

Left, Ben Thompson in 1881 when he was city marshal of Austin. The "Keystone Cops" uniform and pillbox hat are a get-up Timothy Courtright and other early Fort Worth marshals would not have been caught dead wearing. Thompson was better known as a "gun fighter" than a lawman. Bat Masterson said he "possessed a much higher order of intelligence than the average gunfighter . . . of his time." Reproduced in *Human Life* magazine in 1907 (courtesy Library of Congress). Right, twenty-two-year-old John Henry Holliday, better known as "Doc," as he appeared during his Dallas days (1874). The characteristic heavy mustache and piercing eyes are here, but the gaunt, dyspeptic look of later years is missing. He would soon decide he couldn't serve two masters, and gambling won out over dentistry (courtesy Kansas State Historical Society and Gary Roberts, Tifton, Georgia).

Fort Worth's growth during the decade. Up to 1883, the paper said, "The border roughness was exhilarating in a business way but depressing in its social aspects." Afterward:

> Homes were improved. The city began to have a finished appearance. Shrubbery and shade trees were cultivated. Men of wealth built costly residences. Sidewalks sprang into existence in all parts of the city. . . . Church congregations swelled and the social garden budded and blossomed. . . . And life in Fort Worth commenced to adorn itself with comforts and delicacies.

It was, the *Gazette* proclaimed proudly, "an era of public improvement."[28]

On the opposite end of the social spectrum from the gunmen and desperados were the decent, churchgoing folks, though it is estimated that only one in ten Fort Worthers attended religious services.[29] For the pious, there were nine churches at the beginning of the eighties, but they did not draw much business away from the city's sixty or more saloons. Most of the churches shunned the Acre, preferring to locate uptown where saints outnumbered sinners. The notable exception was the Catholic church, known until 1892 as St. Stanislaus Kostka Church and housed in a wood-frame building on Throckmorton between Twelfth and Thirteenth streets. The Catholics may have been braver than the Protestants about locating so close to the Acre because in the grand scheme of things they had been battling Satan much longer than either the Baptists, Methodists, Presbyterians, Episcopalians or Disciples of Christ, all of whom had congregations in the city. On the other hand, the location of the church might have simply reflected the congregation itself: most of the parishioners were recently arrived railroad men and poor immigrants, especially Irish, who settled on the south end of town near the railroad reservation. During the 1880s, St. Stanislaus was the only home for Fort Worth Catholics. In 1888, the parish demonstrated its faith in the future of the city by laying the cornerstone for a magnificent stone Gothic-Revival edifice. The new building, christened St. Patrick's when it held its first mass four years later, continued the close association between the Catholic church and Hell's Half Acre. It was located on two lots just north of St. Stanislaus in the 1200 block of Throckmorton. Just a few blocks to the east at the opposite end of Eleventh Street a well-known brothel stood for many years.[30] At times, parishioners going to early mass passed bleary-eyed customers just going home from a long night of revelry, and on one occasion the Acre lifestyle landed practically on the church doorstep. Two local bawds got into a fight right in front of St. Patrick's, one beating the other senseless with a rock. The police came and hauled them both away, but not before some church members must have wondered if having "money-changers in the Temple" was not a lesser evil than having battling bawds on the front steps.[31]

The German Evangelical Church of North America and the Methodist Evangelical Church also established outposts in the Acre, seeking to serve the spiritual needs of German and black minorities, respectively.[32] Unfortunately, neither found much success trying to find "just ten righteous men in Sodom."[33] The German Church never prospered because its parishioners were soon squeezed out of the Acre as a distinct ethnic group. The Methodists' story is more interesting. St. Paul's Methodist Evangelical congregation put up a building at Ninth and Main streets and issued the Macedonian call to all who would listen. Success, not defeat, caused them to flee the Acre. As the *Star-Telegram* described it, "prosperity came to the congregation and they moved." The Methodists left behind them, however, a name and a building. Both were quickly taken over by a saloon, which did profitable business at that same location for years under the name "The St. Paul."[34]

The Baptists also established a congregation on the edge of the Acre in 1882 when a group of disgruntled members from the older First Baptist Church of Fort Worth founded the Southside Baptist Church. They organized formally on the last day of 1882 and held their first Sunday service two weeks later in a rented hall at the corner of Fifteenth and Houston streets. From the beginning, however, they were uncomfortable with their close proximity to the Acre, and they never intended to be a mission to the Acre's godless residents. They were looking instead for an affordable piece of land within the city limits. As soon as they found a permanent location, they moved farther south across the Texas & Pacific tracks where they built at Broadway and Fifteenth. After 1886 they took their name — Broadway Baptist Church — from this new location. During the three years that Southside Baptist Church and the Acre were close neighbors, the church's influence on the sinners was almost negligible, despite the avowed aim of the church, as stated by its modern historian, to be "an instrument of great good in the community."[35] In later years the legend grew that the church had begun as a mission to the benighted

Throckmorton Street: St. Patrick's Catholic Church after 1889. The church entrance looks straight down Eleventh Street at a notorious whorehouse, perhaps Jessie Reeves', where Eleventh intersected Rusk Street (courtesy W. D. Smith Commercial Photography, Forth Worth).

south end of town, but neither the people of the Acre nor the first parishioners would have agreed.

Despite the presence of five or six denominations and eight or nine congregations in the mid-1880s, Fort Worth could not be considered a church-going community. An unnamed visitor commented in April of 1883, "I have not seen any place more in need of a missionary than Fort Worth." He also noted that "no place in Texas would pay better either."[36] Fort Worth was a prosperous town by any standard, but its morals had not kept pace with its prosperity, and the situation did not improve markedly in the next few years.

The city boasted three religious newspapers in 1880 in addition to the two popular dailies. But none offered much competition to the *Democrat* or the *Standard* for the loyalty of the reading public. Nor did they have much of an impact on Fort Worthers' wicked ways. Another local newspaper on the side of righteousness was the semi-weekly *Temperance Banner*, the organ of the small group of local Prohibitionists. Nationally, the anti-liquor movement was just picking up steam among the old stock, Protestant middle-class Americans, especially outside the larger cities. But it was still far from the fervent crusade it would become after the turn of the century. The first temperance society, the Star of Hope Lodge, was organized in Fort Worth in June 1877 with a beginning membership of one hundred concerned citizens. They held regular meetings every Tuesday night at the Odd Fellows Hall over the City National Bank. Whether out of progressive thinking or just plain necessity, they elected both men and women as officers, probably the first local organization to do so.[37]

The *Temperance Banner* grabbed attention in 1885 by starting a hot debate with the *Cleburne Chronicle* over the state of Fort Worth morals. In those days, Cleburne was a full-fledged rival to Fort Worth, much as Birdville had been in the 1850s. In the verbal volley that ensued between the *Temperance Banner* and the *Chronicle*, objective readers could detect more than a whiff of civic boosterism on the hometown side. The *Temperance Banner* could ordinarily be counted among the city's harshest critics, but this time it found itself in the unaccustomed role of local champion. The *Fort Worth Gazette* appointed itself referee in the dispute and then proceeded to defend the hometown just as vigorously as the *Temperance Banner*.[38] The feud soon flickered out, but it showed that the city had a definite problem

The temperance movement finally reached Fort Worth by the 1890s, here using one of the preeminent symbols of the age—the railroad—to make its point. At this date reformers were more concerned with the evils of "John Barleycorn" than "White Slavery." Note the alphabetical progression of themes popular during the Crusade as one goes down the tracks (courtesy Library of Congress).

with its public image. Not surprisingly, Hell's Half Acre was the root of the problem.

Local defenders of Fort Worth were hard put to explain the Acre. The district had by now expanded beyond its humble origins in the Daggett Addition. In 1881, the *Democrat* made its now-famous observation that "Hell's Half Acre has spread out until it covers two and a half acres. It increases with the balance of the town."[39] In the 1880s, the Acre came to include the lower end of Calhoun and Jones streets, plus a more visible presence on such older streets as Houston and Main. North to south, it stretched from the railroad reservation up to Seventh Street, where a vacant lot at Main and Seventh served as an informal boundary between uptown and downtown.

Between the main thoroughfares of Houston, Main, Rusk, Jones and Calhoun passed the numbered side streets that reached fifteen north of the railroad reservation before the end of the 1880s. Below Seventh, some of these were really little more than alleyways. Here were located the lowest dives, as well as the few residences of those who by circumstance or choice called the Acre home. On the numbered streets and nameless alleys of the Acre were to be found the few Fort Worth cribs.[40] (Unlike some of the larger western cities, Fort Worth never had entire blocks devoted to cribs.) At the geographic center of Hell's Half Acre — Twelfth and Rusk streets — was a concentration of cribs and female boarding houses. In 1885, one could stand in the middle of that intersection, look in any direction, and see nothing but places devoted to prostitution.

Hogan's Alley was the most notorious back street in the Acre. Because it was never elevated to full street status, its exact location is unknown today, but there is no doubt that it ran through the district (probably in the area bounded by Main to Jennings and Thirteenth to Front, or Fifteenth) and "was the scene of frequent assaults and killings in the early days of the city."[41] For a number of years it was occupied largely by blacks who lived in small, tumble-down shacks, showing that segregation in the Acre existed on several levels, racial as well as social. During the 1880s, the nature of the district's population began to undergo a subtle change. Imperceptibly, year by year, it was becoming racially segregated from the rest of Fort Worth. The new image of Hell's Half Acre was of a district of declining property values to be shunned by respectable folks for either living or doing business. In short, it was turning into a genuine urban slum, occupied by citizens lowest on the socio-economic scale. By the end of the century, the majority of the resident population in the Acre would be black, sullying its image still further in the public eye while at the same time reinforcing old racial stereotypes of the worst sort.

In earlier days, when the Acre was a thriving business and residential district, there was no color barrier because there was no "colored" population to speak of. Inevitably, that situation changed through a combination of factors: first, it has been estimated that 5000 black cowboys helped drive cattle up the Chisholm Trail after the Civil War.[42] Some settled in Fort Worth and started families. Added to those, other freedmen came to work as domestics for prosperous whites. When John W. Forney came through Texas in 1872 to drum up support for the railroad, he observed that "whites predominate [in Tarrant County], and the work is done mainly by them." He noted that black field hands were still a relative rarity in Texas compared to the rest of the South.[43] All that began to change, however, with the famous "black exodus of 1879," which brought a huge migration of blacks from the deep South onto the southern plains looking for homesteads. An estimated 20,000 to 40,000 settled in Kansas alone.[44]

The railroads also had a great impact on social patterns in the West after the companies hired thousands of Oriental, Irish and black construction workers to do the heaviest labor for the lowest wages. In every major western rail center large communities of ethnic minorities grew up on the outskirts of town. Fort Worth was no exception. A distinct black community existed on the south end of Fort Worth by the middle of the 1880s. Many, according to one historian, were "transient railroad workers" who arrived after 1876.[45] Others, according to the census survey at the beginning of the decade, were "cattle drivers," "housekeepers" and "cooks." But by far the largest category listed for black residents of that time was "washing and ironing."[46] Judging by the numbers listed, Fort Worth must have been the cleanest and best-pressed cow town in the West.

But the blacks' occupations were less important than their presence in the city at that point. On the unpaved streets and unzoned blocks of the Acre, blacks owned houses or operated businesses, something denied to them uptown. On fire maps of the period, their humble dwellings, starting between Eleventh and Twelfth streets on Rusk and extending south and east, were described as "negro shanties" and "negro tenements." Calhoun and Jones streets, still sparsely populated at the end of the decade, were given over almost entirely to black residences.[47]

A few black businesses could be found on the lower end of Rusk and Main streets, but mainly they were on Calhoun and Jones, interspersed with private residences. Sadly, many of their business enterprises catered to the vice trade. Lottie Freeman, for instance — described as a "colored virago" — owned a dive on Rusk Street and got her name in the papers and on police records frequently.[48] The Bucket of Blood was a "two-story Negro gambling joint [with a] saloon on the first floor," which did a brisk business in the 1880s. To the best recollections of a local judge who never visited the place, it was located at "about either Jones or Calhoun and Twelfth."[49]

The most notorious black establishment in the neighborhood was the Black Elephant, which combined the worst elements of racial segregation, criminal wrongdoing and general moral corruption under one roof of any place in the city. That very reputation also made it a trendy hang-out for some of the daring among the city's white sporting fraternity. The Black Elephant was located at Eighth and Main but the owner never advertised, and as far as the city directory was concerned, it did not even exist. It depended on reputation and word of mouth to keep business booming. The proprietor was a man named West Mayweather, who bragged that "all colors" were welcome in his establishment, especially green because that was the color of the customers' money. For several years, around the turn of the century, the Black Elephant kept its doors open through every cleanup campaign and change in city administration. Its debauched reputation was summed up by the *Fort Worth Record* in 1906: "For foul filth, nothing in the Acre can compare with the Black Elephant."[50]

The sad irony of the situation is that by flouting the color barrier, places like the Black Elephant struck a blow against racial segregation. But their motives and methods made that blow a mockery of genuine equality. Even while it was metamorphosing into a black slum, Hell's Half Acre remained the great melting pot of Fort Worth society, where all races met on an equal footing more or less. Here democracy and the American Dream had found their lowest common denominator — money. As the *Record* expressed it, "Money is the great equalizer in this section."[51]

Lottie Freeman was more fortunate than most blacks because she owned her establishment. Most of her race had to be content working for absentee white landlords who lived on the north end of town and kept their names out of the newspapers.[52] But three prominent men can be identified through city directories and recollections of old-timers. All are remembered as upright men and founding fathers of Fort Worth, not vice landlords. Winfield Scott, Walter Huffman and Captain E. M. Daggett, however, can all be linked to the Acre through their land holdings.

Winfield Scott, the famous cattle baron, parlayed the return from a 14,000-acre Tarrant County ranch into a second fortune in real estate. Late in his very successful life, the *Star-Telegram* reported he "owns business houses in practically every block from the Court house to the Texas & Pacific Passenger Station."[53] Among his other properties was the uptown establishment on Main known as the White Elephant Saloon. He also built the "Winfield Jr. Building" at Twelfth and Main streets, naming it after his son, and the Hamburger Steak Place, a frame shack at Thirteenth and Main, described in 1909 as his "most popular possession." The Century building at Eighth and Rusk streets was one of his assets.[54] Another of his prized properties was the entire 800 block between Main and Rusk, which he acquired around the turn of the century.[55] The property was right in the heart of the Acre, though in 1902 it became the site of the posh Metropolitan Hotel, described as "Fort Worth's Finest" and "the only European hotel in the city."[56] To reflect his image as one of the most powerful men in the city, Scott bought a Georgian-style mansion for his family in 1911.[57]

Between 1870 and 1890, Walter Huffman, the city's first self-made millionaire, earned much of his money in real estate, including several blocks on Main Street down as far as Twelfth.[58] And Captain E. M. Daggett, described in admiring biographies as "one of the real founders of Fort Worth," had his name on the Daggett Addition not because of his civic contributions but because his name also happened to be on the title to every piece of property sold in that section. The lower ends of Main, Rusk, Jones and Calhoun, including the railroad reservation, were all on property that once belonged to Ephraim M. Daggett.[59] Daggett represented the old-fashioned work ethic that brought civilization and prosperity to the frontier through hard work, self-sacrifice and civic-mindedness. His son and only child, however, E. B. Daggett, born in 1838, was of a different bent. Many considered him to be the black sheep of the family, and some of his less savory associations in town gave rise to a lot of gossip. The legal arrangements his father made of his property after he was gone only confirmed the worst gossip. In 1876, when E. M. was an old man, he wrote a will leaving his property to a nephew, who was also his namesake. In 1882, he had this will annulled and wrote another leaving everything to E. B.'s wife Elizabeth and their children. After the old man died on April 19, 1883, the son got nothing.[60] Perhaps E. M. felt his son had gotten too cozy with the wrong kinds of people over the years.

The Daggett connection goes well beyond mere property ownership. According to public records, E. B. Daggett had a very personal interest in the Acre. He knew Madam Porter well enough to post her bail in 1887 when she was charged with "keeping a disorderly house." Miss Porter appealed her first conviction in city court and Daggett, along with W. H. Ward, proprietor of the White Elephant Saloon, put up her appeal bond.[61] Three years later, E. B. Daggett was arrested and charged with "keeping a disorderly house" of his own. He pleaded not guilty and stood trial on November 18, 1890, but a jury of six of his fellow citizens found him guilty. He was fined $200.[62] It was just as well his father was not alive to witness these goings-on. E. B. was hardly a young colt, kicking up his heels at this time; he was a middle-aged businessman of forty-nine when he signed the bond for Mary Porter.

Of course, land holdings alone do not a "vice king" make, at least not in the same sense as Joe Lowe or George Holland, but such holdings did give these three men a vested interest in the Acre's development. Furthermore, it was impossible to own as much as a block in the area without owning land on which sat at least one saloon, gambling hall or worse. It follows that at least in part several substantial fortunes among the city's founding fathers were derived from questionable sources. But nobody worried much about the actual property owners, as opposed to the operators, renters and leaseholders, until long after the turn of the century, when ardent muckrakers and tenacious preachers began to dig into the records. Rumor and innuendo connect other well-known figures with the Acre.[63] But it is doubtful that men like Winfield Scott or Walter Huffman ever spent much time there, particularly after the mid-1880s when the area was increasingly being taken over by blacks.

The Acre was changing and becoming less inviting to proper, Victorian Fort Worthers. Census reports for 1880 and 1900 underscore

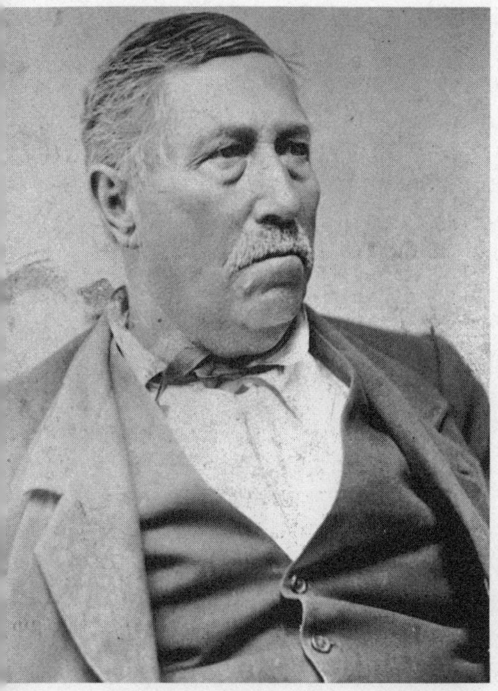

The Acre's Biggest Landlords: Ephraim M. Daggett, Sr. (top left), W. A. Huffman (top right), and Winfield Scott (right). How much of the guilt belongs to those who hold the property deeds? None of the three was ever accused of contributing personally to the reputation of the Acre, but none was a candidate for sainthood either (Daggett and Huffman courtesy Fort Worth Public Library; Scott courtesy Mrs. Roze McCoy Porter, Fort Worth).

this trend, showing a concentration of "colored" residents in the area commonly known as the Acre.[64] Further evidence can be found in statistics published by the *Fort Worth Daily Gazette* in 1890, which show that the city's population was ninety percent white and six percent "colored," out of a total population of 31,000. Where they lived is not detailed, but an educated guess suggests that most lived on the south end of town, and newspaper accounts in the decades of the '80s and '90s support the limited statistical evidence.[65] Even allowing for blatant racial prejudice in the reporting of all-white newspapers, the facts speak for themselves. The *Fort Worth Daily Gazette* in 1887 observed that "it seems likely more than half of the prostitutes in Hell's Half Acre are black."[66]

Fort Worth's major newspapers throughout the period never missed a chance to make mocking or condescending references to black residents of the Acre, a tone used for both the victims and the perpetrators of crimes. Typical of the headlines in the *Democrat* and the *Gazette* in these years were: "Burly Black Assaults a Ten-Year-Old-Girl," and the following classic, "A Black Fiend Attacks an Invalid White Lady in Her Bed, Chokes Her Until the Blood Oozes from Her Mouth and Nose, Accomplishes His Design!!"[67]

Like her contemporary Lottie Freeman, Emeline Gooden regularly had her escapades chronicled in the pages of the *Gazette* and *Democrat*. Called "she-terror of the Third Ward" by the *Gazette*, she lived in the Acre for ten years, earning a living as a prostitute when she was not brawling like a sailor.[68] Her scrapping ways were legendary, and men were her favorite opponents. She would fight with whatever came to hand, but her favorite weapons were bottles and razors. The *Gazette* figured that she averaged thirteen fights per week for a decade. It was said she could "whip her weight in wild cats," back when that expression still had some meaning. "She hardly ever condescends to an encounter with a woman."[69]

Local papers usually reported crimes committed by blacks in an off-handed and insensitive manner, never with the shock or righteous indignation used to describe a stage robbery or a shoot-out among gunmen. One reason for this less-than-spirited treatment was that mayhem among black citizens was not usually carried out with six-shooters and Winchesters but with knives, razors, beer bottles and even an occasional rock or pouring pitcher.[70]

If the newspapers were hard on blacks in the Acre, the all-white police force was even harder. Black Fort Worthers were at the mercy of white officers who did not operate under the constraints imposed by modern civil rights legislation and enlightened attitudes. The city's police force had not always been all-white, however. In 1873, Marshal Ed Terrell had requested a black policeman be added to the small force. The city council considered Terrell's request and agreed to appoint a "Special Policeman" whose job it would be "to arrest all offenders . . . within the city limits . . . of his own color." The marshal suggested a man named Hague Tucker, and the council accepted. But this otherwise enlightened attitude was marred by the conditions of Tucker's employment. He was not to be considered a member of the "regular police force" or to be paid the same as white policemen — $37.50 per month. Whereas white lawmen always appeared before the council to request their monthly pay, Marshal Terrell settled up with Tucker in some unspecified way out of unnamed funds.[71] Tucker's name never appeared again in city council minutes, and his job probably disappeared as soon as Terrell resigned.

Tucker's presence on the force might have made a difference in 1875, when Sol Bragg, a local black man, became the first of his race to be hanged in Tarrant County. There was no trial; the "judge and jury" were a band of white vigilantes. Bragg was accused of assaulting a white woman who came through town on a prairie schooner headed west. The vigilantes took him out to the Cold Spring Road and built a platform under a sycamore tree. As one resident later described it, presiding over the "execution" was none other than Sheriff "Bill" [sic] Henderson.[72] The rough platform continued to stand under the tree for several years afterward, perhaps as a warning to the rest of the city's black population.

During the 1880s, despite the growing black community in Fort Worth, the police force remained all white. The policemen usually patrolled the Acre in pairs and rousted individual blacks on the slightest pretext. Some officers carried brass knuckles and were not above using them to subdue suspects when the situation demanded. One victim of police brass knuckles was Bill Davis, a black man who, on the night of April 16, 1885, got into a scrap with a policeman who thought Davis looked suspicious. In the ensuing fight, Davis managed to more than hold his own: he grabbed the officer's gun and escaped. The entire episode was reported the next day in the *Dallas Herald*.[73]

Newspaper reports indicate another change occurring in the Acre around this same time. The hottest night spots were no longer the dance halls where customers provided their own entertainment for the price of a dance. Variety theaters were the newest rage where "professionals" entertained while the customers watched and drank. Variety shows, often described as "girlie shows," were the crude antecedents of vaudeville. Across the West, they replaced the cowboys' beloved dance halls as public tastes changed and legal action closed down the roughest dance joints. The cowboy had been the biggest customer of the dance halls when the trail drives held Fort Worth's economy in thrall. But the trail drives had declined rapidly since their heyday in the early 1870s, and new customers demanded more cosmopolitan entertainment for their dollar than a spin around the dance floor with a graceless nymph, followed by a round of drinks at the bar. Variety theaters provided eastern-style entertainment for the masses at a price the masses could afford.

Local entrepreneurs had no difficulty shifting to the new form of entertainment. They built theaters and imported traveling variety acts to fill their stages. In every act, the girls were the most important part of the show. What they lacked in charm, they more than made up for in energetic performances and brazen displays of flesh and form. They were euphemistically called "actresses," which gave a bad image to that particular calling for many years. When they took time out for a breather or to entertain individual customers in more private surroundings, singing, juggling and comic acts took the stage.

The city council wrestled with the problem of variety shows, or theaters as they were also called, for several years. In August, 1877, such entertainment was prohibited by ordinance for one month until a new law repealed the old one.[74] The most interesting part of the first ordinance was that the determining factor of what constituted a "variety show or theater" was the participation of women on stage. If women were on the stage, it was a variety show and therefore illegal. It was probably not the disapproval of decent women that quickly got the ordinance repealed, but the financially motivated protest of small-time saloon keepers who were hurt by competition from variety theaters. Women, except under the banner of the Temperance Union, were not an organized force in local politics, and even when organized, still could not vote. In the end, the city won a partial victory by closing down the variety shows on Sundays, but even this relatively mild prohibition was flouted without consequence.[75]

In Fort Worth, the leading entrepreneurs of variety theater were Joe Lowe and George Holland. At one time or another they operated theaters under the names My Theater, Theater Comique, Centennial Theater and Holland's Variety Theater, all appealing primarily to the lower end of the socio-economic scale. They were definitely not high class by anyone's standards.

The typical variety theater was a cheaply constructed, frame structure, "where for a modest admission fee, one could witness an immodest display of unattractive but still alluring" female performers.[76] The charge might be as little as ten cents for one of the bump-and-grind shows in a low-rent Acre dive, or as much as a dollar for one of the big, costumed performances in a theater uptown. Regardless of their location, all the theaters were multi-dimensional operations where drinks were sold and organized gambling permitted on the premises. Although a stage was an essential part of the place, it was seldom the architectural focus of the building. Rather, it was usually small and set off to one side of the main room. The rest of the place was taken up with saloon and gaming rooms. Of such places it was said, "Their environments were more conducive to exciting than to interesting sensations."[77]

The Centennial Theater was one of the major Fort Worth attractions from the mid-1870s to the mid-1880s, with a regional reputation that drew customers from all over the Southwest. Many years later, old-timers remembered, "A visit to Fort Worth was not complete unless a call at the Centennial was made."[78] Many just came to stand at the bar and gawk, but when they left they took with them tales of the wild goings-on that served as far better advertising than anything that ran in the newspapers.

By cow town standards, the Centennial was a fairly impressive, two-story establishment with no hint of the false front that marked the first generation of public buildings. The Centennial was also a cut or two above the average western variety theater of its day, which Bat Masterson described contemptuously as "pine-board affairs that were in general use in frontier towns. A bullet fired from a Colt .45 caliber pistol would go through a half-dozen such buildings."[79] The big Main Street entrance doors had glass panes and a boardwalk ran the length of the building. The place was lit on the inside by gas lamps that put off almost as much heat as light. The lighting system was not only inadequate but dangerous and probably caused the fire that nearly destroyed a chunk of downtown Fort Worth in 1878. Prompt action by the boys of the Panther City fire department saved the Centennial, and insurance repaired the damage in short order. Business hardly missed a beat.[80] Not so fortunate that night were the nearby Occidental Saloon and a female boarding house maintained by Lowe for his actresses. The *Democrat* lamented the next day the passing of the Occidental in these terms: "Finest saloon in Texas licked 'clean up' by the Demon." Lowe was in the Occidental Saloon when the fire started and narrowly escaped with his life. The fire raged for hours, and passengers arriving on the train from the east about 2:30 A.M. "could see the cupola of the courthouse very plainly in the glare and the light from the burning buildings."[81]

Back in action, the Centennial was as good as new, if not bigger and better. On the first floor were the bar, dance floor and theater. The dance floor was at the center of the room with the bar occupying one entire side. The stage was at the rear. The second floor was devoted to gambling and to private rooms for the "actresses." Only customers with a good-sized bankroll or good connections got this far. Circling the major part of the first floor was a gallery where the actresses could sit while not on stage. Patrons were allowed, even encouraged, to visit with the actresses in the gallery. If a man desired more seclusion, a key to the lady's room could be purchased for a dollar. In the room a bottle of beer cost a dollar, and other refreshments could be obtained at equally inflated prices. But for the extra charge, the patron could enjoy his visit undisturbed.[82]

The Centennial did a booming business for Joe Lowe. On any given night, from one to two hundred men might be found there enjoying Lowe's hospitality. Whenever shooting started, as it did on occasion — whether out of sheer exuberance or sometimes meaner intent — patrons and performers alike stampeded for the doors. At such times, however, the management soon had the altercation cleared up and everything back to normal. The customers, most of whom had not gone far, drifted back in and resumed their revelry.

By the 1880s, many of the Centennial's patrons were decked out in "evening clothes" and no longer smelled of horses and cattle. But only a few blocks farther south on Main Street, standards of dress and behavior had not changed much. Toward the end of the decade, the *Gazette* observed, "They still retail pandemonium at a nickel a pan in the Third Ward."[83] Yet even the variety theaters were forced to keep

Main Street, 1881, looking south toward the Texas & Pacific depot (courtesy *Fort Worth Star-Telegram*). "A town of gentility and decorum," as Oliver Knight called it? Or a regular stop on the Outlaw Trail and the Gambler's Circuit?

up with the times. In the mid-1890s, the Standard Theater went up at the corner of Twelfth and Rusk. Its all-brick construction, electric footlights, bar and wine rooms made it the premiere establishment of its kind in the city, a title it held for many years.

A considerably different picture of Fort Worth in the 1880s has been painted by historian Oliver Knight, who described it as "a town of gentility and decorum."[84] But his description does not bear up under close examination. It was particularly questionable below Seventh Street whether, as Knight claimed, Fort Worth had risen above its 1870s cow town roots. Polite folks still settled around Samuels Avenue, north of courthouse square, and westward out Seventh Street. These were the "silk-stocking" neighborhoods. But from Ninth Street down to the railroad reservation the town was still wide open. Most legitimate businesses were located on Main, starting at Weatherford and extending south to Fifth or Sixth streets. From Seventh down to Ninth streets, these entrepreneurs fought it out with the vice trade for the upper hand. Apart from growing larger, the town had not changed much in ten years.

If "Queen City of the Prairies" was the title Fort Worth preferred for its public image, another was used by alarmed police and city health officials: "City of Auger Holes and Morphine Suicides,"[85] a reference to the growing suicide rate among Acre prostitutes, who preferred death to the diseases, shame and poverty that came with their profession. The picture of the carefree, good-hearted western bawd is a concoction of dime novels and Hollywood movies. The truth was much grimmer. Even in the good times, business was fraught with uncertainties for the Acre's female entrepreneurs, not the least of which was constant harassment by the police. Unlike her madam or gentleman, the prostitute could not afford too many fines or too much time off from work for court appearances and nights in jail. Sometimes the streets were practically swept clean by the zealous defenders of law and order. In one September 1881 roundup, twenty-two girls were arrested, spent the night in jail, and were fined five dollars each plus court costs in the Mayor's Court the next day.[86] A few roundups like this over a short period were enough to cause some girls to pack up and skip town for good. Of course, that was the purpose of such sweeps, but they hardly made a dent in the city's prostitute population.

Even when not beset by the law, the prostitute's life in the Acre was far from glamorous. In the 1880s, working conditions were just as grim and living conditions were just as bad as they had been earlier. The parlor houses ameliorated these conditions only slightly for the handful of girls lucky enough and pretty enough to find a home in one of them. Nights spent entertaining customers and days spent recuperating from the night's activities did not leave much time for the finer things of life. The girls lived with fear in many forms. On any given day a prostitute might be beaten up — or worse — by one of her competitors, "stiffed" by a cheap customer or thrown out of her living quarters by her madam or landlord. The madams could terrorize their own girls with virtual impunity. In one highly publicized incident, police had to be called to Dolly Love's (a.k.a., Dolly Wilson's) place because the madam of the house was beating up one of her girls. The next day Dolly was fined less than $20 in city court.[87] If the victim was smart, she used the head start to get out of town, because she knew the local authorities usually backed the madam whenever any disputes arose. As historian Nancy Wilson Ross has put it, "The madam could usually rely upon the local constabulary to come on the double when she called and remove any unwanted troublemakers [male or female]."[88] In fact, the madam in her own house possessed the absolute authority of a sea captain on his ship.

Like fear, violence was a constant companion. The girls saw so much violence that they tended to become blasé about it. Three or four prostitutes were present in the Santa Fe saloon one night when a man was shot in an argument. All of them later testified, but the testimony of Mattie White is particularly revealing. Mattie stated, "I did not scream or make any noise when the shooting was done. I have been around where there was a heap of shooting and have been shot a time or two myself."[89]

Fort Worth newspapers regularly chronicled the brutal lives and shocking ends of girls in the Acre, and the problem was decried by everyone who read their stories. A typical report of the way in which many girls entered the profession ran in an interview in the *Fort Worth Register*. The girl, whose real name was given simply as "Miss Belknap," was living at the time in one of the nicer "female boarding houses" at 1012 Rusk where Madam Porter reigned. She said her working name was Velma Banks, and that she had been at the Rusk Street house about five months since coming to Fort Worth from Dallas. The rest of her story is best told in her own words, as taken down by the reporter for the *Register*:

My home . . . is in a little city in the northern part of the state, where my mother and father now reside. My father treated me brutally, and on one occasion attempted to violate my chastity. I resisted and he struck me, knocking me down, and then kicked me three times; when I got up he knocked me down again and kicked me. I got down stairs, how I cannot tell, after he had threatened to kill me if I told what had occurred. From this time on it was very unpleasant for me, and I finally left home and went to my aunt's to live while I completed my schooling. Shortly thereafter, mother came to me and asked me to leave the city, but gave no reason for doing so, though I believe it was because of fear of my father. As stated before, I went to Dallas, where I secured employment in a factory running a sewing machine, but I was shortly forced to quit this work, as I was physically unable to perform the duties. After this I secured employment in a private family, where I stayed only a few days because the head of the house made insulting propositions to me, and his wife believed his statement in preference to mine. Then I made an appeal to two ministers, begging their assistance in securing employment. They readily promised, and that is as far as the matter went. Some time elapsed and my little means were about exhausted, when I met Mr. Gribble, who knew me at home, and I borrowed $5 from him. This enabled me to prolong the fight, and I came to this city in quest of employment. Having no knowledge of housework or anything else, in fact, I found it difficult. My possessions had dwindled down to five cents when I met Madam Porter, who offered to send me home, but having no home, this kind offer was refused. Then it was that I met Miss Clifton and received the first encouragement. I went to her house, and in a day or so was taken ill and lay in bed for three months, Miss Clifton nursing me and defraying all of my expenses, doctor's fees, drug bills, etc., and made no charge for board. I am very anxious to leave this place and life, but there is a debt of $59 for board hanging over me, which has accumulated since the doctor ceased attendance. This I feel in honor bound to pay, first because it is an honest debt, and lastly, because of the kindness of Miss Clifton in my illness.

All I want is an opportunity to earn a living and be given a chance to complete a course of shorthand which I have already begun. This would take two or three months. Thus prepared I could battle for myself and repay those who assist me. Certainly there is enough charitably inclined people to render this assistance and save a soul from purgatory.[90]

Even allowing for a little journalistic license and a dash of Victorian mawkishness, the story nonetheless rings true for the place and time. The saddest part, however, is the postscript added by the madam, Mildred Clifton, who told the reporter that "once a girl had entered the life, she did not believe it possible to effect a lasting reformation, unless some good man married her and placed her in a good home."[91]

The Madam Porter of the story was Mary Porter, a Fort Worth legend in her own right. Every western town that survived long enough had its famous madam, a woman who was a central figure on the local scene for many years and became a part of local history after she passed on. Denver had Mattie Silks and Dodge City had Dora Hand, just to mention two. In Fort Worth three women vied for the unofficial title, "Queen of the Madams": Mary Porter, Jessie Reeves and Josie Belmont. All three ran houses in the Acre within a block of each other and operated as friendly competitors for the better class of male customers who chose to sample the delights of Rusk Street. As one old-time mayor of another city remarked, "Competition makes for better conditions in the sporting world. One parlor house in a town is no good." It was that gentleman's observation that a town needed *at least* two houses to keep a healthy level of free enterprise going.[92] The most successful madams, judging by the descriptions of those who knew them, were "hard-headed realists, forthright and outspoken, warm-hearted to a fault, generous to the sick and those down on their luck."[93] Based on this rosy description, every town could have used a dozen or more such women plying their trade.

Fort Worth's Big Three were well known in the city's polite districts and even better known in the courts where they were frequent defendants. During periodic police roundups, Madams Porter, Reeves and Belmont were routinely arrested together, appeared in court on the same date, pleaded guilty, paid their fines promptly, then disappeared out the door with a flourish of petticoats and long skirts. This legal charade went on for the better part of two decades while they ruled the roost on Rusk.

Of the three madams, the least is known about Josie Belmont. Josie hardly ever got her name in the papers except in conjunction with Mary and Jessie. One of those rare occasions was in 1881 when she was hauled into the Mayor's Court on a charge of "vagrancy" and fined $31.10. (The odd amount included the fine plus court costs, which were usually more than the fine.[94]) In 1884, Josie was just a "boarder" with another woman named Frankie Brown. But by 1886 Josie was running her own house at 1106 Rusk, right next door to Mary Porter's. Her sister Lottie lived with her. Josie operated her house for the next four or five years before selling out to Mary Porter and moving in with Maud Levan. She continued to make regular appearances in the courts after that, but on the lesser charge of "vagrancy," not "running a disorderly house." Her days as a madam had apparently come to an end.

Jessie Reeves came to her occupation after trying her luck as a circus performer and a monte or faro dealer. As a dealer, she was once shot in the chest by an irate cowboy over a questionable deal. She lived to tell about it, but spent fifteen months convalescing in bed and thereafter decided to give up the dealer's life. Jessie was born and spent her early years in Spain, before immigrating to the United States and turning up in Fort Worth in the early 1880s with her sister. They moved into a house at the corner of Seventh and Main that eventually boasted the first green lawn in the city, a significant touch of class in the 1880s when most westerners regarded grass as something for grazing cattle on. By 1885, she owned a boarding house at Rusk and Eleventh, catty-cornered across the street from Mary Porter's. Jessie's girls, according to local legend, entertained any number of respectable, even prominent local citizens over the years. There were also rumors that Jessie was the special "girlfriend" of one of the most prominent of the city's fathers, a rancher and oil man with a family and a name that eventually graced several local landmarks.[95] The $100 fines she paid in the Mayor's Court every two or three months were easily recouped from her distinguished clientele.

All of Jessie's notoriety was not negative. In the summer of 1888, a roofing works across the street from her boarding house caught fire, quickly turning into a "fiery furnace," as the *Gazette* described it. The fire department raced to the rescue, and the local citizens pitched in to help out of fear that the whole town might go up in flames. At the height of the blaze, Jessie sent over a score of blankets and quilts to be used by the firemen as protection against the intense heat. At one point, her house was also threatened by the leaping flames. The outside walls began to smolder until a well-directed stream of water from the grateful fireman saved the place.[96] Cynical citizens had often accused the police of having special arrangements with local madams, but this was the first time the firemen had ever provided "protection" to a local madam's operation.

Years later, after she had left Fort Worth, Jessie turned over a new leaf and went on the religious lecture circuit. Speaking as a reformed madam, she titillated and shocked audiences with her story

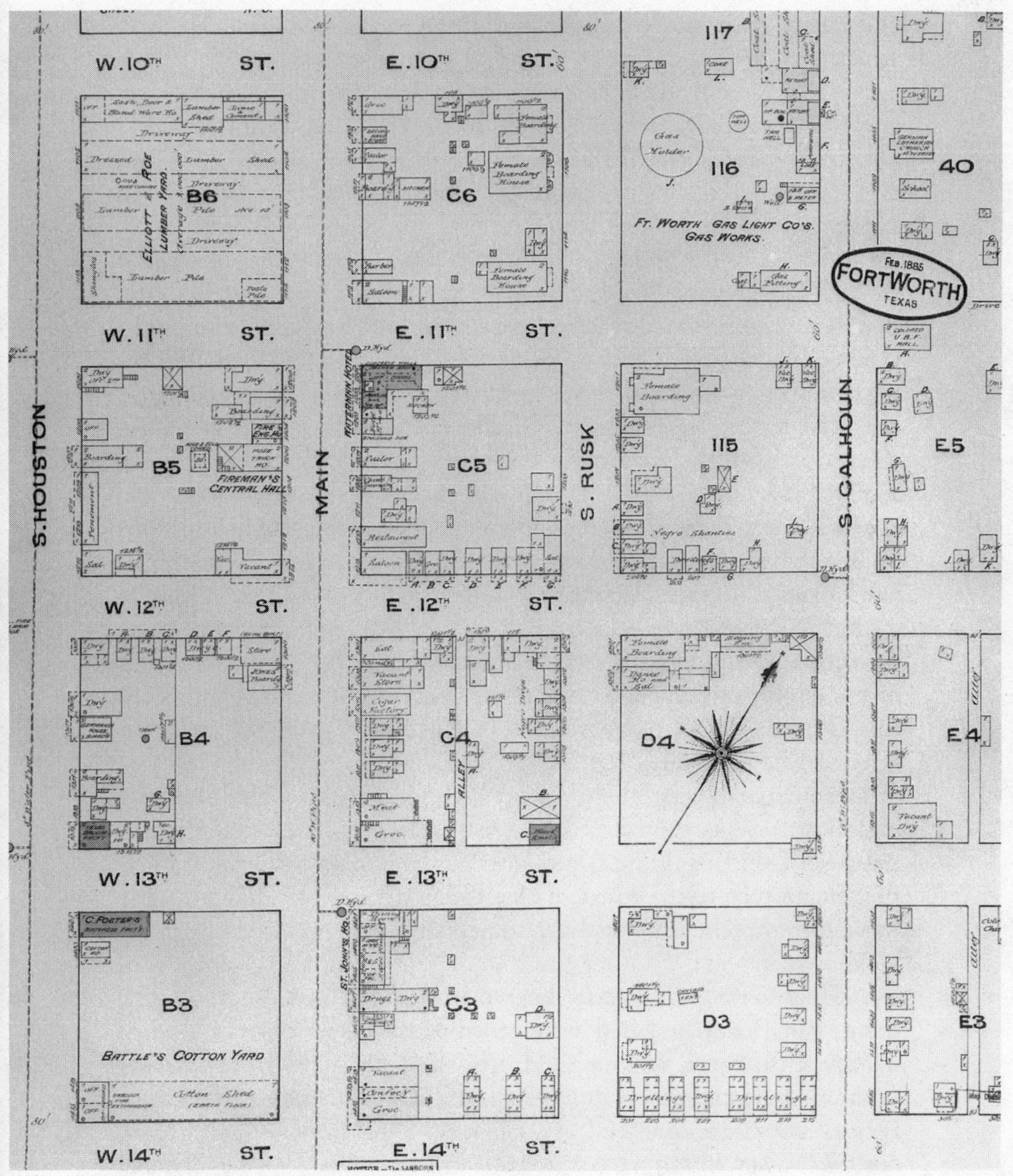

Earliest Sanborn Fire Map of Fort Worth, 1885, showing downtown business district. Where Rusk and Twelfth streets intersect was the heart of Hell's Half Acre—an unrelieved stretch of saloons, dance halls and bordellos (Barker History Center, University of Texas at Austin).

of a misspent life just barely saved from eternal damnation. She also took up the pen to tell of "a career in sin rarely equalled."[97]

Although not the best known of the Big Three, Jessie is the only one for whom a physical description has come down to us. Local historian Mary Daggett Lake describes Jessie as having dark skin and dark hair that she wore in a braid "dropped down her back like a school girl."[98]

Mary Porter is probably the most famous of the local madams for several reasons. First, she has often been confused with Fannie Porter by later writers who never realized there were two Madam Porters doing business in Texas cow towns. She also outlasted Fort Worth's other notorious madams, and she probably knew every prominent man in town on a first-name basis. The doors at 1106 Rusk were still open in 1901, although Mary owed back taxes to the city of $89.25 on property valued at $5,950.[99] During the previous two decades she had appeared frequently in court to answer charges of keeping a disorderly house, selling beer and liquor without a license, even vagrancy. In many cases, the county attorney refused to prosecute so the cases were dismissed. On the rare occasions when she chose to fight the charges, she could depend upon friends like Nat Kramer, the gentleman gambler and sporting man, to post her trial bond. Between 1893 and 1897, she had 130 offenses on record with the County Court, yet she never spent a night in jail.[100] Although her operations were brazen and clearly outside the law, she was practically untouchable. Part of Mary's legend is the story that she was married to Nat Kramer and the two of them lived on East Third Street.[101] Sad to say, for all her notoriety, she left no picture to provide a clue to her appearance. Whether she was tall or short, plump or thin, homely or lovely will probably never be known.

There were other, lesser-known madams in Fort Worth during these years. They included aforementioned Mildred Clifton, Madam Brown (first name unknown), Carrie Barklow, and Dolly Wilson (a.k.a. "Dolly Love"). Will Lake also recalled a woman named Pearl Bebee, whom he described as "a big old slob, heavy-set and blondine."[102] They all ran what were euphemistically described as "female boarding houses" and their names appeared in court records regularly. The exact locations of their houses and their eventual fates have long since been forgotten. But they clearly played second fiddle to the Big Three — Porter, Reeves and Belmont.

All the Fort Worth madams operated under an unwritten agreement with local authorities. The rules governing this quasi-legal arrangement were simple: no public advertising, no fights and regular medical examinations for the girls. These rules were fairly standard all over the West, and as long as they were followed and income was split equitably with the authorities, no one got too exercised over a little friendly prostitution.[103] Money that found its way into local coffers through the Acre was a powerful incentive for city fathers to turn a blind eye toward what was happening down on Rusk Street. The "up-lifters," as B. B. Paddock contemptuously referred to them, did not stand a chance.

There were other factors which made genuine reform in these years impossible. One was Dallas, thirty miles to the east, Fort Worth's chief rival as the entertainment capital of North Texas. The older and larger city had big-time racetrack gambling that Fort Worth lacked. Even Fort Worth's resident gambling fraternity made regular trips to Dallas to bet on the horses.[104] But Fort Worth had something its rival did not, and that was a wide-open resort district that compared favorably with anything the major Kansas cow towns had to offer. Dallas's red-light district, for better or for worse, lacked the reputation of Hell's Half Acre. The rivalry between the two cities went beyond friendly competition. Just how serious it could get was illustrated by a notice which appeared in Fort Worth newspapers in 1883. The city fathers of Cowtown offered professional gamblers from Dallas County rent-free accommodations and $3500 in cash to "remove the seat of their operations to this city." Dallas businessmen were so upset over the potential loss of revenue that they paid a call on their own county attorney, Charles Clint, to persuade him to be more hospitable to the gamblers.[105] Meanwhile, Fort Worth continued to take a permissive, even protective attitude toward all manner of gambling activities. There was a movement among the local sporting fraternity in 1887 to introduce dog fighting into some of the darker corners of the Acre. The *Fort Worth Gazette* blamed the plan on "Dallas sports" and harrumphed that "chicken fighting is bad enough."[106]

Another factor keeping the doors open in the Acre might be called the "upper-crust connection." Slumming in the Acre was a popular sport among the young blades whose fathers ran the city. They provided a persistent source of annoyance to the police with their frequent midnight hack rides down to the south end of Rusk or Main streets. Following the usual scenario, police would be summoned to the site of an "untimely exhibition of hilarity." They would race to the scene only to hear the derisive cries of "the young sports as they drove out of sight, urging their hack driver to greater haste."

Joe Witcher, a veteran policeman by this date, recalled those days many years later:

> Once in a while we would recognize some of the boys and shout their names after them. Many a morning at daylight I've met a bleary-eyed youth sidling around the corner to where I was waiting for the first welcome glimpse of sunrise. "Joe," he would say, "Have you got anything against me this morning?" and when I would nod and smile a little, he'd say, "Now don't tell father and I'll fix up my fine at the end of the week."
>
> I always trusted a man who would make a promise of that sort in those days. In nine instances out of ten he could be trusted to keep his word. Cowboys and businessmen alike were pretty square about such things.[107]

As long as the young men "of the better class" saw Hell's Half Acre as their personal playground, there was little chance of its being shut down permanently. And policemen like Joe Witcher, it must have seemed, were there as much to protect the lawbreakers as the law. They were the crucial link in the chain between vice operators and city government. The *Democrat* recognized this link in 1881 when it paid this back-handed compliment to Witcher: "Joe Witcher, they say, handles the prisoners to a better advantage than any officer who has yet had control of them."[108] One reason Officer Joe was so good with his prisoners is that he knew most of them would be back out on the streets in a few hours, so there was no sense in being too hard-nosed about crime-busting. The same *laissez faire* attitude permeated the entire law enforcement system.

On December 1, 1881, just in time for the Christmas season, the dance halls were allowed to re-open after being closed during one of the periodic clean-up campaigns. Such campaigns were characteristic of Hell's Half Acre's later years, but they did not really pick up steam until after Timothy Courtright's ouster from office. The first time all the dance halls and gambling houses were closed was under the new administration of Mayor R. E. Beckham in 1879. The mayor ordered every ordinance on the books "enforced to the letter," setting a standard for later administrations that was hard to ignore completely, though it was bent considerably.[109] Beckham's 1879 campaign did not last the summer before "the voice of the cowboy [was] heard once again."[110] His successors in city government were not much more successful at making reform stick, despite brave pronouncements like that of County Attorney N. R. Bowlin, who announced in 1885, "Gamblers in Fort Worth Have Got To Go!"[111]

Life in the Acre was still dangerous in the 1880s, even for those who were only passing through. A street car driver and his passenger were shot at one evening by person or persons unknown. Neither was hit, but the passenger had a bullet hole in his coat to show for his brief trip through the district.[112] On October 6, 1887, the *Gazette* reported that "Third Ward Philistines" had robbed another stranger in town. Such reports were so routine during these years that they were more in the nature of updates than news flashes.

Not counting the usual gambling, prostitution and drunkenness, less violent lawlessness continued on a regular basis, too. In February, 1887, a gang of counterfeiters was arrested for running an operation over Isenhower's grocery store at 1016 Main.[113] On any given day or night, greenhorns who came in by rail were likely to be robbed or fleeced by petty criminals as soon as they stepped off the train. The *Fort Worth Gazette* reported that around the platform of the depot, "pickpockets, confidence men, bunco steerers and almost every variety of crook known . . . gather."[114] All were waiting for the same thing: the imminent arrival of another shipment of sheep ready for shearing. It may have been chance or practical considerations that led the Texas & Pacific to place the original railroad station on the south end of town at the edge of the Acre, but it was a decision that benefited every immoral or criminal operator in the Acre after 1876.

By the mid-1880s, Fort Worthers aimed their sights on becoming a major convention city, and a city could not be too strait-laced if it wanted to attract convention business. The annual cattlemen's meeting drew the biggest attendance. During the convention days, the lid was taken completely off, and the town became, for a time, "hot." Naturally, there were some citizens who yelled long and loud. These people would call at the district attorney's office but it seemed this official was ill each time the convention date rolled around and he would disappear for a few days.[115]

Before the end of the decade, conventions replaced the cattle business as the biggest contributor to the Acre's annual income. This was a natural result of the changing economic picture. At the beginning of the 1880s, cattle were still being driven up the Chisholm Trail in large numbers — 250,000 in 1882 alone. But by the end of 1884 the huge drives had virtually ceased.[116] While the cowboy was still an important part of the local scene, conventions of cattlemen, war veterans and political parties had become the big events. They gave the Acre a new lease on life.

Numbers told the story. Cowboys in town never counted more than a few hundred, even during the height of the season. A single convention could draw more visitors during a week than an entire cattle season. In August, 1885, the Third Grand Reunion of Ex-Confederate Soldiers drew 15,000 to Fort Worth for the three-day event.[117] Between November 8th and 10th, 1887, the city was host to Mexican War veterans, most of whom must have been pushing seventy by this date but were still spry enough to enjoy the pleasures of the Acre. Whatever combination of factors attracted the convention business to Fort Worth, the city was justifiably proud of its "great reputation for hospitality" and styled itself "the Convention City" from the middle of the decade on.[118] That reputation was only slightly tarnished in 1888 — a presidential election year — when the city failed in its efforts to attract the state Democratic convention.

In spite of the periodic clean-up campaigns, the Acre flourished. Officials continued to turn a blind eye to it, the sons of the rich continued to patronize it, and juries made up of upstanding citizens refused to convict notorious characters. To the red-blooded men who sat on the juries, gambling and prostitution were not considered crimes — nuisances, yes, but not crimes.

The frustration of officials like City Attorney J. W. Swayne were well documented. In August, 1884, Swayne brought nearly fifty cases before the Mayor's (sometimes known as the Recorder's) Court on charges of violating city ordinances against gambling. He placed his own reputation and that of the city attorney's office on the line against the gamblers and their lawyers. Fort Worth's sporting men had long been in the habit of pleading guilty in the Mayor's Court, paying a small fine and going back to work. The whole process did not take much longer than it took for a stroll down Main Street to the courthouse and back again. When Swayne began to apply the heat to send them to jail, they fought back by demanding jury trials. The first batch of cases all ended in acquittal. The writing was on the wall when out of forty-eight men impaneled for jury duty, not one was found willing to convict.[119]

The gamblers closed ranks behind Nat Kramer, who advised Swayne to give up. To make the medicine go down easier, Kramer told the city attorney that none of the gamblers thought any the less of him for his failure! In fact they admired him for the fight he had made and "did not endorse the slurs thrown out at him."[120] On August 28, Swayne asked the court to dismiss the remaining forty-three cases still on the docket, which was immediately done. The gamblers had scored a stunning victory over the forces of law and order — *vox populi.* Whether because of political machinations or voter dissatisfaction, Swayne was not reelected the following year. Taking his cue from the city attorney, County Attorney W. S. Pendleton announced that he would prosecute no cases on the county level, admitting he was legally powerless in the matter.

For years madams received the same sort of kid-glove treatment from the jury system. Judge J. H. Jackson of the City Court fumed publicly that, "The men who have preached morality for years in this city . . . often get on juries . . . and it is surprising that they will bring in verdicts of not guilty, to the disgust of the court and the officers making the arrest, and this class of wrong-doers are fast getting on the scheme of requiring juries." The judge was particularly incensed over the case of a madam hauled before his court because "she was one of the worst type, one of those who do more to lead young girls astray than those who make their actions more brazenly public." The all-male jury acquitted the woman, leading Jackson to grumble about "that class of violators of the law who will give the court and all connected with it the 'horse laugh'"[121]

Many other prominent citizens agreed with the judge's sense of outrage. Some had already decided to do more than just complain. In 1884, they formed the Law and Order Association and dedicated themselves to suppressing "gambling and other vices." At their first organizational meeting on September 1, a large turnout jammed the courthouse to hear speeches and resolutions against gambling, prostitution and open saloons on Sunday. All the resolutions were carried unanimously. City Judges Edward Hovenkamp and James W. Thomason addressed the crowd on the need to "create a healthy public sentiment on these three evils."

Ed Hovenkamp and Jim Thomason were closely allied with the

city's law-and-order advocates for years. Hovenkamp came to Tarrant County in 1854 and stayed to become one of the city's earliest practicing attorneys. He eventually became a district attorney. Along the way he also helped rear two sons, Thomas D. and M. W., who became well-respected attorneys in their own right. Jim Thomason boarded with policeman W. M. Rea in one of the city's boarding houses in the mid-1880s. In later years he was a deputy sheriff and then a police detective. The credentials of such men gave their cause the stamp of respectability, raising it above mere vigilante status. Other participants in this first meeting helped set up a permanent organization, with Thomas Anderson as president, and W. J. Boaz, K. M. Van Zandt, Sam Seaton and J. W. House as vice presidents. Later there was talk of starting their own newspaper.[122]

Despite its admirable beginnings, the Law and Order Association soon split over which direction to take. One wing wanted to run it as a religious organization, declaring war on horse racing, liquor and even baseball. The other faction favored modest goals of stopping gambling and regulating prostitution. From its perspective thirty miles away, a Dallas newspaper opined, "The extremists will probably drive the society to endorsement of measures which will kill it, so an early demise may be expected."[123]

Eventually the Law and Order Association lost all credibility and, worse, all interest as a news item, its voice drowned out by the sound of cash registers ringing up sales. The insignificance of the Law and Order Association in Fort Worth's history contrasts sharply with the highly visible presence of vigilante committees in other cow towns like Ellsworth, Wichita and Dodge City.[124] The difference was that while law and order sometimes took a beating in Fort Worth, it never broke down to the point where extra-legal measures had to be adopted to keep the lid on crime and vice. Fort Worth's law-and-order advocates never posted signs on the outskirts of town like those posted on the roads into Las Vegas, New Mexico. In bold, black letters, one broadside warned all visitors:

> Notice! To Thieves, Thugs, Fakirs And Bunko-steerers. . . . If found within the limits of this city after Ten O'Clock P.M. this Night You will be Invited to attend a Grand Neck-Tie Party, The Expense of which will be borne by 100 Substantial Citizens[125]

That sign was posted on March 24, 1882, and it is certain that the vigilantes of Las Vegas meant business. Fort Worth preferred to make its own peace with the wilder elements of western society: make them welcome but keep them on the south end of town. And while the city's economic base grew steadily, the uplifters could take some comfort from the march of progress, too. They could point to real improvements in the 1880s in the reorganization of the police force, the growing number of churches and the well-intentioned efforts of the Law and Order Association.

Still, all these reform efforts should not be overestimated, as Oliver Knight did when he wrote that a new city government was able to "clean up the Acre between 1887 and 1889."[126] Newspaper reports and court records show the same old activities going on with the same old zest on the south end of town at the end of the decade, leading the editor of the *Gazette* to offer a new solution to the problem. He called for moving the vice district out of "the heart of the city, where all who come and go may see and hear the crying shame."[127] There was plenty of precedent for such a move in Kansas cow towns like Ellsworth, Wichita and Abilene, where the vice districts were segregated across the river or in the case of Abilene, literally "across the railroad tracks."[128] The opportunity to segregate the Acre had been missed in the late 1870s before it took root within the corporate limits of the city. Now in its second decade it would take dynamite to remove it. The *Gazette's* suggestion did not generate much interest. Hell's Half Acre was part and parcel of Fort Worth proper, separated by nothing more than a vacant lot or an invisible line between uptown and downtown. With such vague boundaries, it is not surprising that both vice and violence spilled out of the Acre and into the uptown district. The most famous clash between downtown and uptown interests took place in 1887, and involved Fort Worth's two most famous gunmen, Luke Short and Timothy Isaiah Courtright.

SIX

"Ful, they've got me!"

LATE IN 1883 LUKE SHORT, FAMOUS GAMBLER AND friend of gunfighters, arrived in Fort Worth. Described as "small in stature, mild of manner, [but] deadly with a six-gun" by one of his modern biographers, Short was a celebrity before he came to Texas.[1] In the West, where a man was often measured by the number of notches on his gun, Luke had only one, and he earned that in a one-sided run-in with a drunk.[2] He preferred to be known as a gambler rather than a gunfighter; gamblers lived longer and usually got along better with the law.

Short was not always a professional gambler and was never much of a gunfighter. Most authorities agree that he was born "somewhere in Mississippi" in 1854. His parents brought him to Texas two years later.[3] Like many boys who grew up in Texas, his first real job was as a cowhand on one of the numerous cattle drives going north to Kansas. He soon tired of the drovers' hard, low-paying labor and turned to more profitable albeit more dangerous pursuits. These included peddling whiskey to the Indians and dealing faro. He was a dabbler, a frontier entrepreneur who was willing to try his hand at anything that caught his fancy or might make him a buck. He tried ranching but found it to be as hard and dirty as cow punching. Horse racing did not keep his interest for very long because it depended as much on the horse as on the man. He liked his games of chance to be more predictable. And all the while he polished his image and honed his skills as a gambler. His nickname "Little Luke" was more a reflection of his carefully cultivated image than of his actual physical stature. At five-feet-six and 150 pounds he was hardly the bantamweight of legend when compared to the other specimens of American manhood of his day. Very few men he crossed paths with actually towered over him. But his soft voice and mild manner contrasted sharply with the blustery, overbearing manner of many men he faced. Beneath the velvet-smooth exterior, however, Luke Short had as much grit and pride as any man.

Before landing in Fort Worth, Short had drifted across the West between frontier towns, making a few friends and a little money but not calling any place home for very long. Among those he called friends were Wyatt Earp, Bat Masterson and Doc Holliday. He met that famous trio quite by coincidence in 1881 when all four men were house dealers at the Oriental Saloon in Tombstone. The fact that four of the West's most notorious gamblers and gunmen were all in the same town, working at the same place at the same time did not go unnoticed. Tombstone residents quickly dubbed this little gambling cabal the "Dodge City Gang" because they had all come to Tombstone by way of Dodge.[4]

In August, 1882, Luke was back in Dodge City holding down a job as a dealer at one of the town's better saloons — the Long Branch. Its owners, William H. Harris and Chalkey M. Beeson, ran honest and peaceable games and — unless one counted the so-called "actresses" — kept out the prostitutes. Short enjoyed his work and thought of making Dodge his permanent home. He even bought a part interest in the Long Branch early in 1883.

But things soon began to unravel. Short joined the wrong side of two rival political factions in the city. The other faction included the owners of the Alamo Saloon, right next door to the Long Branch. The opposition called themselves "reformers" and captured control of the city government in the spring elections of 1883. When the reformers zeroed in on the Long Branch with the intention of forcing Short and his partners out of business, the famous "Dodge City War" resulted. At the center of the controversy were three female actresses employed by Short and arrested by authorities as prostitutes. Short claimed that a double standard had been applied to the Long Branch and threatened retaliation. Nobody was killed, but before it was all over, Short had to bring in some of his gun-toting friends, including Wyatt Earp and Bat Masterson, to protect him. Their presence was sufficient to overawe the local authorities and allow Short to reestablish himself at the Long Branch. Because of their success in ending the "war," the group of friends brought in by Short styled themselves the Dodge City Peace Commission. Once his friends left town, however, Short found his popularity among the townspeople considerably diminished. He may have won the battle, but he lost the war for the goodwill of the community, something that is essential to any gambler's success.

He sold out his interest in the Long Branch and moved to Fort Worth seeking greener pastures and friendlier authorities. The *Dodge City Times* carried a small notice on Wednesday, November 22, 1883, to the effect that Short had left town the previous Friday, headed for Texas: "The authorities in Dallas and Fort Worth are stirring up the gambling fraternity and probably the Celebrated 'peacemakers' have gone there to 'harmonize' and adjust affairs."

Short arrived in Fort Worth sometime in late November, 1883, but, judging by his reception in the newspapers, the city took no notice; his name is not mentioned in either the *Democrat* or the *Gazette* at the time. He had already visited Fort Worth quietly to check out the local opportunities for a man of his calling. He liked what he saw, and when he came back to Dodge it was with the specific purpose of closing out his affairs there so that he could move his gambling operation to Fort Worth.[5]

Whether or not any of Short's Dodge City buddies came to town with him is unclear, although Bat Masterson was reportedly with him when he left Dodge City.[6] Wyatt Earp was also in Dodge City in November 1883 and might have welcomed the chance to renew old acquaintances in Fort Worth. But he had better reasons to head due west to Colorado where he and his "wife" Josie had been living since June of 1883. Josie later recalled, however, that they visited Fort Worth "later that same year [1883]," putting them in the town about the time Luke Short was settling in.[7]

While Josie shopped or stayed in the elegant Mansion House Hotel on Fourth Street between Main and Rusk, Wyatt made the rounds of the clubrooms. At only $2 a day for one of its "well-ventilated, newly-furnished rooms," the Mansion was a bargain, and a well-heeled gambler like Wyatt could appreciate its elegant furnishings and fine foods. They advertised that they offered "special inducements to the commercial traveler," and "the quietude and comfort of a home," all conveniently located "in the business center of the city."[8] (A persuasive fellow like Earp might have convinced the management that an itinerant gambler was the same as a commercial traveler and deserved the discounted rates.) Josie would have enjoyed the homey atmosphere of the place. From the window she could watch the street lamps being lit at night and "street urchins" chasing along behind the ice wagon hoping to grab a piece of ice. The Earps ate their evening meals at the White Elephant Saloon's downstairs dining room before Wyatt disappeared for a long night of gambling, often not returning to the room until one or two in the morning. That was not the main reason Josie remembered Fort Worth long after they had moved on, however. She reminisced that her husband hit a winning streak, "and we were several thousand dollars richer when we left Fort Worth than when we came."[9]

After leaving Dodge City with Short in the fall of '83, Masterson's movements are more difficult to trace, although it is known he showed up in Fort Worth a few months later. Bat and Wyatt both were reported to be familiar figures in the city's better gambling rooms.[10] Their visits must be attributed at least in part to Luke Short's presence; his influence in Fort Worth sporting circles would assure the two outsiders a hospitable welcome in the town's best clubrooms.

It is doubtful that Masterson or Earp spent much time in Hell's Half Acre. Carousing in the Acre would have been below their dignity; they felt more comfortable uptown where the stakes were higher and the clientele more genteel. Like their friend Short, they were members of the western fraternity known as "sports," professional gamblers whose "chief delights [were] wine, women and billiards; their occupation is faro, and occasionally a game of 'draw.'"[11] Sports never exerted themselves too much except in the pursuit of easy money, which is why they were often referred to by their contemporaries as "genteel loafers." Most men took such disparagement in stride because they were proud of their calling. The members of the local fraternity included six men who gave their occupation in the 1880 Census as professional "gamblers."[12] They did more than just dress up and play games. All were married men with families and homes. Part of their image was supporting local charities, the way Joe Lowe supported the Fort Worth firemen, and they also added a touch of ersatz class to frontier communities with their sophisticated manners and fancy dress.

The traditional uniform of the sport consisted of a snow-white shirt, tailored suit, fine jewelry and polished boots. Even in the dirtiest western towns, no genuine sport would go around in muddy boots and certainly not Luke Short.[13] The jewelry of choice among Fort Worth sports included such items as diamond rings, diamond shirt studs and diamond-mounted watch charms.[14]

Card playing was the preferred vocation of the gambler, but he was an expert on the finer points of all sporting events, which explains in part why Wyatt Earp was asked to referee a title fight between Bob Fitzsimmons and Tom Sharkey in 1896, and why Bat Masterson became a newspaper sports writer after he hung up his guns. Other contests favored by the professional sport included wrestling, horse racing and cockfighting, although a dedicated sport would bet on practically any contest where the outcome was in doubt. Sports enjoyed the fast company of their peers, and high-stakes card games were practically a religious sacrament. They tended to make their money off the cowboys and tinhorns, however, who were always eager to test their skills. "That he [the sport] will win is as sure as death and assessments, unless he is completely out of luck, and even then his superior sagacity is usually sufficient to pull him through."[15] A smart sport also made the acquaintance of the town marshal wherever he went and stayed on his good side. Those who did not earned a quick trip to the city jail or a one-way ticket out of town.

Not to be confused with the true sports were the tinhorns who wore names like "the California Kid," "Kid Kinney," and one character, who probably had his name bestowed on him by unimpressed fellow gamblers, "Kid Big Mouth."[16] Like scavengers circling near a fresh kill, these characters hung around the fringes of the sporting fraternity and picked up the gleanings. Their type was seldom seen in the Cattle Exchange or White Elephant except when they worked as dealers under the watchful eye of one of the big sports. Instead, they made their reputations in the low dives and back rooms of the Acre.

The true sport lived for the Big Game — where a pot might reach $4000 — so he could fatten his bankroll, as well as his reputation.[17] One of those legendary contests took place in Fort Worth in August, 1885, and brought Luke Short, Bat Masterson, Wyatt Earp, Timothy Courtright and Charlie Coe together at the same table in the White Elephant.[18] All except Courtright considered themselves sports or at least professional gamblers. Indeed, Courtright may have been the "patsy" at the table, for he was hardly in the same

This photo might be labelled "Luke Short and a Few Close Friends." Instead it is "The Dodge City Peace Commission, 1883": the loyal group of former Dodge gamblers and saloon keepers who backed up Short's power play. Local authorities took a dim view of their presence: "We cannot preserve the peace or enforce the laws. Will you send in two companies of militia at once?" they wired the governor. Back row: W. H. Harris, Luke Short, Bat Masterson, W. F. Petillon; front row: Charles Bassett, Wyatt Earp, M. F. McClain, Neal Brown (courtesy Kansas State Historical Society, Topeka).

league with the others. Masterson's bankroll alone was said to be more than $9000 which, if true, makes this one of the richest games in the history of the West. Coe was the biggest winner, beating Short's full house with four kings on the last hand. Coe said in his memoirs sixteen years later that it was one of the proudest moments in his life.[19] Luke Short was one of the losers that day, but the game gave him a chance to show the locals why he was considered one of the sharpest gamblers in the West. From this date on, Bat and Wyatt played second fiddle to the diminutive Short as an object of Fort Worth curiosity and gossip.

Luke Short had at last reached the stage in life where he was considered a big fish, even if it was only in a small pond like Fort Worth. Heretofore, the locals had seen big-name gamblers pass through town, but none had settled down to stay. And when big money changed hands, it seldom did so all at once as it did at the White Elephant on that famous occasion described by Charles Coe. A gambler might drop a thousand dollars in two weeks as one local sport did in 1879, but that was rare enough to cause comment in the newspaper.[20]

Yet Short's rise to the top of the local gambling fraternity was not without challengers. His two principal rivals for the title of crown prince were Jake Johnson and Nat Kramer. Kramer began his career as a riverboat gambler on the Mississippi and Red rivers. After the Civil War he settled in Fort Worth but also spent a lot of time in Abilene (Kansas), Austin, Dallas and Dodge City. He listed himself at different times as a "speculator" and a "liquor dealer."[21] He preferred the polished surroundings and polite company of the Cattle Exchange and the White Elephant to any of the joints downtown. Kramer's principal distinction as a gambler was that he never took a drink, engaged in a quarrel or carried a weapon. Luke Short once expressed amazement that Kramer could survive so long in their profession without going armed or being called out to defend himself.[22] By avoiding the more violent aspects of the profession, Kramer was able to last fifty years as a gambler, dying peacefully in Fort Worth in 1905. He was unrepentant to the end. Shortly before he died somebody asked him how he would answer for his life as a gambler when he met St. Peter at the pearly gates. "Well," Kramer replied, "I am just going to tell him that I have helped some and I have skinned some. Those I skinned could afford it, and those I helped needed it maybe."[23]

Jake Johnson also enjoyed a long and distinguished career as a local sport, dating back to the mid-1870s when he first came to town. Later he went into partnership with Nat Kramer. Johnson listed himself as a "cattleman and speculator" but also ran saloons and gambling rooms for more than two decades. Between 1877 and the end of the century, Johnson spent almost as much time defending himself in court as he did running his various businesses. On the occasions when charges against him were not dismissed, he pleaded guilty, paid a small fine of $25 or $30 and was soon back on the street. Although Johnson was a sport, he was no dandy, being cut from the same rugged cloth as other cattlemen of his era. On numerous occasions Johnson was hauled into court on charges of "assault" and "aggravated assault," not to mention gambling and selling liquor illegally. His local reputation derived more from his sporting activities than his cattle deals.[24]

Luke Short's arrival cast a shadow over every gambler, however. Why Short picked Fort Worth over bigger and more exciting towns like Denver and Tombstone is difficult to fathom. His biographer states that he came to Fort Worth to "look over the scene and perhaps to invest the money he had made from selling his former establishment [the Long Branch Saloon] in Dodge City."[25] The gambler must have liked what he saw. Like Dodge City, Fort Worth was well located for a gambler to take advantage of the highly profitable Southwest cattle trade. The city was known, in fact, during the 1870s and '80s as a "gamblers' mecca" where some of the best card sharpers in the Southwest made their headquarters.[26] But until Short arrived no one had yet succeeded in establishing dominance over the local gambling scene.

Short soon found the ideal spot for his new headquarters: the White Elephant Saloon, an uptown establishment on Main Street between Second and Third. In the early 1880s the White Elephant was a nondescript establishment whose location placed it a cut above the typical saloons down in the Acre. It fell on hard times in 1884 when it was closed by attachment and the proprietor charged with embezzlement.[27] But after Luke Short set up his headquarters there, all that soon changed. Although Luke did not have the money or the social connections to transform it into a major gathering place for the city's elite, he was the big-name attraction that put the place on the map. In years to come the White Elephant became more than just a saloon; it became a legend in the Southwest, its name synonymous with the best drinking and gambling emporiums in any town. It even outgrew its original quarters.[28] Before the end of the century, the White Elephant Restaurant and Saloon was a fancy, two-story establishment with a large restaurant downstairs and several clubrooms for gambling upstairs. The White Elephant gained the reputation of being the finest in the city and claimed to be the best in Texas, perhaps even the nation![29] To back up this claim it boasted a menu that included "fresh fish, oysters and game," plus "the choicest wines, liquors and cigars" for its gentleman clientele.[30] More important, it was also the scene of some of the richest games in town and a gathering place for high rollers like Short.

Short apparently bought into the White Elephant in 1886 with William and John Ward, who had recently moved up from San Antonio. Bill ran the saloon downstairs while Short handled the gambling operation upstairs. John Ward was a silent partner. Sometime in 1886 or early '87, Jake Johnson — previously a co-owner of the Cattle Exchange clubroom with Nat Kramer — bought one-third of the business, but he, too, remained in the background.[31] Bat Masterson, who knew both Short and Johnson well, called them "business associates," which implies a certain equality but hardly clears the matter up.[32]

Whatever the legal arrangement, Short's practical involvement with the White Elephant consisted of operating the second-floor gambling room. It was here that he popularized the newly fashionable game of keno among Fort Worth residents.

Luke loved the role of the congenial host, welcoming his famous sporting friends to the White Elephant clubroom, making them comfortable and arranging high-stakes games with the local boys like Kramer and Johnson. After Short's arrival, the White Elephant was definitely a hang-out for some of the biggest names among the West's legendary gamblers. One of the men Short welcomed was Richard B. S. Clark, known simply as Dick Clark, whose reputation as a gambler exceeded Wyatt Earp's and Bat Masterson's. Clark was a dues-paying veteran of the circuit and the king of Tombstone's gamblers for several years. It spoke well of the White Elephant and of Short's reputation as proprietor of the clubroom that Clark made the arduous trip all the way from Tombstone to try his skills at Fort Worth's tables.[33] There is no record of how often he came to town or how much he won or lost.

Clark was always welcome at the White Elephant. His kind of gambler brought out the locals and raised the stakes of any game in which he played. Like gunfighters and lawmen, every gambler had a reputation and Clark's was that of a square dealer with an easygoing temperament, and a generous giver to good causes, including down-and-out tinhorns and struggling families.[34] He was both a true gentleman and a true sport. Those qualities, however, did not save him from an agonizing death caused by tuberculosis, alcoholism and drug addiction. He was fifty years old when he died in 1888. The sporting fraternity was poorer for his passing.

The involvement of men like Clark, Earp and Masterson with the White Elephant helped promote the regional reputation of the place, and the flashy opportunities matched the flashy clientele. This was no dive, though it was not exactly elegant either. Decor at the White Elephant might best be termed "frontier kitsch," with a solid mahogany filigree bar forty feet long, mirrored back bar (the pride and joy of the place), cut-glass chandeliers, and a wide, thickly carpeted stairway leading to the second floor where a table stood "stacked six inches high with gold coins."[35] The total effect of the interior was quite a contrast to the bare floors, stained wooden tables and hanging kerosene lamps in Hell's Half Acre. Short, however, did not cater to the clientele from the south end of town. His customers were more likely

"White Elephant" was a common name for western saloons, perhaps because "seeing the elephant" was a universally understood expression in the late-nineteenth century for having an exciting time or finding great adventure. Some were ritzy; some were hole-in-the-wall places like this one in Bingham Canyon, Utah, after the turn of the century. Top: The men here are playing faro (courtesy Denver Public Library, Western History Department). Below, an advertisement for the Fort Worth White Elephant "Saloon and Restaurant" that appeared in the 1881 city directory—a classy place even before Luke Short moved in. In a few years it would be known more for the caliber of its gambling than for the quality of its menu or wine list (courtesy Ed Bartholomew, Fort Davis, Texas).

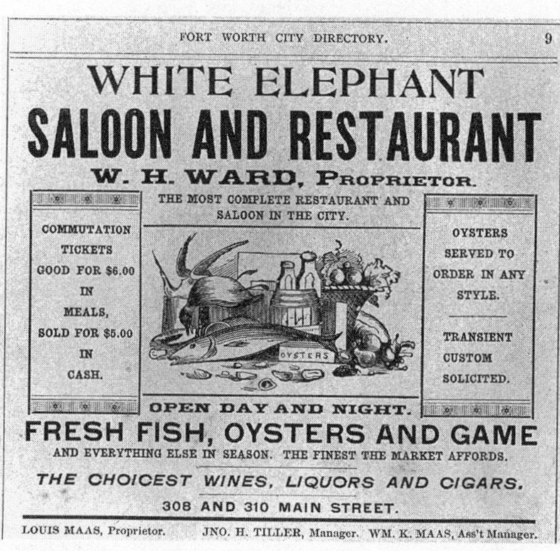

to own cattle than to herd them, to ride trains rather than drive them or hold them up. Luke had his silent friends in the upper strata of Fort Worth society, and they were always welcome at the White Elephant. Belying the myth of frontier egalitarianism, these were very narrowly defined friendships for Luke was never welcome in his guests' homes or private clubs.[36]

Short hired dealers from the seasoned local gamblers, paid them a decent wage, perhaps with incentives, and paid their legal fees when they were arrested, as all of them were sooner or later. Sometimes he paid the bond and told them to leave town because the police would be watching them closely in the future. In these cases, Short had to absorb the lost bail money, sometimes as much as $100, but it was all part of business expenses and new dealers were easy to find. The California Kid worked for Luke in 1887 until he was arrested one time too many. Shortly after getting out on bond in December, 1887, the Kid skipped town.[37]

Luke considered Fort Worth his home. He had married Marie Hettie Bimbo in 1881, and he brought her with him. They had four children eventually, which indicates that Luke was more of a family man than he has been given credit for. They bought a little house at Sixth and Pecan. Unlike Elizabeth Courtright, not much is known about Marie Short. She was never part of her husband's public life, and her origins are obscure.

By 1886 Luke Short — prosperous, satisfied and respected — had made a name for himself around Fort Worth as "the King of the Gamblers."[38] This might have gone on forever had not a joker suddenly appeared in the deck. Timothy Courtright returned that year to reclaim his former place as "Fort Worth's First Citizen."

Trouble between Courtright and Short did not flare into open conflict immediately. At the time of Courtright's troubles with New Mexico authorities Short had been a "substantial friend" of the ex-marshal, even giving him money when he went to stand trial in Albuquerque.[39] But such a gesture hardly constituted a mutual admiration society. Their relationship was based on other things. If not exactly friends, they were at least kindred spirits across the gambling table. They also counted a number of mutual friends, the principal one being Jake Johnson, part owner of the White Elephant and, at different times, a business partner of both men. More important than the friends and acquaintances they shared, the two men had a healthy

The Gambler and the Reform Mayor: Richard B. S. "Dick" Clark (left) was one of the very few famous western characters who was not also a gunman. This gambler confined himself to cards and was very successful in his profession for years. Clark and his more violence-prone friends kept reform-minded officials busy in the 1880s (courtesy C. L. Sonnichsen, Tucson, Arizona). H. S. Broiles was elected mayor four times on a reformist platform, 1886-1889. At one point, his administration proclaimed "the end" of Hell's Half Acre (courtesy Fort Worth Public Library).

respect for each other as professional colleagues. Neither needed to prove anything with a gun.

But the comfortable working relationship would not last long. The problem was Courtright. He could not adjust to his lowered standing in the community. The position of city marshal was adequately filled by W. M. Rea, a popular and respected officer of the law. There was no worthy employment for "an aging two-gun lawman with a shady past."[40] With a wife and three children to support now, his only marketable trade or skill was his fast draw. Courtright also found it difficult to accept the new order of things in the local world of gambling and vice, and the segregation of the refined and the riff-raff who patronized the city's uptown and downtown gaming rooms.

There were other differences. One was the color barrier between downtown and uptown. Blacks could patronize the downtown establishments, but they were *persona non grata* uptown. Uptown gambling was also more elevated in another way. Most downtown establishments were located on the ground level whereas uptown gaming rooms were located on the second floor over restaurants and bars like the White Elephant and its principal rival, Joe Wheat's Stag Saloon at 702 Main.[41]

Fort Worth had come a long way in a decade. In the early days, rich and poor, high-born and low, all rubbed elbows in the same saloons on Rusk and Main streets. Now nice people did their gambling upstairs. Dignified dining had replaced the free lunch counter, and fine wines had replaced rotgut whiskey as the preferred drink with dinner. Moreover, thanks to Luke Short, keno was now the preferred game of the gents uptown while faro and monte still reigned downtown.

Short had picked up keno somewhere during his wanderings and brought a fondness for the game with him when he moved down from Dodge City. He was responsible for the keno craze which practically took over many clubrooms in the next few years, producing huge profits for the owners and operators. After 1883 the local criminal court records contain numerous cases of men charged with "exhibiting a keno table" or "keno bank."[42] Since keno did not require any particular skill on the part of the dealer, Luke could quickly replace those who were hauled off to jail or had simply left town for greener pastures.

Luke Short ruled the roost on the north end of town and probably

The mysterious and alluring Hettie Bimbo Short. She was never a part of her husband's public life like Elizabeth and T. I. Courtright, but Hettie's head-turning beauty belies the rumor that Luke Short made a play for Betty Courtright. Hettie cared tenderly for Luke in his final days, but as soon as he was dead and buried she left town never to return. Possibly taken in Galveston by Rose & Schmelding Photographers, date unknown (courtesy Amon Carter Museum).

Left, a youthful Luke Short, looking more like a serious-minded college student than a man-killer, outlaw and gambler. The photo was probably taken between 1879 and 1880 in Dodge City after some of the rough edges of frontier life had been smoothed off, but before the effects of bad whiskey, stale air and late hours had taken their toll (courtesy Kansas State Historical Society, Topeka).

had some connections downtown, but his image was strictly "uptown." It was a carefully cultivated image: the genteel, impeccably dressed fancy-dan gambler. Wearing a "hogleg" strapped to one leg was hardly in keeping with his dapper appearance, so Short carried his pistol in a specially made trouser pocket, leather-lined for a fast draw. He preferred the Colt .45, commonly known as a "belly gun" because with its five-and-a-half-inch barrel it was "small enough to be stuffed in a belt at the wearer's waist" — or, as in Short's case, carried in a small pocket.[43] Luke always went armed, a fact that was well known among his fellow gamblers. Short's habit was also known by the police, and several times during his tenure in Fort Worth he was arrested for carrying a pistol in violation of local ordinances.[44] Invariably, these cases were not prosecuted by the county attorney and Luke continued to carry his gun, concealed but handy.

Life and business in the Acre, however, was not so classy, but there was money to be made for the right man with a gun. All it took was plenty of brass and some organizational skill, two qualities which a certain former marshal had in abundance.

Like many gunfighters on the downhill side of life, Timothy Courtright had turned to the bottle more and more for solace since his return to Fort Worth. He felt out of place among the gentry at the White Elephant, more at home among the rowdy element in the Acre. He also knew something about larceny and how to trade on a famous name. When he had first returned from his unhappy sojourn in New Mexico and found himself with no job and no prospects, he had opened up the T. I. C. Commercial Detective Agency. Although he had a partner, a man named Charley Bull, it was Courtright's popularity and reputation with a gun that maintained a steady income for the venture. The nature of the work also guaranteed him plenty of free time for gambling and drinking with friends down in the Acre. He had business cards printed up giving his address as the corner of Houston and Second streets and offering his services "to transact any legitimate detective business, such as collecting evidence in criminal cases, finding lost people, collecting bills, etc." They were signed "T. J. [sic] Courtright, President and General Manager." Courtright was rather proud of them and passed them out to friends and clients alike.[45] But his business was shut down abruptly when he was forced to leave town to avoid extradition back to New Mexico.

By mid-1886 he was back trying to reestablish himself, but in spite of his entrepreneurial flair the firm did not prosper. He had a large sign painted on the outside wall of his building facing Weatherford Street and courthouse square. Emblazoned on the brick wall between two second-floor windows, the sign read "T.I.C. Commercial Detective Agency," but in place of the initial "I" was a large, staring eye.[46] It was creative advertising and a real attention-grabber designed to take advantage of a well-known trademark — that of the Pinkerton Detective Agency. They had used the symbol for years to advertise their nationally recognized investigative services.[47]

But borrowing the Pinkerton symbol did not seem to help Courtright's struggling agency. He could not make money doing legitimate business although the timing should have been perfect for him. Law enforcement had fallen on hard times in recent years. The man who was city marshal in 1883, Sam Farmer, spent more time quarreling with local businessman James Maddox than he did catching criminals. Farmer and Maddox came very close to having a shootout on the city streets in 1885.[48] Two years later, the city council even shaved policemen's salaries from $60 to $50 per month and reduced the size of the force as well. The salary cuts announced in April followed two months in which the officers had not been paid at all because their traditional income from fines had been diverted to pay other city expenses.[49] Marshal William Rea's twelve-man police force was angry and demoralized.

Yet the citizenry seemed to have little use for the services of a cowboy-booted gumshoe. Many probably agreed with Bat Masterson's assessment of the ex-marshal as "a sullen, ignorant bully, with no sense of right or wrong."[50] With this sort of reputation it was no wonder that Fort Worth citizens did not beat a path to the door of Timothy Courtright, detective. And what business there was — bill collecting, gathering evidence for divorces and chasing down bail jumpers — hardly paid the liquor bills of a man like Courtright.

So he expanded his operations. Very soon, the T. [I.] C. Commercial Detective Agency was operating as a thinly disguised front for a highly profitable protection racket, possibly the first in the history of the West. The agency's new clients — victims might be a better description — included for the most part proprietors of gambling houses and saloon keepers in the Acre. For a fee, Courtright protected them against over-exuberant cowboys, unfair competition from rivals and harassment from city officials who felt it their job to enforce the laws. Just how he accomplished all this is unclear, but even viewed in the best light, it was an entirely extralegal arrangement. It is not without good reason that one historian has called Courtright "Fort Worth's first gangster."[51]

In addition to his protection racket, Courtright found other ways to put his gun to work. He signed on with the Gould Railroad system as a special detective during the Great Southwest strike of 1886.[52] The duties of a "special detective" were really those of a strikebreaker, and this is how Courtright was perceived by many of the hometown folks. The fact that he was also wearing a deputy U.S. marshal's badge while working for the Gould lines did nothing to increase his popularity.

Helping Courtright protect Missouri Pacific property in Fort Worth were members of the regular police and sheriff's departments, including officers John J. Fulford, Bony Tucker and Joe Witcher. Like Courtright, they were violent men who worked both sides of the law. At various times in their law-enforcement careers, Fulford and Tucker were charged with assault, aggravated assault, gambling and other misdemeanors.[53] Another of Courtright's contemporaries in local law enforcement who enjoyed a checkered career was H. P. Shiel. Shiel, who served one term as marshal before Courtright and later ran for another term unsuccessfully, had a long criminal record that included selling liquor illegally, keeping a disorderly house, assault and using abusive language.[54]

Arrayed against Courtright and his fellow officers in the strike were hundreds of angry railroad workers thrown out of work by the strike and a populace that sympathized with their demands for better treatment from absentee employers. On the afternoon of March 3, 1886, Courtright, Fulford and two other guards were riding a "KATY" (an acronym for Missouri, Kansas & Texas Railway, part of the Missouri Pacific system) train when it was ambushed two miles south of Fort Worth. A dozen or more strikers blocked the track and opened fire with Winchesters when the train slowed to a halt. Fulford and the other two guards were hit in the first fusillade. Only Courtright was able to return the fire. Using his six-guns with telling effect, he drove off the attackers and probably saved the lives of two guards, the third dying of his wounds later.[55] The train's fireman reported that the attackers "seemed particularly anxious to wing

Courtright."[56] Thanks to his skill with the pistols and a good measure of luck, Courtright was unscratched, and he wounded one of the strikers who was subsequently captured.

This episode did not make Courtright a hero to the large number of local workers and their friends and families. A public commendation was given to Fulford, and the slain guard was eulogized, but Courtright had to settle for the gratitude of the Missouri and Pacific.

While the strike raged, Fort Worth was an armed camp with Texas Rangers and state militia patrolling the streets. When it was finally broken, Courtright was richer for his part in it, but his popularity had taken a beating. The fact that he had worked for money as a strikebreaker and not in the line of duty as a member of the regular police force did not sit well with his fellow citizens.

His other line of work — shaking down gamblers and saloon keepers — proved ridiculously easy and far more profitable. On a more modest scale, he used the same methods as the protection mobs during Prohibition forty years later. Courtright ran what amounted to a one-man racket, and he was able to make it work because of his reputation with a gun. In the Acre men still had more fear for the law of the six-gun than the laws of society. The proprietors themselves operated on the shady side of the law. The respectable landowners behind the scene also preferred to pay up rather than attract unfashionable notoriety. So protection deals were made on a monthly or even weekly basis with the fees based on whatever the traffic would bear.

It was all perfectly normal. Many of the establishments were also paying money under the table to "Fort Worth's finest" — or the men of the regular police force — "and possibly a politician or two," according to one historian. But such expenses were easily recouped in the course of a profitable run of greenhorns and suckers. "It was a shaky business," the same historian says, "but the downtown boys were used to operating that way."[57]

According to two contemporary sources, trouble arose when Courtright tried to move uptown to put the squeeze on the high-class gambling rooms like Luke Short's comfortable set-up over the White Elephant.[58] Until that time, the two men had apparently been on cordial terms, as Short emphasized in a public statement he made later. "In the first place," he told a newspaper reporter, "I want to say that it was all of a sudden, all unexpected by me. There had been no previous disagreement between us."[59] Short had no reason to lie about this point and his statement is supported by other accounts affirming that the two had had no run-ins and may even have joined forces since Courtright came back from New Mexico.[60] In any event, their relationship definitely took a turn for the worse when Courtright tried to get the dapper gambler to install him as a "special officer" in the White Elephant. Short laughed at such presumption, telling Courtright he would rather pay him a good salary "to stay away from my house entirely" than to have him hanging around intimidating customers. "Your presence in my house as an officer would ruin my business," Short told him bluntly.[61]

Courtright was not used to being talked to in this way. He had approached Short expecting to find the smaller man a pushover, and the rebuff caught him by surprise. He retreated to think about his next move. He had seriously underestimated how much grit the little man possessed. He should have known better. A survivor of the frontier himself, Short was not about to cave in to threats — even from an ex-marshal and gunslinger. Courtright thought about it and tried a different ploy. He threatened to have Short indicted and the White Elephant closed down for violating the city's anti-gambling ordinance. Short still refused to back down. He would pay his own fines when arrested legally and post bail for his dealers when they were hauled into court. He had no quarrel with legitimate law enforcement. Although Short was no stranger to the protection racket, being squeezed by men who claimed to represent the law was something he had never stood for. He might have even gotten a wry laugh out of the similarity between Courtright's tactics and those of his opponents in the Dodge City War, remembering how that little disagreement had come out in his favor. Courtright had finally met someone he could not buffalo, but he refused to let the matter die.

Like Courtright's scrape with saloon keeper N. H. Wilson ten years earlier, his feud with Short could only end one way — in bloodshed. Each adversary's well-known stubborn streak precluded any other solution. Courtright was determined to skim off a share of the highly profitable White Elephant keno business. Short was determined to protect what was his even though he could absorb the loss. He had demonstrated in the past that he would not be intimidated, no matter how numerous or well-armed the opposition. Once again, he called in reinforcements from among his brothers in the gambling fraternity. He probably sent for Bat Masterson about this time, because that gentleman arrived in town in the winter of 1887.

Of all the men Luke might have called on, Bat was the most likely to drop everything and come on the run. He had taken almost a fraternal interest in Luke ever since their days together dealing faro at the Oriental in Tombstone. Luke and Bat were arguably as close as Wyatt Earp and Doc Holliday. It may even have been Masterson, the debonair *bon vivant*, who helped turn Luke from a "white Indian when I first found him" into a gentleman gambler during their Dodge and Tombstone days.[62] When the chips were down, Bat was the first one Luke sent for to back his play.

Meanwhile, news of bad blood between Short and Courtright had spread up and down the street on both ends of town. The downtown boys watched with more than a passing interest to see how Short's challenge to the system would be answered. Short's supporters whispered that their man had told Courtright to "take the short walk necessary to jump into the Trinity River."[63] Some newspapers later claimed that Courtright had made threats "to make Short bite the dust."[64]

There are two sides to every story and the other side of this one could not be more bizarre. In later years, Betty Courtright maintained that Short had been in love with her so he provoked the deadly fight with her husband. Much later, Courtright's biographer, F. Stanley, claimed that Courtright was the real owner of the White Elephant, and that Short worked for him running the gambling concession on the second floor. According to this pro-Courtright version, when city fathers pressured Courtright to shut down the gambling room, Short balked and threatened to bring in his pals from Dodge City.[65] The pro-Short version of the feud seems much more plausible for several reasons. First, there are no records showing Courtright to have ever had a financial interest in the White Elephant, while there are numerous references to Courtright's protection racket and Short's interest in the business. Furthermore, contemporary newspaper accounts after the showdown depict Courtright as the "outsider" in the affair.[66]

Courtright paid several visits to the White Elephant during the first few weeks of 1887 but received neither money nor satisfaction from Short. The situation had now escalated to the level of a genuine feud. As in most western feuds, pride was more at issue than practical matters. Courtright clearly had more to lose as it stacked up. Not only was his profitable protection racket being threatened, but his reputation was on the line. He brooded over the situation, usually with a bottle in front of him. During one drunken conversation in a downtown bar on February 7, Courtright made two statements that summed up the differences between the old days and the new in Fort Worth. First, he quoted the hoary cliché that "God had made one man superior to the other in physical strength, but when [Samuel] Colt made his pistol it made all men equal." But times were changing. Courtright's second statement that same day indicated that he was not entirely unaware of the change. He said, more to himself than anyone standing nearby, that he had "lived over his time."[67]

This was more than mere fatalism, more even than a reflection on his own career; it was social commentary, however unintentional. The frontier had moved past Fort Worth and it would soon pass into the history books. For a large segment of the population in the West, this meant that behavior which had been accepted as part of the natural order earlier was now being seen as immoral or criminal. The problem for Timothy Courtright and men like him was they were too old to change and too few to stand in the way of progress.

Luke Short, a more flexible man perhaps, made his own peace with the changing times; he dressed like a city gentleman and behaved more like a businessman than a brawler. Yet violence was part of his life. Short had never backed down from a fight and had even provoked a few over the years, but he did not relish confrontations the way some of his contemporaries did. He envied Nat Kramer's peaceable ways and once admitted to being "tired of this business of packing a gun."[68] Perhaps Short was thinking of quitting Fort Worth. He might have decided it was easier to concede gracefully and accept the fact that a town was not big enough for him and a rival; he would be the one to go. Moving on periodically was a natural part of the gambler's lifestyle for many reasons, and smart gamblers knew when to cash in their chips and get out. There would be other days. When he sold his one-third interest in the White Elephant on February 7 to his partner Jake Johnson, he must have gotten a nice bankroll that would help him get set up elsewhere.[69] Under similar circumstances, he had already said goodbye to Tombstone and Dodge City. Fort Worth was not the end of the line. There were plenty of other western boom towns where a sharp gambler could set up shop and live comfortably, including San Antonio, Tascosa and Las Vegas (New Mexico). Maybe he could even return to Fort Worth once Courtright's violent ways and constant drinking took him out of the picture. There is no way of knowing what Short was thinking as he considered his options. The only clue provided by the historical record is the business transaction with Jake Johnson just one day before the showdown.

It may be that Short believed the showdown with Courtright to be inevitable, perhaps explaining why he sold out to Johnson. In the event that the worst happened, and that seemed highly likely if one listened to the talk on the streets, his affairs would be in order. Ironically, selling his interest in the White Elephant could have been the very action that finally provoked Courtright to seek a confrontation. All Courtright had to do was read the front page of the morning newspaper the day he came looking for the dapper gambler. Beforehand, Courtright could have been deterred from seeking a confrontation because of the business relationship between Short and Johnson. (Johnson remained a close friend of Courtright's.) With that obstacle out of the way and with Courtright possibly feeling an urgency to resolve the matter before his reputation suffered further damage or before Short could escape town, he made his decision.

At this stage, a peaceful ending to the feud did not look promising. In fact, the feud showed the inevitability of a Greek tragedy with all of Fort Worth in the role of the audience — the gamblers on the front row. On a practical level, the gamblers in Hell's Half Acre who were following the action did not prefer either Courtright or Short. One was a business competitor while the other was a shakedown artist. As a sporting proposition, Courtright had the flashier reputation with a pistol, but no one had ever seen them both in action. This showdown promised to be a once-in-a-lifetime event.

Like most everything else about the Courtright-Short relationship, there are several versions of what happened next. Three first-person accounts by men involved in the evening's events have survived. One of those accounts, Luke Short's, must be used with great care for obvious reasons. That leaves two reasonably objective descriptions. One comes from Jake Johnson, notorious gambler and convicted felon, and Short's ex-business partner. Johnson claimed to have witnessed the whole thing and was quoted extensively in the newspapers afterwards.[70] Another version of the shootout, quite similar except in some of the details, comes from Bat Masterson, but it did not appear in print until two decades later when faulty memory and active imagination had had a chance to do their work.

Masterson and Johnson were close friends of Short, so it is not surprising that both cast Courtright in the villain's role. Johnson, however, also claimed to be a friend of Courtright, so his account is probably more reliable.[71] It is also important to remember that Johnson's description was given under oath while the events were still fresh in his mind.

The generally accepted sequence of events is this: On the evening of February 8, Luke Short was at his usual station in the clubroom of the White Elephant.[72] Business was slower than usual so he went downstairs to have his shoes "blacked." Later, while Short stood at the mahogany bar having a drink, an unnamed friend came up and warned him that Courtright was looking for him. Short took no action but returned upstairs to his regular duties in the clubroom. Also upstairs that evening were Jake Johnson and Bat Masterson, although later both claimed to be unaware of any trouble between Courtright and Short, and neither was there to protect their gambler friend.

Sometime shortly before 8 o'clock, Courtright arrived at the White Elephant accompanied by his partner Charley Bull. Leaving Bull outside, Courtright stalked into the vestibule and proceeded to cause enough commotion to attract the attention of those sitting in the bar. He demanded to see Short. The message was quickly relayed upstairs. Jake Johnson, who had been playing billiards, was the first to come down and meet him. They stepped outside and talked intently for a few moments while Bull stood quietly to one side. Bull's presence might have been a warning that trouble was brewing, but Courtright still seemed rational and under control, so Johnson agreed to go back in and fetch Short. Courtright waited impatiently outside — a wait that did nothing to improve his disposition. Reaching the end of his patience, he decided to go back inside and find Short himself. He knew just where the gambler would be this time of the evening. A few minutes later, patrons in the bar saw all three men — Courtright, Short and Johnson — come downstairs together. Observers noted that "Johnson's face was white as chalk, and both Courtright and Short appeared very much agitated."[73] Masterson was not with them.

Short by all appearances accompanied the others willingly, pos-

Above, the famous Luke Short back bar from the original White Elephant Saloon as it appeared in 1949 when it was owned by O. L. Shipman of El Paso (posed in front of the bar). After Short's death in 1893 the bar began a long odyssey that saw it grace saloons in San Antonio and Del Rio, an ice cream parlor in Marfa, and finally Shipman's candy shop in El Paso. The bar's features originally included solid mahogany construction, hand-carved decorations, gas lighting and onyx columns (courtesy Art Leibson, El Paso). At right, twenty-five-year-old William B. ("Bat") Masterson as he appeared in his Dodge City days (1878), several years before he came to Fort Worth. Masterson was well acquainted with the White Elephant Saloon from his visits to Fort Worth. This photo was first reproduced in *Human Life* magazine in 1907 (courtesy Library of Congress).

sibly thinking that Courtright had come to negotiate a peaceful settlement with Johnson acting as the honest broker. Instead, he soon realized that the ex-marshal was in a belligerent mood, a state he slipped into easily when he had been drinking. At Courtright's insistence, the three men moved their conversation outside.

At this point in the affair, Courtright had clearly issued a challenge or, in frontier parlance, "called Short out." Having Charley Bull present gave him added confidence, especially since he did not know what Bat Masterson or Jake Johnson might do. Short showed considerable courage going out onto a darkened street where Courtright's partner could be waiting to bushwhack him. Only a fool or a greenhorn would now believe that Courtright had come to parley, and Luke Short was neither. On the other hand, he could only have refused at the risk of being labelled a coward and, thereafter, being washed up in Fort Worth. When Short accepted the demand to move the meeting to the street, the affair had reached the point of no return. Any further talking would simply be prologue.

By this time on a February evening it was quite dark outside, and the flickering gas street lights offered little illumination of the scene. To get out of the traffic coming and going through the White Elephant's entrance, they moved up the block a few feet until they stood on the sidewalk in front of Ella Blackwell's shooting gallery. Oddly, Bull drops out of the picture at this point as either a witness or a participant in the events that followed, although there is no doubt that he hung around to the bitter end. Jake Johnson thus becomes the only witness to the ensuing verbal exchange between Short and Courtright. It would have added a truly bizarre twist to the unfolding drama if Betty Courtright had been working at the shooting gallery that night and witnessed what followed. But she was not on the scene.

Short and Courtright stood facing each other just three or four feet apart. Courtright was still visibly agitated, his thinking muddled by alcohol. Short, perhaps trying to calm him, casually hooked his thumbs in the armholes of his vest. He also assured Courtright that he carried no gun and even made a move to show him by raising his vest. In such a tense atmosphere, every movement took on exaggerated significance.

The conversation ended abruptly. Short's movement toward his vest, the darkened street and a belly full of liquor were all it took to touch off Courtright. He had come looking for a fight, so anything that Short or Johnson did probably would have been taken as a threat. In the back of Courtright's mind was also the knowledge that Short habitually carried his gun in a concealed inner pocket. Courtright would not have lived as long as he did if he had not kept informed of every habit and idiosyncrasy of dangerous opponents. His exclamation, "Don't you pull a gun on me!" was more of a signal than a genuine warning.

Courtright, as was his custom, wore two .45s holstered on his hips. He had never liked the current fashion among so-called gentleman of wearing their guns hidden. Without any further exchange of words, he reached for one of his six-shooters, but his legendary fast draw failed him. Courtright's gun cleared its holster before Short got his own piece out, but from that point on it was all Short. One well-regarded historian has claimed that in the process of drawing his pistol, Courtright caught the hammer of the weapon in his watch chain, "giving Short ample time to clear his own weapon and get off the first shot."[74] Contemporary accounts do not support this theory, but there is no doubt that Short got off the first shot, striking Courtright in the body. He squeezed off four more in quick succession, each staggering the bigger man and knocking him backwards through the shooting gallery doorway. He fell heavily to the floor, half in and half out the door. The infamous gunfighter had never gotten off a shot.

Some said later that Courtright tried to execute the tricky "border shift" before he went down, tossing his gun from right hand to left in one quick motion. He had good reason; one of the first bullets to hit him nearly took the thumb off his right hand and jammed the cylinder on his six-gun. Everything happened so fast and it was so dark there is no way of telling whether Courtright tried the border shift or not. No testimony mentioned such a maneuver, but it is known that Courtright counted the border shift among his repertoire of tricks.[75]

All the action took place "within a few minutes" of the time the men exited the White Elephant. Hearing the shots, the bar customers rushed out to see what happened. The first thing they saw was "Courtright lying on his back gasping for breath [and] Luke Short standing by with his pistol smoking."[76] Within minutes, the law arrived. When the shooting started, Policeman Bony Tucker and two companions were standing in the doorway of the Cabinet Saloon on the next block. Tucker sprinted to the scene, arriving just in time to find Short standing over his adversary. The officer, who knew Luke well, asked him if he had done it. "Short bowed his head and handed his pistol over to him."[77] The sheriff, the marshal and two other officers arrived soon after. No one seemed to notice Jake Johnson. Why so many of the town's law enforcement officers happened to be in the neighborhood is another inexplicable part of the story. At the time, no one seemed to find it odd that so many lawmen reached the scene in a matter of moments.

What did strike people as odd were reports by several onlookers in the shooting gallery that Courtright had never even gotten his pistol out of its holster before Short put the first bullet in him. Some of the same witnesses also claimed that after Courtright fell through the door and hit the floor, obviously dying, Short stood directly over him and pumped four more slugs into him. This sort of behavior did not follow the acceptable script for such gunfights and caused considerable excitement in the crowd as the reports circulated.[78]

Unknown to most Fort Worth citizens, the entire confrontation had been practically custom-made for Short's favorite gunfighting tactics. He created odds in his favor, as was the case when he shot Charlie Storms in Tombstone several years before. On that occasion he had used exactly the same tactics to dispose of another drunken assailant on another darkened street in front of a popular saloon, crowding in close and emptying his pistol into the man before his opponent could get his gun into action.[79] Standing at opposite ends of a street in broad daylight, seeing who had the faster draw and then blazing away until one or the other went down are romanticized creations, not tactics that suited Mr. Short. Anyone who had witnessed that fight in Tombstone on February 25, 1881, would have felt a sense of déjà vu in Fort Worth on the night of February 8, 1887.

The rumblings in the crowd and the general uncertainty over just what had happened convinced Sheriff B. H. Shipp to take charge, arrest Short on the spot with the assistance of Marshal Rea plus Officers Rowan and Bony Tucker, and escort him off to county jail, not the city lockup. Short went along calmly, protesting self-defense. The four-man escort helped persuade the crowd to keep their distance.

Charley Bull was also arrested and hustled off to jail, confirming the suspicions of many people that he and Courtright had come gunning for Short that night. One of the numerous rumors that swept through town right after the shooting also had Bull getting off one shot "in defense of his friend," but this rumor was quickly discredited and Bull was released that same night with no charges filed against him.[80]

Courtright's end was anticlimactic. Lying in the dust and blood on the shooting gallery floor, he was able to gasp just a few words to the nearest friendly face he saw, that of Officer John J. Fulford. As Fulford bent over to pick up Courtright's gun and check for signs of life, the dying man gasped out: "Ful, they've got me." Although they have the ring of a dime-novel prose, Fulford swore these were Courtright's dying words.[81] Whether he uttered any dying words or not, Courtright was a goner. Witnesses said he was dead within five minutes of hitting the floor. It was a true Wild West ending to a true Wild West legend.

Justice still had to be served, however. Short was left in jail for the night despite his protestations of self-defense. The policemen decided to let the magistrates straighten things out in the morning. The crowd, meanwhile, was already turning bellicose. Despite the steady decline in Courtright's reputation in recent years, he was still a popular local figure. And in death his reputation outshone his mean-spirited and larcenous side.

There was enough doubt about Short's safety in the local hoosegow that his old friend Bat Masterson spent the night in the cell with him armed with a pair of pistols. Masterson even convinced the sheriff that the prisoner should also have a pair of pistols in case trouble showed up.[82] The message was clear: any lynch mob wanting Luke Short would have to go through Bat Masterson first.

The night passed without incident, the only visitor besides Masterson being a reporter for the *Fort Worth Gazette*, who got the first interview with the prisoner. The next morning a hastily called jury of inquest met at 10:00 to take testimony. After hearing from just eight witnesses, the judge released Short on a $2000 bond until the grand jury could meet to decide whether to indict. Jake Johnson, W. T. Maddox, Robert McCart and N. A. Steadman signed the bail bond. All were respectable citizens: Johnson the cattleman; McCart and Alex Steadman, two-thirds of the law firm of Wynne, McCart and Steadman (who became judge of the Forty-Eighth District Court a few years later); and Maddox the businessman.

It was a full day for Fort Worth citizens. Timothy Courtright was buried in what turned out to be a major public event — the grandest funeral in Fort Worth history, in fact — that began with the ringing of fire bells at 1:00 P.M. and climaxed in a burial ceremony sometime after 4:00 in the afternoon. The procession to Pioneer Rest Cemetery began at Courtright's residence and wound its way up Main Street and past the courthouse. It included a string of carriages six blocks long following behind the hearse. The route did not go through the Acre, but denizens of that district trooped up to the north end of town where they crowded the streets and rubbed elbows with respectable folks and curious out-of-towners, who must have wondered what sort of honored citizen could cause this sort of mass turnout even in death.[83]

Despite Courtright's shady business dealings and influential connections, he had died a pauper. His friends took up a collection the day of the funeral to pay for it. In later years, a legend grew up that the city had paid for it out of a sense of guilt or obligation, or some such sentiment. But it was the size, not the expense, of Courtright's funeral that struck observers. The turnout for the "has-been" gunfighter reflected more than his past celebrity status in Fort Worth; it also reflected the importance of the shootout itself. The Courtright-Short fight was the most celebrated event in Fort Worth history. In a sense, it was bigger than the city itself. One modern historian has called it "the foremost controversy of the entire West, *indeed of the whole country in 1887* [emphasis added]"[84] Among the estimated 20,000 men killed in illegal gunfights on the frontier between 1830 and 1900, there were no more than a handful that even approached it in terms of significance or notoriety.[85]

Luke Short was never tried for the killing of Timothy Courtright. On reflection it was obvious to local citizens that the shooting was a clear case of self-defense. After hearing the testimony of the few witnesses, the grand jury refused to indict on the evidence, holding that it was a case of justifiable homicide. Since the man on the street had already reached the same conclusion, both the law and popular sentiment were thus satisfied. The fact that Short and Courtright had been carrying guns in violation of city ordinance was completely outweighed by the higher law of self-defense.

Case closed, or almost. There remained the widow and the legend. Elizabeth Courtright did not stay in Fort Worth long after her husband was killed. Barely two weeks after his burial, she packed up her children — Mary, John and the infant Lulu Mae — and moved to California "to join her mother."[86] The widow Courtright could not have taken many good memories with her when she boarded the westbound train on February 16, 1886. She had watched her husband lose in succession: an election, a job, his self-respect, his friends and ultimately his life. She had also buried a child during her years in Fort Worth.[87] It is no wonder she never returned to the city where she had lost so much.

The story of "Longhair Jim" Courtright's death became part of western lore. Among the legends that sprang up in later years was one that claimed it was actually Bat Masterson who killed Courtright that night.[88] Another legend without substance that gained wider acceptance claimed that Courtright's gun had been tampered with before the shootout. The seeds of this rumor were planted by a story in the *Gazette* the morning after the shooting. According to the *Gazette*, "officers who examined Courtright's gun after the duel stated that the chamber of his .45 failed to act correctly."[89] From two lines in the newspaper grew a thoroughly unfounded rumor. Its principal appeal was that it explained why one of the fastest draws in the West had not been able to get off a single shot although his gun was in his hand, a cartridge was in the chamber and the pistol was half-cocked when he died. Nobody could believe that Short was *that* much faster than Courtright, even if Courtright had been drinking heavily before the showdown, which no one claimed to know for sure either. This story added a conspiratorial element to the basic legend. Even without conspiracy theories, the showdown between Timothy Courtright and Luke Short had all the elements a legendary gunfight should have, except that it occurred at eight o'clock at night instead of high noon.

For the second time in his life, Luke Short's name was splashed across national headlines (the first time being the Dodge City War), but the notoriety did nothing to improve his standing in Fort Worth. Both Courtright and Short were part of an era that Fort Worth was trying to live down. Providence had removed Courtright so the city could mourn him, but Short was still around every day, a constant, living reminder of the rough-and-tumble frontier days.

In his defense, it must be said that Short, the gentleman gambler, lived the life of a respectable citizen ordinarily. When Fort Worth built the fabulous Spring Palace in 1890 to show off the state's agricultural products, Short subscribed $250 to the cause. He also paid $5 for a gaming concession at the Palace, however.[90] Even civic-minded gamblers have to earn a living.

For another year or more, Luke continued his association with the White Elephant Saloon, not as an owner, but simply as "proprietor" of the upstairs clubrooms. Then he severed the connection, moving over to the Palais Royal Saloon at 406 Main Street, which was owned by Jake Johnson and Victor S. Foster.[91] He still catered to the better class of gamblers and still ran an honest if profitable game. His old gambling friends from all over the West continued to visit him to take advantage of the city's well-known hospitality. Bat Masterson worked as a dealer in Fort Worth for a time, perhaps even at the Palais Royal, but when he was arrested and charged with "exhibiting a faro bank," he packed up and moved on. A warrant for his arrest remained on the court records for many years.[92]

In 1890 uptown and downtown gambling interests clashed again. This time the combatants were Short and Charlie Wright, the man who replaced Courtright as king of the Acre's bad actors. Wright, a transplanted Chicago dealer, was less a celebrity than Courtright, but still a serious rival to Short. His gambler's pedigree was as long as Short's but not so exciting. Before coming to Fort Worth, Wright ran successful "brace [crooked or illegal] games" in Omaha, Dodge City and Las Vegas. He found a congenial atmosphere in the Acre for his kind of gambling and opened a "skinning house for suckers" over the Bank Saloon at 1608 Main. At least until 1890, Wright and Short were on speaking terms. On several occasions they co-signed fellow gamblers' bail bonds, going together to put up the $100 or $200 required by the city's judges. Short and Wright had also had to eat some of those bonds when the accused gamblers preferred to skip town rather than take their chances with the law.[93] But by 1890 professional and personal differences had erased any previous basis for cooperation.

The war between the uptown and downtown gamblers was still carried on mostly behind the scenes; occasionally it came right out in the open. In the summer of 1890, Short dropped in on Wright's place and broke it up, running out all the patrons in the process. Wright did not take kindly to this affront but declined his option of paying a return visit, possibly out of respect for Short's reputation with a gun. Nothing happened for several months. Then on December 23, 1890, Short paid another visit to Wright's place. This time his rival was waiting for him with a shotgun. He used it, catching Short in the back and the side with a full load of buckshot. It staggered Short but did not kill him. Luke still had enough fight left to put a bullet through

Wright's gun wrist. Then he limped off to find a doctor.[94] Neither man died of his wounds, but Short's left hand was permanently crippled, and thereafter he walked with a distinct limp.

While recuperating, Short offered a self-serving explanation to a newspaper reporter that explained why he wanted to put Wright out of business:

> We have not been friends for two years, and matters were aggravated when he ran a 'brace' game over the Bank Saloon. I have my home in Fort Worth, and everybody who knows me will say that I have never tolerated anything but square gambling houses. I intend to stay here, but I knew full well that if Wright continued as he was doing it would only be a matter of time until public opinion would be closed up with the rest. I have assisted to break up two or three places which were being conducted in a crooked manner, and Sheriff Richardson will tell you the same thing.[95]

Adding insult to injury, Wright filed charges against Short for assault with intent to murder. Short posted $1000 bail; then the legal maneuvering began. Motion after motion was filed by Short's lawyers for continuance or dismissal. More than a year after the incident, the case was tried in county district court. Short was found guilty of aggravated assault and fined a paltry $150, indicating jurors' true feelings about the charges. The little gambler appealed nonetheless. The case was finally dismissed a year and a half later with good reason: Short was dead and Charlie Wright had long since been run out of town for his shady gambling activities.[96]

Fort Worthers had finally come to realize what had been true all along: Short, Wright, Courtright and others of their ilk were all part of the riffraff fringe "who preyed on one another with considerable impunity in the early days of the West."[97] Respectable folks coped with the situation by staying away from the gamblers' haunts, and when one of the bad guys was killed by another member of the fraternity, they considered the loss good riddance.

Short's connections with the uptown boys and his carefully cultivated reputation for charitable giving probably had protected him from being run out of town at the same time as Charlie Wright. Or the town fathers might have been mindful of the $15,000 lawsuit filed by Short against Dodge City, Kansas, for business losses after that town gave him the gate in 1883. The suit had been settled quietly out of court, but only after lawmakers agreed to pay off Short.[98]

Neither his reputation nor his charitable giving could save Short from the cumulative effects of gunshot wounds and years of hard living. He died on September 8, 1893, a thirty-nine-year-old, broken-down gambler and gunfighter. Short spent the last three years of his life in Fort Worth, although he died in a health resort in Geuda Springs, Kansas, where he had gone seeking relief for his various physical ailments.[99] The cause of death was described at the time as "dropsy," an archaic name for the deterioration of the body that accompanies a general breakdown of the major organs. Luke was in considerable pain and discomfort at the end, his hands and feet swollen, his breathing labored.[100] He was a pitiful shell of the man who had dispatched Charlie Storms and Timothy Courtright. He had known he was dying for months, gathered his family around him and made what arrangements he could. Before he left Fort Worth for the last time, he made a final investment, paying $20 for a burial plot in Oakwood Cemetery and a granite headstone.[101] On the stone he had engraved the simple inscription,

Luke Short, 1854–

The last date was to be filled in at the appropriate time.

Luke Short had not only outshot his old rival Courtright, but had outlived him by several years and died in bed. Short's body was brought back to Fort Worth for burial in Oakwood Cemetery, the same graveyard that would eventually hold the remains of Timothy Courtright. After Short's body arrived by train from Kansas, it was put on view in the Gause Funeral Home chapel, then taken to the Mansion House Hotel for the final procession. For several hours on Sunday, September 10, large crowds passed through the chapel to view the remains. The final procession to the cemetery on Sunday afternoon was more than a mile long, according to reports.[102] The grave site was beautified by a profusion of flowers, including one especially large wreath from Nat Kramer. Impressive as it must have been, one is inclined to wonder how many people present were actually grieving friends and how many were curious spectators hoping to get one last look at the famous gambler. Bat Masterson maintained that at his death Short was one of the "most popular sporting men in the country."[103] One tourist who made it a point to attend the funeral and remembered it in his memoirs years later was Wells Fargo detective Fred Dodge, a frequent visitor to Fort Worth on company business.[104]

After Luke's death, Marie Short did not stay long in the town that had only grudgingly accepted her husband. Neither did she stay single for long. She soon married Luke's brother, John Short, and with her new husband and four kids, moved back to Arizona where she had come from originally. She died in Tombstone in 1940.[105]

Short's life after 1887 and even his death were merely postscripts to the era that he and Timothy Courtright had shaped in Fort Worth history. It was actually Courtright's violent death, not Short's peaceful passing that marked the end of the second era in Fort Worth's wild 'n' woolly history. Several other related events reinforce this time as a transitional period. First is the manner of Luke Short's arrest on the night of February 8, 1887. Uniformed policemen — not some rough-and-ready sheriff or quick-draw marshal with a six-gun strapped to his leg and a tin star on his chest — dispersed the crowd and hauled Short off to jail. The times had changed so much since Courtright's days in the marshal's office that after the 1887 city elections, S. M. Farmer, the new chief law officer, announced that he preferred to be known as "Police Chief." Old habits die hard, however, and newspapers continued for many years to refer to the office and the man occupying it as "city marshal." The difference in emphasis, however, is clear.

There were more changes in the air. The day after Courtright died in a hail of bullets, the Texas Senate took up the question of carrying pistols in public. Many Texas towns, including Fort Worth, already had ordinances on the books that carried fines as punishment, but the penalty was seldom enforced. Legislation would apply the prohibition statewide and impose tougher penalties on violators. The House had already taken up the matter in House Bill No. 51, a proposal that included jail sentences of at least thirty days to go along with the fines.

Now it was the Senate's turn, and if ever the time was ripe for reform, this should have been it. Courtright's death was on everyone's mind; one senator referred to it specifically as "a striking example of the results of unlawfully carrying arms."[106] The debate was described as "one of the most interesting discussions of the session." The "pernicious practice" of carrying firearms was roundly denounced, but in the end the gentlemen of the Senate could not agree on an appropriate penalty. The far-sighted House reform measure died in the Senate, although sentiment for gun control remained strong.

In the summer of 1887, after years of debate, the legislature also approved the first constitutional amendment against liquor. In Fort Worth, prohibition reformers had already been at work on public opinion. One local newspaper had commented in 1885, "If there is a place under heaven that ought to have prohibition, it is Fort Worth."[107]

The state amendment was submitted to voters in August, 1887, and brought the largest turnout in state history: 358,897 votes were cast. The measure was defeated, but prohibition candidates continued to run in every state and municipal election until national prohibition was made a part of the United States Constitution in 1919.

The amendment failed on a statewide basis although Fort Worth and Tarrant County voters were in favor — 198 aye votes were counted in the city and more than 500 in the county. Fort Worth was the only city in the state, in fact, to approve it. Even the city's black population turned out in large numbers to vote.[108] In part, this can be attributed to a particularly senseless killing just before the election in one of the city's saloons. It combined the usual elements of guns and liquor.

Mike Haggerty drove a beer wagon for the Texas Brewery Company. One of his best friends and a customer on his delivery route owned a saloon on the corner of Fourth and Houston streets. Early one morning Haggerty stopped his wagon in front of the saloon and strolled inside. His friend the proprietor was still behind the bar, having worked all night. A reporter later described the man as "fatigued and distraught." As Haggerty walked up to the bar he called out a cheery, "Top o' the mornin' to yez." Instead of replying in kind, the proprietor picked up a pistol from under the counter and shot Haggerty dead. For days afterward he was described as a "raving maniac," unable to explain his actions or make rational conversation.[109] This incident must have been very much on the minds of Fort Worth voters when they went to the polls on August 4.

Most surprising of all, prohibition even passed in the Third Ward. The *Fort Worth Gazette* explained that remarkable fact this way:

It should be remembered that the Third Ward is a large one and is peopled by good citizens, among whom the laboring element largely predominates. The classic walks of Hell's Half Acre are to be found in a small corner of the ward and we must admit that the denizens thereof are pre-eminently and distinctively "tough." But they cut no figure in an election. They are not voters because they are not built that way.[110]

City officials moved against gambling, too. Open-door gambling was barred in Fort Worth by ordinance in December, 1887, and, according to one historian, "this time they made it stick."[111] Within a few days after the ordinance was enacted, County Attorney R. L. Carlock got convictions in twenty-four cases, mostly against keno dealers, Luke Short's game. The penalty in each case was a $25 fine, plus ten days in jail in some instances. But there was a certain sham to all the zealous prosecuting and public pronouncements. Most of those caught were small fish and the places closed down were the lowest dives and back rooms. Meanwhile, places like the White Elephant and the Stag Saloon, where "palatial magnificence and luxurious surroundings" were the chief features, continued to operate brazenly.[112] Fort Worth gambling, like the rest of the city's vice, was evolving, and the rougher elements down in the Acre were being squeezed out. The days when a cowboy could saunter into any saloon, purchase a beer and a stack of chips, and have his choice of a place at several tables were practically over. Gambling was not being stamped out; it was being forced behind closed doors, and in the process into fewer and fewer hands. It was becoming organized. Some mistook this development for real improvement.[113]

The attentions of reformers — thwarted in the case of gun control and liquor prohibition — focused on Hell's Half Acre in 1887. Although it was true that the killings of Timothy Courtright and Mike Haggerty had not actually occurred in the Acre, it was still a fact that most of the city's violent crimes took place there. Another brutal killing, which happened only a few days after Courtright's death, helped bring on the latest clean-up campaign against the Acre. More so than the ex-marshal's death, this latest outrage shocked citizens on both ends of town.

The event that took Fort Worth's mind off the shooting of Timothy Courtright was the crucifixion of Sally. For an incident about which so little is known, it has been described in more histories of Fort Worth than any other single crime.[114]

Despite the brutal and lurid nature of the act, it might never have attracted more than passing interest except for the coincidence of timing. Sally, a dance-hall girl with no last name, was found dead in

Hell's Half Acre one morning, nailed to the door of an outhouse behind the hall where she worked. There was never an arrest, never a suspect, never even a clue to indicate who had done it or why — just another particularly grisly mark against Hell's Half Acre. More important than the crime itself was the fact that it occurred just a matter of days after the famous gunfight on Main Street. Suddenly, respectable citizens, who had tried to ignore the seamier side of their city, wondered what was going on. Clearly, rigorous enforcement of laws and a general reform effort were called for before the city sank back to the level of a wide-open cow town.

That possibility loomed still larger following another sensational shooting a little more than a month after the Short-Courtright duel. The scenarios were remarkably similar, right down to the location — the White Elephant Saloon. Again, two rival members of the "sporting fraternity" were involved, Harry Williams and Robert Hayward. Williams, a newcomer to town, had been warned by friends the day of the shooting that Bob Hayward intended to "do him up." On the night of March 15, 1887, Williams was standing in front of the south entrance to the White Elephant when a hack drove up and Hayward got out. When Williams asked if he was looking for him, Hayward said, "Yes, you son of a — !" then drew a .38 Colt. Harry Williams waited until the other man's pistol cleared leather before drawing his own gun. Williams fired first. His shot went through Hayward's right eye, killing him instantly. The dead man never got off a shot. The hack driver, who was the only witness, stated later that it was self-defense.[115] In the aftermath, the cause of their differences was said to have been "money matters," a euphemism for a gamblers' quarrel.[116]

Hayward's killing was the third sensational death in less than six weeks, and the reputation of the "Bloody Third" was threatening to engulf the whole city if something did not change soon. Reformers held out hope for the upcoming city elections.

Shortly before he met his death at the wrong end of a six-shooter, Timothy Courtright had observed that all men were not born equal but Samuel Colt made them so. Two days after Courtright's demise, Dr. Alexander Hadden of the New York Academy of Medicine, reading a scholarly paper before his esteemed colleagues, also stated that "all men are *NOT* born equal; in fact, there is not such a thing as equality." But Dr. Hadden based his conclusion on a scientific study and offered a different remedy than Colt's six-shooter for human inequality. He called for a "good, sensible education . . . and healthy food" to remedy Nature's inequities.[117] The good doctor probably never got any farther west than St. Louis, and never faced a man with a pistol, but his conclusions reflected the changing times and attitudes west of the Mississippi.

Whatever the future held for Fort Worth, however, the turbulent era represented by Luke Short and Timothy Courtright had come to an end.

SEVEN

"Nothing But Brick and Mortar . . ."

THE CHANGING TIMES HAD ALREADY CAUGHT UP WITH Hell's Half Acre. Newspapers now described it as "that dilapidated part of the city" where bums and tramps hung out.[1] When reporters journeyed to the south end of town to work on their stories, they took their cue from Shakespeare's Cassius, coming not to praise the Acre but to bury it. An increasing proportion of the city's population no longer looked benignly on chronic wrongdoing in the Third Ward.

The voters indicated in the spring of 1887 that they were ready for a change, and in no mood to wait for the long-term effects of a good education and proper diet to bring about that change. They preferred direct political action. When the municipal elections of April 1887 were held, the killings of Timothy Courtright, Bob Hayward and Sally "X" were still fresh on everyone's mind. The annual voting ritual took on added significance in the climate of moral outrage that gripped the city. Not surprisingly, voters turned out the old administration and voted in another "reform mayor"; this time it was H. S. Broiles who would lead the city out of the wilderness of two decades of crime.

The marshal's race that year attracted as much interest as the mayor's race. Former marshal S. M. Farmer challenged incumbent W. M. Rea in what developed into the hottest contest in a decade. Rea had been city marshal for the past four years and was blamed for the recent rash of violence and for the continued existence of Hell's Half Acre. The elections were a referendum on the city's crime problems. Ironically, even local gamblers got in on the action, taking bets on who would win the marshal's race. One well-heeled sport wagered $1500 on Farmer.[2] He won, and Fort Worth got a new marshal. Rea announced his retirement from public office right after the election, and the city he had served as a member of the police force since 1879 honored him for "his devotion to duty and fine tact as an officer." It was stated that in retiring he carried "the general goodwill and approbation of his fellow-citizens."[3]

The new marshal and the new mayor did not start off on the best of terms. Broiles had promised voters that he would clean up the Acre with or without the help of the city's police force. He may have overplayed his hand when he pointed the finger at the lawmen as one of the causes of criminal immorality in Fort Worth. He certainly won no allies among the boys on the force by launching a one-man campaign after he took office to "discipline and prune the police force of undesirables." Broiles favored a more professional force modeled on the lines of the big eastern cities. His reforms consisted of, among other things, taking away officers' pistols and replacing them with clubs or nightsticks.[4] Such a proposal did not sit well with men who considered carrying a gun a God-given birthright and furthermore wanted every advantage they could get when they had to go into the Acre. Another of Broiles' reforms sought to end the cozy relationship between policemen and certain disreputable elements in the Acre. Henceforward, policemen were forbidden to leave their beats and enter houses of prostitution "except in the line of duty."[5] This practice, like guaranteed seats at the city's gaming tables, had long been considered one of the perks of the office for marshals and their deputies.

The mayor's clean-up campaign targeted three classes of vice or crime in Fort Worth: wide-open gambling, carrying guns in the city, and abuse of Sunday closing laws. Each class represented an area that was persistently and shamelessly ignored by a substantial number of people, often with the tacit approval of the authorities. Broiles' quixotic war on crime soon ran into opposition, however, particularly the Sunday closing law, which could be debated on valid grounds without having to defend immoral or violent behavior. The loudest protest against enforced Sunday closing came not from the saloon owners but from the city's druggists, who protested that they could not fill prescriptions if they were closed.[6] Since most prescriptions contained a

Just two years after Luke Short plugged Timothy Courtight at 310 Main, guests at the Hotel Worth at Eighth and Main could look up a paved street lined with telephone poles and multi-story brick buildings. Looking in the opposite direction, they could still see Hell's Half Acre in all its shame and glory. On this particular day they were watching a grand parade down Main Street, perhaps one of the big conventions like the Mexican War Veterans or the Cattleman's Association (courtesy W. D. Smith Commercial Photography, Fort Worth).

strong dose of alcohol, it is no wonder they did so much business on Sundays. Nevertheless, the sale of liquor in any form or shape on Sundays was officially banned after August 7, 1887. Practically all the so-called uptown places obeyed the ordinance to the letter, but a "good deal" of whiskey was still being sold in Third Ward saloons after that date. Most people thought it would be next to impossible to convict any barkeeper for doing business on Sunday because witnesses for the accused would be plentiful.[7] No regular customer wanted to help put his friendly local barkeeper in jail.

When the police proved less than vigilant about enforcing reform ordinances, Mayor Broiles took matters into his own hands and appointed special officers with strict instructions to enforce the Sunday closing law. They were told to "raid the low dives of the Acre out of existence."[8] Trouble soon followed, but it came from a surprising direction. Neither the city council nor the police department had been consulted in advance about the mayor's private police force. When some of Broiles' special agents tried to arrest members of the city council who habitually carried pistols, an uproar resulted.[9] The arrests were quietly dropped, but after this episode the working relationship between the mayor and council members cooled considerably.

Mayor Broiles was not entirely alone in his clean-up campaign. He had two important allies in County Attorney R. L. Carlock and District Judge R. E. Beckham. This was Carlock's first stint in public office and as the months went by his resolve wilted like a starched collar in Fort Worth's summer heat. Beckham, on the other hand, was a veteran of past reform campaigns. One of Fort Worth's "good ol' boys" who swapped the city's highest offices around among themselves, he had been elected mayor in 1878 and again in 1886. Beckham's public commitment to reform was well known, but his popularity with the voters rose and fell like a political barometer.

Beckham and Carlock were firmly in Broiles' corner. The same cannot be said of other city officials. In September, 1887, Broiles called a meeting of the police chief (city marshal), the city attorney and the county recorder (judge) to rally their support. He called on his fellow officials "to cooperate with him in a more rigid enforcement of the ordinances." The response was lukewarm, and the meeting ended without progress, "the mayor having the most of the talking."[10]

On that same date, however, Judge Beckham opened the fall

District Court term with a get-tough speech. He followed this with a "request" that all peace officers leave their pistols outside when they came into his courtroom. The *Fort Worth Gazette* explained the judge's reasoning to its readers: "He thinks they [the police] appear to better advantage minus their guns." Strangers would also be less inclined to think "the Fort a tough border town."[11] At first the response to His Honor's speech was surprise, then indignation. Frontier law officers had always worn guns; it was a privilege that came with the office. A frontier peace officer without his gun was only half-dressed, even in a court of law.

To many folks, Beckham's novel ideas about reform targeted the wrong class of citizens. Instead of getting drunks off the street, rounding up bawds and running tinhorn gamblers out of town, Beckham thought reform should start at the top by requiring city officials to be models of propriety. This radical idea took most of the fun and profit out of holding public office. It had not been too many years since city aldermen were identified in the newspaper as owners of brothels, and sworn officers were "winking at the dens of vice and immorality."[12] But now a determined Judge Beckham was trying to turn that comfortable system on its ear with his appeals and directives. In 1889 he charged a grand jury to "look closely into the conduct of *all* public officials, and let no man escape because of high social or financial standing." They should no longer tolerate a system where "the poor wretch, after a night's debauch, was hurried before the magistrate and fined, [while] those whose influence was regarded as important about the time of election were passed unobserved in violation of law."[13]

The public response to Beckham's one-man crusade was pretty much the same response Mayor Broiles had gotten for his own well-intended efforts. Reform was well and good, as long as it did not hurt business or interfere with personal freedom. Part of the problem may also have been that after the uproar over Sally's death and the other two killings died down, local citizens just did not see anything so immoral or bad about their town. Certainly, it was no worse than Kansas City, St. Louis or any other booming western town. A visitor from Kansas City, who was interviewed by a reporter for the *Fort Worth Gazette* in August, 1887, supported this view. The unnamed visitor claimed that he got off the train expecting to find a community where "the nights would be made hideous by nightly 'scrimmages' and which would be followed at breakfast time by the summoning of at least half a dozen coroner's juries which would, with wonderful unanimity, return verdicts reading thus: 'Killed by an act of Providence.'"[14] The Kansas City man went home disappointed with his brief visit to "the Wild West."

It seems likely that the real Fort Worth lay somewhere between the reformers' high-minded ideals and the expectations of the disappointed visitor from Kansas City. Mrs. Octavia Bennett later recalled growing up in Fort Worth during this time, and her memories were of a more peaceful town than popular accounts have portrayed. According to Mrs. Bennett, on special occasions or holidays like Christmas, "cowboys would ride up and down Main Street, yelling at the top of their voices and once or twice we would hear a pistol shot." At such times, respectable citizens kept their doors closed and lights out to avoid becoming targets of the revellers. Contrary to legend, however, this did not happen often "and was not a custom."[15]

A more common problem was expressed by a "Church Woman" in a "Letter to the Editor" the same year. She complained that ladies on the way to church every Sunday were compelled at almost every corner of the public streets to pass a saloon. As if that were not bad enough, they were forced to endure the salacious remarks of young men who congregated on those corners. "Oftentimes the remarks overheard are not of such a nature as ladies should hear, but even if this offensive part is not permitted, such a gathering is a kind of gauntlet which no modest woman likes to run. The attention of the police might be directed to the language and manners of newsboys and bootblacks who haunt these corners."[16]

Far from condemning the Acre, the sanctimonious and often indignant *Fort Worth Gazette* could even find something good to say about the district. "Hell's Half Acre is in Fort Worth and it is a tough place. They cut, shoot and slug each other now and then in that well-advertised district, but then they meet each other face to face, and their victims are never women nor wives."[17] While this stretched civic boosterism a little, the point was well taken — Fort Worth was not a bad place to live. It could be an exciting place, even a violent place, but it was not a bad place. The fact that "the lamb and the lion could lie down together" was demonstrated when Editor Paddock put up $180 bail for Nat Kramer when that gambler was arrested and charged with "exhibiting a faro bank." Kramer's arrest was not surprising; judging by the public record, he probably spent as much time in court as he did in his place of business. What is surprising is to find Paddock's name linked to one of the most notorious Fort Worth gamblers.[18]

A large share of the credit for making Fort Worth a decent place to live and raise a family must go to the unceasing efforts of reformers like Paddock, Broiles, Carlock and Beckham. Between 1887 and 1889, Broiles and Carlock in particular cleaned up the Acre "as no one before them had ever been able to do."[19]

The reformers were aided in their efforts by the changing face of Fort Worth from frontier town to mid-western city. Economics played an important part in the improving moral climate. In the mid-1880s the range-cattle boom collapsed in the United States, and with it came a decline in all the related enterprises on the Great Plains, including red-light districts like Hell's Half Acre. Fortunately, by that time the local economy was more dependant on the railroads than the cattle trails; otherwise Fort Worth might have dried up and blown away like Fort Griffin, Ellsworth and some of the other cow towns.

Fort Worth not only survived the bust in the cattle industry but continued to grow and prosper. A new economy based on meat packing, brewing and transportation saw the declining importance of Hell's Half Acre to the local economy. Credit for this new economic boom must be given to a handful of prominent men, including B. B. Paddock, K. M. Van Zandt and John Peter Smith.

On December 6, 1887, the *Gazette* reported a strange quietness on the city's south end: "The gambling houses were closed last night tighter than wax as far as anyone could discover." Mayor Broiles was justifiably proud of keeping one of his campaign promises.

For years, local officials had been trying to force the gamblers to carry on their operations "behind closed doors," which meant limiting them to small friendly games in back rooms. But trying to distinguish between public and private gambling proved to be unworkable. It was still possible for any stranger arriving in town to find a friendly game to fit the size of his bankroll; this could be accomplished simply by asking on the street. The old division between downtown and uptown interests also continued to make a mockery of enforcement. The only places that were ever shut down were those found in "some obscure quarter of the city."[20] The palatial emporiums uptown, of which the White Elephant was the most notorious, were never subject to raids or mass arrests, although everybody knew what went on upstairs behind the polished, dark-wood doors. When County Attorney Carlock and Judge Beckham teamed up to put an end to this corrupt system they achieved mixed results, despite the proclamation by the *Fort Worth Gazette* that "Open Door Betting House [was] a Thing of the Past in Fort Worth."[21] While some of the cases were prosecuted successfully, one suspects that few of the convictions included the starched-shirt gamblers. The main result was not to put these "Knights of the Green Cloth" behind bars or even out of business, but to persuade them to pack up their tools and leave town. In the roundup of December, 1887, forty-five gamblers who were arrested and posted bond preferred to take the next transportation out of town rather than take their chances in court.[22] Like an ant hill kicked over and stomped flat, these industrious fellows simply moved to another location and were soon back in business on the same scale as before. But where they landed next was of no concern to Fort Worthers. Also like the industrious little ants, the numbers of gamblers never seemed to diminish significantly despite the most rigorous efforts to exterminate them.

Local prohibitionists were also hard at work to improve Fort Worth morals. For church-going folks, liquor consumption failed every test of righteousness: the church denounced drinking as a sin; women attacked the saloon as a menace to family life; reformers saw an unholy alliance between drinking and crime; and businessmen discovered that drinking lowered productivity. Even white racists eventually found a place on the bandwagon, believing that liquor stirred up the primal instincts of Negroes and made them uncontrollable.[23] The Star of Hope Society first brought the national movement to Fort Worth in 1877, but it was not until the 1890s that temperance zealots and the Women's Christian Temperance Union made any headway locally. Most of their early attempts to abolish gambling, close saloons and banish prostitutes had been frustrated by lack of numbers, organization and influence, but they persisted through the hurly-burly years. The WCTU fought for a more moral community on several fronts. One of the most popular measures on the group's agenda was saving innocent young girls from the allure of saloon and bawdy house. The first effort to raise the legal age of consent in Texas for girls from ten years old to sixteen was launched by the Fort Worth Union in 1891. They sent Mrs. Mary M. Clardy to Austin to lobby the legislature. She and her sisters back home had to settle for half a loaf, succeeding through her "heroic efforts" in getting

"The Temperance Crusade—Who Will Win?" A popular theme of reformers in the 1870s: women pleading with a saloon keeper for the souls of their menfolk. The temperance movement, already active in large eastern cities by 1874, had not reached Fort Worth yet (*New York Daily Graphic*, March 5, 1874, courtesy Library of Congress).

the age raised to twelve. Nonetheless, her work made the Fort Worth chapter of the WCTU one of the most respected in the country.[24]

While respectable citizens became more vocal in their opposition to sin, and the city tried to shut down the gambling houses, crime had not adjourned. The years 1886–1889 proved to be banner years for train robbers around Fort Worth. The area had been quiet since the Bass gang was run to earth in 1878. Nine years later a new bunch, the Rube Burrows gang, hit trains on Fort Worth's doorstep. The leaders were brothers Reuben and James Burrows, Alabamans who hung around Fort Worth in 1886 and 1887. Rube was a likeable sort, a temperate man in most things, and a "great storyteller." He owned a ranch near Stephenville that he and his brother worked, but they preferred train robbing to ranching and they were successful at it. On December 1, 1886, they held up a Fort Worth & Denver train at Bellevue, Clay County, and disarmed an entire squad of black soldiers, then made a clean getaway with all the loot and arms they could carry, "leaving them well-supplied with guns [if not money] for years to come."[25]

A number of train robberies in North Texas between December 1886 and September 1887 were blamed on the two Burrows brothers, starting with the Clay County holdup of the Fort Worth & Denver on December 1.[26] On January 23, about sixty-eight miles west of Fort Worth near the small town of Gordon, a seven-man gang stopped a Texas & Pacific train, forced open the express car, and got away with nearly $2000.[27] Desperados struck a third time on June 4, 1887, even closer to Fort Worth. The eastbound Texas & Pacific express from El Paso was boarded and stopped at Mary's Creek, a few miles southwest of Fort Worth near Benbrook. Four robbers made off with $2500, but it was the tactics not the size of the haul that made this robbery memorable. The holdup men stopped the train on a high trestle over Mary's Creek so that only the engine, coal car and express car were off the trestle. All the passenger cars sat high and dry on the bridge, discouraging any curious passengers or crewmen from coming forward to interfere with the gang's work and cutting down on potential witnesses who might identify them later on. After pilfering the safe and mail bags, the thieves disappeared into the surrounding brush without a trace. When the train reached Fort Worth, a sheriff's posse was dispatched accompanied by bloodhounds, but they soon returned without catching sight of the robbers.[28]

The fourth robbery happened on September 20. The same gang hit the same train at the same place using the same tactics. They even found the same crew on the train. This time they got away with $2,725. No one was injured in any of the incidents, and the "trestle tactic" became a favorite of western train robbers from that time on.[29]

After the fourth robbery and another fruitless search for the culprits, Fort Worth was no longer shocked by the news of robberies in the city's backyard. The *Gazette* summed up the feelings of a lot of people when it said, "A thing to be exciting must contain an element of novelty, and the train robbing has become so very common, as to scarcely deserve any uncommon display of headlines in a newspaper."[30] The sheriff and the express company officials were certainly not amused.

A couple of years later, Burrows turned up in Denver and bragged to a newspaper reporter about a couple of train robberies he had pulled at "Bend Brooke [sic]." He estimated the haul from the two jobs at $4000 and $400 respectively. Soon after the holdups, the gang drifted eastward to Missouri and then to Mississippi. Interviewed on one occasion, Burrows attributed his life of crime to having read about the adventures of Jesse James as a boy, and having "an ambition to equal him in daring deeds."[31]

Among the desperados who called the city home during the period was Eugene Bunch, known to history as "Captain Dick" and "the Lone Highwayman." Bunch, a tall, angular man with a long face and a drooping handle-bar moustache, arrived in town in 1885 from Wichita Falls. He neither smoked nor drank, but he did enjoy gambling and sometimes flashed a bankroll of $500. He dabbled in real estate, too, but was usually seen at the gaming tables around town, including the White Elephant's, where faro was his game. As a gambler he lost more often than he won, but no one minded — he always paid his debts promptly. He also wore a brace of pistols á la Timothy Courtright, and like Courtright, he knew how to use them. He had the reputation for being "as nervy a man as ever pulled a gun," although he was never involved in any gunplay in Fort Worth. Fort Worthers knew him as a smooth-talking sport who affected a rather "cool, off-hand manner." Bunch could drop $10 or $500 and shrug it off.

Bunch was generally well-liked and no one ever questioned either the timing or the destination of his frequent trips out of town.[32]

Acquaintances did not make the connection between Captain Dick and the rash of holdups that occurred around Fort Worth in the first half of 1887. Only later would folks recall the odd timing of a couple of events following one of those robberies. After a June 4th holdup, while posses and bloodhounds were still out scouring the countryside, Bunch was "at his accustomed place . . . in front of the faro dealer" in one of the local saloons. He had a "fistful of money," and was "bucking the tiger," gambler's jargon for playing faro.[33] His luck had not improved any, but dropping his bankroll at the faro table did not prevent him from paying $60 cash to R. L. Carlock on June 11 for a parcel of land outside town.[34]

Late in 1887, about the same time the robberies around Fort Worth stopped, Captain Dick pulled up stakes and moved to Gainesville. Soon after, a series of unexplained stage robberies started in the Gainesville area. He certainly got around if we are to believe the legends associated with his exploits, for while he was still living in Gainesville, his name is linked to an El Paso job. According to the story, he hit a train not far from that town using a young woman as an accomplice — not an unknown arrangement among western outlaws. When officers later caught the lady with $1600 of loot, she named Captain Dick as her partner, helping to bring the curtain down on the Texas phase of his career.[35] His next appearance was noted in the *New Orleans Daily Picayune* of November 4, 1888: "The lone highwayman, possibly the same rascal who has for years been in the habit of robbing railway trains and stagecoaches in Texas has now transferred his operations to the railways in the neighborhood of this city."

Captain Dick eventually met his end at the hands of Pinkerton detectives in Louisiana five years after leaving Fort Worth. Since he had never been arrested or charged with any crimes while he lived in Fort Worth, townspeople was surprised to learn of his long criminal record. In fact, Bunch was never connected to any local robberies except through circumstantial evidence.[36] Like many badmen, his reputation grew after his death, and he was dubbed the "Prince of Outlaws."[37] Although most Fort Worthers had long since forgotten him when the news of his death arrived, the newspaper gave him a nice write-up, describing him as a man of "commanding, knightly appearance . . . universally thought to be a high-minded, honorable man."[38]

The flurry of train robberies around Fort Worth in 1887 was

A pair of outlaw brothers, Reuben (left) and James (right) Burrows. Alabama-born, they came to Texas to become train robbers. Their outlaw careers came to an end in 1889 when Jim died of consumption in prison and Rube was shot by a railroad detective. Lasting fame eluded them (from *Train Robberies and Train Robbers* by William A. Pinkerton, 1907).

never solved. Neither was the last big robbery of the decade. On September 24, 1889, five men held up the northbound Santa Fe train near Crowley. They got at least $1000 from the Wells Fargo & Company express car, including three bags of Mexican silver.[39] The unidentified gang made it look ridiculously easy for no trace of them was ever found and the money was never recovered.

What made all these robberies curious, as well as tiresome, was that none of the outlaw gangs could ever be run to ground nor their headquarters located. Outlaw gangs traditionally had a base of operations, like Sam Bass' headquarters in the Cross Timbers near Denton or the more famous Hole-in-the-Wall, Brown's Hole and Robber's Roost retreats on the northern "Outlaw Trail" — all in the tri-state area of Utah, Wyoming and Colorado. But none of these gangs seemed to originate at or retreat to any particular location between jobs. The realization slowly dawned that the most obvious sanctuary was not some hideaway in a creek bed or up a draw outside of town, but right in Fort Worth's favorite playground. After a while the finger of suspicion pointed at Hell's Half Acre as soon as a robbery occurred nearby, and for good reason. Sooner or later most of the shady characters in the Southwest paid the Acre a visit, and some of those who never got there during life had their names associated with the Acre after death. Countless western communities claim universal right of proprietorship to legendary desperados with scant evidence that they had ever lived there or had even passed through.

During these years Fort Worth played host to a remarkable collection of characters, including the real Frank James, an ersatz Billy the Kid, and perhaps the ghost of Jesse James. Frank James, the reformed train and bank robber and older brother of Jesse James, visited Fort Worth in November, 1888. This was several years after the James gang broke up and his brother was killed. By this time Frank had gone straight and was regarded as something of an expert on outlaws and their methods. He received celebrity treatment during his one known visit to Fort Worth and repaid the city's kindness by offering his opinions on Dick Bunch, whose exploits were just then coming to light.[40] But the locals were more interested in the exploits of the legendary James gang who were already ranked among the most famous outlaws of all time. That fame brought the universal right to proprietorship into effect. Only three years before, a Dallas newspaper had reported the rumor that Jesse James was under arrest and lodged in the Fort Worth jail, despite the fact that he had been shot in the back in Missouri in 1882. No one knew who started the rumor, but the Fort Worth sheriff vigorously denied it.[41]

The ersatz Billy the Kid was a drifter who came to town after the heyday of the western badmen and claimed to be the genuine article. He arrived in town in 1890 and was arrested for carrying a pistol but skipped before he could be brought to trial. No one got too excited about the little affair because the real Billy the Kid had died in Fort Sumner, New Mexico, on July 14, 1881, shot by Sheriff Pat Garrett. Copycat Billy was never seen in Fort Worth again.[42] It was indicative of the times that Fort Worth's most newsworthy badmen were now out-of-towners, and either retired or cheap imitations of the real thing.

All the gunmen who passed through the Acre were not hardened criminals. Henry Andrew "Heck" Thomas, who later won fame as a U.S. marshal in the Indian Territory, lived in Fort Worth from 1878 until 1885. He worked as the resident agent for the Texas Express Company most of that time, a promotion he won for his heroic actions during Sam Bass' reign of terror. When the Texas Express Company faltered financially, he went into business for himself, opening the Fort Worth Detective Association. He had already run for city marshal twice, first in 1883 then again in 1885. Both times he lost to William Rea, although the Third Ward gave him a majority of its votes in both races. He lost the 1885 race by the slimmest of margins when the judges closed the polls nine minutes early to avert violence. At the time Thomas had forty-one men standing in line waiting to cast their ballots for him — more than enough to carry the day. The story made headlines as far away as Galveston where the *Galveston Daily News* called it the "most hotly contested election ever held in the city."[43] As a defeated candidate for city marshal who then opens his own detective agency, Thomas took a page from the book of his old friend Timothy Courtright but with a happier ending. Heck still had many friends in Fort Worth who urged him to run for sheriff on the Democratic ticket in 1886 or seek an appointment to the Texas Rangers. He was a shoo-in for either, they said. Thomas was not interested. Instead, he moved to Oklahoma and put on a U.S. marshal's badge.[44] Cut from the same cloth as Timothy Courtright, Heck Thomas won a different kind of fame because all his shootouts were on the right side of the law.

Mayor Broiles' clean-up drive reached its peak in 1889. The *Gazette* reported that Judge Beckham had charged a new grand jury "with emphasis upon the importance of suppressing gambling and closing gambling houses."[45] The jury acted swiftly. One month later the *Gazette* triumphantly carried this story:

> The *Gazette* can say most positively that 'Hell's Half Acre' is no more. This plague spot of Fort Worth had been wiped out completely and everlastingly. A *Gazette* reporter found Saturday night that Main Street from 11th to 12th was all quiet. East on 12th the change was marvelous. On 12th to Jones, not a woman to be seen, no oaths, no fights, no robberies — nothing but vacant houses; up Jones to 11th, down 11th and back again to Main and still not a Mother Hubbard-clad woman could be seen.[46]

Reports of the Acre's demise were premature, but for the first time in two decades things were relatively quiet at the south end of town and stayed that way after Mayor Broiles left office in 1890.

Quiet was not necessarily law-abiding, however. An editorial in the newspaper in 1890 complained that "street robbery is too frequent in Fort Worth," then went on to ask rhetorically, "Cannot the authorities put an end to it, for highwaymen are not good immigration agents."[47] But Fort Worth authorities were after bigger fish.

In the summer of 1890 the grand jury reconvened and set out after bars and saloons that had long ignored the Sunday closing law. The jury announced a target date after which, it was promised, indictments would be handed down against every saloon, gambling den, dive and "theater of low women" that stayed open on Sunday. At first it seemed to be the same old story. The previous year, during the crack-down on gambling, the county attorney had proclaimed that as of Sunday, September 15, all local saloons were "hermetically sealed" in accordance with his orders. Citizens as far away as Austin followed this news with interest because of Fort Worth's reputation as "the Paris of the Plains."[48] After a decent period of respect for County Attorney B. P. Ayres' orders, business was back to normal. Ayres turned over the county attorney's office to O. W. Gillespie after the municipal elections of 1890. That summer Gillespie charged a new grand jury to enforce the Sunday closing law. Howls of indignation immediately arose from the saloon keepers, who recommended that officials "pay a little more attention to the sanitary conditions of your city, your sidewalks and your streets, and in heaven's name let us alone."[49] When word of their protest got out, over 1200 honest businessmen, "including every firm on Main and Houston streets with few exceptions," signed a petition to the city council "to move these places off of public streets."[50]

The grand jury pressed ahead with its plans, publishing notice of its intention to indict Acre property owners "for renting places to parties of ill-repute" — the first time any clean-up campaign had threatened the root of the problem and Fort Worth's most solid citizens.[51] If property owners were not safe from indictment, what hope did gamblers, madams and saloon keepers have? Several familiar characters in the Acre began to pack up and leave town, turning stretches of Rusk and Calhoun into passable imitations of a ghost town. Adding to the overall effect, many of the gamblers who stayed moved their operations behind closed doors, prostitutes stayed off the streets and saloon keepers began closing on Sundays. One of those threatened with eviction was Mary Porter, owner of several adjacent lots on Rusk Street. Her properties were occupied by houses, at least one of them a "female boarding house." She was notified that the city would take over her house on November 1. But Mary was too tough to join the stampede of those leaving town. She had weathered other reform campaigns, and she would ride this one out, too.

Broiles had turned the reins of municipal government over to W. S. Pendleton in the sweeping electoral changes of 1890. Under Pendleton and his immediate successors, the torch of reform passed to new hands outside city government. The religious community finally made its voice heard. For years that voice had been drowned out by the din from saloons, dance halls and variety theaters. But there was new "Reformation" at work in the city. The *Gazette* reported in 1890 that half a dozen church buildings were either under construction or just completed. The Baptists, Methodists, Catholics and Presbyterians had all moved into new houses of worship; the Episcopalians had broken ground for a $75,000 building. All this construction reflected a growing religious spirit at work in the Paris of the Plains.[52]

The expanding congregations were a welcome sign, but more important was the attention focused on Hell's Half Acre. The reformers had a new paladin, the ardent and outspoken minister of the Southside Baptist Church, A. E. Baten. Baten took over the pulpit of the little congregation across the tracks in 1890, but he did not really hit his stride until the summer of 1893 when he preached a series of blistering sermons on "Municipal Meanness in Fort Worth." He attacked not only the "dives that have so long disgraced the city" but also a city administration that tolerated and even encouraged vice and corruption in Fort Worth.[53] The main, statewide Baptist organ picked up his sermons and reprinted them, as it did his subsequent claim of a "great moral victory" after the city council passed another of its endless ordinances to shut down the worst spots in the Acre. When this law proved as ineffective as previous efforts, Baten abruptly resigned his pastorate, announcing his intention to become an evangelist. Baten's timing was probably more than coincidence.[54] He was not the first preacher that Hell's Half Acre had defeated, nor the last Baptist preacher to stake his reputation on shutting down the Acre.

There were other developments in the holy crusade against the Acre in the 1890s, characterized by the adoption of a new strategy. Now reformers based their approach on two popular reform movements of the day — the social gospel and the settlement houses. The social gospel was a movement among Protestant churches to address the problems of an increasingly urbanized and industrialized society.

By improving men's living conditions and physical surroundings, believers hoped to save more souls. Related to this high-minded ideal, but with more secular orientation, was the settlement house movement. The last two decades of the nineteenth century were the heyday of that program in the United States. The basic idea came from England, by way of New York City and Chicago, before it reached the frontier in greatly diluted form. Settlement houses sought to provide comprehensive social services to the urban poor and slum-dwelling ethnic minorities. In addition to meals and beds, their services included reading rooms, boys' clubs, gymnasia, education classes and child care. The movement reached Fort Worth around 1890 when the Union Bethel Mission on Fourteenth Street and the Women's Industrial Home on West Ireland opened their doors.

The Union Bethel Mission tried to assure a skeptical neighborhood that its purpose was to elevate and reform the people of the Acre. For years various self-proclaimed reformers had waged war on the Acre in attempts to wipe it out and scatter its inhabitants. Such efforts had all failed sooner or later, so it was understandable that Third Ward residents greeted the arrival of the Mission with hostility and suspicion. One saloon keeper sent a cynical note to the Mission soon after it opened, saying he wished more such "schools" would open in the Acre, as it helped to draw a crowd to the neighborhood and his receipts had gone up to $200 a day.[55]

After the city forced Madam Porter to vacate her first bagnio in November, 1890, the Union Bethel Mission was offered the house on a rental basis. They expanded their operations to the new Rusk Street location with more Sunday school classes and more reading rooms. Madam Porter soon opened her doors at another location on Rusk Street, however.

Meanwhile, the Women's Industrial Home was also getting into the act. The objects of their attention were the "poor down-trodden sisters" who worked in the Acre "without hope of reform or rest."[56] The women had first planned to locate on Samuels Avenue near the Orphan's Home, but when they learned that Madam Porter's place would be offered for rent by the city, they rushed to lay claim to it. They even sent circulars describing the Home to the girls at Madam Porter's and then followed with a visit en masse to the brothel to make their pitch in person. The working girls must have been surprised when the committee showed up on their doorstep. But they took it in stride, even assuring the reformers that their work was "a needed one," and the bawds were anxious to see it succeed.

Since the Bethel Mission had already established its claim to the house, the Women's Industrial Home decided to locate at 117 West Ireland. There, Mrs. Delia Collins, Mrs. L. J. Clayton and Colonel A. J. Chambers' wife founded Fort Worth's first home for single and "fallen" women.

While this was going on, special interests groups in the Acre were not standing by idly. On September 26, 1890, the saloon men met and formed a defensive organization that they named the Fort Worth Liquor Dealers' Association. The immediate cause behind their organization was the closing of all saloons on September 19 with threat of prosecution under the Sunday closing law. A similar group had existed in 1888, but died for lack of a worthwhile cause to hold them together. Two years later they had their cause: the Sunday closing law. Forty-seven men attended the first meeting of the revived association at the Germania Hall on North Houston. Those attending did not deem it wise to publicize their get-together; in fact, "very few outside those engaged in the interested trade were aware of it."[57]

The presiding officer was H. P. Shiel, one of the city's first policemen back in the 1870s but a man whose frequent appearances in court since then had been on the opposite side of the law. In subsequent meetings the men elected officers, drew up an agenda, and passed resolutions to send to the city council. Their basic purpose, they explained in one of the resolutions, was defensive, or "self-protection." They rightly recognized the "church folk" as their number-one enemy and challenged them to look to their own homes if they wanted to save souls.

Other residents of the Acre took the high road in the battle between commercial interests and the forces of reform. For the first time, the Acre's substantial black population made its voice heard in city hall. The 1890 Census had showed that six percent of Fort Worth's population was black, and most of that population was concentrated in the Third Ward.[58] For years they had either been forgotten or maligned by more powerful interests in the city. Finally in the 1890s they organized the Afro-American Citizens' Conference and the Colored Progressive Club. The Afro-American Citizens' Conference met regularly at several locations, including city hall. On January 8, 1897, they announced the agenda for their next meeting: they would discuss "open gambling houses for the colored people and running a colored man or colored man's representative for City Council from the Third Ward."[59]

After the turn of the century, black professionals and businessmen like Bill "Gooseneck" McDonald began to have an impact on the Acre, but in the 1890s most white citizens probably agreed with the bigoted opinion offered by outlaw Sam Bass years before: "God never made a Negro man or woman that will not steal nor a [Negro] woman that will not sell her virtue for $.50 or give it away if she can't get the money."[60]

As the nineteenth century waned, times were changing and events in Fort Worth mirrored national trends. The United States Census Bureau announced the official "closing" of the frontier; the Indian wars were over; and technology brought railroads, which in turn brought goods and services. "Robber barons" were largely replacing gun-toting outlaws and red-skinned savages as the nation's principal villains. Immigration was up, with most of the so-called "new immigrants" coming from southern and eastern Europe. More than 5000 came through the nation's ports in 1890 alone. Their culture, their religion and their languages were markedly different from the northern and western European stock who had settled the country in earlier decades.

The influx of Orientals through the West Coast in the same period caused an even greater cultural shock. Between 1850 and 1882 (when the U.S. Congress passed the Exclusion Act forbidding further Chinese immigration), some 200,000 Chinese settled in the port cities and mining camps of the far West. Some followed the railroads eastward and put down roots in the Midwest and Southwest though their numbers were hardly significant. In 1870 census reports for Texas showed only twenty-five Chinese compared to 629 Indians and 253,475 "Colored" residents.[61]

Fort Worth, as a major railroad hub, attracted a few Orientals from the late 1870s onward but they received a very cautious reception from local employers. One prominent railroad man noted, "They are good hands, but keen after their interest, and ready to demand an increase of wages [on any pretext]."[62] As it turned out, the Chinese would have a lasting impact on Fort Worth, and on Hell's Half Acre in particular, where they joined the existing minorities of poor blacks and Irishmen living in the city's slum district. In 1878 the *Daily Democrat* noted there were at least twelve Chinese in Fort Worth, although the city directory that same year listed just two residents, Gee Hop and San Wah, both of whom operated laundry services.[63] The *Democrat* referred to them cruelly as "Chinks" and "chin-ee-men" and called for their early departure. But they did not depart; instead, their numbers continued to grow steadily through the 1890s until by 1905 about sixty Chinese were living in Fort Worth's own "Little Chinatown."[64]

Chinese newcomers established a large boarding house on Houston Street, just south of Fourteenth, and another at Fourteenth and Calhoun.[65] White residents eyed these two locations with suspicion but did not molest the inhabitants. By choice or circumstance, Fort Worth's Chinese population confined themselves to the three enterprises usually associated with their race at that time: opium, hand laundries and restaurants — only two of which were legal. Opium, whose addictive properties and debilitating physical effects were well known, was an illegal drug, but authorities were ambivalent about enforcing this law, as they were so many other laws on the frontier. On one hand, the *Gazette* reported in 1887 without comment that "A Chinaman was fined $25 by the Recorder [court] yesterday for running an opium dive on Houston Street." On the other hand, only a few years later another Fort Worth newspaper reported: "The [police] officers do not molest the yellow-skinned men for 'hitting the pipe,' for the reason that they are privileged to do so if they desire. It's just a habit of the people from the Orient, just like drinking whiskey is a custom of lots of people of other nationalities."[66]

It seems probable, if not provable, that it was the Chinese who introduced opium smoking to Fort Worth. The influx of Chinese immigrants and the discovery that the city had a new problem happened too close chronologically to be mere coincidence. The fact that the practice was so closely identified with a foreign race helps explain why it did not achieve greater acceptance among whites who had no qualms about using alcohol or morphine. To a simple cowboy who had grown up around liquor and drinking, opium, with its mind-altering effects, was frightening. As one workingman in the far Northwest explained, "It was different from drunks. With a drunk he was out, and you knew where he was. But with pipe-smokers, well, it was as though they had gone some place you or nobody could follow. They were *really* gone."[67] Being illegal was not the principal deterrent where opium was concerned.

There was nothing illegal, of course, about the hand-laundry business, but because it was monopolized by the Chinese, it was sneeringly dismissed as "a sort of Washee-Washee Tong" whose services the city could do without. "This country wants washing bills which it can read," one newspaper editor commented bluntly, "even if it can't pay for them."[68] The Chinese restaurants, as the third business activity entered into by that race, rather easily attracted a cross-section of respectable patrons, bringing them into the mainstream of the city's business and social activity.

Chinese influence in the Acre went deeper than their small numbers might indicate. Forced by necessity into the lowest socioeconomic stratum, they soon carved out their own niche in two of the Acre's traditional enterprises — prostitution and gambling. Among the first Chinese to get nabbed by the law were You Lee and Hop Lee, both of whom operated laundries in the main business district. On the side, however, they ran other interests. In 1888 they were convicted of running a disorderly house, location unspecified.[69]

The opium trade also attracted a wider clientele than Orientals, and was cause for strong moral, as well as official, concern. After the turn of the century the newspapers began complaining of "Chinese opium dens" operating in the heart of the city where there was a "communion of white and yellow brethren."[70] Obviously, the Acre's denizens had overcome their earlier fears of the strange Oriental drug. In fact, opium abuse made a comfortable accommodation with the Acre's other illicit activities. Charles Ambrose, one of the district's better-known entrepreneurs in the early 1890s, ran a combination "disorderly house" and "hop joint" on lower Main. In May, 1893, he was arrested and hauled before the county court on both charges. The court found him guilty and fined him $200 plus court costs. It was noted that Ambrose himself was "a confirmed opium fiend, beyond redemption [who had] practiced all forms of the opium habit." He was also a member of the Knights of Pythias and his fraternal brothers had tried previously to cure him but to no avail. When he proved unable to come up with "the fine and trimmings," he was sentenced to two years' hard labor on the county roads.[71] Ambrose's story shows that opium had clearly made the crossover from an exotic minority problem to a general plague on the Acre even before the end of the century.

The tide of American progress that brought strange new immigrants to Fort Worth also brought new industry. The Texas Brewing Company — the city's first large industry — was built in 1890 and located on Jones Street between Ninth and Twelfth, almost in the heart of the Acre. Before the end of the decade, the plant was turning out enough beer to fill 3000 freight cars a year, and making an annual payroll of $100,000. Now the Acre's drinkers could enjoy the hometown brew, and even hoist a few in salute to the city's largest employer, all in the name of civic pride.

The economic boom of the previous decade continued into the 1890s. In 1893 construction began on the present-day county courthouse, a pink granite monument to the city's faith in the future. That same year on the south end of town at Tenth and Throckmorton, a new city hall opened, just close enough to keep a watchful eye on the Acre without actually being in hostile territory.

The growth in city government did not make a dent in the familiar problems associated with the Acre. The chief form of death in the Acre during this era was suicide, and the victims were not the rough, tough cowboys traditionally associated with the district, but the soiled doves who lived on the edge of society and seldom had more than a tenuous grip on life in the best of times. Suicide was hardly a new problem in the Acre at this late date. It was as old as the district itself and was first brought to the public's attention in 1876. On November 29 of that year, the *Democrat* reported, "Another Soiled Dove Crosses the River. . . . The last suicide of such nature was about two weeks ago." In the years since that headline, the problem had grown to such proportions that two and three a night were regularly reported. On the night of May 29, 1888, three girls, two white and one black, attempted to snuff out their lives by ingesting various poisons. The newspaper did not mention their names but reported gratuitously that they were "all of ill fame."[72] By December of the same year, the *Daily Gazette* felt obliged to call it a "suicide craze" when four women took morphine overdoses on the same night.[73] Three of the women, including the notorious Emeline Gooden, were saved by "hard-working" doctors who rushed to the rescue, but the fourth woman was not so fortunate.[74] Headlines and stories like these

By the end of the century local tipplers could try a remarkable variety of brews, including the product of the Anheuser-Busch Brewing Association (top), and the locally made product of the Texas Brewing Company (bottom). The Texas Brewing Company was one of the first success stories of the Fort Worth Board of Trade in the transformation from trail town to modern city. The unpaved streets (top) were still characteristic of south Fort Worth even at this late date (about 1905). Horse-drawn wagons made their deliveries in the city (top, courtesy Fort Worth Public Library and Amon Carter Museum; bottom, courtesy W. D. Smith Commercial Photography, Fort Worth).

said more about what life was really like in the Acre than all the colorful legends about boisterous Saturday nights and barroom brawls.

Unfortunately, death by suicide was one of only two times the demimondes of the Acre received public attention; the other was when they were arrested for plying their trade. Public notice at both times was confined to a few lines in the newspaper, notably lacking in any expression of sympathy. Most of the stories chronicling life and death among the painted women were written in sardonic, world-weary tones, like the following headline in the *Daily Democrat* on September 22, 1880: "Tumble-down Angel Tries to Climb Golden Stairs." Similarly the *Gazette* described the death of Lulu Andrews in 1885: "Weary of Life, Diseased, Destitute, Deserted, and Despondent, Lulu Andrews Seeks Death."[75]

For girls of the Acre, it was a simple matter to take a massive overdose of a drug that was already on hand or readily available. Morphine was most often the narcotic involved. It was cheaper than whiskey and packed twice the kick when used in non-fatal doses.[76] For permanent results, ten to fifteen grains of morphine would usually send a girl over the river.[77] In the case of Dora Doyle, fifteen grains of morphine was a sufficient dose to bid farewell to this world on the night of February 9, 1897.[78] Dora was already addicted to both morphine and cocaine. Clyde Riggin, one of Mary Porter's girls, took an overdose on the night of May 31, 1897, after a quarrel with her lover. The newspapers called it "the old story: the lover took a walk and the woman took the poison."[79]

For reasons of their own, some suicide-minded females chose a bloodier method. Grace Myers shot herself through the breast with a .38 revolver on the night of March 9, 1897, missing her heart by a fraction of an inch. Grace chose to take her life at her place of employment, the Blue Goose Saloon. Possibly because she was drunk at the time and her aim was off, she did not accomplish her purpose. Doctors from the nearby Fort Worth Medical College got there in time to save her life, and she was expected to recover. The *Register* reported on March 11 that "she will live to shoot another day."

Still, for Grace, Clyde, Dora and many others like them, the reasons for their desperate actions are not hard to fathom. They were a product of the lives they led — hardened, cynical, old beyond their years. The *Morning Register,* perhaps trying to put the best face on things, reported with ghoulish humor in 1897 that Fort Worth's suicide rate could hardly compare to Chicago's, where the record was forty in the first twenty-five days of June "with more anticipated before the end of the month." That statistic included eight suicides in a single day.[80]

The most depressing aspect of the suicide epidemic in the Acre was not the sameness of the methods but the frequency of the occurrences. On an average of two or three times a week for more than a decade the newspapers reported a suicide or attempted suicide among the working girls of the Acre. These accounts far outnumbered reports of fights, knifings and shootings among the male denizens. After a while, they lost the ability to shock; indeed, they barely qualified as news.

Having made the decision to end their lives, most of the girls chose the drug route, possibly because it left a prettier corpse. The drugs of choice were usually morphine or laudanum or some combination of the two. Laudanum, potent and popular, was made by mixing opium in a tincture with alcohol and water. Securing the desired narcotics was no problem since in those days morphine, laudanum and others were routinely sold over the counter, often without a prescription. They retailed for as little as ten cents a shot, no questions asked. An 1878 ledger for Daggett and Hatcher's Mercantile Store lists opium and morphine right alongside the less dangerous medications like epsom salts, quinine, calomel and ipecac.[81] While pure opium could not be bought legally without a prescription, many doctors prescribed opium and its various derivatives for every unspecified "female complaint." But the girls of the Acre did not have to depend on doctors to satisfy their cravings. With no more trouble than it took to walk down the street, they could get whatever they wanted, if not from the neighborhood drugstore, then from one of the city's Chinese-run opium dens.

Not surprisingly, many of the prostitutes who worked the Acre were addicted to drugs long before they overdosed. While every girl was not an addict, one suspects that a large percentage wandered around in a perpetual fog. Drug-induced euphoria would explain much of the hurly-burly, round-the-clock commotion that the Acre was famous for in those days. In one sad but unremarkable case, Helen Harris, described as "a confirmed cocaine fiend," was found at 2:00 in the morning "loaded to the guards . . . in one of the streets in the Acre executing the sun dance over an imaginary snake, yelling as if the imps of hades were after her."[82] Police carted her off to jail. Just three months later, Lillian Sayles and Mary Prince, described as "two dusky damsels devoid of decency and devoted to deviltry," went on a similar spree at 1:30 in the morning. The *Morning Register* reported their antics the next day: "[They] decided to do a midnight war dance in the Acre, and as a sequel to their festivities will this morn tell Judge Jackson how the play came about. . . . Their wearing apparel looked as if they had been chased through a Trinity River bottom before the business end of a Texas cyclone."[83]

Fort Worth newspapers show very few drug-related incidents before about 1890. The change after that date was part of a national pattern played out in countless communities across the country. In the mid-1880s pure cocaine began to be sold in the United States over the counter, to be consumed by sniffing, smoking, injecting, rubbing, eating or mixing with alcoholic drinks. Medical opinion of the day considered it safe, non-addictive and free from bad after-effects.[84]

When William Rea was police chief he once told a newspaper reporter that of the eight prostitutes currently confined in the city jail, five were "habitual users" of cocaine. He went on to say that the average number of addicts among female prisoners would run to about the same proportion throughout the year.[85] Rea described one of the unfortunate girls in his custody who was soon to be released back on the streets: "Five years ago she was one of the handsomest girls in our city, of good character. Now she is a moral and mental wreck, made so by the use of the drug [cocaine]. The habit she contracted no one knows how."[86]

Among such girls there was no place to go but down.

• •

When Grace Myers shot herself, she was fortunate not just that her aim was off but that the Fort Worth Medical College was located nearby — right on the edge of the Acre, in fact, at Seventh and Rusk streets. Grace was just one of many Acre victims who owed their lives to the quick response of the college staff on numerous occasions between 1895 and 1903. Doctors often rushed to the scene to treat patients; at other times, when the emergency was not so great, patients were taken to the college for treatment.

The institution occupied a two-story brick building that had been the Tarrant County Courthouse from 1893 to 1894 when the courthouse moved to new quarters at Weatherford and Main. The school provided medical services and a bit of respectability to the neighborhood. The Acre provided the medical school with most of its patients "for treatment and demonstration." Cadavers, as well as more lively subjects, were a necessity for any medical school, although these could usually be secured only on a catch-as-catch-can basis.

Students sat in a large amphitheater on the first floor of the building and observed while their instructors diagnosed and treated patients, and performed autopsies on subjects who had probably been walking up and down Rusk Street just a few hours earlier. Students' dissecting rooms were on the second floor and sometimes doctors-to-be got a little "rambunctious" after long hours of learning. In the summer months when the dissecting rooms grew hot and stuffy the students would open the windows facing the intersection of Rusk and Seventh. What followed next was sworn to later by Dr. Kent Kibbie of the college, who claimed students amused themselves by tossing spare pieces of cadavers out the windows so that they landed on the street — or worse — below. This bit of tomfoolery never failed to have the desired effect of frightening unsuspecting pedestrians, "particularly Negroes."[87]

During the second year of the college's operation on Rusk Street, the newspaper reported that victims of crime or suicide attempts were usually rushed to the Fort Worth Medical College for emergency treatment.[88] When Dora Doyle attempted to take her life at her home on the corner of Thirteenth and Jones, "she was attended by students of the Medical College."[89] Although her exact occupation was not stated, Dora's description as "one more unfortunate" clearly indicated her profession to readers of the *Register*.

In 1903 the College moved to a new location at Fifth and Calhoun, farther removed from the Acre but still close enough to maintain a working relationship.

• •

If the Acre was slowly being cleaned up in the 1890s, it was less the result of improving morals than of urban renewal in action. For years, respectable citizens had decried the outward appearance of the district as much as its low moral standards. There was certainly a connection between the two. The *Gazette* noted in 1887 that "some splendid street improvement is being done in Hell's Half Acre. If the improvement could only reach to the morals of the frisky citizens of that quarter, there would indeed be reason to rejoice."[90] Among the significant improvements that year was an official decision to extend city fire protection to the district.[91] But this decision promised to preserve the eyesore rather than hurry its end.

The fact that the problem lay squarely between the uptown business district and the train station made it worse. As the *Gazette* said, "No other city in the Union would exhibit to strangers its vilest corners as an introduction. A ride up Rusk Street from the [Union] Depot makes an impression on strangers that has cost Fort Worth more than its people will ever know. If only a half-dozen of Mrs. O'Leary's cows [believed to have been the cause of the famous Chicago fire] could be turned loose in this city it would be worth millions."[92]

In spite of the Acre, the city progressively remade itself from a dusty trail town into a modern city. By the middle of the 1890s there were eighty-five miles of graded and paved streets and fifty-three miles of sewer lines. The city-owned electric light company provided much-needed street lighting on the main thoroughfares and sold electricity to private street railway companies. More than 36,000 citizens took advantage of these services or alternately complained that they were inadequate.

As urban renewal worked its magic, the south end of Fort Worth also began to put on a new face; or as the *Morning Register* put it, "The march of improvement goes steadily onward. One by one the old ramshackle buildings, that have caused the eyes of loyal Fort Worthers to weaken and have given a bad impression to visitors, are being displaced by modern brick structures."[93] In 1893 C. C. Lawson, the city's long-time restaurateur who had served Timothy Courtright his most famous meal, announced plans to build a new restaurant on Main Street between Eleventh and Twelfth. The deal he made with the former owner for $10,400 included both the lot and construction of a brick building to house his business.[94] It was a good deal for both Mr. Lawson and the Acre.

Reform of the Acre was closely tied to this public facelift. In the real estate boom of the 1890s (which saw property values rise dramatically all over the city), property in the Acre began to look more desirable to the legitimate businessman. After the Lawson deal was announced, the *Daily Gazette* reported mysteriously, "There are quite a number of other important deals pending but as they are as yet in an

Looking north on Main Street in 1906 from the tower of the Texas & Pacific depot. Looking down on sin was something the Reverend J. T. Upchurch was very good at after "more than 12 years experience in personal rescue work." This photo was part of a series of articles by Upchurch about Hell's Half Acre to appear in *The Purity Journal* in 1906. Below, latter-day cribs (about 1906) captured by Upchurch's prying camera. The times have changed since the wild and woolly days, but the basics are the same: one-room apartments, usually attached to the side or back of a big saloon. The exact location and name of the saloon are both unknown (both photos courtesy Dallas Historical Society).

incipient state it is requested not to mention them for the present."[95] Property in the Acre was undervalued because of the stigma of the district's reputation. Many of the Acre's most venerable establishments had been thrown up in the boom times of the late seventies. They were little more than shanties to begin with, never intended for permanent or for respectable occupancy, and by the mid-nineties they not only constituted an eyesore, they were a public hazard. For years those ugly ramshackle buildings with their unsavory residents had scared potential buyers off. Now they represented good investments, and real estate transactions like the following were news: "Yesterday several small frame buildings in the Third Ward were sold and will be removed to other portions of the city. It is possible that these removals are to make room for more pretentious buildings."[96] Real estate agents and prospective sellers were even using the more neutral term "Third Ward" for the district because calling it "the Acre" might remind buyers of the district's sordid past.

City officials were more than disinterested observers. Some of the town's progressive citizens suggested that instead of just tearing down the worst buildings with the prospect of the same sort of structures springing up again in their place, the local government take the lead in rebuilding the area for housing and legitimate businesses. Apart from improving the city's appearance, the ultimate benefit would come when "the population [of the Acre] retires in disorder from the field, for it flees from the refining encroachment and influence of legitimate businesses, as the traditional bat is supposed to flee from a burning building."[97] Or to quote one irate letter-writer to the *Daily Democrat*, "Nothing but brick and mortar will effectually supplant the present population."[98]

This was not entirely true. The south end of Fort Worth, that area once known as the Daggett Addition, then as the Third Ward, and now primarily as the Acre, was still a residential community if one got off the main streets. Counted among the residents were some good, moral people. Furthermore, wholesome entertainment was not totally unknown there. In the spring of 1897, residents of the Third Ward organized a baseball team for boys under sixteen, then petitioned to join the city school boys' league.[99] Such honest and well-intentioned efforts did little to change the image of the Third Ward, however. Reformers still placed their hopes in new buildings and new businesses.

The physical improvements in the Acre were best represented by the glamorous Metropolitan Hotel, which took up almost the entire block between Main and Rusk from Eighth to Ninth streets. Winfield Scott began building it in 1898 as "a first-class hostelry where even the most genteel visitors could be comfortable."[100] By the time the hotel was completed in 1905, it rose to three full stories, all in red brick. Besides the fact that it towered over every other building in the Acre, it was only a five-minute ride from the depot. Visitors getting off the train could hardly miss it. The cattle-baron-turned-hotel-builder first leased the hotel to Ella Moore, then sold it to her later. Ella and her husband John, a city alderman, were well-known as legitimate business people in the Acre, still a rare breed at this date. John ran the Standard Theater on Rusk and Twelfth streets and the Palace Hotel saloon. Mrs. Moore had operated the Palace Hotel at 1201 Main and the Atlanta House at 1114 Main before taking over the Metropolitan.

Despite its location on the wrong end of town, the Metropolitan offered such luxurious amenities as electricity, gas, steam heat and artesian baths — all for a dollar a day. Business was so good that Mrs. Moore had to take on extra help in the first two years.[101]

The urban renewal that saw respectable businesses like the Metropolitan begin to replace the old dives and shacks was also seen as an alternative to another frequently proposed remedy: moving the Acre's population to a reservation outside the heart of the city. The idea of localizing or colonizing urban vice populations became a popular one in the enlightened atmosphere of the late nineteenth century. Similar proposals were entertained in towns as divergent as Waco and New Orleans. Though it never got past the planning stages, the idea was tossed around Fort Worth for years to come. At one point city fathers went so far as to designate an area in what is now the Riverside neighborhood as a location for the proposed reservation.

On April 6, 1897, the *Morning Register* reported on the positive changes in downtown Fort Worth: "The growth of business is ever in the direction of lower Main Street." Would urban renewal succeed where reform had failed?

While activities in the Acre went on at a reduced level in the 1890s, the banner of reform was passed on. It had first been raised by the city's newspapers, then passed on to the mayor's office and the church pulpits. Now it came to rest in the city courts. The new self-proclaimed champion of urban reform was Judge J. H. Jackson of

The Metropolitan Hotel, above, part of the renaissance occuring in the Acre around the turn of the century. "The Metro is one of the leading hotels in the city," according to a 1907 advertisement. "Of modern construction, up-to-date in every particular and conducted upon the European plan . . . popular with traveling men and visitors to Fort Worth" (courtesy Mrs. Barty Duncan, Fort Worth). Below, the Fort Worth Medical College in 1903, after it moved into new quarters at Fifth and Calhoun streets, abandoning its old two-story building at Seventh and Rusk. No longer the "emergency clinic" for the Acre by this date (courtesy Mrs. Barty Duncan, Fort Worth).

the City Court who even criticized the record of his own venue (before he took over the bench, of course) for going easy on lawbreakers. He did not stop there. Jackson saved his sharpest barbs for the good citizens who sat on the juries, who heard the evidence and still failed to convict.[102] On a scale of metaphors, Judge Jackson was somewhere between a "loose cannon" and a "hanging judge." He was tough on all manner of criminals who appeared before him, but he was also so contentious and critical of the system that he alienated many of those who should have been allies, including police, fellow judges and elected officials.

Jackson's one-man campaign to make the City Court "what it really ought to be" was side-tracked at the end of May, 1897, when the Judge came down with a mysterious ailment that brought him close to death. By the middle of July, however, he had recovered and was back on the bench battling with the Fort Worth police department over how vigorously to prosecute gambling and other "petty" vices. Jackson wanted to crack down, while the police wanted to dismiss most of the pending cases for lack of evidence. The judge's specific target was the long-standing, venerable practice of fining local gamblers a monthly fee for the privilege of operating. This had been going on for so many years that there had never been an outcry against it. Fort Worth gamblers were charged under the city's vagrancy ordinance and paid a maximum $6 fine into the city coffers each month. Jackson intended to see them fined $10 "per tin horn per offense" every time they came before his bench. He took his case to the public on the front pages of the *Fort Worth Register,* defending his relationship with the city police department but denouncing the situation where "gamblers live at the sufferance of those whose duty it is to enforce the laws."[103]

The result of all the uproar was that fines in police court went up a few dollars per arrest, and the number of arrests rose briefly, but gamblers and prostitutes continued to operate as usual. Jackson discovered what all of his predecessors in city government had found in the 1870s and '80s — that any official attempt to shut down or strictly regulate the Acre was sure to be blocked by two facts: the district, with all its related business and social connections, controlled too many votes for elected officials to challenge; and it was a rich source of municipal revenue that furnished a good proportion of the city's income. Whenever the city treasury needed a boost, wholesale raids and fines could always be depended on, and Acre owners and operators accepted such practices as reasonable business expenses.

Meanwhile, more exciting events in the Acre captured the public's attention in 1897. For a few days it seemed the hands of time were turned backward to the early days when card play and gunplay went hand-in-hand. In the end, one of the Acre's last homegrown characters died. Mike Crummer was his real name, but he was better known in the Acre by the moniker "Colorado Kid." Crummer died in approved Wild West fashion, shot in a dispute over a faro game. The incident attracted quite a bit of attention in the March 24 edition of the *Fort Worth Morning Register*.

According to witnesses, Crummer had been gambling in the Old Oak Club over the Corner Saloon at Sixth and Main streets on the afternoon of March 23. Shortly after 3:00 P.M. he got into an altercation with a dealer named Charley Walker. The verbal dispute soon turned into gunplay which left the Colorado Kid fatally wounded. Walker was placed in jail but released the next day after witnesses corroborated his plea of self-defense.

The Kid lingered on his deathbed for twenty-four hours before expiring. His obituary described him as "a drifter, known all over the Southwest as a gambler . . . generally regarded as a dangerous and desperate man . . . also a 'coke fiend.'"[104] Yet Crummer's passing was not entirely unmourned. His fellow Acre gamblers collected a pot to pay for his March 25 funeral.

The Colorado Kid was an anachronism from the Acre's early days when violence over matters of cards or honor was a regular occurrence. To those who recalled former times in Hell's Half Acre, the list of arrests in the middle of the final decade of the nineteenth century must have seemed pretty tame by comparison: a wild chase by three officers and a detective trying to arrest a suspicious-looking black; a "serious cutting affray" between two men at a saloon on South Main Street; a prostitute high on cocaine arrested for discharging firearms in the city limits.

One consistent fact about law enforcement in Fort Worth was the names of the men who executed the laws. For thirty years — 1879 to 1909 — the office of city marshal or police chief belonged to just three men and rotated among them as though it were a private club. S. M. "Sam" Farmer, W. M. Rea and J. H. Maddox all held the office at different times and for more than one term. All were elected as reform candidates at one time or another, and all accommodated themselves to the criminal element in the city before their terms were up. William Rea was typical of this small fraternity. A long-time resident, he first joined the force as a patrolman in the early days under Timothy Courtright. He was eventually elected police chief three times and sheriff four times. Rea, distinguished by his full white beard and soulful eyes, looked like a cross between abolitionist John Brown and Santa Claus. He wore his five-pointed police chief's badge with pride and dignity, and his commitment to reform was genuine. Years before it was popular, he advocated a state reformatory for youthful offenders as an alternative to their being imprisoned with hardened convicts.[105] In dealing with old-time vices, however, progressive ideas made little headway against the entrenched interests in prostitution, gambling and liquor sales.

Rea, Farmer, Maddox and others like them represented only the front line in the fight against crime and vice. It was a broad campaign conducted on many fronts. Public opinion, as expressed in the newspapers, and the courts were also part of the fight. Throughout the 1890s, Fort Worth newspapers depicted a new and improved city that no longer deserved the title "Paris of the Plains." Court records upheld their partisan claims that there was indeed a healthier moral climate in the city, at least insofar as the judicial system could make it so. In the early 1890s the size of the fines which were levied by the courts against repeat offenders among the gamblers and madams began to increase. To these bigger fines were added more jail sentences and "road sentences" (assignment to county road details) before the decade was out. This had never been a part of the standard operating procedure in Fort Worth before. The county court slapped well-known gamblers Nat Kramer and Jake Johnson with $50 fines for doing business as usual in 1894.[106] On previous appearances in court, a guilty plea had brought fines of no more than $10 to $20. Kramer had already been brought down a few pegs when he was charged with betting on an election, although he got out of that one.[107] Prominent madams Porter, Reeves and Belmont were now being arrested for "vagrancy," traditionally a charge leveled only against common streetwalkers, rather than the more respectable charge of "keeping a disorderly house."[108] The biggest shock, however, must have been the addition of jail sentences to the trifling fines that were usually handed

Left, William Marian Rea in 1914, the year he retired as Sheriff of Tarrant County. He also served as police chief (three times) and deputy sheriff during his long tenure in public office beginning in 1879. Besides being one of the most popular officers in Fort Worth history, he enjoyed universal respect among his peers (courtesy Brian Perkins, Fort Worth). Right, Buckley B. Paddock, 1889 or '90, after he had become more than just the fiery newspaper editor and civic booster; he is a city father now, president of the Spring Palace and a suitable subject for one of the photographic Swartz brothers—whether John, Charles or David is unknown (courtesy Amon Carter Museum and Mrs. C. W. Hutchison, Fort Worth).

down. Nat Kramer, for instance, was given a ten-day term in 1894 for gambling. Kramer pleaded not guilty to the charge but was convicted on the evidence. He appealed, but a second jury also found him guilty.[109]

Finally, lawmakers began to enforce some of the more obscure laws on the books. More significantly, those laws were being enforced against the high and the mighty who heretofore had enjoyed virtual immunity from such official harassment. Witness what happened to Nat Kramer in 1890: he was arrested for riding in a carriage with a prostitute. The charge was based on the nearly forgotten ordinance making it a crime to be seen in public in the company of a known prostitute.[110] Luke Short in his later years also found himself in court more and more frequently for gambling and other criminal activities.[111] Luke did not live long enough to see how it would all turn out, but his fellow gamblers Kramer and Johnson were witnesses to the slow death of the Acre's Golden Age, Kramer dying in 1905 and Johnson in 1909.

As the 1890s wound to a close, the Acre seemed destined to fade into seedy obscurity if not honest respectability. Cowboys no longer hurrahed the town before tying up their horses in front of one of the Acre's drinking and gambling establishments. They also left town more quietly than in former days. Most of the visitors to the district were now transients, killing a few hours between trains, or dirt farmers hoping to kick some of the dust off their boots, or young stallions looking to kick up their heels. Most of the crimes were petty and unglamorous, like the "corpse scam" run at Union Station in March 1897. Small-time con artists, known as "sure-thing men," were content to work the trains until the police ran them out of town. The law also made it hot on card sharps like "Eat-'Em-Up-Jake," who were given the choice of leaving on the next train or being locked up, fined, and photographed for the mug book, a practice which was just coming into vogue at the end of the century.

The true desperados were all gone now — men like Timothy Courtright, Luke Short, Captain Dick Bunch and Sam Bass. They had made the Acre legendary in earlier years but now were either dead, behind bars or out of Texas. Among those who were now behind bars was a character named Texas Tom Redmond. Redmond was well-known among Fort Worth's sporting fraternity from his frequent visits to the best club rooms over the years and because he could "stack chips with the best of them."[112] When he outgrew Fort Worth he moved his base of operations to Chicago. There his career came to an end in 1890. He was convicted of murder and sentenced to life in the penitentiary. Another desperado had fallen by the wayside.

For a brief spell in 1901, however, the march of progress seemed to stop and the days of the old gunfighters returned to Fort Worth. The biggest manhunt in the nation focused on the city. The objects of all this attention were the legendary Butch Cassidy and his Wild Bunch.

Jennings Avenue, about 1905, looking north from Twelfth Street. A mixture of the old and the new is apparent: telephone lines and electric street cars side-by-side with horse-drawn buggies. The back side of St. Patrick's Church can be seen in right background. Hell's Half Acre is just three blocks to the east (right), though by this date its former glory has long since faded (courtesy Fort Worth Public Library and Amon Carter Museum).

EIGHT

The End of the Line

IF, AS THEY SAY, ONE PICTURE IS WORTH A THOUSAND words, it is not surprising that it took just one photograph to bring about the downfall of the West's most successful outlaw gang. The gang was Butch Cassidy's Wild Bunch, and the picture was taken in John Swartz' studio on the edge of Hell's Half Acre in 1900. How Cassidy's Wild Bunch and John Swartz got together makes for one of the most interesting and hotly debated episodes in the history of the West. It also provides a fitting climax to the first era of Hell's Half Acre.

The Wild Bunch was legendary both before and after their historic date with John Swartz in Fort Worth. They were the last of the great nineteenth-century outlaw gangs, the inheritors of the James-Younger and Dalton legends among western badmen. Compared to those earlier gangs, the Wild Bunch came to a less bloody and less spectacular end, but their hauls from a series of successful robberies were bigger. The Wild Bunch's status among outlaws reached mythical proportions, assuring them a place in history even before pulp fiction writers and Hollywood filmmakers got hold of them.[1] It just added to the legend that the Wild Bunch were singularly successful at what they did — robbing banks and trains and getting away scot-free.

Formed sometime in 1896 in the triangle where Wyoming, Utah and Colorado meet, the gang acquired their nickname not from their criminal activities but from their hell-raising escapades in an area known as "the Strip," just south of Fort Duchesne, Wyoming.[2] They liked to make regular forays into the Strip for a little drinking and dancing, "and no one dared to stand in their way."[3]

When the boys were not raising hell in town, they were stealing horses, rustling cattle or robbing banks and trains and managing to stay one jump ahead of the law by crossing back and forth between Wyoming and Colorado. Soon every unsolved crime in the area was laid at their doorstep. By the time they robbed the Montpelier, Idaho, bank on August 13, 1896, Robert Leroy Parker — a.k.a. George Parker, a.k.a. Butch Cassidy — had the nucleus of the gang in place. After the Montpelier job, his leadership was never challenged.

In popular legend, Cassidy's right-hand man was Harry Longabaugh, also known as the Sundance Kid. In the beginning, however, that position belonged to William Ellsworth "Elzy" Lay, according to Lula Parker Betenson, Butch's sister.[4] Lay might have remained Cassidy's top lieutenant had his outlaw career not been cut short following the attempted holdup of a train at Folsom, New Mexico, in 1898. He was captured and sent to the New Mexico state prison. Longabaugh inherited the job. Harvey Logan, or Kid Curry, another outlaw notorious even before hooking up with Cassidy, was also a member of the Wild Bunch nucleus. What is more intriguing though is that he may have been Cassidy's most trusted lieutenant, not Longabaugh as legend has it.[5]

Logan and Lay are stories unto themselves. Logan has been called the "wildest and toughest member of the Wild Bunch," and also "the executioner of the Wild Bunch."[6] Either way, he had a deadly reputation with a six-gun. He also had a nasty temper, a contempt for all laws, and a fondness for the soiled doves he picked up in sporting houses in every town the gang visited. Elzy Lay was a more shadowy character who seems not to have made much of a name for himself apart from the Wild Bunch. His reputation says he was "the educated outlaw," and some chroniclers credit him with being the true brains behind the gang.[7]

Depending on the job and their availability, a number of part-timers, including Ben Kilpatrick, Tom O'Day, Will Carver, Robert Lee, Walt Puntency, Joe Walker, Flatnose George Curry, and others of no particular distinction, dropped in and out of the gang. All were identified at the scene of one or more Wild Bunch robberies. In fact, up to fifty different men have been mentioned by various sources as being associated with the Wild Bunch at one time or another.

Undoubtedly, the two most famous members of the gang in the long view of history were Parker and Longabaugh.[8] They were as different as night and day but nonetheless hit it off from the beginning. Longabaugh was a horse thief and a train robber long before he threw in with Parker. He held up his first train in 1892 and showed himself even then to bear a charmed life. On that first job the other participants were all caught and put away for long terms; only Longabaugh managed to escape and luck stayed with him in later years after he joined the Wild Bunch.

The swarthy, fun-loving Longabaugh was an integral part of the gang for most of its history, although it was not until Hollywood aggrandized the story that he was elevated to folk-hero status and equality with Butch Cassidy. Cassidy respected him for his skill with either rifle or pistol but disapproved of Longabaugh's excessive drinking — when Longabaugh drank he tended to talk too much, and this could be fatal for an outlaw gang that was never more than one jump ahead of the law. Like the genial Cassidy, Longabaugh was not known as a killer, though some sources describe him as "the fastest gun in the West."[9] Longabaugh was fast on the draw with the ladies as well. This habit brought him more grief than his pistols, however, because he suffered from a venereal disease which frequently laid him low, a condition known as "catching cold" in whorehouse euphemism.[10] The nickname "Sundance Kid" came from a stretch he served in the Sundance, Wyoming, jail for horse stealing while still a teenager.[11]

Butch Cassidy has been called "one of only two American outlaws who were outsized legends *during* their careers."[12] He came from an unusual background for a feared robber and gunman. Butch was born in Utah and raised in a strict Mormon family, close-knit and intensely loyal to each other. At an early age he fell in with the wrong crowd, however, and quickly found rustling cows more exciting and profitable than punching cows for a living. By his twenty-fourth birthday, he had robbed his first bank in Telluride, Colorado. Following that robbery he went straight for a long spell. A streak of innate decency ran through his character, but he loved the excitement of the outlaw life too much to give it up permanently. He kept his criminal life and straight life separate. During law-abiding stretches he could be loyal to his employers and always prided himself on being a man of his word. He eschewed liquor, making him a double oddity as an outlaw prince: a man who disliked gunplay and did not drink. One other piece of the Butch Cassidy legend completes the picture of the bandit folk hero: he loved children, or at least displayed an abiding concern for their welfare, according to his sister.[13]

But the traits that have endeared him to countless historians and outlaw buffs over the years were his intelligence, his good-natured roguishness, his wry sense of humor and not the least a penchant for writing articulate and expressive letters about himself. Most western outlaws, by comparison, were dull-witted, mean-spirited and loutish. In short, Robert Leroy Parker was a likeable fellow whom anyone could call friend, and many did. His crimes tended more toward the mischievous than the brutal, though he had a long list of them to his name.

In 1894 he began serving a two-year stretch in the Wyoming state penitentiary for horse stealing. After he came out in January of 1896 he organized the Wild Bunch and turned his attentions exclusively to train and bank robbing. The gang's career lasted approximately five years, longer than almost every other outlaw group that operated during the post-Civil War train-robbing era.[14] While many gangs became highly efficient at the business of plundering express cars and passenger coaches, none brought quite the flair or proficiency to it that the Wild Bunch did. And at the center stood the inestimable Robert Leroy Parker. Although he led perhaps the most feared outlaw gang in the West, Cassidy never killed a man. Nor was he ever linked to any female companion for any length of time.

The alias "Butch Cassidy" evolved from an unlikely combination of influences and incidents in his youth. He borrowed the last name from a small-time rustler, Mike Cassidy, with whom he served his apprenticeship as an outlaw. Some years later he worked for awhile in a butcher shop in Rock Springs, Wyoming, where he picked up the nickname "Butch."[15] It was a proper outlaw's name and as an alias it brought no reproach down upon his honest, hard-working Mormon family. No one knows exactly what happened to Mike Cassidy, although there is an intriguing possibility that he may be the same Mike Cassidy who turned up in Fort Worth in the late-1880s. That Cassidy was an unscrupulous character with a mysterious past who went into the saloon business locally and then promptly began breaking every liquor ordinance on the books. He lived in Fort Worth many years with his wife and family, running a series of cheap saloons and living at a number of different addresses on the south or Hell's Half Acre end of town. Judging from court records, his criminal career in Fort Worth was limited to violations of various liquor ordinances. *If* he were the same Mike Cassidy as Butch's Utah mentor, however, he certainly would have provided a valuable friend to an outlaw on the lam when Butch and the boys came to Fort Worth at the turn of the century.[16]

Butch Cassidy ran his gang fairly but strictly as a business operation, which may be why he preferred the more businesslike moniker "Train Robbing Syndicate" to the romantic "Wild Bunch" with which the popular press tagged them. All bank and train jobs were carefully screened beforehand, and periodic "vacations" were scheduled to allow the members to relax and to let the heat die down. Among the favored vacation spots were Denver, San Antonio and, at least once, Fort Worth. The gang was always on its best behavior whenever they visited these places to avoid drawing attention to themselves, although events in Fort Worth proved to be the cause of their ultimate downfall.

On the periphery of the Wild Bunch were a coterie of tough females named Laura Bullion, Lillie Davis, Etta Place, Annie Rogers, Maud Walker and Fannie Porter.[17] Fannie Porter, a Texas madam, may have served as the entree to the gang for the other women. She is described by historian James D. Horan as "a hard, shrewd woman who made a small fortune hiding out train robbers, outlaws, horse thieves and killers for a price. She was well-known to the law but more than once she had chased an officer from her place with a broom."[18] William Pinkerton (son of the agency founder) was well acquainted with Fannie, having interviewed her in person while he was pursuing the Wild Bunch. Fannie's place in history is so closely identified with the Wild Bunch that when they broke up, she dropped out of sight although she did not change her name or occupation after they were gone.[19]

Laura Bullion, one of the girls that Fannie introduced to gang members, grew up on a farm near Knickerbocker, Texas, about twenty miles southwest of San Angelo in Rio Concho country. When she was a little girl in the 1880s, her mother once brought her to Fort Worth. Years later, she still remembered being frightened by the crowded streets.[20] On the other hand, it is doubtful if she was much frightened by the sight of men with guns. Knickerbocker at this time was a center of outlaw activity in Texas. It was home to the outlaw Ketchum family, Tom "Black Jack" Ketchum and his brother Sam. The Kilpatrick brothers, Ben and George, as well as Will Carver were frequent visitors to the area. Even Laura's father, Ed Bullion, was a notorious train robber who was killed while pulling a job at Stein's Pass, New Mexico, in December, 1897.[21] It is no wonder that little Laura wound up on the wrong side of the law as soon as she was old enough to pick her own friends. After she left home she worked as a prostitute for Fannie before becoming the common-law wife of Will Carver, a morose and surly misogynist who got his start running a gambling operation in San Angelo before he hit the "Outlaw Trail." She was only twenty-six or twenty-seven, but far from young by the standards of her profession. She used the name Della Rose on occasion, which is how she got the title "Rose of the Wild Bunch." She was also known as Clara Haye and Laura Casey.[22] Laura became "available" after Carver died in a shootout in 1901. There is a legend that Ben Kilpatrick and the Sundance Kid rolled dice for the widow, with Kilpatrick the winner, but there is little evidence to support this tale and little reason to believe it since the Sundance Kid was already hooked up with Etta Place by this time.[23] More likely, Ben Kilpatrick simply took up with the lady because she was good-looking and well-known to the gang as a trustworthy moll.[24]

Annie Rogers was another Texas girl who went bad and found herself keeping company with a member of the Wild Bunch. She met Harvey Logan while working in Fannie Porter's San Antonio establishment and did not seem to mind that another one of the girls had prior claim to him. This sort of "claim-jumping" occurred all the time in Annie's profession and was the cause of more fights among the sisterhood than money, name-calling or differences of opinion. Love blossomed almost immediately under the watchful eye of Madam Porter, who never discouraged her girls from getting romantically involved with the regular clientele. Annie saw in the diminutive gunfighter with the Groucho Marx mustache an exciting companion and a ticket out of her sullied surroundings. But like so many girls in her situation she made the mistake of thinking she could tame her outlaw. She followed him all over the West for nearly a year, hoping to settle down to a normal domestic life back in Texas. Her hopes were never realized. Eventually the law separated them when Logan was arrested in Tennessee. Annie returned sadly to Texas but wrote him touching love letters while he was in jail. She never did reform, however, and spent time in a "woman's home" in Fort Worth before escaping and heading south again.[25]

Lillie Davis, who sometimes enjoyed the company of Will Carver when he was not robbing banks and trains, hailed from Palestine, Texas. When she decided that the rural, small-town life was not to her liking, she found her way to San Antonio and entered the service of Fannie Porter. As soon as the glamour wore off she began looking for a man to rescue her from the oldest profession. She latched onto Carver as her personal ticket to respectability, admitting later that love had nothing to do with it. She claimed they were married in a festive whorehouse wedding in Fort Worth in 1900, but no record of such a marriage has ever turned up.[26] Before the year was out, he had "divorced" her and sent her home with money and gifts and one last farewell kiss.[27] The money was soon spent, the gifts all hocked and the kiss left a bitter aftertaste in her mouth. When the Pinkertons came calling in the winter of 1901, Lillie was ready to tell all she knew about the Wild Bunch: their aliases, habits, hideouts, previous jobs, everything. Her information, motivated more by jealousy than civic duty, helped provide the detectives with the first real profile of the gang that they had.

Maud Walker is the least known of the Wild Bunch's women. Like the others, she was a Fannie Porter alumna who paired up with one gang member, Harvey Logan. Her real name was Beulah Phinburg according to the loquacious Lillie Davis, and she came from St. Louis. The match-up only lasted a few weeks, just long enough for Maud and Harvey to accompany Will and Lillie on a wild honeymoon trip up to Idaho that mixed business with pleasure. Maud never succeeded in getting her outlaw to say "I do," and when he moved on, she was left with nothing.[28]

Closest to Butch and Sundance was Etta Place. Ironically, of the six women identified with the gang in Texas, only Etta could not claim deep roots in the Lone Star State. One writer calls her "truly the mystery woman of the Wild Bunch story" because there is so much romantic speculation about her but so little hard information.[29] Some sources claim she was born out of wedlock to an American mother and an English father named George Capel, alias George Ingerfield, who was himself illegitimate.[30] If true, this provides an interesting connection between Etta and the English-born Fannie Porter. It may also explain another story about her — that she was never a prostitute but served as sort of a companion and housekeeper for Fannie before running off with Butch and Sundance.

Etta was a fairly late addition to the gang's female hangers-on. She did not fit the pattern of the typical outlaw's moll, starting with her classic good looks. William Goldman, the veteran screenwriter who turned the story of Butch Cassidy and the Sundance Kid into a hugely popular movie, always swore she looked just like glamorous screen star Jeanne Crain. She certainly looked too elegant to be labelled a common whore. For Goldman the answer was simple: "To me, she had to be a schoolteacher."[31] And by some accounts, this is exactly what she was before hooking up with the Wild Bunch. Etta was also close to Fannie Porter, whether on a professional basis or purely personal, however, is uncertain.

Fannie Porter, the best-known accomplice of the Wild Bunch, always kept the welcome mat out at her house for members of the gang. Fannie's professional title was "madam" and her business establishment was described as a "sporting house," two Victorian euphemisms that confirm she was more than a common prostitute or gang follower.[32] Fannie ran a high-class bordello in San Antonio's vice district but probably visited Fort Worth on occasion. There has been considerable historical confusion over whether Fannie's house was in San Antonio or Fort Worth since both cities possessed a vice district with the name Hell's Half Acre. Surviving criminal records and additional supporting references in the Pinkerton files, however, indicate that Fannie was living in San Antonio at the time of the gang's last visit to Texas.[33]

There is also evidence, however, that at some point in her career Madam Porter was in Fort Worth. The road between San Antonio and Fort Worth was well traveled even in that day, both by persons with legitimate interests and by shady characters anxious to stay one jump ahead of the law. The Gamblers' Circuit and the Outlaw Trail ran through both towns. Fannie Porter's "Fort Worth connection" comes from Lillie Davis as told to William Pinkerton. According to Lillie, Fannie liked to sleep on fine sheets and her favorites came from "the best store in Fort Worth." Those sheets were destroyed one night when Harvey Logan came in drunk and collapsed on her bed still wearing his spurs.[34] The sheets could have been brought to Fannie from Fort Worth by Butch or some other member of the gang; they

Stately madam: Fannie Porter, probably taken in San Antonio in 1901 when William Pinkerton came to her sporting house looking for information on the Wild Bunch. The only known picture of Fannie belies the image of a "hard, shrewd" woman capable of chasing lawmen from her premises with a broom (courtesy Pinkerton's, Inc., Archives).

were certainly fond of her and magnanimous enough to bestow such a gift.

While the Wild Bunch's principal area of operation was the tri-state area of Wyoming, Utah and Colorado, all of their favorite molls lived in Texas. This line of reasoning leads to two conclusions: one is that Texas produced particularly fine molls in those days, but the second and by far the more important is that the gang spent more time in Texas than the historical record indicates. They never pulled a job in the Lone Star State, however, much to the regret of historically minded Texans today.

Under Parker's expert leadership the gang established a familiar pattern that became its signature. First, passengers on trains hit by the gang were never robbed or molested. This kindness may have sprung from a chivalric regard for their persons, as Butch Cassidy's defenders would have us believe, or it may have been because shaking down all the passengers would take too much time and delay a fast getaway; besides, the return was never worth the effort. Whatever their reasons, this practice placed them in sharp contrast to earlier train robbers like Sam Bass and his gang who concentrated most of their attentions on shaking down the passengers when they were on the rampage in the mid-1870s. Second, when persuasion did not secure what they came for, the Wild Bunch resorted to dynamite to open express cars and the heavy iron safes inside. Most train crews readily cooperated when faced with a charge of dynamite attached to a short fuse. Cassidy may even have been the gang's explosives expert, underscoring his crucial leadership role. Third, the Wild Bunch always made their getaway on relays of fresh horses stationed in advance on the escape route, allowing the robbers to outdistance their pursuers easily. Western historian Jim Dullenty calls this practice, "probably Cassidy's greatest contribution to outlawry."[35]

By 1900 a variety of law enforcement officers and private agencies were after the Wild Bunch, including the Pinkertons, Wells Fargo, Union Pacific railroad detectives, and U.S. marshals. In the days before the FBI and the Federal Marshals Service, the Pinkerton Detective Agency, with headquarters in New York City and Chicago, provided the only national organization that investigated and aggressively pursued criminals across state borders. After the Wilcox, Wyoming, train robbery on June 2, 1899, the Union Pacific Railroad brought in the Pinkertons to help catch the thieves. The head of the agency's Denver office, James McParland, was in charge of the manhunt until William Pinkerton came down from Chicago to take personal charge.[36]

Among those most determined to end the Wild Bunch's career was Wells Fargo and Company, often described as the era's most powerful private institution west of the Mississippi River. Wells Fargo operated a vast network of express lines and banks all across the West, some of which had been victimized by Cassidy. The company also maintained its own highly efficient investigative arm. One of its most famous detectives, Fred Dodge, was assigned to run down Butch Cassidy and his gang after the Tipton, Wyoming, train robbery of August 29, 1900. With lawmen closing in on the usual hideouts — Brown's Hole, Wyoming, and Robber's Roost, Utah — a new haunt had to be found, at least until some of the heat was off the old places.

Members of the gang came to Fort Worth in late September or early October, 1900, on the run following their latest job, a holdup of the First National Bank of Winnemucca, Nevada, on September 19. Four members are believed to have participated in this particular robbery: Butch, Sundance, Will Carver and Harvey Logan, although only the first three were definitely placed at the scene of the crime by eyewitnesses.[37] Logan, it seems, did not actually enter the bank but stayed outside on the street as a lookout. His presence was later presumed by law officers because posses reported four men on the run and Logan was a well-known confederate of the other three. Will Carver was supposed to be on his honeymoon at this time, but he and Logan had stashed Lillie Davis and Maud Walker in a Denver hotel before joining up with the others.

The actual holdup came off without a hitch, but trouble had already come from an unexpected source as they rode into Winnemucca. Carver tangled with a skunk that refused to yield the right of way. As Cassidy's sister later told it, "the skunk fired first." The lingering effects of the one-sided duel got the bank employees' attention more than the guns that the outlaws brandished.[38] The gang on this occasion decided to dispense with the masks they had always worn when robbing trains and in previous bank holdups. That careless decision later allowed authorities to identify them by the descriptions bank employees provided.

The robbers galloped out of town with a sheriff's posse hot on their trail. Posses from neighboring communities soon joined in the manhunt. They headed northeast toward Idaho, taking a trail that led them through Soldier's Pass and the Clover Valley. At Clover Valley they switched to fresh horses. One of the animals they left behind was a beautiful white horse that Cassidy particularly liked.[39] The four men outdistanced their pursuers, then apparently turned and headed south toward Texas. They were a thousand miles from Fort Worth at that point.

When news of this latest robbery spread, Pinkerton agents joined in the search. As the manhunt expanded across several states, most law agencies had to rely on unverified reports that it *was* the Wild Bunch they were looking for. Details about how many robbers there were, their identities and physical descriptions, remained vague and sometimes conflicting in early reports. Three months after the Winnemucca robbery the identity of all the robbers had still not been clearly established. Not until January, 1901, was Cassidy a serious suspect, and not until February was his picture put on a wanted poster by the Pinkerton's Chicago office.[40] Doubts continued to be expressed about Cassidy's participation, but the Pinkertons expanded their hunt to include him and his companions.[41] Eight months after the robbery, the first wanted posters were circulated that named Will Carver and Harvey Logan as suspects. They came out of the Denver office and were chiefly notable for the outdated description of Carver as "smelling like a polecat."[42] The reward on Carver eventually reached $5000 and carried the ominous notation "dead or alive."[43] In the meantime, the Pinkertons had furnished every bank in the country with a list of serial numbers on the stolen bank notes.

The loot from the First National Bank of Winnemucca totaled somewhere between $29,000 and $33,000 in gold and bank notes. The bank notes were unsigned, but this minor problem was soon solved with ink pens and a little unlicensed autographing. Somewhere on the road south, the gang divided up the gold and currency, then split up. They would rendezvous in Fort Worth. Will Carver and Harvey Logan stopped in Denver just long enough to pick up their girls — Lillie and Maud — whom they had left there with spending money but no explanation a week earlier. The girls' irritation at being abandoned for that length of time may have been considerably mollified by the sight of "six or seven sacks full of twenty dollar gold pieces . . . and a big pile of paper money." From Denver, the two outlaws and their ladies took the Fort Worth & Denver City train to Fort Worth.[44]

The route Cassidy and Longabaugh took is uncertain, but somehow the four robbers wound up in Cowtown at the same time and made contact with each other. Here also they were joined by Ben Kilpatrick, who may have come up from San Antonio, where he liked to divide his time equally between the local bars and fleshpots. The beeline they took to Fort Worth and the ease with which they melted into the local population probably indicates that they had been in town before. If so, there are no first-hand descriptions of earlier visits, just vague references in secondary works, one of which claims that Butch and Sundance at least had been guests on more than one occasion at the Market Hotel at Twelfth and Calhoun streets.[45] One thing is certain: the gang was on the run after they left Winnemucca but hardly in an aimless or panicked fashion. Cassidy always planned every detail of a job, including the hideout. Fort Worth was far to the south of their usual operating area, and they never maintained a regular hideout here, but the city was a well-known stop on the Outlaw Trail where the forces of law and order were not too inquisitive about strangers, and it was on the way to Fannie Porter's place in San Antonio as well. These two reasons alone may have been sufficient to bring Butch Cassidy and company to the city on the Trinity River that fall.

Alternative explanations are just as speculative, including the possibility that it was the Texas connection between the Wild Bunch and their female followers that brought them to Fort Worth. Having run from their pursuers for a thousand miles, they may have just "run out of gas" when they reached Fort Worth, or perhaps they felt it was time to stop and enjoy some of their ill-gotten loot. The fact that they stopped and settled down for a spell leads one to believe that some of their women were with them.

Having arrived in Fort Worth, the five outlaws were in no hurry to leave. Here, hundreds of miles from the scene of the crime, they felt safe enough to walk down the street in broad daylight, sleep in real beds, even take off their guns. For a while they were safe as sheriff's posses, railroad detectives, Wells Fargo and Pinkerton men scoured their usual haunts in Utah, Nevada and Wyoming.

Just where they hid out is another one of those interminable questions about their visit. Respected historian and outlaw authority Eugene Cunningham says they lived at the Randall Apartments, at least "for a time," but provides no source for this statement. Furthermore, the list of boarding-house proprietors in Fort Worth in 1900 does not include anyone by this name.[46] Fortunately, Harvey Logan provides a clue. Logan told a *Knoxville Sentinel* reporter in 1903 that "we rented an apartment and were living in style."[47] This statement concurs with a published account by historian James D. Horan that they stayed in a boarding house known as Maddox Flats. The 1901 *Fort Worth City Directory* lists a Maddox Flats in the heart of the Acre at 1014½ Main Street, the "½" indicating an upstairs address over a private residence or possibly a business.

The proprietor of the apartment house was Mrs. Elizabeth Maddox, also described as "Lizzie," who lived on the premises. In his jailhouse interviews in Tennessee, Logan described the proprietor as "an old Negro woman," but the census records for 1900 show that Elizabeth Maddox and her husband K. C. were both white. Logan may have been remembering either a cleaning lady or a landlady as opposed to the proprietor when he told his story. Anyone who broke the law as frequently and as casually as Logan did, however, would not have worried much about the strict historical accuracy of his recollections.

Although the gang spent at least two months in Fort Worth, no one seemed to notice them. This may be explained in part because none of the local newspapers in Dallas or Fort Worth ran an account of the Winnemucca robbery, even though the Wild Bunch was notorious by this time. The local papers tended to report only big train robberies, not bank robberies, in their national news columns largely because of the influence of the great railroad and express companies with their vast networks of local offices. It was news when the Union Pacific was robbed. Bank robberies, even when they were "national banks," seldom made national news unless they were spectacularly bloody affairs like the James-Younger raid on Northfield, Minnesota, or the Dalton raid on Coffeyville, Kansas. The Winnemucca job did not qualify as either spectacular or bloody, although in the amount of money taken it was one of the largest robberies in the history of the West.[48] Local newspapers in the fall of 1900 were full of news about the coming of Buffalo Bill's Wild West Show, about the deadly hurricane that struck Galveston in September, and about the presidential election coming up in November. The Wild Bunch was not front-page copy and local news of a more mundane nature filled the back pages, which is probably the way Butch preferred it.

Perhaps posing as North Texas cattlemen who had sold their

herds and were celebrating their good fortune, they made the usual rounds of saloons, sporting houses and gambling parlors, being careful to stay out of trouble with the local authorities.[49] Hell's Half Acre was an easy place to get lost in, and the Wild Bunch was not wanted for any crimes locally. As long they behaved they were not likely to attract attention.

Buffalo Bill's Wild West Show arrived in town on October 10 and stayed just long enough to put on two performances. Judging from the newspaper coverage, it was the biggest event of the year. According to the *Fort Worth Register,* by October 10 "there were many strangers in town," so it was easy for five more strangers on the run from the law to get lost in the crowd. It is even likely that some of the boys attended the show. More than 11,000 others did.[50]

With time weighing heavily on their hands, the gang went on a buying spree, purchasing all new clothes for themselves. Harvey Logan also began spending his time in the Acre bars, getting drunk and gambling.[51] At some point, he and Will Carver tired of the company of Lillie Davis and Maud Walker and sent them packing. Lillie went home to Palestine, Texas, but did not soon forget how Logan had jilted her.

After more than two months in town, the boys must have gotten restless for new adventures. This is the only way to explain what happened next. Letting their natural caution slip, they decided to have their picture taken in a group, sort of a "family portrait" of the Wild Bunch. The decision was not unanimous; Harvey Logan for one counseled against it.[52] But the others overruled him. What harm was there in a little group picture? Logan knew the answer to that one: boyish high spirits or just plain carelessness had ended the careers of many outlaws.

The reckless decision to have the photograph made is a curious one that many have attempted to explain. According to one account, in the course of a "friendly scuffle," the boys succeeded in totally destroying each other's hats. There was nothing to do but adjourn to a hat store to purchase new ones. Somebody tried on a derby as a joke, then someone suggested that they all buy "iron hats" (or derbies) and get their picture taken.[53] It has also been suggested that they just collectively succumbed to a whim to pose for posterity's sake. As Cassidy allegedly recalled the moment, "We were passing the place [Swartz's] and thought it would be a good joke to have our pictures taken."[54] A third explanation, offered here for the first time, points the finger at Harry Longabaugh. Sundance was a notoriously fancy dresser who, according to his biographer, was the only member of the Wild Bunch to own monogrammed shirts.[55] He enjoyed dressing up, and it may well be that the idea of putting on the dog and having a portrait made came from Longabaugh. Whatever the case, they were soon posed in front of a false backdrop, the resulting effect being that of a cozy Victorian family portrait.

The five men sat for the now-famous group photo in the Fort Worth studio of John Swartz. The photographer was a well-known local figure, having come to Fort Worth from Fort Griffin, Texas, where he was proprietor of the Planter's Hotel in 1878.[56] He belonged to a family of professional photographers who owned studios in Fort Worth and other Texas cities for the better part of forty years, from the mid-1880s through the second decade of the twentieth century. There were three brothers, John, Charles and David. All worked in the business, sometimes in partnership and sometimes alone. The trio had photographed Fort Worth and its citizens for years, achieving a reputation as the city's premier photographers. Although they were not the only professional photographers in the city in 1900, they could point with pride to fifteen years of experience. John and David were working as partners in 1888 and 1889 when they took the official pictures of the Spring Palace, as well as life-sized photos of Texas' largest pumpkins at the same 1889 exposition.

As a professional photographer, therefore, John Swartz could honestly claim that he had experience in dealing with historical and larger-than-life subjects before he met the Wild Bunch. In 1900 his business, the Swartz View Company, was at 705 Main Street with the studio upstairs over the gallery. Since it was only a short walk from Maddox Flats, the boys must have strolled past it many times before they came calling as customers.

John was no stranger to what might be called "criminal photography," or photography of the notorious. In 1885, after the murder trial of J. T. Stevens, the defendant, the jury and the deputy in charge all trooped down to the Swartz brothers' studio and had their picture taken together, "the prisoner in the center."[57] Fifteen years had passed since then, and John Swartz had gone out on his own. Now he was preparing to take the most important picture of his life. He did not recognize the five nattily dressed men as locals, but he may have

The legendary portrait by John Swartz (above) that brought the curtain down on the West's last outlaw gang. Striped suits and derby hats were not standard apparel for western badmen. Sitting (left to right) Harry Longabaugh, Ben Kilpatrick, Butch Cassidy; standing (left to right) Will Carver, Harvey Logan, alias Kid Curry. Annie Rogers and Harvey Logan (right) in a wedding-like portrait with the proud bride and a reluctant gentleman looking uncomfortable in his store-bought clothes. There is no record of Annie and Harvey ever being married, however; Harvey was too fickle and too footloose. This photograph probably taken in John Swartz's Fort Worth studio (both photos courtesy Jim Dullenty of Hamilton, Montana).

suspected that this was no ordinary photo session because afterward he proudly placed a large copy of the picture in the front window of his gallery where it could be seen by all passers-by. The boys liked the photograph so much, they placed an order for fifty prints, telling Swartz they would be back to pick them up.[58] This compounded their original folly.

If they had been willing to settle for a cheap, albeit inferior quality, tintype, they could have paid Mr. Swartz and left with their portrait a few minutes after it was taken. But this was a special occasion and they wanted one of the high-class studio photographs done with the newer dry-plate process. Naturally, cost was no object for the high-living bank robbers. The result, however, was that they had to wait until the next day to pick up their photographs, and the dry-plate process which allowed innumerable copies to be made, also allowed the photographer to keep the negative, put a copy of the photo in his window and later make additional copies for law officers.

The Wild Bunch continued to hang around Fort Worth after the famous photo session, spending their loot from the Winnemucca bank and mapping out future plans. Their latest consort was Annie Rogers, Harvey Logan's new girlfriend. Logan and Rogers made another visit to Swartz' Studio to pose for the camera as a respectable pair of strait-laced lovers.[59]

Annie and Harvey, like Etta and Sundance, were probably common-law husband and wife, with Fannie Porter getting the credit as matchmaker for both couples. As far as is known neither couple ever tied the matrimonial knot legally, but the picture of Harvey and Annie in their Sunday best bears more than a passing resemblance to a typical studio wedding portrait. One thing this picture proves, along with a slightly later photo of Etta and Sundance taken in De Young's New York studio, is that the Wild Bunch members certainly had good taste in women. Both Etta and Annie are beauties by the standards of any era.

It is probable that the recklessness of having their photo taken would never have backfired if they had not started passing forged bank notes from the Winnemucca job. The notes could be identified easily by an alert bank teller or by Fort Worth police. It would not take too long to bring the Pinkerton and Wells Fargo detectives down on them once word of their whereabouts got out. Cassidy may have had a premonition that the law was closing in. According to his sister's memoirs, he realized his time was running out and planned to use his share of the money from recent jobs to skip the country.[60] It was accepted that wherever he went, the Sundance Kid would also go since they were a pair. With Etta Place added in, they became the "little family of three" that Butch refers to in a later letter.[61]

About this time Cassidy announced to the group his decision to break up the gang and head off to South America. Why South America? It was not such a strange choice for a notorious outlaw hoping to start over, and it was certainly less strange than his first choice — Australia.[62] There was some precedent from an earlier outlaw pair, Timothy Courtright and Jim McIntire, who had, according to reports, spent some time "south of the border" while on the lam from the law in the mid-1880s.[63] The principal appeal of South America was that "the frontier was still bigger than the law and there were no Pinkerton detectives."[64] Or as Cassidy himself explained it in a letter to friends in Utah, "The U.S. was to [sic] small for me. The last two years I was there, I was restless, I wanted to see more of the world. I had seen all of the U.S. that I thought was good. . . ."[65] Cassidy's nature was such that no town or territory could satisfy him for long. He craved adventure, and he liked to stay on the move. Sooner or later, even when the law was not after him, the wanderlust in him started rising and he was off to new places.

On another mischievous whim while in Fort Worth, Butch sent a collection of pictures to a young boy in Winnemucca, Nevada, whom the gang had befriended when they were casing the First National Bank there. Ten-year-old Vic Button did not know he was running errands for wanted outlaws until after they held up the bank. He rode off with them for a way, and as a gesture of thanks Cassidy gave Vic his favorite white horse when they changed mounts at Clover Valley. The boy had admired the horse ever since he first saw it, and Cassidy had grown quite fond of young Button. The boy's gratitude for the outlaw's gift knew no bounds; in his eyes, Cassidy became a western Robin Hood when he finally found out the outlaw's true identity.

Now Butch decided to send him some pictures, among them the group photo taken at Swartz' Studio. The only one that interested young Vic, however, was a view of Butch posed with an Indian chief. Vic saved this one and put the rest away in a trunk where they remained forgotten for years. In 1914, Vic Button, then a grown man, took them out and gave them to the sheriff of Humboldt County as a memento of the Wild Bunch's famous visit to Winnemucca. The group picture wound up on the wall of the First National Bank of Winnemucca, where it still hangs today, although the bank has been renamed the First Interstate Bank of Nevada.[66] Other stories that Butch himself sent the famous photograph back to the bank as a wry expression of thanks are pure fancy, the stuff of legends.[67]

The picture which Butch sent Vic Button was not the proximate cause of the gang's downfall, although Cassidy's lack of prudence in mailing it across country was almost as remarkable as having posed for it in the first place. The picture that did cause the downfall of the gang and forced them to make a hasty departure from Fort Worth was the copy that John Swartz displayed in his gallery window. But for that photo, the boys might have stayed in Fort Worth indefinitely. Their idyllic vacation, however, was cut short. When Mr. Swartz placed the photograph of the Wild Bunch in his show window, he set in motion a chain of events that did not end until all the gang members were either dead or out of the country.

Once again, there are conflicting accounts of just how the photo led lawmen to them. Credit belongs to either a passing Pinkerton detective or Wells Fargo agent; different sources credit one or the other for breaking the case wide open. Both agencies had been tracking the gang for a long time, and when one of their operatives saw the photo in the window he was able to identify at least some of the outlaws. Some historians credit Fred Dodge, famed Wells Fargo detective, with the discovery.[68] Wells Fargo maintained an office in Fort Worth for many years — in 1900 that office was at 817 Main Street, and the agent was Nicholas J. McGinnis. McGinnis did not conduct criminal investigations, however. That job was left to roving detectives like Fred Dodge. Dodge may have spotted the gang just as they were emerging from the studio after having their picture taken, or he may have spotted the picture some time later after it had been placed on display. Either way, he might have recognized Will Carver and hurriedly notified both his superiors and the Fort Worth police. The resulting investigation turned up no robbers, but it did turn up some of the loot from the Winnemucca bank job, which was enough to focus the vast manhunt on Fort Worth. Long before the law enforcement officers and private detectives could descend on the city en masse, however, the objects of their search had cleared out.

Other historians credit Pinkerton company detectives with the discovery, and first-hand testimony about the affair provides a strong link. In his jailhouse interviews, Harvey Logan told the reporter how the gang happened to leave Fort Worth in a big hurry: "One day one of us saw a Pinkerton detective on the street and in thirty minutes the apartment was empty." Logan said the old black woman in charge of the apartment did not know when they went, "but found [a copy of] the picture for the Pinkerton men."[69] One can only assume the gang members must have been in a big hurry to clear out if they left such incriminating evidence behind. From this point the Pinkertons took the lead in putting the Wild Bunch out of business once and for all. They assigned their best operatives to the case, pursued all leads and spared no expense to run the gang to ground. Twenty years earlier, the agency had lost out to the Texas Rangers in bringing Sam Bass and his confederates to justice, and they seemed determined not to let that happen again. Even William Pinkerton himself left his office in Chicago and took to the field.[70]

The first "Wanted" poster bearing a reproduction of the famous photograph was distributed by the Pinkertons' Denver office on May 15, 1901. Ultimately, 15,000 of the circulars were spread across the country from Pinkerton headquarters in Chicago and proved crucial in capturing the outlaws. Part of the delay in getting the posters out came from the problem of identifying all five men. Carver and Logan were well known to authorities, but the others — Kilpatrick, Cassidy and Longabaugh — were not.[71]

From Fort Worth, the gang split up, spreading out across Texas. At least three members high-tailed it directly to San Antonio and the safety of Fannie Porter's: Carver, Logan and Kilpatrick celebrated Christmas 1900 there before moving on to San Angelo and then Knickerbocker, Texas. They adopted the well-worn disguise of horse buyers, but it is doubtful if they fooled too many people, particularly if, as reported, they tried to use the preposterous line that they were "buying polo ponies for an outfit in Iowa."[72] Meanwhile, Butch and Sundance, probably accompanied by Etta, took off in a different direction.

It is doubtful that the Wild Bunch ever saw Fort Worth again. Historian James Horan claims that Butch, Sundance and Etta Place boarded a ship in New York City on February 20, 1901, that took them to South America.[73] While the timing of their departure is disputed, there is no doubt that the three eventually wound up in South America where they soon resumed their criminal career. Stealing other people's money and thumbing their noses at the law seemed to be ingrained in the two men, and Etta was content to tag along wherever they went.

Until recently, most authorities agreed that Butch and Sundance met their end in South America, shot down by Bolivian soldiers. But there have always been doubters who maintain that the legendary robbers did not really go out in a hail of bullets but slipped back into the United States after a few years and lived out the rest of their lives in peaceful obscurity out West somewhere.[74] One legend about Cassidy includes his return to Fort Worth. According to an elderly Mormon man, who claimed to have met Butch when he was a boy, the reformed outlaw once "worked for his father in Fort Worth as a traveling salesman."[75] This apocryphal story does not include the father's name nor when it is supposed to have occurred. It would have to have been before 1937 when by all accounts Butch finally passed from the scene once and for all. This story would also fit another part of the Butch Cassidy legend that says in later years he was hit hard by the Great Depression and forced to make money by "working at odd jobs and by *peddling* the . . . various inventions" of a close friend.[76] However, the same source says that Butch lived out his later years in the Northwest. If he visited Fort Worth as a traveling salesman or "peddler" he certainly had a large territory. The Mormon account is another odd-fitting part in the intriguing puzzle.

Even more intriguing is the story that there is a rock in an abandoned "potter's field" somewhere west of Fort Worth with the name "R. L. Parker" carved on it.[77] The possibility that this might be *the* Robert Leroy Parker, better known as Butch Cassidy, does not square with family stories or independent reports that Butch died in Spokane, Washington, his burial place known only to a few tight-lipped family members.[78]

There is even less historical consensus, if that is possible, regarding the ultimate fate of Etta Place, the third member of the outlaw trio who eluded the grasp of every Pinkerton agent, U.S. marshal and sheriff's posse in the United States. Her claim to being the mystery woman of the Wild Bunch is only enhanced by questions about her fate after she reached South America.[79] It seems clear that both Butch and Sundance regarded her quite fondly, although the exact nature of their three-way relationship is unknown. Was she an accomplice who could shoot and ride like a man and rode with the gang on more than one occasion? Was she just a friend and companion who cared for Sundance during his frequent bouts with venereal disease? Was she actually Harry Longabaugh's cousin? All of these theories have been suggested with varying degrees of credibility.[80]

Butch probably recognized her for what she was, if we are to believe words credited to him by one source. The story goes that he once told an acquaintance during their stay in South America, "She was the best housekeeper on the Pampas, but she was a whore at heart."[81]

As a subject for biography, Etta Place lived the sort of life that encourages writers to make up their own endings. She may have died an unknown death in South America with Butch and Sundance. Most so-called authorities believe she returned to the United States, with or without Sundance — take your choice — around 1907. According to these writers, she was suffering from "acute appendicitis" (some say venereal disease, some even claim pregnancy) that was operated on successfully in Denver; some say in New York City. There are no medical records in either place to prove it. Thereafter, she lived out her life in quiet solitude as a prostitute or a schoolteacher, in Denver or in Marion, Oregon, or in some other western city. Recent research has led some historians to believe she married and moved to Paraguay where she raised children and later died.[82] If the latter is true, it would complete the South American connection for the gang: Argentina, Bolivia, Paraguay.

The most absorbing legend about Etta Place has her dying in Fort Worth many years later, the victim of a fire in a run-down boarding house that she owned and operated under the alias Eunice Gray.[83]

The violent adventures of the other members of the Wild Bunch after they fled Fort Worth are easier to trace. Harvey Logan (alias Kid Curry) was arrested at Knoxville, Tennessee, in 1901, for shooting two local policemen. He was tried, however, for train robbery, convicted and sentenced to twenty years at hard labor in the federal penitentiary in Illinois. Before he could be transferred, he pulled a daring escape from the Knox County jail and headed west again. The Pinkertons traced him to Colorado where he, or someone who looked just like him, was killed in 1904 trying to rob a train. The Pinkertons closed the case at that point, but three years later reopened it when Logan was reported in South America with Butch and Sundance. Although the exact date and location are still debated, there is no doubt that Logan met his end still on the run from justice.[84]

Will Carver was shot down by Sheriff E. S. Bryant while resisting arrest in Sonora, Texas, on April 2, 1901.[85] Ben Kilpatrick and his current inamorata Laura Bullion were arrested in St. Louis in 1901 for passing forged bank notes. The St. Louis police had a hard time identifying the two and finally had to send Kilpatrick to jail under his alias "John Arnold." Laura proved more cooperative and told Chief of Detectives William Desmond her story, including the fact that she had been Will Carver's girlfriend and that she had met Kilpatrick in Fort Worth. When the St. Louis newspaper reported her story, they erroneously referred to the tall Texan as "Harry Longabaugh," thus compounding the confusion.[86] The courts sentenced Kilpatrick/Arnold/Longabaugh to prison for fifteen years; Bullion got five years. Neither served a full sentence. When Kilpatrick got out in 1912, he immediately resumed his outlaw ways. He tried to hold up a train at Sanderson, Texas, but he must have gotten soft during his stay in prison. The express messenger was able to distract his attention, then hit him over the head with an ice mallet, killing him instantly.

One might conclude from all this that the Wild Bunch collectively was greater than the sum of its parts. One might also conclude that without the steadying hand of Butch Cassidy to direct the gang's activities, the individual members' careless habits made them easy targets for the law. The short and unsuccessful careers of the Wild Bunch members after Butch Cassidy deserted them for South America is the best argument for his natural leadership abilities.

It is unfortunate that Fort Worth could never adopt Butch and Sundance as genuine hometown heroes, but the primary evidence for their connection to the city is too scanty. The popular legend is much bigger than the facts warrant. This is not to diminish Fort Worth's place in the life and legend of the Wild Bunch, however. Fort Worth can still claim that the city was the last time and place that the principal members of the outlaw gang were all together. The events of 1901 provide a fitting end to the heyday of Hell's Half Acre and close out the frontier era in the city's history.

• •

How much had the Acre changed over its twenty-five years? The following reminiscence by an old-timer, told many years after an 1899 visit, paints a picture of a considerably tamer Acre than legend has it.

> In October 1899 I unintentionally spent three weeks in what was known as Hell's Half Acre. We drove into Fort Worth after dark and were directed to a hotel. It was somewhere near the old Union Station. Seemed nice.
>
> There were a lot of trainmen and wives living there. I could look from my upstairs window on to some small cottages where women were gossiping and gloating over roses they had received.
>
> At nights I'd see big, black, horse-drawn carriages stop at the doors. Finely dressed men wearing stovepipe hats would go inside. Sometimes the carriages waited.
>
> We contacted a friend who lived in Fort Worth and she told us where we were and gave us the cold shoulder.[87]

That a man could stay in the Acre for three weeks without realizing what sort of neighborhood he was in says something about his powers of observation. It also says a great deal about how much the Acre had changed over the years. It may not have improved much, but it had changed.

Some of the people associated with Hell's Half Acre in its earlier years had also changed with the passage of time. In 1901, Joe P. Witcher, a member of the original police force in the 1870s and an occasional defendant in the city courts in later years, became captain of the police department. Witcher represented the frontier era when a lawman could wear a badge and still be on a first-name basis with gamblers and madams, yet crack some heads when the situation demanded. But by 1901 the city was more than willing to forgive and forget Joe's past indiscretions and elect him to the city's highest law enforcement office. Their faith was well placed for he served ably for a number of years before retiring with honors.

The case of Jessie Reeves also demonstrates that people as well as neighborhoods can change. After years as a well-known Acre madam, she was walking down Dauphin Street one day when she heard someone singing hymns through an open doorway. She entered and met a gospel minister named Burr to whom she unburdened her soul. He

The mysterious Etta Place posed with Harry Longabaugh at DeYoung's Studio in New York City, February, 1901, shortly before they left for South America. William Pinkerton called her "Mrs. Kid Longbaugh [sic] of the Wild Bunch." Others have called her an exact look-alike for Hollywood actress Jeanne Crain, who has been described as "the sexiest woman in the movies" in the 1940s and '50s (courtesy Jim Dullenty, Hamilton, Montana). Above, Jeanne Crain, a studio publicity photo (courtesy Eddie Brandt, North Hollywood, California).

Advertisement for Charles L. Swartz's rival photographic studio, after he and brother John went their separate ways. Their studios were just one block apart on Main and Houston streets (courtesy Tarrant County Historical Commission and Amon Carter Museum).

helped her turn over a new leaf and eventually leave the city to start a new life back east. In 1900 her name was back in the newspapers, but this time as a writer for *Rescue and Mission Work*, published in New York City and distributed all over the country. Her story was so inspiring and her name so well-known that it was reprinted in both Fort Worth and Dallas newspapers.[88]

When the Wild Bunch said their final farewells to Hell's Half Acre, it was not dead, just somnolent. Last rites would not take place until 1919. But it was surely fading fast. In the same year that Butch, Sundance and Etta sailed for South America, local newspapers reported that the gambling houses were all shut down, and "there is a general impression that the closing will be permanent."[89] The Progressive Era, which coincided with the first two decades of the twentieth century, brought a new nationwide commitment, both public and private, to the cause of reform. Anti-vice crusades were eagerly launched in major cities from New York to San Francisco in 1901.

And in the same Fort Worth courts where judges and juries used to wink at the goings-on in the Acre back in the days when the city's economy depended on the cowboys' good will, a new morality appropriate to the new century now seemed in vogue. If one case symbolized the change, it was that of Mrs. Mattie Black, who won a $5000 law suit against Mr. Frank DeBuque, manager of the Standard Theater and Bar at the corner of Rusk and Twelfth streets. DeBuque had come to Fort Worth in 1897 and had taken over the Standard Theater that same year. He soon had business booming, due at least in part to the preferential treatment he gave the city's young bloods. These untamed sons of some of Fort Worth's best families had their own special side entrance and were allowed to run up tabs at the bar.

DeBuque always claimed, then and later, that he ran one of the nicer places in town, "there being no smoking allowed among women, no drinks sold to those already intoxicated, no bare anatomies exposed on stage, and no swearing, profane language allowed, or coarse vulgarities."[90] These same house rules would have been sufficient in earlier years to win public commendation for DeBuque. But Mrs. Black charged him with serving four drinks to her underage son on Christmas Eve, 1898, and a jury of Fort Worth citizens agreed.[91] It was not so much the conviction as the size of the award that got the attention of the other theater and saloon operators in the city. The cost of doing business was finally becoming prohibitive.

If conclusive evidence is needed that the Acre was not what it used to be, Fort Worth police records provide it: There was only one murder in the entire city during the twelve-month period ending on March 21, 1901. Fort Worth's days as "the Paris of the Plains" were history.

NINE

Epilogue

HELL'S HALF ACRE DID NOT REALLY DIE IN 1900 OR 1901, though it no longer found its way onto the front pages of the newspapers the way it once had. The fact that Hell's Half Acre did not conveniently go away should not be too surprising. The real world never works that way; it has neatly wrapped eras and endings only in history books. This truism is reflected in the old adage that "reform is a process, not an act." Hell's Half Acre proved the truth of that adage by lingering through World War I, defying the best efforts of twentieth-century reformers just as it had nineteenth-century reformers. The intimate association between the Acre and certain prominent citizens continued during these years. As late as 1911, the First Baptist Church board approved a statement in the minutes that no member be retained on the church rolls "who has any interest, directly or indirectly, in a disorderly house of any kind or class."[1]

Among the reformers defeated by the Acre after 1900 were County Attorney Jeff McLean, who was gunned down in broad daylight by an Acre gambler in 1906; and J. T. Upchurch, who was head of the Baracha Home for Unwed Mothers and published the first photographs of the Acre in his *Purity Journal*. It finally took the combined efforts of an odd pair of allies to bring about what newspaper editors, marshals, mayors and judges had been unable to effect over more than four decades. The odd couple who joined forces to defeat the Acre were a Baptist preacher and the U.S. Army.

The preacher, J. Frank Norris, arrived in Fort Worth in 1909 as the pulpit minister of the First Baptist Church. His reputation as a reformer and a flamboyant sermonizer had preceded him, but it was only after three relatively quiet years in the Fort Worth vineyard that he broke loose and declared war on Hell's Half Acre. Five years later the army came to Fort Worth in force for the first time since Major Ripley Arnold had established a small outpost on the Trinity River some sixty-eight years earlier. The Army set up a training camp on the outskirts of west Fort Worth and called it Camp Bowie. In 1849 Major Arnold's principal enemies had been the Indians who preyed on the settlers. In 1917, the Army had to deal with a different type of enemy: the prostitutes and saloon keepers who preyed on young recruits. Determined to keep the boy soldiers who came to Camp Bowie pure in body, mind and spirit, the Army declared war on Hell's Half Acre. The combined attacks of religious fundamentalists and government prosecutors were more than the Acre could resist. The final battle, with the Preacher and the Army on one side and the Acre's never-say-die denizens on the other, is a fascinating story, but one that deserves a separate telling.

Between 1900 and World War I the Acre still had enough life left in it to raise an occasional tempest. The assassination of Jeff McLean — for there is no other word to describe it — was the most sensational murder in Fort Worth since the Courtright-Short shootout some twenty years earlier. In the aftermath of the public outcry, the state legislature in Austin passed the first statewide anti-gambling law. Following the death of Timothy Courtright in 1886, the legislature had tried to pass the first statewide gun-control law, but on that occasion the forces of law and order were not strong enough to prevail. This time outrage produced action.

Other, more subtle changes were also taking place in the Acre. The growth of drug use, particularly opium, represented a significant change from frontier days when rotgut whiskey was the principal "mind-altering substance" dispensed in the Acre. The newspapers after the turn of the century only made occasional references to drug usage, but these can be seen today as a warning flag that the twentieth century, with its more cosmopolitan vices, had arrived in the West.

Another event marking the end of the old days was the passing of Mary Porter. Madam Porter, as she proudly called herself, was the last of Fort Worth's Big Three Madams to give up the fight. She had first opened her doors on Rusk Street when the cowboy was king, and she had kept them open after a new century and a new attitude toward her particular line of work had arrived. Business had declined to the point before the end where Mary even found it hard to pay her taxes. Finally, in November, 1906, she was served with a "summons" she could not ignore. Few noted her passing or what it represented. Her house and property on Rusk Street were put up for public auction. J. C. Ingram paid $35,000 for everything, and the property was soon converted to legitimate commercial uses.[2] When Mary died a big part of Hell's Half Acre died with her. Along with Jessie Reeves and Josie Belmont, she had maintained a certain level of tarnished class and brazen honesty in a disreputable profession. Her passing marked another long step downward in the decline of Hell's Half Acre

At least the public face of the Acre was improving somewhat. For several years, the good merchants of Rusk Street had pressured city fathers to change the name of their street to something with less sordid connotations. Finally, in 1910 their efforts were rewarded when the City Council changed the name of Rusk Street to Commerce Street, partly out of deference to the memory of a great founding father of the state.

The darker corners of the Acre also underwent a renaissance during these years. Thirty-two buildings in "the district" between Main and Jennings, from Thirteenth to Front streets, were razed in 1909 on orders of the city fire commissioner and city engineer. Besides being the scene of frequent assaults and killings for many years, it was reported that the small wooden structures — many no longer inhabited — were fire traps.[3] Those that still sheltered inhabitants were mostly homes to hoboes, drunks and Negroes who were all callously displaced in the name of progress.

• •

But the legends! They bloomed and grew like flowers in a hothouse garden. There were legends about Butch Cassidy and the Sundance Kid, about Etta Place and Sally (the whore with no last name) and many others. Lots of legends grew up around famous characters who spent time here, like Luke Short, Sam Bass and the Wild Bunch; some who *might* have spent time here, like Doc Holliday and Fannie Porter; and some who definitely did not, like Billy the Kid and Jesse James. They were all incorporated into the Grand Legend of Hell's Half Acre with only the slightest historical screening. Rules regarding

By the 1890s Fort Worth saloons had lost most of their Wild West flavor. Places like W. S. Wright's looked more like storefronts than saloons, and customers no longer tended to be "armed and dangerous." Note sign in window: "No minors allowed" (courtesy Mrs. Barty Duncan, Fort Worth). Below, a small, turn-of-the-century bar in the Acre, name and address unknown, serving some of the local boys on a quiet afternoon. Dozens of similar neighborhood taverns operated on the side streets of the Acre without ever getting their names in the newspaper (courtesy Ruby Schmidt, Fort Worth).

Lower Main Street in the early 1960s, looking westward: a long, last look before the wrecking ball does its work to what was once Hell's Half Acre. Even at this late date, bars, theaters, cheap hotels and drifters still predominate. After 1965 the Tarrant County Convention Center completely covered this area. Right: the Acre never had much use for fences or limits of any kind. Top: note the beautiful gabled windows and other architectural details that date from the turn of the century renaissance in the district (courtesy Mark and Lee Angle, Lee Angle Photography, Inc., Fort Worth).

right of proprietorship to the West's most famous characters were never too clear, and the legends die hard. The word of an old-timer that he knew or met a genuine legend is sufficient grounds for any history-minded community to lay claim to one of the famous.

Fort Worth appropriated a few western legends and created a few of its own. Among the former were Sam Bass and the Wild Bunch, none of whom ever regarded Fort Worth as their principal stomping grounds. If Wyatt Earp had spent a bit more time here or made a bigger splash on the local scene, he too would have been embraced by the city as an adopted son. By contrast, all of Timothy Courtright's so-called fame is associated with Fort Worth, but he is the best example of a locally created legend. T. I. Courtright as "Fort Worth's First Citizen" and the "Two-gun Marshal who cleaned up the Acre" never existed; he is the creation of local historians and hack writers who have spent years trying to create a figure the equal of Wild Bill Hickok or Wyatt Earp. Courtright was never a major player in the cast of western gunmen on par with those two.

In the twentieth century, long after a "closed" sign was hung on the frontier, the legends continue to roll on just like "Old Man River." One of the more curious concerns Euday Bowman, the brilliant jazz man who wrote "Twelfth Street Rag" among other well-known tunes. According to local lore, Bowman composed "Twelfth Street Rag" about the street of the same name in the Acre while living here after the turn of the century. The truth of the matter is, Bowman had a St. Louis street in mind when he wrote the song, but many citizens of Fort Worth, including newspapermen who should have known better, accepted the legend in later years as gospel truth.[4] Fannie Porter's legend has proved even more indestructible. As late as 1990 a respected Fort Worth columnist assured his readers that the notorious madam once maintained a place in Fort Worth, although "considerable research has failed to turn up any listing of her or her house in the old city directories." Nonetheless, he went on, "the existence of both has been verified."[5] It would be nice to know where and when for the historical record.

A different sort of legend is played out every year in the "new" White Elephant Saloon in the city's Northside district. There, every February 8, the famous shootout between Luke Short and Longhair Jim Courtright is re-enacted — complete with "historic" dialogue — before an appreciative, if semi-inebriated audience. It is all grand fun, even if history does get somewhat trampled underfoot in the process. The historian takes part in such spectacles somewhat shamefacedly, knowing in his heart of hearts that any direct quotes attributed to the outlaws and other western characters must always be taken with a large measure of salt. The times, the circumstances and the people involved were hardly conducive to leaving behind an accurate historical record. At the most, what the historian hopes for is a sense of the moment, a feeling of the dialogue, perhaps an understanding of the persons involved. It is enough.

Delbert Willis, long-time writer and editor of the old *Fort Worth Press*, probably provided the best epitaph for Hell's Half Acre. He ended one of his many columns about the Acre with the following image:

> The red lamps of the evening no longer glow over Rusk Street, the one-time scarlet thoroughfare of the Acre. Only a faded memory to old men, and a few old women, are the tinkling crystal chandeliers which hung like jewelled pendants from the parlor ceilings. And the player pianos which blared out ballads for dancing with the girls of the evening. . . . Those were bold days of a bold era . . . and they gave the Acre a fancy name from coast to coast.[6]

This is the way we choose to remember Hell's Half Acre.

• •

The lessons of Hell's Half Acre, as opposed to the legends, are fewer but more enlightening. As a red-light district, the Acre never measured up to the likes of San Francisco's Barbary Coast or Storyville in New Orleans or New York's Tenderloin district. But by cow town standards it was quite a place. Change the names and some of the particulars and Fort Worth's story is just like many other western cow towns during the same period: gambling was open, fighting and prostitution were rampant, defiance of the law was endemic and city government was a caricature. Fort Worth, in fact, was the mirror image of half a dozen cow towns in Kansas, beginning with Abilene and including Dodge City and Ellsworth. The well-traveled routes up the Chisholm and other cattle trails were practically a commute. Texas cowboys were notorious troublemakers in Kansas towns during the 1870s, and those same villages sent some of the worst gamblers, madams and others of their like down the trail to Fort Worth. It is not surprising that the Dodge City Gang's best-known members (Short, Masterson and Earp) spent time in Fort Worth. What is surprising is that more of their brethren did not follow.

During the heyday of Hell's Half Acre, Fort Worth was a regular stop on the Gamblers' Circuit and an unofficial stop on the Outlaw Trail. These aspects of local history have largely been ignored by the legend-makers. What attracted the many gamblers and outlaws to Fort Worth is as interesting as the individual stories of the famous who came here. Following the Gamblers' Circuit or the Outlaw Trail, they shuttled back and forth between a handful of communities where they felt welcome and found the same brand of hospitality in a dozen or more well-known towns.

Linking Fort Worth's name with such rip-snortin' places as Dodge, Denver and Tombstone definitely enhances the city's legendary status and helps explain why so many famous characters passed through. Fort Worth offered two things for the criminally inclined: economic opportunity and a tolerant citizenry. Fort Worth citizens tolerated the excesses of Hell's Half Acre long after the citizens of Dodge and Abilene, to name just two, had cleaned up their towns. The reasons for this are hard to explain. Perhaps it is because the Acre was a more fully integrated part of the city — economically, socially and politically — than similar red-light districts in those Kansas towns. Or perhaps it was something in the nature of Texans themselves. As Betty Dooley, a present-day Washington lobbyist, has observed: "I've come to believe that the morons, thieves, and cutthroats who with their women settled Texas have passed on genetically a spirit of independence, courage, and tenacity."[7] And one might add just plain orneriness to that list of characteristics. In any case, Fort Worthers were slow to give up their frontier ways.

Hard as this may be for Dallas to take, Fort Worth was definitely wilder 'n' woollier during these years than its sister city. The caliber of gambling, the comeliness of the prostitutes and the friendliness of the barkeeps may not be much to brag about nowadays, but in those days such things were a badge of civic pride. Never mind that all claims were relative; Fort Worth held bragging rights over Dallas. Hell's Half Acre was known far and wide. The *Graham* [Texas] *Gazette* clucked in 1889 what a shame it was for our "beautiful city that such a den of infamy is allowed to exist right in its center, in open defiance of the laws of God and man."[8] Many Fort Worthers were not sure it was such a shame and detected a note of jealousy in the *Gazette's* moralizing. A century later Fort Worth citizens are still in a position to point with great pride to what their city has become compared with countless Grahams. Fort Worth did not turn out so badly, it seems, for a city that began with a "den of infamy" at its center.

The dark side of Hell's Half Acre is also a part of the city's legacy. It is true that crime in the Acre recognized neither color nor sex, and even age was seldom a hindrance to local lawlessness. Black, white and yellow, male and female, teenagers and oldsters were all busy making a buck and exercising their God-given freedoms to say, act and think pretty much as they pleased. They were allowed a free rein because freedom was the most precious commodity in the West. That they abused the privilege of breaking some laws was to be expected. The population of Hell's Half Acre kept breaking the law and thumbing their noses at conventional morality until they finally wore out their welcome in the city, but it took a long time. The legendary tenderloin gave way to a slum district that was eventually bulldozed to make room for a modern convention center.

The last lesson of Hell's Half Acre is that the complete history of such a district can never be told. As the *Graham Gazette* said in 1889, "Many of the dark deeds perpetrated in this locality are publicly known, but others are not."[9] And, it is safe to say, they will probably never be known. Where the historical record ends, the legends begin.

• •

Some hapless souls are led astray,
While some themselves, seek out the way.
Some fall, unthinking, in the pit,
While others seek about for it.
'Tis probable, if Satan should
Strive for the universal good,
And close his gates and bar them well,
Some souls would still break into Hell.

— from *Rube Burrow, King of Outlaws,* 1890

Notes

COMPLETE BIBLIOGRAPHIC INFORMATION FOR THE following sources can be found in the bibliography.

Introduction

1. Quoted in Mark Thomas Connally, *The Response to Prostitution in the Progressive Era*, p. 11.

2. *Fort Worth Star-Telegram*, May 12, 1990, A.M. edition.

3. B. B. Paddock, *Early Days in Fort Worth*, p. 31.

4. J. A. Sharpe, "The Criminal Past: The Face of Crime in Later Medieval England," *History Today* (January, 1988), p. 19.

1. "Dress and Delight Days"

1. *Fort Worth Daily Democrat*, April 10, April 17, 1877.

2. According to western lore, the term "red-light district" originated in Dodge City, Kansas, when the town was a rail terminus on the Santa Fe line. Railroad men would visit the bawdy houses and leave their red lanterns outside while they took care of business inside. The sight of one of these lanterns hanging outside a house was as good as a neon sign for advertising purposes. Whether myth or fact, this explanation is now firmly ensconced in the history of the West. See, Harry Sinclair Drago, *Notorious Ladies of the Frontier*, p. 256. Also, Fred and Jo Mazzulla, *Brass Checks and Red Lights*, p. 4. Compare, Paul I. Wellman, *The Trampling Herd*, p. 195. Wellman offers a slightly different version of the same story, saying that in the beginning red glass was used in the entrance of one of the favorite Dodge City honky tonks, the Old Red Light House, and from there came to be applied generically to all such establishments. Drago also cites the traditional story but moves the origin of the term back even further to Chicago's early days when working girls congregated on market days

to service the farmers who came to town to sell their produce. The girls advertised by hanging red lanterns on their wagons. True westerners stoutly deny the latter story.

Some five hundred miles south of Dodge City on the opposite end of the Chisholm Trail, Fort Worth was no stranger to red lanterns in its early days. Like Dodge City, Fort Worth was a town built on cattle and railroads. In the 1870s, red lanterns often hung outside notorious houses on the south end of town. At least one early resident, Octavia Bennett, still remembered those days almost a century later. Interview with Mrs. Octavia Bennett, June 6, 1952, Fort Worth, Texas (Transcript in possession of Tarrant County Historical Society, Fort Worth). Gradually, the term "red-light" came to signify a particular type of district where prostitution was just one of a variety of vices offered to paying customers.

3. "Texas Writers' Project, Research Data: Fort Worth and Tarrant County, Texas" (Fort Worth: Fort Worth Public Library Unit, 1941), vol. 51, p. 20,100. Hereafter referred to as "Texas Writers' Project."

4. Unfortunately, the confusion this has created for later historians of the West knows no bounds. James D. Horan may be the writer most guilty of muddying the waters by confusing Hell's Half Acre in Fort Worth with the district of the same name in San Antonio in several books: *The Desperate Men*, *The Wild Bunch* and *Pictorial History of the Wild West* (with Paul Sann). Robert Elman in *Badmen of the West* commits the same mistake. Horan is the historian who started the story that Butch Cassidy's famous bicycle-riding episode romantically depicted in the 1969 movie "Butch Cassidy and the Sundance Kid" took place in Fort Worth's Hell's Half Acre. No such event ever occurred on the streets of Fort Worth.

5. Noah Smithwick, *The Evolution of a State*, p. 171.

6. This derivation is not as far-fetched as it may seem. Between December 31, 1862, and January 2, 1863, 85,000 Union and Confederate soldiers fought around Murfreesboro, Tennessee, for control of middle Tennessee's railroads and rich farmland. At the climax of the battle on December 31, Union and Confederate soldiers fought a desperate hand-to-hand battle for control of a salient in the center of the Union line. The fighting was so intense in such a constricted area that soldiers on both sides christened it "Hell's Half Acre." Among the Confederates who took part in the fighting for Hell's Half Acre were members of the First Texas Brigade, McCown's Division commanded by Brigadier General M. D. Ector. See, James Lee McDonough, *Stones River — Bloody Winter in Tennessee*, pp. 86, 131, 149 and 253.

7. Technically, the Chisholm Trail did not come as far south as Fort Worth; it only crossed the Oklahoma Territory starting at the Red River. South of the Red River it merged with several "feeder trails," one of which came through Fort Worth. However, to the cowboys of that day as well as in the popular imagination today, the whole distance from Abilene, Kansas, to San Antonio, was known as the Chisholm Trail, thus making Jesse Chisholm one of the most unlikely and unjustified heroes in western history. See, Don Worcester, *The Chisholm Trail, High Road of the Cattle Kingdom*.

8. Robert Sturmberg, *History of San Antonio*, p. 135.

9. *Ibid.*

10. Nat Washer, "When the Washer Brothers Came to Town," *In Old Fort Worth: The Story of a City and Its People as Published in the News-Tribune in 1976 and 1977*, Mack Williams, ed. (Fort Worth: Mack Williams, 1986), p. 81. Williams reprinted columns on Fort Worth history in three tabloid editions of the *News-Tribune* (1975, 1976, 1986). Hereafter cited as *In Old Fort Worth* with date of publication.

11. *Fort Worth Democrat*, July 18, 1881.

12. Thomas Jefferson Rusk (1803–1857) was a signer of the Texas Declaration of Independence, Secretary of War during the Revolution, and veteran of the Battle of San Jacinto. After Texas joined the Union in 1845, he was appointed one of the first two U.S. Senators. In 1911, the city changed the name of Rusk Street to Commerce to separate the stigma of the street's notorious past from the honored name of a genuine Texas hero. Cynics at the time claimed that respectable businessmen on the street cared nothing about a Texas hero's good name but cared a great deal about the negative image associated with that name and their street. Other cities in the West, e.g. Denver, had the same problem with some street names from early in their history.

13. "How Fort Worth Came to Be Called 'The Panther City,'" *Fort Worth Register*, January 19, 1902. The same story is related in less detail in Oliver Knight, *Fort Worth: Outpost on the Trinity*, p. 81–82. The story of the panther may well be apocryphal, as it was first told in a Dallas newspaper when the two cities were intense rivals. The alligator story was locally generated. An interesting postscript, which appeared in newspapers, told how two shady characters were arrested in the city a short time after the alligator was bagged. The men were charged with running a house of ill-repute. The *Democrat* announced that the accused would appear in court to "prove their innocence, defy the allegation, and if necessary, eat the alligator!" (*Fort Worth Democrat*, February 28, 1879).

14. Wayne Gard, *Sam Bass*, p. 104.

15. Ordinance No. 205, passed by City Council, August 19, 1879, in "Fort Worth City Ordinances," Book A, No. 1, April 5, 1873–No. 298, December 28, 1882 (City Secretary's Office, Fort Worth City Hall). Hereafter cited as Ordinance with number and date passed. Unless otherwise indicated, all references can be found in Book A.

16. Sam Smith, "When Every House Had a Water Barrel," *In Old Fort Worth* (1986), p. 103. Smith recorded his recollections in 1965 when he was eighty-two years old.

17. "The First Time I Saw Fort Worth," *In Old Fort Worth* (1976), p. 2. In 1949 Samuel Houston Cowan wrote this account of the city he first saw seventy-one years earlier. That account is preserved in the private files of Mack Williams as well as in the *Fort Worth News-Tribune's* pages, although the latter is no longer a publishing newspaper.

18. Quoted in Gard, *Sam Bass*, p. 234.

19. Oliver Knight, *Fort Worth*, p. 70.

20. Sam Smith, "When Every House Had a Water Barrel," *In Old Fort Worth* (1986), p. 103.

21. *Ibid.*

22. *Fort Worth Daily Gazette*, September 19, September 25, 1885. (This was the famous "Hog-Law Election.")

23. *Fort Worth Record and Register*, August 27, 1905, excerpted in "Texas Writers' Project," vol. 33, pp. 13,122–13,123.

24. *Fort Worth Democrat* (Weekly), May 10, 1873.

25. The Trinity Billiard Hall (see advertisement in "Fort Worth City Directory," 1878–79).

26. This forerunner of the modern cash register was invented in James Ritty's Dayton, Ohio, saloon because Ritty suspected his bartenders were dipping their fingers in the till. Ritty secured a patent for his invention in 1879. In 1884 a friend purchased Ritty's idea, added a bell, and Dayton's National Cash Register Company was born along with phrases like "ringing up a sale." See, Joseph Nathan Kane, *Famous First Facts*, pp. 153–54; also George Will, "First a Box, then a Bell . . . ," *Fort Worth Star-Telegram*, April 6, 1989, A.M. edition, p. 21, sec. 1.

27. As a result of a state law in July 1879, all saloons had to have a bell register upon which every drink sold on the premises was "punched" to make a tax record for the saloon keeper to pay revenues upon such drinks (*Fort Worth Daily Democrat*, July 16, 1879).

28. Tarrant County Criminal Docket, County Court, 1878–79, 1879–81 (Special Collections, University of Texas at Arlington).

29. Forbes Parkhill, *The Wildest of the West*, p. 75. See also, Time-Life Books [Jim Hicks, et al.], *The Gamblers*, in *The Old West* series, pp. 162–63.

30. *Fort Worth City Directory*, 1878–79.

31. *Dodge City* [Kansas] *Globe*, September 10, 1878.

32. Paula Mitchell Marks, *And Die in the West: The Story of the O.K. Corral Gunfight*, pp. 338–41 ff.

33. *The Knoxville* [Tennessee] *News-Sentinel*, January 19, 1930, p. 1 C.

34. *Fort Worth Daily Democrat*, September 4, 1876.

35. "Where the West Begins," (Introductory Essay) "Texas Writers' Project," vol. 51, p. 20,368.

36. *Dallas Daily Herald*, April 20, 1877, p. 3.

37. *Fort Worth Record and Register*, October 12, 1908 (cited in "Texas Writers' Project," vol. 33, p. 13,135).

38. Quoted in *Fort Worth Star-Telegram*, April 20, 1915.

39. Time-Life Books, *The Gamblers*, p. 156.

40. The legend is repeated in numerous sources. See, Janet L. Schmelzer, *Where the West Begins: Fort Worth and Tarrant County*, p. 46.

41. See various entries in Tarrant County Criminal Docket, County Court, 1879–1881 (Special Collections, University of Texas at Arlington).

42. Thomas Penfield, *Western Sheriffs and Marshals*, p. xi. See also, J. B. Roberts, "Memories of an Early Police Reporter," *In Old Fort Worth* (1976), p. 28.

43. Minutes of the City Council of Fort Worth, April 8, 1873, Book A, April 4, 1873–January 1, 1878 (City Secretary's Office, Fort Worth City Hall). Hereafter cited as Minutes of City Council with date. Unless otherwise indicated, all references can be found in Book A.

44. Time-Life Books, *The Gamblers*, p. 185.

45. *Fort Worth Record and Register*, "Old Fort Worth and the New City," August 27, 1905 (cited in "Texas Writers' Project," vol. 33, p. 13,123).

46. *Junction City* [Kansas] *Union*, July 8, 1871.

47. *Dallas Daily Herald*, August 12 (p. 2), August 15 (p. 3), August 16 (p. 4), 1877.

48. Elliot West, "Wicked Dodge City," *American History Illustrated*, Special Edition, vol. 17, no. 4, p. 27.

49. The black prostitutes like Pokey Negro shared the same historical fate as the black cowboy. They were both forgotten characters in the history of the West, probably the prostitute more than the cowboy because at least the black cowboy was earning an honest living wage, which made him a more respectable subject for writers. While the black cowboy is represented in western lore in the persons of Bill Pickett and Nat Love, the black prostitute has no one to represent her. Neither her name nor her presence has been preserved in the historical record. William Loren Katz, *The Black West*, pp. 183–87.

50. "Register of Persons Committed to City Prison, 1886–1889" (Special Collections, Tarrant County Junior College, Northeast Campus, Fort Worth).

51. *Fort Worth Democrat*, November 1, 1881, p. 4.

52. *Dallas Herald*, July 1, 1880 (citing the 1880 Census).

53. Sanborn Fire Maps of Fort Worth, 1885, 1889 (New York: Sanborn Map & Publishing Co., Ltd.), in Barker History Center, University of Texas at Austin.

54. Drago, *Notorious Ladies*, p. 129. See also Forbes Parkhill, *The Wildest of the West*, p. 21. No one, so far as can be discovered, has documented the prices charged by Fort Worth's crib girls. But judging by the comparable prices charged for drinks, criminal fines, and the like, Fort Worth prices were in line with those in cities like Denver, Abilene and Dodge.

55. *Dallas Daily Herald*, May 15, 1877, p. 4.

56. Minutes of City Council, July 7, 1874.

57. *Fort Worth Daily Democrat*, April 5, 1879.

58. *Fort Worth City Directories*, 1877 and 1878.

59. David C. Humphrey, "Prostitution and Public Policy in Austin, Texas, 1870–1915," *Southwestern Historical Quarterly* (April, 1983), p. 496.

60. Hilary Evans, *Harlots, Whores and Hookers*, p. 11. Also, Raymond Schuessler, "Bawdy Houses of the Old West," *True West* (May, 1984), p. 28.

61. *Fort Worth Daily Democrat*, March 7, 1879, and April 5, 1879.

62. Humphrey, "Prostitution and Public Policy in Austin," pp. 488, 490 (Table 1). For relative population figures of Fort Worth and Austin, see *Dallas Morning News* (Belo Corporation), *Texas Almanac*, 1968–69.

63. For the standard costume worn by Denver's girls, see, Parkhill, *The Wildest of the West*, p. 21; for Fort Worth's girls, see *Fort Worth Gazette*, October 10, 1889.

64. *Dallas Daily Herald*, August 1, 1877 (reprinted from *Fort Worth Democrat*, no date given).

65. Minutes of City Council, April 8, 1873.

66. *Fort Worth Democrat*, February 5, 1877, p. 3.

67. *Ibid.*, July 7, 1877, p. 2.

68. *Fort Worth Record*, February 19, 1921.

69. James C. Shaw, *North from Texas: Incidents in the Early Life of a Range Cowman in Texas, Dakota, and Wyoming, 1852–1883*, p. vii.

70. *Fort Worth Star-Telegram*, June 13, 1983, p. 3 B.

71. Thanks to Tom Blevins' remarkable memory and his powers of description, the Two Minnies was reincarnated a century later as the club of the Ramada Inn Central, a motel on Fort Worth's near east side which has changed names more than once. When it was owned by Ramada Inn, this story was included in promotional literature the management gave out. The original story came from the personal files of Mr. Bill Jary, long-time local author and historian. (Interview with Bill Jary, June, 1983).

72. Mack Williams, "In Old Fort Worth: Relaxing in Hell's Half Acre," *The News-Tribune* (Fort Worth), March 20, 1981.

2. "The Wages of Sin Are a Damned Sight Better Than the Wages of Virtue"

1. A. Von Steinwehr, *The Centennial Gazetteer of the United States*, n. p. The *Gazetteer* is based on the 1870 census reports. The T&P advertisement, signed by George Noble, general superintendent, and two other railroad officials, is cited in Mary Daggett Lake, "1876 Fort Worth Map Shows City as Village," *Fort Worth Star-Telegram*, November 21, 1937. The chapter title is attributed to Whitney Rupp, famous western gambler. Quoted in Drago, *Notorious Ladies of the Frontier*, p. 111.

2. Denton C. Limbaugh, "City Government," (Introductory Essay) "Texas Writers' Project," vol. 45, p. 17,979.

3. J. B. Roberts, "Memories of an Early Police Reporter," *In Old Fort Worth* (1976), p. 28. Not for another forty years did a leading minister, J. Frank Norris, take after the saloons and other vice establishments with a genuine zeal.

4. Woody Phipps, "Salvation in Saddle Bags," (essay) "Texas Writers' Project," vol. 49, pp. 19,236–19,237.

5. *Fort Worth Democrat*, July 31, 1878, p. 6.

6. "The First Time I Saw Fort Worth," memoirs of Mrs. Fannie Vincent, *In Old Fort Worth* (1976), p. 4. Vincent first came to Fort Worth in 1872, making her one of the earliest unofficial observers of the local scene. She dictated her recollections eighty-two years later.

7. Sam Smith, "When Every House Had a Water Barrel," *In Old Fort Worth* (1986), p. 103.

8. Unnamed source, quoted in *Fort Worth Star-Telegram*, October 30, 1949, p. 8, sec. 1.

9. *Dallas Daily Herald*, July 15, 1876.

10. This suspicious-sounding story originated with B. B. Paddock in the pages of his newspaper during those hot summer days of 1876 when the town was gripped by railroad fever. It has been repeated uncritically by many historians since then. See *Fort Worth Daily Democrat*, July 8, 1876, p. 2; also, Knight, *Fort Worth*, p. 85.

11. *Fort Worth Daily Democrat*, July 16, 1876, p. 4.

12. *Dallas Daily Herald*, July 18, 1876.

13. Quoted in *Fort Worth Star-Telegram*, "Fort Worth's First Hundred Years," October 30, 1949, p. 2.

14. Knight, *Fort Worth*, p. 87.

15. Paddock, *History of Texas*, vol. 2, p. 611.

16. *Fort Worth Democrat*, July 7, 1876, p. 3.

17. Paddock, *Early Days in Fort Worth*, p. 25.

18. *Ibid.* For an account of overland travel by stage, see, Thomas H. Peterson, "Cash Up or No Go: The Stagecoach Era in Arizona," *Journal of Arizona History*, pp. 205–22.

19. See, Wayne Gard, *Sam Bass*, p. 104; also, James B. Gillett, *Six Years with the Texas Rangers*, 1875–1881, p. 116.

20. Ewald H. Keller, "The Blacksmith: A Mighty Man Was He," *In Old Fort Worth* (1986), pp. 99–100. Ewald Keller was eighty-three years old in 1936 when he dictated his recollections to a reporter; he had first come to Fort Worth in 1873 walking thirty miles from Dallas.

21. Interview with E. H. Keller, May 24, 1938, in "Texas Writers' Project," vol. 2, p. 508.

22. Brookes Baker, *Map of Fort Worth, Texas, Centennial Edition, Compiled from Deed Records and Actual Surveys*, vol. 1 of 2.

23. David R. Copeland, "Hell's Half Acre: Fort Worth's First Amusement Center, 1873–1889," (unpublished thesis in Master of Arts History program, Texas Christian University, 1969, copy on file with Fort Worth Public Library).

24. *Dallas Daily Herald*, July 15, 1876, p. 1.

25. *Ibid.*

26. *Ibid*, July 20, 1876, p. 1.

27. *Topeka* [Kansas] *Daily Commonwealth*, September 17, 1872; Ed Bartholomew, *Wyatt Earp, 1848–1880: The Untold Story*, p. 47.

28. Bartholomew, *Wyatt Earp, 1848–1880*, p.47.

29. *Ibid.*, p. 202.

30. The unofficial title "Queen City of the Prairies" was coined in 1876 by T&P Railroad promoters and popularized in the early 1880s by Walter A. Huffman, Fort Worth's first homegrown millionaire, who made his money in railroads and real estate. It was picked up and widely quoted by newspapers around the country. The exact origin of Fort Worth's other name, "The Paris of the Plains," is unknown, though it came into popular usage when the Chisholm Trail was still the major route for driving cattle northward to Kansas railheads. See, Gard, *The Chisholm Trail*, p. 146.

31. Minutes of City Council, October 2, 1877.

32. Nancy Wilson Ross, *Westward the Women*, p. 125.

33. *Fort Worth Daily Democrat*, October 19, 1877, p. 4.

34. Howard W. Peak, Jr., "My Recollections of Fort Worth," "Texas Writers' Project," vol. 9, p. 48.

35. Robert R. Dykstra, *The Cattle Towns*, p. 355.

36. Colby Dixon Hall, *History of Texas Christian University: A College of the Cattle Frontier*, p. 29.

37. *Fort Worth Daily Democrat*, February 10, 1878.

38. *Fort Worth Democrat-Advance*, February 1, 1882.

39. This is probably the same saloon owner referred to by B. B. Paddock in his

Early Days in Fort Worth as "Henry Byrne." See, Paddock, *Early Days in Fort Worth*, p. 31. In his recollections of Henry Byrne's [sic] place, Paddock says about thirty members of a whist club, who held their regular games in the rear of the saloon, were once indicted by city authorities for violating the anti-gambling ordinance. For Paddock this represented the extremes to which overzealous reformers went with their clean-up crusades.

40. Interview with Mr. George Gause, May 23, 1938, "Texas Writers' Project," vol. 2, p. 460; see also *Fort Worth City Directories*, 1877 and 1878–79.

41. That first city directory of 1876 apparently no longer exists. The earliest extant city directory of 1877 is now on microfilm in the Fort Worth Public Library collections. The present quotation from the 1876 directory is cited in Mary Daggett Lake, "1876 Fort Worth Map Shows City as a Village," *Fort Worth Star-Telegram*, November 21, 1937. That directory, according to Lake, was in private hands, but she did not identify the owner. Its whereabouts at this date are unknown.

42. Fort Worth's reputation as a drinking man's town and one of "America's hottest cities" has persisted even up to the present day. An article in the February 6, 1989, issue of *Newsweek* magazine cited a survey showing that Fort Worth had "one tavern for every 26 people, compared with one per 3,500 in Dallas." As Fort Worth officials were quick to point out in an indignant "Letter to the Editor," based on the city's population of almost a half a million people, that would mean there were 16,859 taverns doing business locally! And that number is close to the *total* number of business firms in Fort Worth. The magazine acknowledged their mistake, blaming their figures on a University of Texas at Arlington urban affairs professor. Fort Worth's mayor at the time did concede that "bars and taverns are one part of [our] history." *Fort Worth Star-Telegram*, May 23, 1989, p. 1, sec. 1.

43. Smith, "When Every House Had a Water Barrel," *In Old Fort Worth*, p. 103.

44. The Headlight Bar's slogan is quoted in Knight, *Fort Worth*, p. 89.

45. *Fort Worth City Directories*, 1877, and 1878–79; also Charles Ellis Mitchell, "When Every Man Carried a Six-Shooter," *In Old Fort Worth* (1986), p. 46.

46. See *Fort Worth City Directories*, 1877–1882.

47. See advertisement in *Fort Worth Democrat*, November 5, 1881, p. 3.

48. For shootout between N. H. Wilson and T. I. Courtright in 1877, see Chapter 3. For troubles between Luke Short and Charlie Wright, owner of the Bank Exchange Saloon in 1890, see Chapter 6.

49. *Fort Worth Star-Telegram*, undated clipping in Tarrant County Historical Society files.

50. *Ibid.*

51. "Reminiscences of Ida Van Zandt Jarvis," "Texas Writers' Project," vol. 1, p. 107.

52. "Reminiscences of Dewitt Reddick," *Ibid.*, vol. 1, pp. 129–30.

3. "Better to be Undressed Than Unarmed"

1. William MacLeod Raine, *Guns of the Frontier*, p. 15.

2. "Texas Writers' Project," vol. 46, p. 18,346.

3. "Reminiscences of Ida Van Zandt Jarvis," "Texas Writers' Project," vol. 1, p. 107.

4. *Fort Worth Star-Telegram*, October 9, 1921.

5. "Reminiscences of Joe Witcher," "Texas Writers' Project," vol. 1, p. 161.

6. John Gross, ed., *Rudyard Kipling, the Man, His Work and His World*, p. 75.

7. Mitchell, "When Every Man Carried a Six-Shooter," *In Old Fort Worth* (1986), p. 46.

8. Ordinance No. 13, passed April 9, 1873.

9. Ordinance No. 164, passed July 20, 1878.

10. *Fort Worth Democrat*, January 24, 1878.

11. Dodge City counted fifteen killings in 1872–73, its first year as a cow town. Ellsworth, Kansas, had a modest eight homicides to its discredit in the first year (1867) such records were kept. In Abilene, posted notices against carrying guns were often riddled with bullets before the sun set on them, and the city's first jail was destroyed by rampaging cowboys before it could even open for business. Unfortunately, no statistics exist today for the number of homicides in Fort Worth during any year of the late nineteenth century, the era when Hell's Half Acre was in full flower. The city newspapers of those days report lots of violence but little of it fatal. For statistics on Dodge City and Ellsworth, see, Robert R. Dykstra, *The Cattle Towns*, p. 113; also, Howard R. Lamar, ed., *The Reader's Encyclopedia of the American West*, pp. 182–83.

12. Gard, *The Chisholm Trail*, p. 237.

13. Knight, *Fort Worth*, p. 60.

14. P. J. R. MacTosh, "Fort Worth's Centennial," *Texas Weekly*, August 15, 1936, pp. 9–10. This story invites skepticism because the present courthouse was completed in 1895, long after the era when cowboys galloped up and down Main Street shooting off their guns. Moreover, it would have required some pretty slick shooting by a tipsy cowboy on a moving horse to hit the clock face some 160 feet above the ground.

15. Frank X. Tolbert, "Story of George, Cowtown Knight" in *Dallas Morning News*, June 6, 1959, p. 12, sec. 1. The legend, as recounted by Tolbert, claims that Luke Short was the sharp-eyed gunman who shot off St. George's mailed fist. Little Luke was a tightly wound gambler who was not given to such high jinks. There is no record of his ever "hurrahing" any town he visited.

16. *Fort Worth Star-Telegram*, October 9, 1921.

17. Knight, *Fort Worth*, p. 60.

18. Joe P. Witcher, "1879 Policeman Tells How It Was," *In Old Fort Worth* (1975), p. 7.

19. This is the second verse of "The Dying Cowboy," origin unknown. The lyrics and tune were later adapted to the popular ballad, "The Streets of Laredo." For the original lyrics, see, J. M. Parker, *An Aged Wanderer, A Life Sketch*, p. 23.

20. *Fort Worth Gazette*, May 17, 1887.

21. Paddock, *History of Texas: Fort Worth and the Texas Northwest Edition*, vol. 2 of 4, pp. 876–77.

22. J. C. Terrell, *Reminiscences of the Early Days of Fort Worth*, p. 11.

23. *Fort Worth Standard*, July 13, 1876, p. 3.

24. In his memoirs, B. B. Paddock quotes a Fort Worth stage driver who grumbled that his job had become "monotonous and uninteresting" after local authorities

put an end to a rash of stage robberies in the late 1870s. Paddock, *History of Texas: Fort Worth and the Texas Northwest Edition*, vol. 2 of 4, p. 876. An unscientific comparison of newspaper accounts then and now also leads to the inescapable conclusion that Fort Worth in those days was a safer place to live than it is today, even making allowance for the relative difference in population. At the very least, violence in those days seemed to be less random and less often directed against innocent citizens.

25. Unidentified edition of the *Dallas Herald* quoted in *Dallas Morning News*, December 23, 1949.

26. *Ibid.*

27. *Ibid.*

28. *Fort Worth Daily Democrat*, April 11, 1877; Minutes of City Council, April 10, April 17, 1877.

29. Information on local courts comes from the City Directory, 1877, and the Fort Worth City Ordinances, Book A.

30. Minutes of City Council, April 12, 1873.

31. *Ibid.*, April 22, 1873.

32. *Ibid.*, April 10, May 13, 1873; January 11, 1876.

33. *Ibid.*, November 11, 1873.

34. *Ibid.*, April 28, May 12, 1874. The city finally settled with poor Ed Terrell for his 1873 services by paying him sixty dollars, less $21.39 for "disallowed items." Out of his original expense account of $75, Ed finally realized $38.61. See minutes of City Council, October 13, 1874.

35. Roberts, "Memories of an Early Police Reporter," *In Old Fort Worth* (1976), p. 28. During his thirty-five years of reporting local news, Roberts worked at various times for the *Standard*, the *Post*, the *Democrat* and the *Gazette*. He later wrote his recollections of the years 1873 to 1904.

36. Interview with Mrs. Octavia Bennett, Fort Worth, June 6, 1952 (Tarrant County Historical Society files).

37. Mitchell, "When Every Man Carried a Six-Shooter," *In Old Fort Worth* (1986), p. 46.

38. Minutes of City Council, February 8, 1876.

39. *Ibid*, December 14, 1875.

40. *Fort Worth Democrat Weekly*, March 7, 1874.

41. Ordinance No. 92, passed December 26, 1876, and Ordinance No. 99, passed February 27, 1877.

42. Ordinance No. 75, passed May 9, 1876.

43. Minutes of City Council, February 27, 1877.

44. *Fort Worth Democrat* (Daily), July 7, 1876, p. 3.

45. *Ibid.*, December 20, 1876.

46. *Dallas Daily Herald*, December 21, 1876, p. 1.

47. Ordinance No. 11, passed April 8, 1873.

48. Gard, *The Chisholm Trail*, p. 159.

49. Joseph McCoy, *Historic Sketches of the Cattle Trade of the West and Southwest*, pp. 139–41.

50. Roberts, "Memories of an Early Police Reporter," *In Old Fort Worth* (1976), p. 28.

51. Eddie Foy and Alvin F. Harlow, "Clowning through Life," *Collier's* (January 8, 1927), p. 26.

52. *Dallas Daily Herald*, October 13, 1877.

53. This quotation and the entire description of the Red Light come from the *Fort Worth Daily Democrat*, November 29, 1878. The *Democrat* singled out the Red Light as the worst example of Fort Worth's dance-hall saloons.

54. *Fort Worth Democrat*, July 10, 1878.

55. Tarrant County Criminal Docket, County Court, 1878–79, 1879–81, 1886–87. See also *Fort Worth City Directory*, 1877.

56. W. B. Masterson, *Famous Gunfighters of the Western Frontier*, p. 10.

57. Robert K. DeArment, *Knights of the Green Cloth*, p. 138.

58. Bartholomew, *Wyatt Earp, 1848–1880*, p. 94.

59. *Ibid.*, p. 91. Wyatt Earp mentions this shoot-out in his *Memoirs*, written half a century later. According to Wyatt he was the law officer who arrested Rowdy Joe Lowe and took him off to jail. Wyatt's version does not agree with the *Wichita Eagle*, which is not surprising to those who have made a study of Wyatt Earp.

60. *Wichita* [Kansas] *Eagle*, December 18, 1873.

61. *Fort Worth Democrat* (Daily), October 1, 1876.

62. Minutes of City Council, November 14, 1876.

63. *Ibid.*

64. Quoted in *Jacksboro* [Texas] *Echo*, May 18, 1877.

65. Bartholomew, *Wyatt Earp, 1848–1880*, p. 306.

66. Among Lowe's other theater interests were the My Theater and the Theater Comique. For descriptions of Lowe's various civic contributions and run-ins with the law, see *Fort Worth Daily Democrat*, January 7, 1877; September 10, December 7, 1878; January 1, January 20, 1879. See also, *Fort Worth City Directories*, 1877–1879.

67. *Fort Worth Daily Democrat*, December 7, 1878.

68. *Fort Worth Democrat*, April 26, 1879.

69. *Fort Worth Daily Democrat*, September 10, 1878.

70. Bill O'Neal, *Encyclopedia of Western Gunfighters*, p. 197.

71. Anonymous, "Rugged Marshal in Fort Worth History," *The Pecan Press* (College Station: Texas Pecan Growers), July, 1983, p. 1 ("Hell's Half Acre" file, Fort Worth Public Library).

72. Essay by Sheldon F. Gauthier, "Texas Writers' Project," vol. 34, p. 13,470.

73. Paddock, *Early Days in Fort Worth*, p. 31. Writing before World War I Paddock also noted that the tango, bunny hug, turkey trot "and other fancy stunts" were unknown in the "old days."

74. Gauthier, "Texas Writers' Project," vol. 34, p. 13,470.

75. *Dallas Daily Herald*, April 27, 1877, p. 3.

76. *Ibid.*, September 16, 1877, p. 3.

77. *Ibid.*, June 20, 1877, p. 3.

78. Ordinance No. 15, passed April 9, 1873. (The fines for violating this particular ordinance ranged from $1 to $50.)

79. *Fort Worth Democrat*, August 14 and September 10, 1878.

80. *Dallas Daily Herald*, September 29, 1877, p. 3.

81. *Ibid.*, September 25, 1877, p. 2.

82. Roberts, "Memories of an Early Police Reporter," *In Old Fort Worth* (1976), p. 28.

4. "Lord Make Us Good But Not Right Now": The Timothy Courtright Years, 1876–1886

1. The use of the proper name Timothy Isaiah Courtright instead of the better known appellation "Longhair Jim" is a conscious decision on this author's part to counterbalance the usual tendency to focus on the misnomer (he was *never* named "Jim") and the myth ("Two-gun marshal of Fort Worth"). While the use of the man's full name may seem an affectation, it does serve the purpose of showing Courtright as a historical character and not just a legendary gunfighter. Legends are one-dimensional whereas Timothy Isaiah Courtright was both more and less than his considerable legend. The chapter title is from a quotation attributed to St. Augustine, Bishop of Hippo, in the days of his youth. St. Augustine lived A. D. 354–430.

2. See, F. Stanley [Father Stanley Crocchiola], *Longhair Jim Courtright, Two-Gun Marshal of Fort Worth*, p. 58; Williams, "In Old Fort Worth" (regular column) "Beginning a New Series on the Life of Jim Courtright," *Fort Worth News-Tribune*, October 3, 1986, p. 10 A; Anonymous, "Rugged Marshal in Fort Worth History," *The Pecan Press*, July, 1983, p. 1. Williams, *The Pecan Press* and probably every other account since F. Stanley's biography almost certainly derive their information from that source. Stanley, who did not use footnotes, says that "Following his discharge from the army about 1870–71, Courtright and Betty seem to have joined one of the Wild West shows [i.e., that were touring Eastern cities]" (p. 58). Later, on the same page, Stanley talks about how after Courtright left Fort Worth in 1881 or 1882 (he does not specify) "he tried his luck *again* [emphasis added] with Buffalo Bill's Wild West Show. Betty, a crack shot, was also with the show." He goes on to say Courtright left the show in Virginia City, Nevada, after a serious shooting accident put him in the hospital and caused a falling-out with his employer, Buffalo Bill. Subsequent writers have extrapolated from these two passages that both of Courtright's forays into Wild West shows were with Buffalo Bill — in the early 1870s and again in the 1880s. The first of these connections is impossible because in the early 1870s Buffalo Bill was splitting his time between the western plains and the eastern stage. On the stage he starred in the "Buffalo Bill Connection," which never even got as far west as the Mississippi River. No one has ever claimed Mr. and Mrs. Courtright were on the stage back east at any time in their lives. Therefore, T. I. Courtright *must* have been with Buffalo Bill's show in the early 1880s, it would seem. The wealth of detail provided by F. Stanley, despite lack of documentation, gives this claim the ring of truth. Yet the chronology and movements for Jim, Betty and Buffalo Bill do not coincide. Jim departed Fort Worth in late 1881 or '82. Betty stayed behind in Fort Worth with the children. Jim's destination was New Mexico, where he intended to take a job as marshal at Lake Valley mining camp. He had two more known employers up to the spring of 1883, when he got in a scrape with the law and came back to Fort Worth. Meanwhile, Buffalo Bill staged his first "Wild West Show"

in 1883, in Omaha, Nebraska, and continued to stage these extravaganzas for the next thirty years. It is difficult to see how Courtright had time to tour with any show after 1883 — he died in February, 1887 — much less with Betty, who did not leave Fort Worth with her children until she moved to California as a widow in 1887. Courtright's exact whereabouts are unaccounted for in much of 1884 and 1885 when he was on the run from the law and carrying a price on his head. But it is equally hard to imagine a wanted man touring under his own name with the world-famous Wild West Show. This whole episode is a prime example of the Courtright "mythology," which largely began with Father Crocchiola's 1957 biography. Before he was "discovered," Courtright was a little-known local lawman who died in a spectacular shootout. But it only takes one popular biography to create a legend.

3. Reelected twice, Courtright would serve until 1879. Contrary to popular legend, he was never a U.S. Marshal, although he did serve briefly as a deputy marshal during the KATY Railroad strike of 1885. Unfortunately for the historical record, the legend is quite literally carved in stone, being part of the epitaph on his tombstone in Oakwood Cemetery. This mistake was perpetrated by descendants who had him re-interred and a new marker placed on his grave in 1954.

4. Quoted in *Fort Worth Democrat*, July 7, 1876, p. 2.

5. *Fort Worth Daily Democrat*, March 30, 1879.

6. Lyle W. Dorsett, "Bosses and Machines in Urban America," in *Forums in History*, reprinted in Charlotte Rike and Anthony Picchioni, *Readings in American History*, vol. 2, p. 56.

7. Hendricks, *Bad Man of the West*, pp. 66–67.

8. *Fort Worth Standard*, April 27, 1876, p. 3.

9. Modern writers, caught up in the mythology of the "Two-gun Marshal of Fort Worth," have apparently never checked the actual voting tallies, and therefore have failed to appreciate just how close Courtright's first race was. Courtright's election record in four races (1876–79) does not indicate he was the local favorite as he has so often been depicted. F. Stanley only adds to the misunderstanding by confusing the marshal's first race in 1876 with his first *reelection* campaign the following year. In the second campaign, as one of eleven candidates, he received 387 votes out of a total of 915 votes cast. In the 1877 election, Courtright had more than twice as many votes as his nearest opponent. See, Stanley, *Longhair Jim Courtright*, p. 65. Compare *Fort Worth Democrat*, April 8, 1876, p. 3 and *Fort Worth Standard*, April 27, 1876, p. 3.

10. Bartholomew, *Wyatt Earp, 1848–1880*, p. 246.

11. Minutes of City Council, February 11, 1875.

12. Ordinance No. 27, passed April 12, 1873.

13. Minutes of City Council, May 9, June 19, 1876; Ordinance No. 136, passed December 25, 1877.

14. Louis C. Bradford, "Among the Cow-boys," *Lippincott Magazine* (June, 1881), p. 570.

15. Joseph G. Rosa, *The Gunfighter, Man or Myth?*, p. 87.

16. Drago, *Wild, Woolly, and Wicked*, pp. 56–71.

17. City of Fort Worth vs. Madame Porter, October 26, 1887, Case No. 4299, Criminal Minutes, County Court, 1886–87 (Special Collections, University of Texas at Arlington).

18. Ordinance No. 117, passed July 24, 1877.

19. Henry Steele Commager, Marcus Cunliffe and Maldwyn A. Jones, eds., *The West: An Illustrated History*, p. 189.

20. Joseph McCoy, the man who put Abilene, Kansas, on the map, did not invent the profitable system of "fees and fines" used in Abilene, Fort Worth and elsewhere. This same system was used in Leavenworth, Kansas, at least as early as 1861, six years before the first long drive up the Chisholm Trail. See *Leavenworth Daily Times*, December 11, 1861. (Cited in Joseph Snell, *Painted Ladies of the Cowtown Frontier*, p. 5.)

21. Leon C. Metz, *The Shooters*, p. 13.

22. Rosa, *The Gunfighter*, p. 87.

23. Ordinance No. 136, passed December 25, 1877.

24. Ordinance No. 164, passed July 20, 1878; amended by Ordinance No. 181, passed November 7, 1878. (A $2.50 fee was substituted for the original 15% on December 30, 1879.)

25. *Fort Worth Morning Register*, June 3, 1897, p. 3.

26. Minutes of City Council, September 13, 1876.

27. Jay Scott, "Marshal of Fort Worth," *True Western Adventures* (December, 1959), pp. 23–24.

28. June White, "Recollections of Fort Worth: 'We Still Wonder How They Built It, Paid for It,'" *Fort Worth News-Tribune*, September 30, 1988, p. 1 B.

29. *Ibid.*

30. William Cox, *Luke Short and His Era*, p. 152.

31. Ordinance No. 6, passed April 8, 1873.

32. Williams, "In Old Fort Worth . . . Series on Jim Courtright," *Fort Worth News-Tribune*, October 10, 1986, p. 10 A.

33. There were two jails at this location during Courtright's tenure as marshal. The first one was constructed in 1873, after the city incorporated, by Major J. H. Healey for $497. The city outgrew that structure, and it was replaced in 1878 by a new structure which cost twice as much, took more than a year to complete, and was still beset by legal and structural problems after that. Both were cramped log structures, with no toilet facilities, no running water and a single, barred window for light and ventilation. The second city jail consisted of two small cells on the ground level and a dungeon below. When filled to overflowing on a hot summer night, it must have resembled the infamous "Black Hole of Calcutta." There was a separate county jail after May, 1877, which was part of the new courthouse and cost thousands of dollars. See, Richard Selcer, "Tarrant County Jail Controversy: Something Old, Something New," *Fort Worth Star-Telegram* ("Lifestyle Section"), May 28, 1989, p. 1.

34. Bud Shrake, "Old Days on a Mule Cart," *Fort Worth Press*, September 1, 1957. See also, Williams, "Fort Worth Police Wore Confederate Gray Until '89," *In Old Fort Worth* (1975), p. 10.

35. Minutes of City Council, June 5, 1877.

36. *Ibid.*, December 8, 1877.

37. *Ibid.*, October 2, 1877.

38. *Ibid.*, December 8, 1877. Fort Worth's first public hospital, St. Joseph's, did not open its doors until 1889. It was operated by the Sisters of the Incarnate Word.

39. *Dallas Daily Herald*, October 3, 1876.

40. *Ibid.*, May 17, 1877. The *Dallas Daily Herald* reported on May 31 that the new jail "has been accepted" by Fort Worth officials, but the wording left unclear just when that event took place — some days before is all that can be inferred.

41. Williams, "Fort Worth Police," *In Old Fort Worth*, (1975), p. 10.

42. *Dallas Daily Herald*, June 28, 1877.

43. *Ibid.*, June 24, 1877.

44. *Ibid.*, July 17 and August 18, 1877.

45. *Ibid.*, October 13, 1877.

46. Hendricks, *Bad Man of the West*, p. 27. See also, John F. Wukovitz, "Gunfighters and Lawmen," *Wild West* (August, 1988), p. 61.

47. Minutes of City Council, January 23, 1877.

48. *Ibid.*, September 25, 1877.

49. Williams, "Fort Worth Police," *In Old Fort Worth* (1975), p. 10. A rare photograph exists today of one of those early Fort Worth police forces, dressed all in gray and looking like a reunion of Confederate Gettysburg veterans right after the Civil War.

50. *Ibid.*

51. *Ibid.* On April 22, 1873, the City Council ordered that each police officer wear a star in plain sight.

52. *Fort Worth Daily Democrat*, March 19–21, 1879.

53. Ordinance No. 125, passed September 11, 1877.

54. *Dallas Daily Herald*, June 17, 1877.

55. State of Texas vs. H. P. Shiel, August 25, 1879, November 26, 1879, Tarrant County Criminal Docket, County Court, 1879–1881; State of Texas vs. H. P. Shiel, June 14, 1886, Tarrant County Criminal Minutes, County Court, 1886–1887; State of Texas vs. H. P. Shiel, July 11, 1889, May 8, 1890, Tarrant County Criminal Minutes, County Court, 1889–1890; State of Texas vs. Joe Witcher, March 22, 1881, Tarrant County Criminal Docket, County Court, 1879–1881; State of Texas vs. Bony Tucker, February 8, 1887; Tarrant Count Criminal Minutes, County Court, 1886–1887; State of Texas vs. J. J. Fulford, January 7, 1888, January 7, 1889, Tarrant County Criminal Minutes, County Court, 1887–1889 (all in Special Collections, University of Texas at Arlington).

56. *Fort Worth Democrat*, April 10, 1878, p. 1.

57. Richard B. Hubbard served as governor of Texas from 1876 to 1879, during which time he waged a successful war against the state's numerous lawbreakers. Although a former Confederate himself, the governor had little sympathy for the lawless ex-Confederates who flooded into Texas after the Civil War — men like John Wesley Hardin, Bill Longley, Ben Thompson, and King Fisher, all of whom met their end in Texas while Hubbard was in office. Paul Bolton, *Governors of Texas*; also, Ross Phares, *The Governors of Texas*, pp. 109–11.

58. Knight, *Fort Worth*, p. 102. The Deadwood (Dakota Territory) stage may have been more famous in the history of the West, but no route was longer or more dangerous than this one. Fort Worth became the eastern terminus in 1878.

59. Gard, *Sam Bass*, pp. 106–07.

60. *Ibid.*

61. *Fort Worth Daily Democrat*, March 1, 1879.

62. Paddock, *History of Texas: Fort Worth and the Texas Northwest Edition*, vol. 2, p. 876.

63. *Fort Worth Daily Democrat*, March 20, 1879.

64. Gard, *Sam Bass*, p. 48.

65. *Ibid.*, p. 145.

66. *Ibid.*, pp. 97, 232. Davis was later reported to be living under an assumed name in Nicaragua. He told a visitor there in 1920, "I haven't seen Texas since '77. I lit a shuck out of Fort Worth in early winter that year . . . been here ever since."

67. *Ibid.*, p. 108.

68. *Ibid.*, p. 104.

69. *Ibid*, p. 107. See also, Anonymous, *Authentic History of Sam Bass and His Gang*, p. 44.

70. O'Neal's authoritative *Encyclopedia of Western Gunfighters* does not even mention Bass's stage robberies in Texas, although the earliest biographies credit him with at least nine before he switched to trains. See, Charles L. Martin, *A Sketch of Sam Bass, the Bandit, A Graphic Narrative*; also, Anonymous, *Authentic History of Sam Bass*.

71. Martin, *A Sketch of Sam Bass*, pp. 53–54.

72. Howard R. Lamar, ed., *The Reader's Encyclopedia of the American West*, p. 80.

73. James B. Gillett, *Six Years with the Texas Rangers, 1875–1881*, p. 116.

74. Martin, *A Sketch of Sam Bass*, p. 118.

75. Minutes of City Council, June 7, 1878, Book B, January 15, 1878–December 30, 1879.

76. Gard, *Sam Bass*, p. 112.

77. *Ibid.*, pp. 118–19.

78. *Life and Adventures of Sam Bass*, p. 54.

79. Bartholomew, *Biographical Album of Western Gunfighters*.

80. George Cormack, "Shootout at Round Rock," *San Antonio Express-News*, May 8, 1976, p. 4 A.

81. Richard Dillon, *Wells, Fargo Detective: A Biography of James B. Hume*, p. 234.

82. Lamar, *The Reader's Encyclopedia*, p. 80.

83. Gard, *Sam Bass*, p. 180; Gillett, *Six Years with the Texas Rangers*, pp. 117–18.

84. It is doubtful if any Fort Worth citizens realized at the time how close their city had come to making history in a big way. As it was, the city mourned (celebrated?) Bass' passing in its own way. The El Paso Hotel put a scruffy-looking hat on display in the bar which they claimed was "the identical hat which Sam Bass wore at the time of his capture." The hat, described as "a limp one with a low crown and a wide brim," belonged to a traveling hat salesman out of St. Louis. The salesman was vague on exactly how and where he got the head gear, but he arrived in Fort Worth showing it off just three weeks after Bass met his end. Since the El Paso bar was one of the most popular "watering holes" in Fort Worth at the time, the hat drew considerable attention, which probably did not hurt the bar's or the salesman's business any. See, Gard, *Sam Bass*, p. 240.

85. Mack Williams, "Business Before Law Enforcement, Courtright Told," *The News-Tribune* [Fort Worth], October 10, 1986, p. 10 A.

86. *Fort Worth Daily Democrat*, March 1, 1879.

87. Paddock, *History of Texas*, vol. 2, p. 876.

88. Roberts, "Memories," *In Old Fort Worth* (1976), p. 29.

89. *Fort Worth Democrat*, February 5, 1877.

90. *Fort Worth Daily Democrat*, September 13, 1876.

91. Tarrant County (Texas) District Court Records, Case No. 1664 (Special Collections, University of Texas at Arlington). See also, Bartholomew, *Wyatt Earp, 1848–1880*, p. 226.

92. Minutes of City Council, June 5, June 19, 1877.

93. *Ibid.*, September 11, November 20, 1877.

94. Quoted in Gard, *The Chisholm Trail*, p. 238.

95. *Fort Worth Daily Democrat*, April 18, 1879.

96. *Ibid.*, April 24, 1879.

97. Gard, *The Chisholm Trail*, p. 238.

98. Knight, *Fort Worth*, p. 113.

99. *Ibid.*, p. 117.

100. Glenn Shirley, *Heck Thomas: Frontier Marshal*, p. 32.

101. James McIntire, *Early Days in Texas: A Trip to Hell and Heaven*, p. 137. This section of McIntire's memoirs reads like a handbook for running a wide-open frontier town in the 1870s and '80s.

102. *Fort Worth Daily Democrat*, March 19, 1879.

103. *Ibid.*, March 30, 1879.

104. *Ibid.*, March 26, 1879.

105. Cox, *Luke Short and His Era*, p. 162. See also, Maurice Kildare, "American Valley Went Up in Smoke," *Frontier Times* No. 98 (October–November, 1975), p. 56; and Eugene Cunningham, "Courtright the Longhaired," *True West*, No. 21 (May–June, 1957), p. 36.

106. State of Texas vs. T. I. Courtright, November 3, December 1, 1880, Tarrant County Criminal Docket, County Court, 1878–79 (Special Collections, University of Texas at Arlington).

107. Bartholomew, *Wyatt Earp, 1848–1880*, p. 226.

108. *Ibid.*

109. John Ireland was the eighteenth governor of Texas, serving from January, 1883, to January, 1887. His nickname while he was governor was "Oxcart John" because of his opposition to state subsidies for the railroads and other progressive measures. See, Phares, *The Governors of Texas*, pp. 115–17.

110. Shirley, *Heck Thomas*, p. 36; F. Stanley, *Longhair Jim Courtright*, pp. 146–47.

111. Nat Washer, "When the Washer Brothers Came to Town," *In Old Fort Worth* (1986), p. 81. See also *Fort Worth City Directory*, 1883–84, 1885–86.

112. *Fort Worth City Directory*, 1885–86. John Laneri is one of the true colorful characters of Fort Worth history. He worked his way up to hotel manager from ordinary barkeep at the Ginnochio in the early 1880s. He stayed at the Ginnochio for more than a decade, running its entire operation including restaurant and saloon. In

the latter capacity he achieved quite a reputation for himself, being hauled into court on numerous occasions for "disturbing the peace" and for selling liquor when it was against the law (e.g., on Sundays and election days). Eventually, he made the transition to respectable businessman when he founded the Fort Worth Macaroni Company in 1899, and then Our Best Macaroni in 1905. Between these dates, he also helped organize the city's Chamber of Commerce. Interview with Mrs. Ruby Schmidt, past president of Tarrant County Historical Society (1988). See also Criminal Minutes, County Court for Tarrant County, 1887–89, 1889–1890. vols. 153 and 154 TAR (Special Collections, University of Texas at Arlington).

113. Shirley, *Heck Thomas*, p. 37.

114. This establishment is sometimes cited as Lawler's Cafe, near Third and Main streets. Their advertising claimed this was "where the world's best chicken sandwich sold for $.10." (Both restaurant and ad cited in "Jim Courtright, Fort Worth Marshal, Lived and Died by Gun," *Fort Worth Star-Telegram*, no date, Fort Worth Public Library files.) See also, Mack Williams, "In Old Fort Worth," part 4 of Courtright series, *Fort Worth News-Tribune*, October 24, 1986, p. 10 A.

115. For Thomas, see, Shirley, *Heck Thomas*, p. 38. For the Woodys, see, Williams, "In Old Fort Worth," *Fort Worth News-Tribune*, October 24, 1986, p. 10 A.

116. Scott, "Marshal of Fort Worth," *True Western Adventures*, p. 69.

117. Fort Worth newspapers reported both Courtright and McIntire in Guatemala in 1885, then retracted the story, blaming the mistake on Dallas and New Orleans newspapers. See *Fort Worth Daily Gazette*, April 13, 1885 (p. 5); April 21, 1885 (p. 1); April 26, 1885 (pp. 5, 6). Years later, several historians still believe that Courtright went to *South* (not Central) America while he was on the run. See, Cunningham, "Courtright the Longhaired," *True West*, No. 21 (May–June, 1957) p. 36; and Metz, *The Shooters*, p. 170.

118. *Dallas Weekly Herald*, August 27, 1885, p. 6.

119. *Ibid.*

120. Holland was one of the city's pioneers who had been many things over the years, including newspaper publisher, owner of fine race horses and traveling salesman, but it was as a theater owner that he was best known. At various times he ran theaters in Fort Worth under the names "My Own," "Holland's Free Show Pavilion," and "Holland's Variety Theater." He was successful enough to be the subject of rumors in the 1880s that he was the richest man in the county "as far as ready money was concerned." (See Mary Daggett Lake Papers, Series 4, Box 2, File 9 [Genealogy and Local History Department, Fort Worth Public Library]). Holland's theaters had such sleazy reputations that on more than one occasion he had trouble getting a liquor license from the city. (See, *Fort Worth Morning Register*, June 2, June 3 [p. 4] 1897.) His place on Eleventh Street between Main and Rusk was one of the busiest places in the Acre for years. Sometimes, it was said, business deals struck in the saloon or theater were concluded in one of the "female boarding houses" right behind the building.

121. Interview with J. H. Hagerty, "Texas Writers' Project," vol. 70, p. 27,959. But Holland's standing in the community was solid enough that such criticisms did not bother him and were probably good for business.

122. Williams, "Courtright Ambushes Train Robbers, Makes Enemies," *The News-Tribune* (Fort Worth), October 31, 1986, p. 14 B.

5. "The Gamblers Must Go!"

1. The three-minute gunfight that made history occurred in Tombstone, Arizona, on October 26, 1881. When it was over, three men were dead and two men seriously wounded. The *Fort Worth Democrat* for November 12, 1881 (p. 4), carried the first detailed local account of the shootout between Doc Holliday and the Earps on one side versus the Clantons, McLaurys and Billy Claiborne on the other. The *Democrat* credits its version of events with the description of the Earps as "Texas men" to a private letter sent from Tombstone to "a gentleman in San Francisco" and printed in the *Globe-Democrat* in that city. The *Democrat's* account is strongly anti-Earp-and-Holliday in tone.

2. Bartholomew, *Wyatt Earp, 1848–1880*, pp. 198, 208, 307; also, Schoenberger, *The Gunfighters*, p. 38.

3. Bartholomew, *Wyatt Earp, 1848–1880*, pp. 12, 54, 134, 208, 305; *Fort Worth City Directory*, 1878–79 (Fort Worth Public Library); *Fort Worth Democrat*, January 17, 1879.

4. Bartholomew, *Wyatt Earp, 1848–1880*, pp. 46, 134, 208, 300.

5. *Ibid.*, p. 307.

6. *Las Vegas* [New Mexico Territory] *Optic*, December 30, 1879.

7. *Dodge City* [Kansas] *Times*, May 14, 1878; see also, Schoenberger, *The Gunfighters*, pp. 33–34.

8. Schoenberger, *The Gunfighters*, p. 38; see also, Howard Bryan, *Wildest of the Wild West*, p. 139.

9. Boyer, ed., *I Married Wyatt Earp*, p. 117–23.

10. Nyle H. Miller and Joseph W. Snell, *Why the West Was Wild*, pp. 161–62; Boyer, ed., *I Married Wyatt Earp*, p. 118.

11. Bartholomew, *Wyatt Earp, 1848–1880*, pp. 208, 226; Tarrant County Criminal Minutes, County Court, 1886–1887, Case No. 4302, October 19, 1887 (Special Collections, University of Texas at Arlington).

12. Marks, *And Die in the West: The Story of the O.K. Corral Gunfight*, p. 254.

13. Stanley, *Dave Rudabaugh, Border Ruffian*, p. 22. No other historian or biographer of Doc Holliday agrees with Stanley on this point. See, Pat Jahns, *The Frontier World of Doc Holliday* and Ramon F. Adams, ed., *Six-guns and Saddle Leather, A Bibliography*. Adams offers a devastating critique of Stanley's book (item no. 2095). The depression, which Stanley claims drove Holliday to emigrate to Fort Worth, did not hit until the fall of 1873. By that time Holliday is listed in the *Dallas City Directory* in dental practice with Dr. John A. Seegar on Elm Street. Stanley also claims, without evidence, that Holliday first started wearing sidearms in Fort Worth. No doubt if he visited Fort Worth as a gambler, he came armed, but it is extremely doubtful Holliday went unarmed previous to this time.

14. It is likely that John Henry Holliday knew the Earp family even before he left Griffin, Georgia, as two of the town's residents were Daniel and Obedience Earp, aunt and uncle to the five famous Earp brothers. See, Albert S. Pendleton, Jr., and

Susan McKey Thomas, "Doc Holliday's Georgia Background," *The Journal of Arizona History*, vol. 14, no. 3 (Autumn, 1973), p. 195.

15. Reported in the *Dallas Morning News*, December 23, 1949.

16. *Dallas Times Herald*, February 7, 1964, p. 23.

17. Boyer, ed., *I Married Wyatt Earp*, p. 112.

18. *Ibid.*, p. 116.

19. Robert M. Wright, *Dodge City: The Cowboy Capital and the Great Southwest* (cited in Joseph G. Rosa, *The Gunfighter, Man or Myth?*, p. 130).

20. Bryan, *Wildest of the Wild West*, pp. 4, 108, 134.

21. *Ibid.*, p. 144.

22. *Fort Worth Democrat-Advance*, January 27, 1882; Rosa, *The Gunfighter*, p. 130; O'Neal, *Encyclopedia of Western Gunfighters*, p. 223.

23. Bryan, *Wildest of the Wild West*, pp. 144–45.

24. Paddock, *History of Texas: Fort Worth and the Texas Northwest*, p. 875. Neither of Thompson's two standard biographers, William M. Walton or Floyd Streeter, mentions Thompson ever being in Fort Worth, but there is no reason to doubt Paddock's memory of events. The movements of most of the West's major figures are but poorly known and even less documented. See, William M. Walton, *Life and Adventures of Ben Thompson* and Floyd B. Streeter, *Ben Thompson, Man with a Gun*.

25. Robert K. DeArment, *Knights of the Green Cloth*, p. 9.

26. That picture of Thompson dressed to the nines like a polished eastern dude is still the best-known photo of the man. Unfortunately for this study, it was taken twenty years before he began visiting Fort Worth on a regular basis. Lauran Paine, *Texas Ben Thompson*, p. 47.

27. Oliver Knight, *Fort Worth: Outpost on the Trinity*, p. 123.

28. *Fort Worth Daily Gazette*, May 22, 1887.

29. *Fort Worth Gazette*, April 25, 1885.

30. J. T. Upchurch, "The Lawless Liquor Traffic and the Infamous Traffic in Girls," *The Purity Journal*, vol. 2, no. 9 (March, 1906), p. 6. *The Purity Journal* (published in Arlington, Texas) was such an obscure, local and narrowly focused publication. The only known surviving copies are in the files of the Dallas Historical Society.

31. *Fort Worth Morning Register*, May 16, 1897.

32. *Fort Worth City Directories*, 1881–1887 (Fort Worth Public Library).

33. *Genesis*, 18:20 ff., tells the story of how Lot pleaded with God to save the wicked city of Sodom if he could find as few as ten righteous men in the city.

34. *Fort Worth Star-Telegram*, January 11, 1909.

35. James Leo Garrett, Jr., *Living Stones: The Centennial History of Broadway Baptist Church*, vol. 1, pp. 37–38.

36. Letter to *Texas Baptist* from "L.R.S.," April 19, 1883, p. 2 (Texas Baptist Historical Collection, Southwestern Baptist Theological Seminary, Fort Worth).

37. Fort Worth City Directory, 1878–79, pp. 24–25.

38. *Fort Worth Gazette*, April 25, 1885.

39. *Fort Worth Daily Democrat*, July 18, 1881.

40. *The Purity Journal*, pp. 7–8 (note photographs).

41. *Fort Worth Star-Telegram*, May 26, 1909.

42. William Loren Katz, *The Black West*, p. 146.

43. John W. Forney, *What I Saw in Texas*, p. 24.

44. Katz, *The Black West*, p. 170.

45. Donovan Duncan Tidwell, "A History of the West Fork Baptist Association (Texas)," Th.D. dissertation, Southwestern Baptist Theological Seminary, 1940, p. 105.

46. 1880 Census Report for Tarrant County, microfilm, Fort Worth Public Library.

47. The 1880 census does not show a significant concentration of black residents on the south end of town, although even at that early date the racial mixture of the Acre is apparent. Since the 1890 Census records are lost, there is not another census profile of the city available until 1900. But the earliest Sanborn Fire Maps of the city, 1885 and 1889, definitely show the existence of a black community east of Rusk Street and south of Twelfth. The greatest concentration of black citizens in that decade was on Calhoun Street, the first block east of Rusk. Fort Worth's first "Colored City Directory," published in 1906, gives a better picture of black population growth on the south end of town than does the 1900 census report. Among other things, the Directory shows that practically all the "colored" businesses by that date were located between Thirteenth and Fifteenth streets, from Rusk to Calhoun, that is, the Hell's Half Acre district. Copy of "Colored City Directory" in possession of Tarrant County Historical Society.

48. *Fort Worth Daily Gazette*, February 25, 1887. Tarrant County Criminal Minutes, County Court, 1886–1887, 1887–1889, 1889–1890 (Special Collections, University of Texas at Arlington).

49. Interview with Judge Irby Dunklin, May, 1938, "Texas Writers' Project," vol. 2, p. 526.

50. *Fort Worth Record*, December 30, 1906.

51. *Ibid.*

52. They also kept their names out of the history books, and since property records that far back no longer exist, only educated guesses can be made today about the identity of the absentee landlords. All that has come down to us today are stories that were whispered around or passed down among family members, but those stories paint a picture of respectable, church-going, family men who, over the course of two decades or more, made sizeable fortunes in Hell's Half Acre real estate. Some were prominent enough to have their names placed later on public buildings and other local landmarks.

53. *Fort Worth Star-Telegram*, January 11, 1909.

54. *Ibid.*

55. Mack Williams, "Hotel Corner for a Century," *In Old Fort Worth* (1986), p. 78.

56. *Ibid.*, p. 77.

57. "Thistle Hill," as the mansion was named by its original owner, still stands today at the intersection of Pennsylvania and Summit avenues, a magnificent monument to high society, western style. It is registered as a Texas Historical Landmark and listed on the National Register of Historic Places. See, Judy Alter, *Thistle Hill: The History and the House*.

58. Williams, "Fort Worth's First Millionaire," *In Old Fort Worth*, pp. 57–58.

59. "Texas Writers' Project," vol. 2, p. 592; see also biographical entry in Fort Worth *City Guide*; and Brookes Baker, *Map of Fort Worth, Texas Centennial Edition*.

60. Copies of Daggett's last will and testament, original and revised, in possession of Ruby Schmidt, Fort Worth.

61. Tarrant County Criminal Minutes, Case No. 4299, October 26, 1887.

62. *Ibid.*, Case No. 6578, November 18, November 24, 1890.

63. Although there is no mention in the public records of personal connections between some of the shady ladies of the Acre and certain well-known business and civic leaders, stories about the relationships have floated around for years, losing nothing in the telling. Alas, the overwhelming majority must be relegated to the category of unattributed rumors. Shady relationships between public men and ladies of the evening are part of the web of whisperings and innuendo that compose the frontier heritage of every civilized community before the mythmakers whitewash the reputations of the founding fathers. The frequently heard term "lusty Texans" describes more than their two-fisted, rough-and-tumble approach to business.

64. There are problems inherent in trying to draw conclusions from the census reports. The 1880 census is heavily damaged in the early part, the later pages do not always include street names in the margins and specific street addresses are never given, making it difficult to tell from the data just where the respondents lived. What the 1880 census does show is that Fort Worth was still an overwhelmingly white town. Sixth Street was the only street where blacks predominated, and then only from Main Street eastward. Above Sixth Street there were practically no black residents on any street, although in some cases blacks in white residential areas are enumerated as "laborers." The 1890 census schedules for Tarrant County do not exist. They were destroyed, along with ninety-nine percent of the census records for the rest of the country in a disastrous fire in the Commerce Department Building, Washington, D.C., on January 21, 1921. This is a particularly tragic loss to researchers because this was the only census until 1970 to use a "family schedule," i.e., a separate schedule for each family enumerated instead of a continuous listing. See, Val. D. Greenwood, *The Researchers' Guide to American Genealogy;* also, Arlene Eakle and John Cerny, eds., *The Source: A Guidebook of American Genealogy*. The 1900 census, therefore, is the first one to show a significant black population, concentrated now in the area south of Ninth and east of Main — the heart of Hell's Half Acre.

65. See *Fort Worth Daily Gazette,* September 28, 1890, p. 3. More exact figures are impossible to provide because there were no surveys, polls or other statistical studies done of the district's population. The *Gazette*'s information is probably garnered from census reports, which would have concluded in June of 1890.

66. *Fort Worth Daily Gazette,* April 1, 1887.

67. "Burly Black . . . ," *Fort Worth Daily Gazette,* March 4, 1885, p. 5; "Black Fiend . . . ," *Fort Worth Daily Democrat,* September 5, 1879.

68. *Fort Worth Daily Gazette,* March 14, 1887.

69. *Ibid.* (Emeline was eventually stabbed by a jealous rival. She survived, then tried to take her own life with an overdose of morphine. She survived again and lived to fight another day. *Fort Worth Daily Gazette,* March 5 and December 6, 1888.)

70. *Fort Worth Gazette,* June 2, 1887 (p. 8), April 18, 1887 (p. 8).

71. Minutes of the City Council, April 23, 1873.

72. Interview with J. L. Terry, June 2, 1938, "Texas Writers' Project," vol. 2, pp. 535–36. Terry refers to Henderson as "Bill"; records indicate the sheriff at the time was John M. Henderson.

73. *Dallas Herald,* April 17, 1885.

74. Ordinance No. 120, passed August 29, 1877; and Ordinance No. 123, passed September 11, 1877.

75. Ordinance No. 124, passed September 11, 1877.

76. Nat Washer, "When the Washer Brothers Came to Town," *In Old Fort Worth* (1986), p. 81.

77. *Ibid.*

78. "Where the West Begins" (introductory essay), "Texas Writers' Project," vol. 51, p. 20,355.

79. Bat Masterson, "Famous Gun Fighters of the Western Frontier — Wyatt Earp," *Human Life* Magazine (February, 1907), p. 9.

80. *Fort Worth Daily Democrat,* December 31, 1878.

81. *Ibid.*

82. *Ibid.*

83. *Fort Worth Gazette,* May 24, 1887, p. 5.

84. Knight, *Fort Worth,* p. 123.

85. *Fort Worth Daily Democrat,* December 7, 1880.

86. *Ibid.*, September 18, 1881.

87. *Fort Worth Morning Register,* July 27, 1897, p. 5.

88. Nancy Wilson Ross, *Westward the Women,* p. 131.

89. *Fort Worth Gazette,* August 26, 1884, p. 8.

90. *Fort Worth Morning Register,* October 18, 1900.

91. *Ibid.*

92. Ross, *Westward the Women,* p. 135.

93. *Ibid.*

94. *Fort Worth Democrat,* November 3, 1881, p. 1.

95. The Mary Lake Daggett Papers (Fort Worth Public Library) include this enigmatic reference to Jessie: "S. B. Burnett was her man." Samuel Burk Burnett — friend of governors, presidents and Indian chiefs — was one of the legendary cattle barons who helped build Fort Worth, and founder of the Texas and Southwestern Cattle Raisers Association. Burkburnett, Texas, the Burk Burnett Building and Burnett Park (both in Fort Worth) are named for him. Like many references in Lake's papers, no source or further explanation is given for this comment. According to Ruby Schmidt (interview, May, 1990), Lake must have heard the rumor about Burnett from family members or from one of the old-timers who often sent her tidbits for her newspaper columns.

Mary Daggett Lake (1881–1955) was the daughter of E. M. (Bud) Daggett, Jr., and the grandniece of E. M. Daggett, Sr. She married prominent cattleman Will F.

Lake in 1899, which gave her access to many of the stories passed around the cattleman's fraternity and the pioneer families of Fort Worth. For many years she wrote a regular column for the *Fort Worth Star-Telegram*, specializing in local history. After her death, her papers were acquired by the Tarrant County Historical Society and eventually deposited with the Fort Public Library where they remain.

96. *Fort Worth Daily Gazette*, June 16, 1888.

97. *Fort Worth Morning Register*, September, 26, 1900, p. 8.

98. Mary Daggett Lake Papers, Series II, "State and Local History," Box 2, Folder 6.

99. Taxes Delinquent to City of Fort Worth on Real Estate, 1898, vol. 49, p. 85, Receipts Nos. 2015 and 1096 (Records Office, County Courthouse, Fort Worth).

100. This surprisingly large number includes all listings for arrests made, charges filed and court appearances between 1893 and 1897, suggesting that there is probably some duplication in the entries. See Tarrant County Index to Criminal Minutes, 1893-1897 (Special Collections, University of Texas at Arlington).

101. This story cannot be verified in local marriage records, city directories or newspapers, nor does it jibe with the life of a woman who was known to be running a "boarding house" in 1901, five years before her death. See Mary Daggett Lake Papers, Series II, "State and Local History," Box 5, Folder 3.

102. *Ibid.*

103. Ross, *Westward the Women*, p. 135.

104. *Fort Worth Daily Democrat*, April 14, 1882; see also, *Dallas Daily Times-Herald*, November 9, 1889.

105. "Texas Writers' Project," vol. 51, p. 20,100.

106. *Fort Worth Weekly Gazette*, February 19, 1887, p. 8.

107. Joe P. Witcher, "1879 Policeman Tells How It Was," *In Old Fort Worth* (1975), p. 7.

108. *Fort Worth Democrat*, December 3, 1881, p. 1.

109. *Fort Worth Daily Democrat*, April 27, 1879.

110. *Ibid.*, June 15, 1879.

111. *Ibid.*, May 2, 1885, p. 5; see also, *Dallas Weekly Herald*, May 7, 1885.

112. *Fort Worth Daily Gazette*, February 23, 1887.

113. *Fort Worth Weekly Gazette*, February 8, 1887, p. 8.

114. *Fort Worth Daily Gazette*, May 17, 1887; see also, *Fort Worth Democrat*, February 26, 1887.

115. "Texas Writers' Project," vol. 70, p. 27,959.

116. Wayne Gard, *The Chisholm Trail*, pp. 253–59.

117. *Fort Worth Daily Gazette*, August 6, August 7, 1885 (p. 1, both dates).

118. *Ibid.*, September 26, 1887, p. 2.

119. *Dallas Weekly Herald*, September 4, 1884, p. 2.

120. *Ibid.*

121. *Fort Worth Morning Register*, May 11, 1897, p. 5.

122. *Dallas Daily Herald*, September 2, 1884.

123. *Ibid.*

124. Paul I. Wellman, *The Trampling Herd*, pp. 172 ff.

125. Broadside in the collections of New Mexico State Museum, Santa Fe.
126. Knight, *Fort Worth,* pp. 115–17.
127. *Fort Worth Daily Gazette,* September 23, 1889.
128. Wellman, *The Trampling Herd,* p. 158.

6. "Ful, they've got me!"

1. Wayne T. Walker, "Killer in Fancy Pants," *True West* (September–October, 1956), p. 14.

2. On February 25, 1881, Short was accosted by a drunken gambler named Charlie Storms as he left the Oriental Saloon in Tombstone, Arizona. Before Storms could get his gun out of his holster, Short shoved his own piece against the gambler's chest and emptied the cylinder. A grand jury subsequently refused to indict and the matter was buried along with Storms. This is the only *documented* killing by Short prior to 1887. See, O'Neal, *Encyclopedia of Western Gunfighters,* pp. 284–85. Short's substantial legend has it, however, that he killed eleven men during his career: six white men and five Indians. See also, Bartholomew, *Biographical Album of Western Gunfighters.*

3. See, William R. Cox, *Luke Short, Famous Gambler of the Old West,* p. 7; also, Schoenberger, *The Gunfighters,* p. 133; and O'Neal *Encyclopedia of Western Gunfighters,* p. 284. Compare, Bartholomew, *Biographical Album of Western Gunfighters,* n.p. Bartholomew says Short was born in Arkansas and then moved to Texas.

4. Schoenberger, *The Gunfighters,* p. 136.

5. *Ford County* [Kansas] *Globe,* November 20, 1883.

6. Both the *Ford County Globe,* for November 20, 1883, and the *Dodge City Times,* of November 22, 1883, reported that the two men left town together; the *Globe* specifically said they were headed for Fort Worth.

7. Boyer, ed., *I Married Wyatt Earp,* p. 118.

8. *Ibid.*, p. 121. The four-story Mansion House was located on Fourth Street between Main and Rusk. It was one of the best hotels in the city in the 1880s judging by its advertisements in the Fort Worth City Directories, 1883–84, 1888, 1889 and 1890.

9. Boyer, ed., *I Married Wyatt Earp,* p. 123.

10. Robert K. DeArment (*Bat Masterson, the Man and the Legend,* pp. 294–95) quotes Charles "Rusty" Coe, another well-traveled professional gambler, who has been described as "the most successful and also the most feared gambler of them all." See, Tom Bailey, "King of Cards," *New Magazine for Men,* vol. 17 (May, 1958), p. 13.

11. *Daily Free Press* of Bodie, California (cited in Roger D. McGrath, *Gunfighters, Highwaymen and Vigilantes,* p. 114).

12. 1880 Census for Tarrant County, Supervisor's District No. 8, Enumeration District No. 89, p. 52; Sup. Dist. No. 3, Enum. Dist. No. 90, pp. 11, 51.

13. On the evening of February 8, 1887, when Timothy Courtright came looking for him, Luke Short was in the bar area of the White Elephant, getting his boots polished. He did not go out to meet Courtright until he had finished. See *Fort Worth Gazette,* February 9, 1887, p. 8.

14. "Texas Writers' Project," vol. 51, p. 20,355.

15. McGrath, *Gunfighters, Highwaymen and Vigilantes,* p. 114.

16. Tarrant County Index to Criminal Minutes, 1893–1897 (Special Collections, University of Texas at Arlington).

17. McGrath, *Gunfighters,* p. 114.

18. DeArment, *Bat Masterson,* p. 295.

19. Charles Coe's story was written for him by Hugh Walters and published in 1903 under the title *My Life as a Card Shark.* What eventually became of that work, or if it still exists today, is a mystery. The Library of Congress has no record of it, nor is it listed in the standard bibliographies of western outlaws and gunmen. See, for example, *Six Guns and Saddle Leather, Burs Under the Saddle* and *More Burs Under the Saddle,* all by Ramon F. Adams, ed. According to DeArment, surviving copies of *My Life as a Card Shark,* if there are any, must be in private hands. (DeArment to author, December 8, 1990). DeArment's references to Coe are from Bailey, "King of Cards," *New Magazine for Men* (May, 1958), p. 12.

20. *Fort Worth Democrat,* June 15, 1879.

21. *Fort Worth City Directories,* 1881–82 and 1886–87 (Genealogy and Local History Room, Fort Worth Public Library [Main Branch]).

22. Herbert Asbury, *Sucker's Progress: An Informal History of Gambling in America from the Colonies to Canfield,* pp. 337–38.

23. *Ibid.*, p. 338.

24. *Fort Worth City Directories,* 1883–1900. See also, Tarrant County Criminal Docket, County Court, 1876–1879 and 1879–1881, no case numbers given, only trial dates: May 25, 1877; January 27, 1879; December 1, December 6, 1880; January 28, March 22 and April 25, 1881. Also Tarrant County Criminal Minutes, County Court, 1886–1887, 1887–1889, and 1889–1890, Case Nos. 2837 (March 29, 1886) and 2922 (April 15, 1886); Case No. 5315 (January 7, 1889); and Case Nos. 6141 (January 9, 1890), 6141 (January 13, 1890), and 6728 (September 8, 1890). After 1895, Johnson made at least seven appearances in County Court on various charges, but these records are fragmentary and incomplete. (Index to Criminal Minutes, 1895–1981).

25. Cox, *Luke Short: Famous Gambler of the West,* p. 147.

26. Described in *Fort Worth Press,* November 21, 1927.

27. *Dallas Weekly Herald,* October 9, 1884.

28. From the mid-1880s until the mid-1890s, the White Elephant was located at 308–310 Main Street. Some time between 1892 and 1895 it relocated to the 600 block of Main Street. From then on its address was listed variously at every even number between 604 and 612 Main, with no rhyme or reason to the numbering. See *City Directories,* 1885–1910.

29. One of the writer-editors for the "Texas Writers' Project" quotes unnamed sources in calling the White Elephant, "the most magnificent combination saloon, gambling house and restaurant in the nation — bar none." (See "Where the West Begins," vol. 51, p. 20,353). Other writers are less effusive. See, Cox, *Luke Short: Famous Gambler,* p. 147.

30. Advertisement in *City Directory,* 1881, p. 9.

31. For the Ward brothers' involvement, see *Fort Worth City Directory* listing for "White Elephant," 1886–87; also 1890–91 and 1892–93. John Ward became a city alderman in 1887, was reelected in 1888 for the first and last time and may have

helped provide some official protection for the White Elephant's shadier operations in those years. See, Knight, *Fort Worth,* p. 269. Jake Johnson's interest is revealed in the *Fort Worth Gazette,* February 8, 1887, p. 8. Johnson's former interest with Nat Kramer in the Cattle Exchange Saloon is revealed in the *City Directory,* 1883–84. Cox claims that Short was only an "employee" at the White Elephant in 1885, citing *Morrison & Fournoy's Directory of Fort Worth,* but this cannot be verified in the microfilmed city directory of that year. See, Cox, *Luke Short: Famous Gambler,* p. 147. What is certain is that there were three active owners of the White Elephant by the early part of 1887, although the exact legal rights and obligations of each are impossible to determine from the sketchy historical record.

32. Masterson, "Famous Gunfighters of the Western Frontier — Luke Short," *Human Life Magazine* (April, 1907), p. 20.

33. DeArment, *Knights of the Green Cloth,* pp. 101, 129, 137.

34. *Ibid.*, p. 128.

35. "Where the West Begins" (introductory essay), "Texas Writers' Project," vol. 51, pp. 20,345–20,355.

36. Cox, *Luke Short and His Era,* p. 165.

37. Tarrant County Criminal Minutes, County Court, 1887–1889, Case Nos. 4389, 4511, 4479 (December 3, 1887). Case No. 4389 was continued to January 14, 1888, when it was marked "unable to arrest . . . remain on file til arrested."

38. Cox, *Luke Short and His Era,* p. 158.

39. Masterson, "Famous Gunfighters," *Human Life Magazine* (April, 1907), p. 22; *Dallas Morning News,* February 10, 1887, p. 1. (For a fuller treatment of their relationship, see endnote 60.)

40. Cox, *Luke Short: Famous Gambler,* p. 153.

41. Williams, *In Old Fort Worth* (1975), p. 27.

42. Tarrant County Criminal Minutes, County Court, 1886–1887 (vol. 152) and 1887–1889 (vol. 153), Case Nos. 3878 (December 6, 1886, vol. 152); and 4472, 4501, 4209 (December 3, 1887, vol. 152); Case Nos. 4212, 4198, 4183, 4197, 4205, 4206, 4207 (December 3, 1887, vol. 153).

43. Time-Life Books, *The Gamblers,* p. 176. See also, jailhouse interview with Luke Short, *Fort Worth Daily Gazette,* February 9, 1887, p. 8. The night of Courtright's shooting, police took a Colt .45 off Short, according to the *Gazette.* When Short died six years later, his estate included that pistol and the deed to the property at Sixth and Pecan. Eventually, the pistol passed into the hands of Luke Short, III (interview with Ruby Schmidt of Fort Worth, based on her conversations with Luke Short, III.)

44. Tarrant County Criminal Minutes, County Court, 1886–1887, 1887–1889 and 1889–1890, Case No. 4052 (April 15, 1887); Case No. 4261 (October 15, 1887); Case No. 4606 (November 3, 1888); Case No. 6270 (January 13, 1890).

45. *Denver Republican,* April 27, 1885, p. 2. Jim McIntire had one of these cards on his person when he was arrested in Denver in 1885.

46. The same sign, much faded but still legible, was still there as late as 1929, according to F. Stanley — an odd "monument" to an odd kind of hero. Eventually, time and weather eradicated all vestige of the sign, though the building continued to stand for many years.

47. As its advertising symbol and slogan, the Pinkerton Detective Agency used a large, staring eye and the motto "We Never Sleep." Allan Pinkerton, the first detective on the Chicago police force, founded the legendary agency in Chicago in 1850. Pinkerton was an immigrant from Glasgow, Scotland, who achieved national recognition in the Civil War as a spymaster and protector of President Lincoln. Pinkerton died in 1884, the same year Courtright opened his detective agency. His legacy probably included the term "private eye," used ever since for members of the profession.

48. Shirley, *Heck Thomas,* pp. 35–36. Shirley reports this confrontation complete with dialogue, but he gets the date wrong; this incident could not have occurred any later than 1883 because W. M. Rea replaced Farmer as city marshal in April of that year.

49. *Fort Worth Daily Gazette,* April 26, 1885, p. 5; April 28, p. 6; and April 29, p. 8.

50. Masterson, "Famous Gunfighters," *Human Life Magazine* (April, 1907), p. 22.

51. Hendricks, *Bad Man of the West,* p. 213.

52. Jay Gould, one of the wealthiest railroad barons in the country, owned several lines in Texas in 1886, including the Texas & Pacific and the KATY (Missouri, Kansas and Texas). His brutal labor policies made it possible for the Knights of Labor to organize his workers in the 1880s. When Gould set out to break the union, a bloody series of strikes occurred, which saw scores injured, hundreds of thousands of dollars of property destroyed, and eventually martial law proclaimed by the governor of Texas.

53. Criminal Minutes, County Court, 1886–1887 and 1887–1889. For J. J. Fulford, Case Nos. 4621 and 5289 (January 7, 1888). For Bony Tucker, Case No. 3836 (February 8, 1887).

54. Tarrant County Criminal Docket, County Court, 1879–1891, pp. 6, 29 (no case numbers given). See also, Tarrant County Criminal Minutes, County Court 1886–1887, 1889–1890, Case No. 3706 (June 14, 1886); Case No. 3925 (April 4, 1887); Case No. 5765 (July 11, 1889); Case No. unmarked (May 8, 1890); Case No. 6603 (September 10, 1890); Case No. 6516 (September 8, 1890, and November 6, 1890); Case No. 6689 (September 9, 1890); Case No. 6721 (September 13, 1890).

55. Williams, "Courtright Ambushes Train Robbers, Makes Enemies," *Fort Worth News-Tribune,* October 31, 1986, p. 14 B.

56. *Fort Worth Daily Gazette,* April 4, 1886, p. 1.

57. Cox, *Luke Short: Famous Gambler,* p. 154.

58. *Dallas Daily Herald,* February 9, 1887, p. 1. See also, *Dallas Morning News,* February 9, 1887, p. 1; and Masterson, "Famous Gunfighters," *Human Life Magazine* (April, 1907), p. 22.

59. *Fort Worth Daily Gazette,* February 9, 1887, p. 8.

60. Short's statement agrees with what Bat Masterson said about Short being a "substantial friend of Courtright's during his [earlier] trouble at Fort Worth" (Masterson, "Famous Gunfighters," *Human Life Magazine* [April, 1907], p. 22), and with Howard W. Peak, Jr.'s, recollection that Courtright and Short had been former partners "in the management of a gambling house over a shooting gallery" before the

White Elephant feud erupted. (See, Peak, "My Recollections of Fort Worth," "Texas Writers' Project," vol. 9, p. 48.) Peak's recollections were written many years later. He could have been thinking of the White Elephant Saloon, which was next door to a shooting gallery and had gambling rooms on the second floor. If so, this adds a new wrinkle to the relationship. The possibility that their relationship was something less than cordial is suggested by a Dallas newspaper that claimed while Courtright was on the run from New Mexico authorities, "certain prominent Fort Worth parties" had tried to hire the fugitive gunman to "put Short out of the way." The same source said that Courtright came back to town, "but the scheme miscarried and was dropped." (See *Dallas Morning News,* February 9, 1887, p. 1.) The next day's edition of the same newspaper carried the report that Short had given money to Courtright when he went back to New Mexico to stand trial. All of this goes to show that contemporaries were as confused about the real nature of the two men's relationship as historians are today.

61. Masterson, "Famous Gunfighters," *Human Life Magazine* (April, 1907), p. 22.

62. *Ibid.*, p. 9.

63. Testimony given by W. A. James before Justice Smith at the coroner's inquest on February 9, 1887. (Cited in *Fort Worth Daily Gazette,* February 10, 1887, p. 5. Quoted slightly differently in Eugene Cunningham, *Triggernometry: A Gallery of Gunfighters,* p. 214.)

64. *Dallas Morning News,* February 9, 1887, p. 1.

65. F. Stanley (Father Stanley Crocchiola), *Longhair Jim Courtright,* p. 211.

66. *Dallas Morning News,* February 9, February 10, 1887, p. 1 (both dates). There is also the credibility of Stanley's biography, which is riddled with inaccuracies and distortions on the subject's life in Fort Worth. Finally, Short's side had something in later years that Courtright's did not: a living, breathing descendant ready to defend the family name against all challengers. The Courtright reputation had no such champion among family descendants in the twentieth century. Luke Short, III, the grandson of the famous gambler, was still alive until recently. He was born Charles William Borger in Tombstone, Arizona, on March 24, 1909, but in his later years came to identify himself so closely with the legend of his grandfather that he began calling himself Luke Short, III, and wearing the black frock coat, string tie and Stetson habitually worn by the first Luke Short. He claimed to have been raised by his grandfather's widow. For many years he lived in Sierra Vista, Arizona, but attended the reenactment of the gunfight every year at the "new" White Elephant Saloon at 106 East Exchange Ave. (See *Fort Worth Star-Telegram,* February 9, 1987, A.M. edition) Luke, III, staunchly defended his grandfather's honor and his role in the events of February 8, 1887. A descendant of Timothy Courtright lives today in San Clemente, California, and is said to be working on a new biography of him, but she has not devoted her life to perpetuating the family legends as did Luke Short, III. (Correspondence with C. L. Sonnichsen, Arizona Historical Society, Tucson, Arizona, June 8, 1989, author's files.)

67. Testimony of W. A. Jones at coroner's inquest, *Fort Worth Daily Gazette,* February 10, 1887, p. 5.

68. Asbury, *Sucker's Progress,* p. 338.

69. This curious transaction is reported without any details or explanation in the *Fort Worth Daily Gazette,* February 8, 1887, p. 1.

70. *Ibid.*, February 10, 1887, p. 5; also *Dallas Morning News,* February 10, 1887, p. 1.

71. Johnson is described as "a friend of Courtright" in the *Dallas Morning News* account of the shooting, February 10, 1887, p. 1.

72. The following description of events is reconstructed from four primary sources: The report of the coroner's inquest in the *Fort Worth Daily Gazette,* February 10, 1887; stories in the *Dallas Morning News,* February 10, 1887, and *Dallas Daily Herald,* February 9, 1887; Luke Short's own account in the *Fort Worth Daily Gazette,* February 9, 1887; and Bat Masterson's recollections, first published in *Human Life Magazine* in 1907. Yet another version of what happened that night might be described as "quasi-primary" because it was set down long after the fact and comes from an unnamed "informant" who related it to Howard W. Peak, Jr. Peak, a Fort Worth resident at the time, did not witness any of the events that he recorded more than four decades later. His informant, "who saw Courtright gasp his last breath," was sitting with another friend in the White Elephant bar that night, the two of them "engaged in a conversation." See, Peak, "The Killing of Courtwright" [sic], "Texas Writers' Project," vol. 1, p. 102. Peak, reportedly the first white child born in Fort Worth (1856), was a distinguished author and local historian for many years. He died in 1939 and was buried in Oakwood Cemetery, leaving behind a wealth of collected and first-hand material related to Fort Worth history. The material in the "Texas Writers' Project" is taken from his "Carnegie Library Scrapbook" (Fort Worth Public Library).

73. Peak, "The Killing of Courtwright" [sic], "Texas Writers' Project," vol. 1, p. 102.

74. Schoenberger, *The Gunfighters,* p. 143.

75. Contrary to popular notion, Courtright did not "invent" the maneuver of flipping the gun from one hand to the other, known as the "border shift." Among earlier practitioners was Ed Masterson, Bat's brother, who once used it successfully in a gunfight with Bob Shaw in a Dodge City bar (See, Wellman, *The Trampling Herd,* pp. 196–97). In reference to Courtright and the border shift, see, Carl Breihan, "How Well Do You Know These Western Badmen?" *Frontier Times* (Winter, 1961), p. 29.

76. Peak, "Texas Writers' Project," vol. 1, p. 102.

77. *Ibid.*

78. From testimony given at coroner's inquest. See *Fort Worth Daily Gazette,* February 10, 1887, p. 5.

79. Masterson, "Famous Gunfighters," *Human Life Magazine* (April, 1907), p. 10. For a fuller account of the Tombstone fight and the events leading up to it, see, DeArment, *Bat Masterson,* pp. 198–99; and Cox, *Luke Short: Famous Gambler,* pp. 72–76. Both secondary accounts refer to Masterson as their primary source.

80. *Dallas Morning News,* February 9, 1887, p. 1; and *Fort Worth Daily Gazette,* February 9, 1887, p. 8.

81. These were the exact words quoted by Officer Fulford at the coroner's inquest the day after the shooting (*Fort Worth Daily Gazette,* February 10, 1887, p. 5). However, that night, Officer Bony Tucker told a newspaper reporter, "When I reached him [Courtright] he was dying, and though I bent over and spoke to him, he

never articulated a syllable." (*Fort Worth Daily Gazette,* February 9, 1887, p. 8.) Tucker's statement was given immediately after the event; Fulford's testimony was given under oath.

82. Alfred Henry Lewis, "The King of the Gun-Players, William Barclay Masterson," *Human Life Magazine* (November, 1907), p. 10.

83. Courtright's body was eventually moved to Oakwood Cemetery, Fort Worth, where it rests today. His grave did not have a headstone until May, 1954, when his granddaughter paid to have one put up. However, here good intentions went awry when she had the stonecutter put on the headstone that her grandfather had been a "U.S. Marshal." The stone still carries that incorrect legend today, puzzling historians and hoodwinking sightseers.

84. Cox, *Luke Short and His Era,* p. 153.

85. Thomas Penfield, *Western Sheriffs and Marshals,* p. xii.

86. *Fort Worth Daily Gazette,* February 25, 1887, p. 3.

87. "Funeral Notice" in Mary Daggett Lake Papers, Series IV, Box 1, File 25, "Courtright Family Misc., 1878–1904" (Fort Worth Public Library).

88. Ed Bartholomew states in his authoritative *Biographical Album of Western Gunfighters*: "As late as 1958, I have been told that it was Bat Masterson who killed Courtright, and not Short" (Luke Short entry in *Album*).

89. *Fort Worth Daily Gazette,* February 9, 1887.

90. Paddock, *Account Book,* 1889–1891, pp. 121, 177 (Barker History Center, University of Texas at Austin).

91. *Fort Worth City Directories,* 1888, 1889 and 1890.

92. Tarrant County Criminal Minutes, County Court, 1887–1889, Case No. 4124 (January 14, 1888).

93. *Ibid.*, Case Nos. 4389, 4511, 4479 (December 3, 1887).

94. *Fort Worth Daily Gazette,* December 24, 1890.

95. *Ibid.*, December 25, 1890.

96. See Tarrant County District Court Records, State of Texas vs. Luke Short for "Assault with intent to murder," Case No. 6199. The case was first filed on January 31, 1891, then dragged out for most of that year because of various legal maneuvers by Short's lawyers. It was finally dismissed on October 23, 1893. (Criminal Courts Building, Fort Worth) Luke Short had already died in September, 1893.

97. Lewis Atherton, *The Cattle Kings,* p. 39.

98. Drago, *Great American Cattle Trails,* p. 216.

99. According to the *Fort Worth Gazette* (September 9, 1893, p. 6), Short died in Geuda Springs, Arkansas, an error corrected by William Cox in *Luke Short: Famous Gambler,* pp. 175–76. Geuda Springs was a hamlet just north of the Kansas-Oklahoma border. The nearest town was Arkansas City, Kansas, which may account for the confusion.

100. The modern medical diagnosis for Luke Short's illness would probably be edema, a very treatable condition caused by any combination of factors, including gradual failure of the liver and kidneys. Apparently it was practically an occupational hazard for gamblers: Doc Holliday and Richard B. S. Clark also suffered from it. Although the *Geuda Springs Herald* for September 8 states that Short died of "dropsy," a descendant of the man who ran the boarding house where Short was staying when

he died claimed many years later that it was Bright's disease that killed him. (See correspondence between M. C. Ward and William R. Cox, in Cox, *Luke Short: Famous Gambler,* p. 176.)

101. For years, a local legend has persisted that Luke bought the plot in Oakwood for a mysterious, unnamed prostitute who occupied a special place in his heart. Unfortunately, he died first, and her name and ultimate fate remain unknown. At least that is the story. No doubt it has been encouraged by the almost complete lack of information about his wife Hettie and their relationship (interview with Ruby Schmidt, Fort Worth, May, 1989).

102. *Fort Worth Daily Gazette, September* 11, 1893, p. 2. Compare, Cox's description of Short's passing: "There was no parade of the fire department or grieving citizens in Fort Worth, as had been the case when Jim Courtright died. There was merely a simple interment, unrecorded in the public prints." (Cox, *Luke Short: Famous Gambler,* p. 177.)

103. Masterson, "Famous Gunfighters," *Human Life Magazine* (April, 1907), p. 24. (As a close friend and fellow gambler, Masterson can be forgiven a little eulogizing.)

104. Carolyn Lake, ed., *Under Cover for Wells Fargo: The Unvarnished Recollections of Fred Dodge,* p. 233.

105. Interview with Ruby Schmidt, Fort Worth, July 27, 1989 (based on her conversations with Luke Short, III).

106. *Fort Worth Daily Gazette,* February 10, 1887, p. 1.

107. *Ibid.*, September 12, 1885, p. 5.

108. J. B. Roberts, "Memories of an Early Police Reporter," *In Old Fort Worth* (1976), p. 29.

109. *Ibid.*

110. *Fort Worth Daily Gazette,* August 20, 1887, p. 2.

111. The prohibition against open-door gambling is reported in the *Fort Worth Daily Gazette,* December 6, 1887. The historian quoted is Cox, *Luke Short: Famous Gambler,* p. 167.

112. *Ibid.*, September 10, 1889 (quoting Judge R. E. Beckham).

113. In announcing the December clean-up campaign, the ecstatic *Gazette* reported, "[the] Open-Door Betting House [is] a Thing of the Past in Fort Worth," and "the gambling houses were closed . . . tighter than wax as far as anyone could discover." See *Fort Worth Daily Gazette,* December 6, 1887.

114. The original source for this famous story remains Oliver Knight (*Fort Worth,* p. 136). Every other writer for nearly forty years has "borrowed" from Knight's work. Although Knight's research has never been questioned, no one has ever cited an original newspaper or other documentary source for the story.

115. *Fort Worth Daily Gazette,* March 17 (p. 8), March 18 (p. 8), 1887.

116. *Ibid.*, March 17, 1887, p. 8.

117. *Fort Worth Daily Gazette,* February 10, 1887, p. 4.

7. "Nothing But Brick and Mortar . . ."

1. *Fort Worth Daily Gazette*, November 21, 1887.
2. *Ibid.*, April 6, 1887, p. 8.

3. *Ibid.*, April 12, 1887, p. 8. Rea's retirement did not last long. He ran for the marshal's office again and was reelected in 1889. After that, he postponed his retirement for many years.

4. *Ibid.*, October 1, 1887, p. 8.

5. Mack Williams, "Fort Worth Police Wore Confederate Gray Until '89," *In Old Fort Worth* (1975), p. 10.

6. *Fort Worth Daily Gazette*, August 22, 1887.

7. *Ibid.*, August 15, 1887, p. 8.

8. *Ibid.*, August 28, 1887.

9. *Ibid.*, September, 3, 1887, p. 8.

10. *Ibid.*, September 13, 1887, p. 8.

11. *Ibid.*, September 14, 1887, p. 2.

12. For "owners" see *Fort Worth Daily Democrat*, April 26, 1879, p. 3; and for "winking," see *Fort Worth Democrat*, February 5, 1877, p. 3.

13. *Fort Worth Daily Gazette*, September 10, 1889.

14. *Ibid.*, August 12, 1887, p. 6.

15. Interview with Mrs. Octavia Bennett, June 6, 1952 (in personal files of Mrs. Ruby Schmidt, Fort Worth).

16. *Fort Worth Daily Gazette*, March 6, 1887, p. 8.

17. *Ibid.*, September 9, 1887, p. 2.

18. Tarrant County Criminal Minutes, County Court, 1886–1887, Case Nos. 2829, 3177; Tarrant County Criminal Minutes, 1887–1890, Case No. 6725; Tarrant County Criminal Minutes, 1893–1894, Case Nos. 9018, 9440, 9568, 9667, 8441, 9888, 9885, 10575, 11932, 11934; and Tarrant County Index to Criminal Minutes, 1895–1918, 33 separate entries, no dates or descriptions of cases. For specific cases where B. B. Paddock posted bail, see Tarrant County Criminal Minutes, 1893–1894, Case Nos. 11932 and 11934. (Special Collections, University of Texas at Arlington).

19. Knight, *Fort Worth*, p. 136.

20. *Fort Worth Daily Gazette*, September 10, 1889.

21. *Ibid.*, December 6, 1887.

22. *Ibid.*

23. Samuel Elliot Morrison, Henry Steele Commager and William E. Leuchtenburg, *The Growth of the American Republic*, vol. 2, p. 285.

24. The WCTU rose to prominence in the 1880s under its redoubtable founder Miss Frances Willard and won many converts in its fight against demon drink. The ladies also waged crusades to found homes for fallen women, win female suffrage and establish Mother's Day as a national holiday. The union's proudest crusade was the one that culminated in the adoption of the Eighteenth Amendment in 1919. In modern times the WCTU has campaigned to "Let Freedom Ring: Freedom from Alcohol, Tobacco, Obscenity and Atheism." For information on Mary Clardy and the WCTU in Texas, see, Helen B. Gardener, "A Battle for Sound Morality," *The Arena* (November, 1895), p. 408.

25. Ed Bartholomew, *Biographical Album of Western Gunfighters*.

26. *Ibid.* This was the same occasion they disarmed the squad of soldiers.

27. *Fort Worth Daily Gazette*, January 24, 1887.

28. *Ibid.*, June 5, 1887.

29. Richard Patterson, *Historical Atlas of the Outlaw West*, p. 171.

30. *Fort Worth Daily Gazette*, September 21, 1887.

31. *Field and Farm Journal* (Denver, Colorado), December 7, 1889, p. 6.

32. In fact, there is some question whether he ever established a residence in Fort Worth. He was not listed in any city directory for the 1880s. This may mean that he did not live within the city limits or that he was not around when the information was compiled. Even if he never established legal residence but only lived with someone as a transient boarder, he should have been listed, however. On the other hand, those early city directories are by no means the final word on who lived in Fort Worth at that time. The strongest evidence that Bunch lived in Fort Worth in the 1880s is a newspaper story about him which appeared in the *Morning Register* on March 3, 1897 (p. 5), and contained the foregoing descriptions of him.

33. *Fort Worth Morning Register*, March 3, 1897, p. 5. The expression "bucking the tiger" to describe faro players came from the fact that some of the decks in those days showed tigers on the aces. Faro players "bucked the tiger"; monte players "piked the game." DeArment, *Knights of the Green Cloth*, p. 398 (footnote).

34. Deed Record, Tarrant County, Texas, vol. 51, p. 354. Cited in Rick Miller, *The Train Robbing Bunch*, p. 65 (footnote).

35. A generation of Fort Worth school children have grown up reading this story in their seventh-grade social studies textbooks. The exact origins of the story are unknown, although it circulated long before inclusion in Rosa May Henson and Golda Ruth Phillips' *The Fort Worth Story, Yesterday and Today*, James M. Bailey and Nancy O. Vick, eds., pp. 29–30.

36. The presence of both Bunch and the Burrows brothers in Fort Worth around this time, plus the coincidence of the series of unsolved train robberies, has confused later historians about just who was responsible. The robberies could have been the work of Bunch or the Burrows boys, or possibly Bunch may have been a member of the Burrows gang, although this has never been suggested before now. One noted outlaw authority simply dismisses the whole controversy this way: "During their [the Burrows brothers] rampage . . . a man from north Texas, Captain Eugene Bunch, was also robbing trains and was killed in Louisiana." See, Bartholomew, *Biographical Album of Western Gunfighters*, alphabetical listing for Burrows.

37. *New Orleans Daily Picayune*, August 19, 1892. Cited in Miller, *The Train Robbing Bunch*, p. 137.

38. *Fort Worth Daily Gazette*, August 25, 1892.

39. *Ibid.*, September 25, 1889.

40. *Fort Worth Weekly Democrat*, April 7, 1883, p. 4; *Fort Worth Daily Gazette*, April 26, 1885, p. 6. For a full account of Thomas' career, see, Glenn Shirley, *Heck Thomas*.

41. *Dallas Weekly Herald*, October 29, 1885.

42. There was more than one Billy the Kid running around the West during this time. Las Vegas, New Mexico, declared another "Kid" *persona non grata* in March, 1882, a year after his more notorious namesake was killed. This counterfeit Billy was also wanted for counterfeiting currency. His real name was William Wilson. Billy Claiborne of O.K. Corral fame was also known as "Billy the Kid" around Tombstone. It almost seems as if everyone named William with an itch to become

famous and a criminal record after 1881 adopted the moniker "Billy the Kid." See, Howard Bryan, *Wildest of the Wild West*, p. 5; and Paula Marks, *And Die in the West*, p. 2. For Fort Worth's "Billy the Kid," see Tarrant County Criminal Minutes, County Court, 1889–1890, Case No. 6621, July 8, 1890.

43. Beth Thomas Meeks with Bonnie Speer, *Heck Thomas, My Papa*, pp. 12–15. Born in 1899, Meeks was still alive at the time of this writing. She is the daughter of the famed Oklahoma lawman and based her book on family stories and her father's personal papers.

44. *Fort Worth Daily Gazette*, November 17, 1888.

45. *Ibid.*, September 10, 1889.

46. Quoted in *Fort Worth Star-Telegram*, October 30, 1949, p. 24.

47. *Fort Worth Daily Gazette*, September 27, 1890, p. 8.

48. *Austin Daily Statesman*, September 18, 1889.

49. *Fort Worth Daily Gazette*, September 27, 1890, p. 8.

50. *Ibid.*, September 30, 1890, p. 4.

51. *Ibid.*, November 2, 1890.

52. *Ibid.*, May 15, 1890.

53. *Baptist Standard*, November 2, 1899, p. 6. Cited in James Leo Garrett, Jr., *Living Stones: The Centennial History of Broadway Baptist Church*, p. 69 (and footnote).

54. Garrett, *Living Stones: The Centennial History of Broadway Baptist Church*, pp. 69–70.

55. *Fort Worth Daily Gazette*, September 30, 1890, p. 4.

56. *Ibid.*, November 2, 1890, p. 16.

57. *Ibid.*, September 27, 1890, p. 8.

58. *Ibid.*, September 28, 1890, p. 3.

59. *Fort Worth Morning Register*, January 8, 1897, p. 8.

60. Charles L. Martin, *A Sketch of Sam Bass*, p. xviii.

61. *Centennial Gazetteer of the United States*, 1873. For an essay on Chinese immigration, see, Ruth Conner, "Charlie Sam and The Sojourners," *Journal of Arizona History*, vol. 14 (Winter, 1973), pp. 303–16.

62. John W. Forney, *What I Saw in Texas*, p. 24.

63. *Fort Worth Daily Democrat*, November 8, 1878.

64. *Fort Worth Record and Register*, August 5, 1906.

65. *Ibid.*

66. *Fort Worth Daily Gazette*, March 11, 1887, p. 8. *Fort Worth Record and Register*, March 16, 1906.

67. Nancy Wilson Ross, *Westward the Women*, p. 131.

68. Quoted in *Fort Worth Star-Telegram*, April 26, 1931. *Fort Worth Daily Democrat*, February 26, 1879.

69. Criminal Minutes, 1887–1889, Case Nos. 5128 and 5132 (November 3, 1888).

70. *Fort Worth Record and Register*, March 16, 1906.

71. *Fort Worth Daily Gazette*, May 9, 1893, p. 8; May 10, 1893, pp. 5–6; May 11, 1893, p. 2.

72. *Fort Worth Daily Gazette*, May 30, 1888.

73. *Ibid.*, December 6, 1888.

74. *Ibid.*, December 7, 1888.

75. *Ibid.*, September 13, 1885.

76. Richard O'Connor, *Bat Masterson*, pp. 209–10.

77. The earliest reports of suicides in the late 1870s all cite morphine overdose as the cause. Its easy availability dated from the Civil War when North and South manufactured or imported immense quantities for military use. After the war it was impossible to put the genie back in the bottle as morphine use crossed all state, sexual and social boundaries.

78. *Fort Worth Morning Register*, February 10, 1897, p. 8.

79. *Ibid.*, June 1, 1897, p. 8.

80. *Ibid.*, June 27, 1897, p. 2.

81. The Ledger Book is microfilmed and in possession of Tarrant County Historical Commission. The original ledger was given to J. C. Terrill to use in collecting debts owed to Daggett and Hatcher. From Terrill it passed into the hands of his granddaughter, Josephine Smith Hudson, and from her to the Tarrant County Historical Commission.

82. *Fort Worth Morning Register*, April 9, 1897, p. 5.

83. *Ibid.*, July 3, 1897, p. 5.

84. Dr. David F. Musto, *The American Disease*. Cited in *Parade* Magazine Sunday Supplement, "Intelligence Report," July 31, 1988, p. 13.

85. *Fort Worth Register*, n.d., 1901 (Fort Worth Public Library files, "Hell's Half Acre").

86. *Ibid.*

87. *Fort Worth Star-Telegram*, undated article by Blair Justice (in Ruby Schmidt's files).

88. *Fort Worth Morning Register*, February 6, 1897.

89. *Ibid.*, February 10, 1897, p. 8.

90. *Fort Worth Daily Gazette*, October 1, 1887.

91. *Dallas Daily Herald*, December 8, 1887.

92. *Fort Worth Daily Gazette*, September 27, 1890, p. 8.

93. *Fort Worth Morning Register*, May 4, 1897, p. 3.

94. *Fort Worth Daily Gazette*, May 11, 1893, p. 2.

95. *Ibid.*

96. *Ibid.*

97. *Ibid.*, October 6, 1890, p. 8.

98. *Ibid.*

99. *Fort Worth Morning Register*, May 12, 1897, p. 1.

100. Williams, "Murder at the Metropolitan," *In Old Fort Worth* (1975), p. 25.

101. In later years, the Acre's violent history haunted the Metropolitan like an ancient Egyptian curse. On January 13, 1913, a man was killed in the main lobby by a jealous rival over the affections of a lady. Twenty years later, the lobby was the scene of another shooting which again involved a romantic triangle. See, Williams, "Murder at the Metropolitan," *In Old Fort Worth* (1975), p. 25.

102. *Fort Worth Morning Register*, May 11, 1897, p. 5.

103. *Ibid.*, July 14, 1897, p. 1.

104. *Ibid.*, March 26, 1897, p. 5.

105. Williams, "Policemen Had Their Own Union," *In Old Fort Worth* (1975), p. 10.

106. Criminal Minutes, 1893–1894 (March, 1894).

107. *Ibid.*, Case No. 8441 (May 1, 1893).

108. Criminal Minutes, 1889–1890, Case Nos. 5896, 5893 (September 2, 1889); 5894 (November 4, 1889); 6265, 6272, 6273 (January 10, 1890); 6473 (May 7, 1890); 6475 (May 13, 1890); 6676, 6677 (September 1, 1890); 6724, 6745, 6746 (September 13, 1890). Compare, *Fort Worth Daily Gazette*, April 5, 1887.

109. *Ibid.*, Case Nos. 11932 and 11934 (March 20, 1894).

110. Criminal Minutes, 1889–1890, Case No. 6725 (September 13, 1890). The case was dropped because the county prosecutor refused to prosecute, but Kramer still had to appear in court.

111. Criminal Minutes, 1887–1889, Case Nos. 4475 (November 3, 1888); 4769 (April 18, 1888); 5198 (November 8, 1888). Criminal Minutes, 1889–1890, Case Nos. 6270 (January 13, 1890); 6582 (July 8, 1890).

112. *Fort Worth Morning Register*, April 30, 1897, p. 5.

8. The End of the Line

1. Novelist and screenwriter William Goldman completed the process of "Robinhooding" the Wild Bunch (as J. Frank Dobie called it), in his 1969 script for *Butch Cassidy and the Sundance Kid.* Actually, the film's original title was to be "The Sundance Kid and Butch Cassidy" because Paul Newman was signed to play the Kid. But when Newman had trouble playing the character and said he preferred to take the title's other role, the billing was reversed to reflect Newman's superstar status. However, author Goldman always preferred the original title with the accent on the Sundance Kid. That billing would have had a major revisionist effect on the popular legend. See, David Zinman, *Fifty Grand Movies of the 1960s and 1970s*, pp. 127–28.

2. Although there is a strong consensus on the date, there is some confusion about the precise location where the gang was born. Charles Kelly, the first chronicler of the Wild Bunch, claims they assembled at Brown's Hole, Wyoming. *The Outlaw Trail: The Story of Butch Cassidy and the "Wild Bunch,"* pp. 84–86. Pearl Baker, who was friends with many of the people who knew the outlaws, points to the Robbers Roost area of Utah. See, Baker, *The Wild Bunch at Robbers Roost*, p. 61 ff. Lula Parker Betenson, the sister of Butch Cassidy, said they organized in the vicinity of Rock Springs, Wyoming, a wild railroad town in the 1890s. See, Betenson, *Butch Cassidy, My Brother*, as told to Dora Flack, p. 75. James D. Horan, claiming to base his research on Pinkerton files, places the gang's birthplace in the Hole-in-the-Wall region of Wyoming. See, *Desperate Men*, pp. 200–01. The only dissenting voice on the date the Wild Bunch was organized comes from William A. Pinkerton. Pinkerton, the famous detective and long-time pursuer of the gang, wrote in his memoirs that the gang began operating in 1895. See, *Train Robberies and Train Robbers*, p. 65.

3. Betenson, *Butch Cassidy*, p. 76; Kelly, *The Outlaw Trail: A History of Butch Cassidy and His Wild Bunch* p. 84.

4. Mrs. Betenson, a true character in her own right, claimed in a series of interviews with Dora Flack in mid-1970 that her brother had told her, "There were

a lot of good friends, but Elzy Lay was the best, always dependable and level-headed." Betenson, *Butch Cassidy,* p. 187.

5. James D. Horan, *The Wild Bunch,* pp. 43 ff.

6. For a contemporary's opinion of Harvey Logan and the source of the quotation calling him "the executioner of the Wild Bunch," see George Bolds, one of the few gunmen who lived long enough to add to the historiography of the era. Cited in Richard Patterson, *Historical Atlas of the Outlaw West,* p. 69. See also, Kelly, *The Outlaw Trail,* p. 285.

7. Lay's name is sometimes incorrectly written "Elza," but this spelling is ahistorical. Edward M. Kirby, *The Saga of Butch Cassidy and the Wild Bunch,* p. 12. See also, Robert Redford, *The Outlaw Trail,* p. 134.

8. Despite a large fraternity of Wild Bunch scholars and students, all western historians are not equally impressed with the legend of Butch Cassidy and the Sundance Kid. In particular, longtime historian Ed Bartholomew is convinced that Butch and Sundance are largely the product of romantic mythmaking by writers Charles Kelly and James D. Horan, aided and abetted by Hollywood scriptwriters. In this view, Kelly's original 1938 account of the gang is so much "hoopla" over nothing, and Horan's later stories fall in the category of historical "opera." Bartholomew is the lonely voice of the debunker who believes that whatever fame and success the Wild Bunch enjoyed should properly be credited to Harvey Logan and Bill Carver. This minority opinion is somewhat supported by the recollections of Joe LeFors, the famed Wyoming lawman who chased the Wild Bunch all over the country in the late 1890s, yet in his memoirs mentioned Cassidy only once and Harry Longabaugh not at all. See, Joe LeFors, *Wyoming Peace Officer, An Autobiography*. Opinions of Ed Bartholomew came from correspondence with this author, December 5, 1988, in author's files.

9. Jay Robert Nash, *Bloodletters and Bad Men,* p. 117.

10. According to a Pinkerton report dated March 6, 1903, Longabaugh had the previous May checked into an upstate New York sanatarium seeking a cure for his condition, but nothing more is known about this episode in his life. See, Edward M. Kirby, *The Rise and Fall of the Sundance Kid,* pp. 96–97; and Carl Sifakis, *The Encyclopedia of American Crime,* p. 573.

11. Bill O'Neal, *Encyclopedia of Western Gunfighters,* p. 190.

12. William Goldman, *Adventures in the Screen Trade,* p. 284.

13. Betenson, *Butch Cassidy,* p. 130.

14. By comparison, the reign of the James-Younger gang lasted a decade and a half (1866–1881) while that of the Daltons lasted only about eighteen months (1891–1892).

15. Betenson, *Butch Cassidy,* p. 251. An alternative explanation comes from the unpublished manuscript of William T. Phillips, who claimed to be the real "Butch Cassidy" before he died in the 1930s. Phillips says he coined the moniker himself because he was always given the job of shooting and butchering game in the cow camps where he worked. Matt Warner, another reformed outlaw who lived to a ripe old age and claimed to have ridden with Cassidy in the early years, says Butch got the nickname when the kickback from a gun he was firing knocked him on his tail, much to the amusement of those watching. See, Matt Warner, *Last of the Bandit Riders*. For

both Phillips and Warner, see, Larry Pointer, *In Search of Butch Cassidy*, p. 262 (footnote 8).

16. The earliest history of the Wild Bunch, and still the standard source, says that rustler Mike Cassidy left Utah at some unknown date to avoid prosecution and was last reported in Mexico. (See, Kelly, *The Outlaw Trail*, p. 12). Fort Worth's Mike Cassidy was sometimes called "Mikey Mike" and hailed from Ireland originally. His activities before coming to Fort Worth are unknown. Therefore the possible connection to Butch Cassidy is based on his name and criminal propensities, their presence in Fort Worth at the same time and the lack of any solid information about his past. See Tarrant County Criminal Minutes, County Court 1887–1889: Case Nos. 3897, 3905; 1889–1890, Case Nos. 6547, 6713; 1902–1909, Case Nos. 26232, 26229, 26230, 23877, 23878, 10424, 9832, 30260, 35575, 36391, 37627 (Special Collections, University of Texas at Arlington). See also, *Fort Worth City Directories*, 1890–1912 (Fort Worth Public Library); and Tarrant County Census Records, 1900.

17. Other females, whom writer and editor Jim Dullenty calls "the real women in Butch's life," were Josie and "Queen Anne" Bassett, Dora Lamorreaux, Maud Davis and Mary Calvert. All were associated with Cassidy in Wyoming. From correspondence with Jim Dullenty, Hamilton, Montana, October, 1987, in the author's files. Dullenty is a founder and former president of the National Association for Outlaw and Lawman History; also the former editor of *True West*, *Frontier Times*, and *Old West* magazines.

18. Horan, *The Wild Bunch*, p. 109.

19. Other historians have tried to trace Fannie Porter, with limited success. One of the more successful, Ed Bartholomew of Fort Davis, Texas, claims she was born "Ann Porter" in New Orleans in 1859 and moved to Dallas in 1878. He says "she supposedly died in El Paso, Texas, in 1912." (Correspondence with Mr. Bartholomew, August 3, 1987.) Other evidence from census records leads this writer to believe she was born in England in 1873. See, U.S. Census, 1900, Bexar County, Texas, Precinct 3, Supervisor's District No. 5, Enumeration District No. 82.

20. Horan, *The Wild Bunch*, p. 43.

21. F. Stanley, *No Tears for Black Jack Ketchum*, p. 48.

22. James D. Horan and Paul Sann, *Pictorial History of the Wild West*, p. 200.

23. Leon C. Metz, *The Shooters*, p. 121.

24. Eugene Cunningham, *Triggernometry*, p. 348.

25. *Fort Worth Morning Register*, July 7, 1901, p. 3.

26. Lillie made this claim to William A. Pinkerton on December 5, 1901, according to a memorandum in the Pinkerton Archives, New York. She also told the detective she had kept a copy of the marriage certificate to show her father. Several historians have searched local courthouse records for a reference to the marriage without success. See, Dale T. Schoenberger, "The Wild Bunch: A New Look at a Legend," *National Tombstone Epitaph*, vol. 16 (April, 1989), p. 15.

27. Horan muddies the water again in his discussion of Lillie Davis. Writing in 1954 (*Pictorial History of the Wild West* with Paul Sann), he pairs her up with Harvey Logan, saying "Harvey soon tired of Lillie and sent her away with $167 in gold coins." (p. 221) A little further on Horan writes, "Once, after an all-night drinking party, he and Lillie fell inside the door of Fannie's place" (*Ibid.*). In *The Pinkertons* (1967),

Horan quotes directly from William Pinkerton's files in calling Maud Walker "Kid Curry's girl." Lillie told Pinkerton she was married to Carver, adding, "I did not love Will and did not marry him for love" (p. 386). Considering the later date of the second book and the footnote reference to a primary source, one has to go with Maud and Harvey/Curry as one couple and Lillie and Will as another.

28. Horan, *The Pinkertons,* pp. 385–86.

29. Kirby, *Saga,* pp. 41–42.

30. Carl W. Breihan, *Lawmen and Robbers,* p. 73. Ingerfield was also one of the numerous aliases used by Butch Cassidy.

31. William Goldman, *Adventures in the Screen Trade,* p. 283.

32. Fannie's sporting house left its mark on history in yet another way. Like many bars and bordellos, Fannie's place issued small, metal tokens that were only good on her premises. They were accepted as legal tender for a variety of purposes from gambling chips to cash for buying drinks to payment for a visit with the ladies of the house. Only the tonier establishments doing a high-volume business could afford to have their own tokens made up, but enough of these businesses existed to make the little round- or octagonal-shaped slugs a familiar sight in the West for many years. They provide a meager historical record for places that did not tend to get listed in city directories or on tax rolls, such as Fannie Porter's. The only primary evidence that exists today to show that Fannie Porter's really did exist is one of these tokens. The tokens are much sought-after collectors' items today, being bought, sold, and traded just like stamps or coins. A surviving token from Fannie Porter's is stamped "Good for One." Tokens with the stamp of the White Elephant Restaurant and Bar are also in collectors' hands. See, Gordon Yowell, "Money of the Merchants," *Frontier Times* (February–March, 1966), p. 37.

33. Much of the controversy derives from the fact that not only did Fort Worth and San Antonio both have a Hell's Half Acre, but both also had a madam named Porter. Fort Worth's Madam Porter, however, was Mary, not Fannie, and she operated her business in Fort Worth from the 1880s until the early 1900s. See *Fort Worth Daily Gazette,* April 5, 1887; and *Fort Worth Register,* October 18, 1900. Fannie Porter's presence in San Antonio in the 1880s and 1890s can be traced through U.S. Census records and her arrest record in that city. (District Clerk's Office, Bexar County [Texas], 1888 and 1891.) When William Pinkerton interviewed Fannie and her girls in December, 1901, it was at her house in San Antonio (memo, Pinkerton Archives). See also, Schoenberger, "The Wild Bunch," *National Tombstone Epitaph,* p. 15. The matter is thoroughly confused in several books. For instance, in *Desperate Men* (1949), Horan places Fannie Porter's Sporting House in Fort Worth, where he says the famous bicycle-riding episode portrayed in the Robert Redford-Paul Newman movie took place. However, in *Pictorial History of the Wild West* (1954), written with Paul Sann, he is quite emphatic in placing Fannie's place and the bicycle-riding episode in San Antonio.

34. Horan, *The Pinkertons,* p. 386.

35. Correspondence with Jim Dullenty, October, 1987, author's files.

36. Horan, *The Pinkertons,* pp. 384–86.

37. See account by Edward A. Ducker, at the time a young lawyer just starting his legal career in Winnemucca; he later became a Justice of the Nevada Supreme

Court. In, Franklin Reynolds, "The Winnemucca Bank Robbery," *Frontier Times,* vol. 16 (December, 1938), pp. 93–96. Compare, account of George S. Nixon, a cashier and part-owner of the Winnemucca bank when it was robbed and later a U.S. Senator from Nevada. The journals he kept all his life indicated considerable doubt whether it was Cassidy and friends who robbed him in 1900. In, Lee Berk, "Butch Cassidy Didn't Do It — Winnemucca," *Old West* (Fall, 1983), pp. 22–27 ff.

38. There is also some question about this part of the story. It was never mentioned by George Nixon in his journals, but is cited by James D. Horan in his works, based on the Pinkerton files, in addition to the reference by Parker's sister. See, Betenson, *Butch Cassidy,* pp. 148–49; also, Horan and Sann, *Pictorial History of the Wild West,* pp. 199–200.

39. John McLain, "Robbery Recalled," *Grit* Magazine (October 22, 1972). Cited in Edward M. Kirby, *The Saga of Butch Cassidy and the Wild Bunch,* p. 37.

40. Horan, *The Pinkertons,* p. 387.

41. Lee Berk, "Butch Cassidy Didn't Do It — Winnemucca," pp. 23–27 ff.

42. Betenson, *Butch Cassidy,* p. 149.

43. Stanley, *No Tears for Black Jack Ketchum,* p. 90.

44. Horan, *The Pinkertons,* pp. 384–86.

45. *Dallas Observer,* vol. 42, no. 36, no date, p. 1 F. The Old Market Hotel was torn down along with the rest of Hell's Half Acre in 1965. No hotel records or guest registers survive today.

46. *Morrison & Fourmy's Fort Worth City Directory* for 1899–1900 lists two boarding houses owned by persons named "Randle," the Ware Boardinghouse at 107 East Belknap, Charles W. Randle, proprietor; and the Randle House at 214 West Weatherford, John A. Randle, proprietor. Both addresses are on the opposite end of town from Hell's Half Acre.

47. Interviews with W. P. Chandler, a reporter for the *Knoxville Sentinel* in 1901, when Logan was being held in that city. Chandler's interviews and reminiscences were later collected in a scrap book which served as the basis of a series of articles by Bert Vincent in the *Knoxville News-Sentinel* in 1930. See "The Story of Harvey Logan, Notorious Bandit," January 19, 1930, p. 1.

48. By contrast, the Wild Bunch's last train robbery at Tipton, Wyoming, on August 29, 1900, made the front page of the local newspapers the very next day. *Dallas Times Herald,* August 30, 1900, p. 1.

49. Alan Swallow, ed., *The Wild Bunch,* p. 85. Swallow's account of the gang was one of the first and is still considered one of the best. Unfortunately, however, there is no documentation.

50. *Fort Worth Register,* October 11, 1900, p. 8.

51. Horan and Sann, *Pictorial History,* p. 220.

52. Swallow, *The Wild Bunch,* p. 15.

53. Art Chapman, "Butch Cassidy," *The Elks Magazine* (April, 1930), p. 32.

54. Horan and Sann, *Pictorial History,* p. 220.

55. Kirby, *Saga,* p. 17.

56. *Fort Worth Daily Democrat,* July 7, 1878, p. 1.

57. *Dallas Weekly Herald,* June 25, 1885, p. 4.

58. Jeff Barton, *Dynamite and Six-Shooter,* p. 139.

59. This picture is less famous than the group shot of the Wild Bunch, but is generally attributed to John Swartz, and therefore was probably also taken in the late or fall-early winter, 1900. Besides the similar composition and quality, it comes from the same Noah Rose Collection (University of Oklahoma).

60. Betenson, *Butch Cassidy*, p. 148.

61. Steve Lacy and Jim Dullenty, "Revealing Letters of Outlaw Butch Cassidy," *Old West* (Winter, 1984), p. 13.

62. Kirby, *Saga*, p. 37.

63. For reports of Courtright and McIntire being in Guatemala or Central America, see Chapter 4.

64. Horan, *The Wild Bunch*, p. 114.

65. Lacy and Dullenty, "Revealing Letters of Outlaw Butch Cassidy," *Old West* (Winter, 1984), p. 13.

66. The story of Vic Button and the famous photograph is confirmed by Vic Button's daughter, who was still living when this book went to press. (Telephone interview with Mrs. Lenore Conway of Sacramento, California, February, 1986.) See also, letter from I. V. Button to Pearl Baker, December 28, 1970, cited in Larry Pointer, *In Search of Butch Cassidy*, p. 171, footnote. According to Button, when he first saw the photograph, he was only able to identify Cassidy and Carver from among the five men.

67. One version of this story is contained in Betenson, *Butch Cassidy*, p. 144. The editor of Betenson's memoir softens her account somewhat by beginning it with "It is said that Butch wrote back to the bank. . . ." According to Betenson, the photo that Butch sent back to Winnemucca put the Pinkertons on their trail again by placing the gang in Texas. This version, however, goes against the story handed down in the Button family. Their version is much more convincing because it comes from a still-living descendant. Butch's sister, on the other hand, is no longer alive and may not have even gotten the story directly from her brother. A lot of her stories were accumulated over the years from many unidentified sources. Undercutting her story still further is the fact that the degree of foolishness attributed to Butch for sending the picture back to Vic Button becomes even more incredible if we are to believe he sent it back directly to the bank instead of the boy. Butch was often impulsive but never stupid.

68. During a career which spanned four decades, Dodge was a frequent visitor to Fort Worth and helped track down some of the most famous outlaws in the West. Six volumes of his journals, together with diaries and correspondence, were in the possession of the Lake family for many years before Carolyn Lake edited them for publication. See, Carolyn Lake, ed., *Under Cover for Wells Fargo, the Unvarnished Recollections of Fred Dodge.* The main problems with the Wells Fargo theory are that the episode does not appear in any standard histories of the company, and no adequate explanation has ever been offered why Fred Dodge was in Fort Worth at the time. Was he tipped off? Was he here on other business? Was it just serendipity? The detective kept copious journals, diaries and correspondence all his life, and after his death these were turned into the book by Carolyn Lake. In those writings Dodge never mentions being on the trail of the Wild Bunch, and it is hard to believe such an event as this would not have stuck in his mind. Equally incredible is that if indeed Wells Fargo

helped track down the gang to its final hideout and flush them out, historians of the company would not mention that feat. See, Lucius Beebe and Charles Clegg, *U.S. West: The Saga of Wells Fargo*; and Edward Hungerford, *Wells Fargo: Advancing the Frontier*. For references to Fred Dodge, see Kelly, *The Outlaw Trail,* p. 281; Franklin Reynolds, "The Picture that Trapped the Wild Bunch," *Denver Post,* July 18, 1948; and Jeff Barton, *Dynamite and Six-Shooter,* p. 139. James D. Horan in *Desperate Men,* p. 242, cites a "Wells Fargo detective posing as a gambler," but does not give his name. What makes this reference doubly interesting is that Horan based it on Pinkerton archives. Horan does one of his unexplained flip-flops by introducing a new character into the story in *The Pinkertons* (p. 386) where he says that "either a [Pinkerton] operative *or* a Union Pacific detective" was the first to discover the photograph (p. 386).

69. Bert Vincent, *Knoxville* [Tennessee] *News-Sentinel,* January 19, 1930, p. 1.

70. Though the Pinkertons were active, even dogged in pursuing the Wild Bunch, there are some problems nonetheless with the theory that one of their operatives flushed the gang out of their hiding place in Fort Worth thanks to the Swartz photo. The biggest problem is that the sharp-eyed agent, whoever he was, has never been named by any writer, which is remarkable since he should have become an instant hero and a legend in Pinkerton history. The second problem is that the agency never maintained an office in Fort Worth — their nearest offices were in Kansas City, Missouri, and Denver, Colorado — and Pinkerton agents were not numerous enough for the odds to be in favor of finding one in Fort Worth by sheer coincidence.

71. These circulars plus later reproductions in the form of prints, book illustrations and museum displays, and finally a movie poster, have given this photograph a notoriety far beyond its immediate impact on the career of the Wild Bunch. One historian says it has been reproduced "more times than any other picture in Western history" (Metz, *The Shooters,* p. 124) The notoriety of the photograph had another effect, too, this one on the Swartz family business. In 1901 Charles Swartz began advertising his own studio, which was one street over from brother John's, with this come-on: "Beats Them All in Group Photos" (*Fort Worth City Directory,* 1901–02).

72. Barton, *Dynamite and Six-Shooter,* p. 140.

73. This is another one of Horan's questionable "facts" since he stated in another book some twenty years earlier that the two men participated in another train holdup on July 7, 1903. Several respected authors also say that Cassidy took part in a holdup at Wagner, Montana, on July 3, 1901, but it seems more likely that both Cassidy and Longabaugh were safely in South America by that time. A compromise scenario has both men going to South America, but one *or both* coming back to take part in the Wagner job. For authorities who think that Cassidy or Longabaugh or both were present at the Wagner holdup, see, Charles Kelly, *The Outlaw Trail* (both); Jay Robert Nash, *Bloodletters and Bad Men* (both); Leon C. Metz, *The Shooters* (both); and Larry Pointer, *In Search of Butch Cassidy* (both). Some authorities claim that Cassidy took part but that Longabaugh was already in South America with Etta Place. Included in this group are Edward M. Kirby, *The Rise & Fall of the Sundance Kid*; Robert Elman, *Badmen of the West*; Carl W. Breihan, *Lawmen and Robbers;* and the mysterious manuscript by William Thadeus Phillips, "Bandit Invincible." Alan Swallow, *The Wild Bunch,* says that neither was there; and Horan and Sann, *Pictorial History,* stake out the solitary

position that Longabaugh was a part of the gang that hit the train at Wagner but not Cassidy. The hard evidence to back up any of these claims is quite scanty.

74. This version is supported by several reported sightings as late as the 1930s, a handful of letters and Lula Parker Betenson's memories. Gradually, historical consensus has come around to the view that Butch, and perhaps Sundance, too, returned to the United States and lived out quiet, unrecognized and law-abiding lives for many years. In later years, the two men who offered the most credible claims to being the "real" Robert Leroy Parker and Harry Longabaugh were William Thadeus Phillips and Hiram Bebee, respectively. For the best accounts of their respective claims and the entire lives of Parker and Longabaugh, see, Phillips, "The Bandit Invincible, the Story of Butch Cassidy," unpublished manuscript with introduction by Jim Dullenty, in possession of Jim Dullenty; and Edward M. Kirby, *The Rise and Fall of the Sundance Kid*. Phillips claims that Longabaugh died in the shootout in Bolivia but that Cassidy made it back to the States safely. Kirby claims that both made it back safely and lived to a ripe, old age. Lula Parker Betenson also claims that both survived the *federales*' bullets and returned to the United States, parted company, and were finally reunited along with Etta Place in Mexico quite by accident many years later. Larry Pointer, basing his conclusions mostly on the Phillips manuscript, also agrees that the two outlaws survived their stay in South America. The "truth," whatever it is, will never be established. Mythic gunfighters never really die.

75. Correspondence with Ed Bartholomew, Fort Davis, Texas, September 23, 1988 (in author's files). This is probably a mix-up with John Monroe Parker, a footloose cowboy who died broke and alone in 1917. He spent the last years of his life wandering the West selling a slim volume of his memoirs in order to raise enough money to live on. He usually signed his name "Roe" or "R. Parker;" the coincidence of two R. Parkers with cowboy backgrounds and rootless lifestyles probably accounts for any mix-up many years later. See, J. M. Parker, *An Aged Wanderer, A Life Sketch*.

76. Pointer, *In Search of Butch Cassidy*, p. 242.

77. Correspondence with Ed Bartholomew, September 23, 1988, author's files.

78. Betenson, *Butch Cassidy*, p. 195.

79. Not until 1986 did an account of her life claiming to be documented and accompanied by childhood photographs appear in print (Carl W. Breihan, *Lawmen and Robbers*, pp. 71–73). The more famous photograph of her posed in glamorous style with the Sundance Kid, coupled with the wildly fictionalized movie *Butch Cassidy and the Sundance Kid*, have only added to the public's fascination with her.

80. In addition to Breihan, *Lawmen and Robbers*, see, Carl Sifakis, *The Encyclopedia of American Crime*, pp. 573–74.

81. Cassidy reportedly made this statement to Percy A. Seibert in Bolivia. Seibert told it to James A. Horan, who included it in *The Authentic Wild West: The Outlaws*, p. 282. See also, Schoenberger, "The Wild Bunch," *National Tombstone Epitaph* (April, 1989), p. 15, and Sifakis, *Encyclopedia of American Crime*, p. 130. Jim Dullenty does not believe this story (correspondence with author, October, 1987).

82. Correspondence with Jim Dullenty, October, 1987, author's files.

83. See, Delbert Willis, "Woman Dies in Fire in Small E. 15th Hotel," *Fort Worth Press*, January 26, 1962, p. 1. Willis was the long-time city editor of the now defunct *Fort Worth Press*. He spent many hours talking to Eunice Gray and after her death claimed that she and Etta Place were one and the same person. Probably not

true, but part of Eunice's story paralleled Etta's in one respect. In talking about her troubles with a local preacher, she told Willis, "He called me up and told me he was going to run me out of town. I told him it wasn't necessary. I was nailing up my place and going on a trip *to South America* [emphasis added].

84. Like the other principals of the Wild Bunch, Logan's end is the subject of some dispute. Pinkerton agent Lowell Spence, who had been on Logan's trail the longest and tracked him down in Tennessee, identified the body showed to him by authorities in Colorado as being definitely Logan's. In 1907, however, William Pinkerton wrote an agency memorandum stating that Logan was still alive with Cassidy and Longabaugh in South America. As a result, Logan's file was reopened. See, Larry Pointer, *In Search of Butch Cassidy,* p. 200 and footnote. Supporting the theory that Logan died in South America around 1910 or 1911, is Pearl Baker, *The Wild Bunch at Robbers Roost,* pp. 107–08. For the traditional theory that he died in Colorado in 1904, see, Kelly, *The Outlaw Trail,* p. 286, and O'Neal, *Encyclopedia of Western Gunfighters,* pp. 183–87.

85. One curiosity associated with Carver's death is that he died in precisely the same manner as Timothy Courtright fourteen years earlier. Like Courtright, Carver was on the losing end of a gunfight in which his gun hand was shattered by the first shot; he then attempted the "border shift," but was riddled with lead before he could effect that particular maneuver. Despite their grandiose reputations with a gun, neither Courtright nor Carver got off a shot in their last gunfight. See, Ed Bartholomew, *Black Jack Ketchum, Last of the Hold-up Kings,* p. 91.

86. *St. Louis Post-Dispatch,* November 7, 1901 (cited in Schoenberger, "The Wild Bunch," *National Tombstone Epitaph* [June, 1989], p. 12).

87. *Fort Worth Star-Telegram,* October 30, ?? (rest of date obliterated on copy in Fort Worth Public Library files; see "Hell's Half Acre" file).

88. *Fort Worth Register,* September 25, 1900; *Dallas Daily Times Herald,* September 26, 1900, p. 6.

89. *Fort Worth Register,* January 2, 1901, p. 2.

90. "The Underworld of Fort Worth, Texas, or Hell's Half Acre," interview with Frank DeBuque (Tarrant County Historical Society files).

91. *Fort Worth Register,* January 30, 1901, p. 8.

9. Epilogue

1. Roy Emerson Falls, *A Biography of J. Frank Norris, 1877–1952,* pp. 31–33. See also, Jerry Flemmons, "Smiting a Sinful World," *Plowboys, Cowboys and Slanted Pigs,* pp. 75–89.

2. Tarrant County Deed Records, vol. 252, p. 463 (Fort Worth, County Administrative Building, Tax Research/Refund Office).

3. *Fort Worth Star-Telegram,* May 26, 1909.

4. *Ibid.*, June 1, 1936.

5. *Ibid.*, Ed Brice's column, August 23, 1990, P.M. edition, p. 2, sec. 4.

6. *Fort Worth Press,* February 27, 1952.

7. Craig Clifford and Tom Pilkington, eds., *Range Wars,* p. 91.

8. Quoted in *Fort Worth Daily Gazette,* April 18, 1889.

9. *Ibid.*

Bibliography

Books

Adams, Ramon F., ed. *Burs Under the Saddle*. Norman: University of Oklahoma Press, 1989.

____________ . *More Burs Under the Saddle*. Norman: University of Oklahoma Press, 1979.

____________ . *Six-Guns and Saddle Leather*. Cleveland: John T. Zubal, 1982.

Agee, G. W. *Rube Burrow, King of Outlaws*. Chicago: Henneberry Company, 1890.

Alter, Judy. *Thistle Hill: The History and the House*. Fort Worth: Texas Christian University Press, 1988.

Asbury, Herbert. *The Barbary Coast: An Informal History of the San Francisco Underworld*. New York: Alfred A. Knopf, 1933.

____________ . *Sucker's Progress: An Informal History of Gambling in America from the Colonies to Canfield*. New York: Patterson Smith, 1969.

Atherton, Lewis. *The Cattle Kings*. Lincoln, Nebraska: University of Nebraska Press, 1972.

Authentic History of Sam Bass and His Gang. Author unknown. Denton, Texas, 1878. Reprinted by *Frontier Times*, Bandera, Texas, 1950.

Baker, Pearl. *The Wild Bunch at Robbers Roost*. New York: Abelard-Schuman, 1971.

Bancroft, Caroline. *Six Racy Madams of Colorado*. Boulder, Colorado: privately printed, 1965.

Bartholomew, Ed. *Biographical Album of Western Gunfighters*. Houston: Frontier Press, 1958.

____________. *Black Jack Ketchum, Last of the Hold-up Kings*. Houston: Frontier Press of Texas, 1955.

____________. *Wyatt Earp, 1848 to 1880: The Untold Story*. Toyahvale, Texas: Frontier Book Company, 1963.

____________. *Wyatt Earp, 1879 to 1882, The Man and the Myth*. Toyahvale, Texas: Frontier Book Company, 1964.

Barton, Jeff. *Dynamite and Six-Shooter*. Santa Fe, New Mexico: Palomino Press, 1970.

Beebe, Lucius, and Charles Clegg. *U.S. West: The Saga of Wells Fargo*. New York: Bonanza Books, 1949.

Betenson, Lula Parker, as told to Dora Flack. *Butch Cassidy, My Brother*. Provo, Utah: Brigham Young University Press, 1975.

Biggers, Don H. *German Pioneers in Texas*. Austin: Eakin Publications, Inc. for the Fredericksburg Publishing Company, Inc., 1983.

Bolton, Paul. *Governors of Texas*. San Angelo: San Angelo Standard-Times, 1947.

Book of Fort Worth, The. Fort Worth: The Fort Worth Record, 1913.

Boyer, Glenn G., ed. *I Married Wyatt Earp: The Recollections of Josephine Sarah Marcus Earp*. Tucson: University of Arizona Press, 1981.

Breihan, Carl W. *Lawmen and Robbers*. Caldwell, Idaho: Caxton Printers, Ltd., 1986.

Brekke, Alan Lee. *Kid Curry, Train Robber*. Privately Printed, 1989.

Brown, Dee. *The Gentle Tamers: Women of the Old West*. Lincoln: University of Nebraska Press, 1981.

____________ with Martin F. Schmidt. *Trail Driving Days*. New York: Ballantine Books, 1974.

Brown, Robert L. *Saloons of the American West*. Silverton, Colorado: Sundance Books, 1978.

Bryan, Howard. *Wildest of the Wild West*. Santa Fe, New Mexico: Clear Light Publishers, 1988.

Centennial Gazetteer of the United States. A. Von Steinwehr, ed. Philadelphia: Ziegler & McCurdy, 1873.

Clifford, Craig and Tom Pilkington, eds. *Range Wars: Heated Debates, Sober Reflections, and Other Assessments of Texas Writing*. Dallas: Southern Methodist University Press, 1989.

Commager, Henry Steele, Marcus Cunliffe and Maldwyn A. Jones, eds. *The West, An Illustrated History*. New York: Promontory Press, 1976.

Connally, Mark Thomas. *The Response to Prostitution in the Progressive Era*. Chapel Hill: University of North Carolina Press, 1980.

Cox, William R. *Luke Short: Famous Gambler of the Old West*. New York: The Fireside Press, 1961. (Also published under the title *Luke Short and His Era*. Garden City, New York: Doubleday & Company, 1961, with different pagination).

Cunningham, Eugene. *Triggernometry: A Gallery of Gunfighters*. Caldwell, Idaho: Caxton Printers, 1982.

DeArment, Robert K. *Bat Masterson: The Man and the Legend*. Norman: University of Oklahoma Press, 1980.

____________. *Knights of the Green Cloth*. Norman: University of Oklahoma Press, 1982.

Dillon, Richard. *Wells Fargo Detective: A Biography of James B. Hume*. Reno: University of Nevada Press, 1986.

Dorsett, Lyle W. "Bosses and Machines in Urban America." In *Forums in History*. New York: Forum Press, 1974. Reprinted in Charlotte Rike and Anthony Picchioni. *Readings in American History*, Vol. 2. Lexington, Massachusetts: Ginn Press, 1987, 2nd edition.

Drago, Harry Sinclair. *Great American Cattle Trails*. New York: Dodd, Mead & Company, 1965.

____________. *Notorious Ladies of the Frontier*. New York: Dodd, Mead & Company, 1969.

____________. *Wild, Woolly, and Wicked*. New York: Clarkson Potter, Inc., 1960.

Durham, Philip, and Everett L. Jones. *The Negro Cowboys*. Lincoln: University of Nebraska Press, 1983.

Dykstra, Robert R. *The Cattle Towns*. Lincoln: University of Nebraska Press, 1983.

Eakle, Arlene and John Cerny, eds. *The Source: A Guidebook of American Genealogy*. Salt Lake City: Ancestry Publishing, 1984.

Eaton, John. *Will Carver, Outlaw*. San Angelo, Texas: Anchor Publishing Company, 1972.

Elman, Robert. *Badmen of the West*. Secaucus, New Jersey: Castle Books, Book Sales, Inc., 1974.

Emmett, Chris. *Shanghai Pierce: A Fair Likeness*. Norman: University of Oklahoma Press, 1953.

Emrich, Duncan. *It's an Old West Custom*. Kingwood (Surrey), England: The World's Work, Ltd., 1951.

Evans, Hilary. *Harlots, Whores and Hookers*. New York: Taplinger Publishing Company, 1979.

Falls, Roy Emerson. *A Biography of J. Frank Norris, 1877–1952*. Euless, Texas: privately printed, 1975.

Flemmons, Jerry. *Cowboys, Plowboys and Slanted Pigs*. Fort Worth: Texas Christian University Press, 1984.

Forney, John W. *What I Saw in Texas*. Philadelphia: Ringwalt & Brown, 1872.

Gard, Wayne. *The Chisholm Trail*. Norman: University of Oklahoma Press, 1954.

____________. *Frontier Justice*. Norman: University of Oklahoma Press, 1981.

____________. *Sam Bass*. Lincoln: University of Nebraska Press, 1969.

Garrett, James Leo, Jr. *Living Stones: The Centennial History of Broadway Baptist Church*. 2 vols. Fort Worth: Broadway Baptist Church, 1984.

Gillett, James B. *Six Years with the Texas Rangers, 1875–1881*. Lincoln: University of Nebraska Press, 1976.

Goldman, William. *Adventures in the Screen Trade*. New York: Warner Books, 1983.

Greenwood, Val D. *The Researchers' Guide to American Genealogy*. Baltimore: Genealogical Publishing, 1973.

Gross, John, ed. *Rudyard Kipling, the Man, His Work and His World*. London: Weidenfield and Nicolson, 1972.

Hall, Colby Dixon. *History of Texas Christian University: A College of the Cattle Frontier*. Fort Worth: Texas Christian University Press, 1947.

Hendricks, George D. *Bad Man of the West*. San Antonio, Texas: Naylor Company, 1950.

Henson, Rosa May and Golda Ruth Phillips. *The Fort Worth Story, Yesterday and Today*, James M. Bailey and Nancy O. Vick, eds. Fort Worth: Fort Worth Public Schools, 1967.

Horan, James D. *The Authentic West: The Outlaws*. New York: Crown Publishing, 1980.

____________. *The Desperate Men*. New York: Bonanza Books, 1949.

____________. *The Pinkertons: The Detective Dynasty that Made History*. New York: Crown Publishers, Inc., 1969.

___________ . *The Wild Bunch*. New York: New American Library, Signet Books, 1958.

___________ and Paul Sann. *Pictorial History of the Wild West*. New York: Bonanza Books, 1981.

Hungerford, Edward. *Wells Fargo: Advancing the American Frontier*. New York: Random House, 1949.

Jahns, Pat. *The Frontier World of Doc Holliday*. New York: Hastings House Publishers, 1957.

Kane, Joseph Nathan. *Famous First Facts*. New York: H. W. Wilson, 1981.

Katz, William Loren. *The Black West*. Garden City, New York: Doubleday Anchor Books, 1973 (revised edition).

Kelly, Charles. *The Outlaw Trail: A History of Butch Cassidy and His Wild Bunch*. New York: Bonanza Books, 1938 (revised edition).

Kirby, Edward M. *The Rise & Fall of the Sundance Kid*. Iola, Wisconsin: Western Publications, 1983.

___________ . *The Saga of Butch Cassidy and the Wild Bunch*. Palmer Lake, Colorado: The Filter Press, 1977.

Knight, Oliver. *Fort Worth: Outpost on the Trinity*. Norman: University of Oklahoma Press, 1953.

Lake, Carolyn, ed. *Undercover for Wells Fargo: The Unvarnished Recollections of Fred Dodge*. Boston: Houghton Mifflin Company, 1969.

Lamar, Howard R., ed. *The Reader's Encyclopedia of the American West*. New York: Thomas Y. Crowell Company, 1977.

LeFors, Joe. *Wyoming Peace Officer*, An *Autobiography*. Laramie, Wyoming: Laramie Printers, 1953.

Life and Adventures of Sam Bass: The Notorious Union Pacific and Texas Train Robber. . . . Author unknown. Dallas: Dallas Commercial Steam Print, 1878.

Limerick, Patricia Nelson. *The Legacy of Conquest: The Unbroken Past of the American West*. New York: W. W. Norton & Company, 1987.

Lomax, John A. *Cowboy Songs and Frontier Ballads*. New York: Macmillan, 1919.

Marks, Paula Mitchell. *And Die in the West: The Story of the O.K. Corral Gunfight*. New York: William Morrow and Company, 1989.

Martin, Charles L. *A Sketch of Sam Bass, The Bandit: A Graphic Narrative*. Norman: University of Oklahoma Press, 1956.

Martin, Cy. *Whiskey and Wild Women*. New York: Hart Publishing Company, 1974.

Masterston, W. B. *Famous Gunfighters of the Western Frontier*. Houston: Frontier Press, 1957 (reprint of 1907 articles in *Human Life* Magazine).

Mazulla, Fred and Jo. *Brass Checks and Red Lights*. Denver: privately printed, 1966.

McCoy, Joseph. *Historic Sketches of the Cattle Trade of the West and Southwest.* Kansas City: Ramsey, Millett & Hudson, 1874.

McDonough, James Lee. *Stones River — Bloody Winter in Tennessee.* Knoxville: University of Tennessee Press, 1980.

McGrath, Roger D. *Gunfighters, Highwaymen and Vigilantes*. Los Angeles: University of California Press, 1984.

McIntire, James. *Early Days in Texas: A Trip to Hell and Heaven*. Kansas City: McIntire Publishing Company, 1902.

Meeks, Beth Thomas with Bonnie Speer. *Heck Thomas, My Papa.* Norman, Oklahoma: Levite of Apache, 1988.

Metz, Leon Claire. *The Shooters*. El Paso: Mangan Books, 1983.

Miller, Ronald Dean. *Shady Ladies of the West*. Tucson: Westernlore Press, 1985.

Miller, Nyle H. and Joseph W. Snell. *Great Gunfighters of the Kansas Cowtowns, 1867–1886*. Lincoln: University of Nebraska Press, 1967.

____________. *Why the West Was Wild*. Topeka: Kansas State Historical Society, 1963.

Miller, Rick. *Bounty Hunter*. College Station, Texas: Creative Publishing, 1988.

____________. *The Train Robbing Bunch*. College Station, Texas: Creative Publishing Company, 1983.

Morn, Frank. *The Eye That Never Sleeps: A History of the Pinkerton National Detective Agency*. Bloomington: Indiana University Press, 1982.

Morrison, Samuel Elliot, Henry Steele Commager and William E. Leuchtenburg. *The Growth of the American Republic*. 2 vols. New York: Oxford University Press, 1969.

Musto, David F. *The American Disease*. New York: Oxford University Press, 1988.

Myres, Sandra L. *Westering Women and the Frontier Experience, 1800–1915*. Albuquerque: University of New Mexico Press, 1982.

Nash, Jay Robert. *Bloodletters and Bad Men*. New York: M. Evans and Company, Inc., 1973.

Noel, Thomas J. *The City and the Saloon: Denver, 1858–1916*. Lincoln: University of Nebraska Press, 1985.

O'Connor, Richard. *Bat Masterson*. Garden City, New York: Doubleday & Company, 1957.

O'Neal, Bill. *Encyclopedia of Western Gunfighters*. Norman: University of Oklahoma Press, 1979.

Paddock, B. B. *Early Days in Fort Worth, Much of Which I Saw and Part of Which I Was*. Fort Worth: n. p., n. d. (Copy in possession of Fort Worth Public Library, Local History and Genealogy Room).

__________. *History of Texas: Fort Worth and the Texas Northwest Edition*. 4 vols. New York: Lewis Publishing Company, 1922.

Paine, Lauran. *Texas Ben Thompson*. Los Angeles: Westernlore Press, 1966.

Parker, J. M. *An Aged Wanderer, A Life Sketch*. San Angelo, Texas: Headquarters, Elkhorn Wagon Yard, n.d.

Parkhill, Forbes. *The Wildest of the West*. New York: Henry Holt & Company, 1951.

Patterson, Richard. *Historical Atlas of the Outlaw West*. Boulder, Colorado: Johnson Books, 1985.

__________. *Train Robbery: The Birth, Flowering and Decline of a Notorious Western Enterprise*. Boulder, Colorado: Johnson Books, 1981.

Penfield, Thomas. *Western Sheriffs and Marshals*. New York: Grosset & Dunlap Publishers, 1955.

Phares, Ross. *The Governors of Texas*. Gretna, Louisiana: Pelican Publishing, 1976.

Pinkerton, William A. *Train Robberies and Train Robbers*. Fort Davis, Texas: Frontier Book Company, 1968.

Pivar, David J. *Purity Crusade: Sexual Morality and Social Control, 1868–1900*. Westport, Connecticut: Greenwood Press, 1973.

Pointer, Larry. *In Search of Butch Cassidy*. Norman: University of Oklahoma Press, 1978.

Prassel, Frank Richard. *The Western Peace Officer: A Legacy of Law and Order*. Norman: University of Oklahoma Press, 1975.

Raine, William MacLeod. *Guns of the Frontier*. Boston: Houghton Mifflin Company, 1940.

Rosa, Joseph G. *The Gunfighter, Man or Myth?* Norman: University of Oklahoma Press, 1973.

____________. *Rowdy Joe Lowe*. Norman: University of Oklahoma Press, 1989.

Rosen, Ruth. *The Lost Sisterhood: Prostitution in America, 1900–1918*. Baltimore: Johns Hopkins University Press, 1982.

Ross, Nancy Wilson. *Westward the Women*. New York: Random House, 1970.

Rowan, Richard Wilmer. *The Pinkertons, A Detective Dynasty*. Boston: Little, Brown and Company, 1931.

Samuels, Charles and Louise. *Once Upon a Stage: The Merry World of Vaudeville*. New York: Dodd, Mead & Company, 1974.

Schmelzer, Janet L. *Where the West Begins: Fort Worth and Tarrant County*. Northridge, California: Windsor Publications, 1985.

Schmidt, Ruby, ed. *Fort Worth and Tarrant County, A Historical Guide*. Fort Worth: Texas Christian University Press, 1984.

Schoenberger, Dale T. *The Gunfighters*. Caldwell, Idaho: Caxton Printers, 1976.

Shaw, James C. *North from Texas: Incidents in the Early Life of a Range Cowman in Texas, Dakota, and Wyoming, 1852–1883*. Evanston, Illinois: Branding Iron Press, 1952.

Shirley, Glenn. *Heck Thomas, Frontier Marshal*. Norman: University of Oklahoma Press, 1981.

Sifakis, Carl. *The Encyclopedia of American Crime*. New York: Facts on File, Inc., 1973.

Siringo, Charles A. *A Cowboy Detective*. Lincoln: University of Nebraska Press, 1988.

Smithwick, Noah. *The Evolution of a State*. Austin: University of Texas Press, 1983.

Snell, Joseph W. *Painted Ladies of the Cowtown Frontier*. Kansas City, Missouri: Kansas City Posse of the Westerners, 1965.

Stanley, F. [Father Stanley Crocchiola]. *Dave Rudabaugh, Border Ruffian*. Denver: World Press, Inc., 1961.

____________. *Longhair Jim Courtright: Two Gun Marshal of Fort Worth*. Denver: World Press, Inc., 1957.

____________. *No Tears for Black Jack Ketchum*. Denver: World Press, Inc., 1958.

Streeter, Floyd B. *Ben Thompson, Man with a Gun*. New York: Frederick Fell, Inc. 1957.

____________. *Prairie Trails and Cowtowns.* New York: Devin-Adair, 1963.

Sturmberg, Robert. *History of San Antonio.* San Antonio: St. Joseph's Society, 1920.

Swallow, Alan, ed. *The Wild Bunch.* Denver: Sage Books, 1966.

Talbot, Robert H. *Cowtown — Metropolis: Case Study of a City's Growth and Structure.* Fort Worth: Leo Potishman Foundation, Texas Christian University, 1956.

Terrell, J. C. *Reminiscences of the Early Days of Fort Worth.* Fort Worth: Texas Printing Company, 1906.

Texas Almanac, 1968–69. Dallas Morning News (Belo Corporation).

Time-Life Books. *The Gamblers.* In *The Old West* Series. (Jim Hicks, et al., eds.). Alexandria, Virginia: Time-Life Books, 1978.

Virgines, George E. *Western Legends and Lore.* Wauwatosa, Wisconsin: Pine Mountain Press (Leather Stocking Books), 1984.

Walton, William M. *Life and Adventures of Ben Thompson, the Famous Texan.* Houston: Frontier Press of Texas, 1954.

Warner, Matt. *Last of the Bandit Riders.* New York: Bonanza Books, 1938.

Waters, Frank. *The Earp Brothers of Tombstone: The Story of Mrs. Virgil Earp.* New York: C. N. Potter, 1960.

Wellman, Paul I. *The Trampling Herd.* New York: Carrick and Evans, 1939.

Williams, Mack, ed. *The News-Tribune in Old Fort Worth, "A Bicentennial Memory Book."* Fort Worth: Mack and Madeline Williams, 1975.

____________. ed. *The News-Tribune In Old Fort Worth.* Fort Worth: Mack and Madeline Williams, 1976.

____________. ed. *In Old Fort Worth: The Story of a City and Its People as Published in the News-Tribune in 1976 and 1977.* Fort Worth: Mack and Madeline Williams, 1986.

Worcester, Don. *The Chisholm Trail, High Road of the Cattle Kingdom.* Lincoln: University of Nebraska Press with Amon Carter Museum [Fort Worth], 1980.

Wright, Robert M. *Dodge City: The Cowboy Capital and the Great Southwest.* Wichita, Kansas: no publisher, 1913.

Zinman, David. *Fifty Grand Movies of the 1960s and 1970s.* New York: Crown Publishers, Inc., 1986.

Newspapers

Austin Daily Statesman, 1889.

Baptist Standard (Fort Worth), 1899.

Dallas Daily Times-Herald, 1889–1900.

Dallas Herald (weekly and daily), 1876–1887.

Dallas Morning News, 1887.

Dallas Observer, Vol. 42, No. 36., no date (In Fort Worth Public Library Files).

Denver [Colorado] *Post*, 1948.

Denver [Colorado] *Republican*, 1885.

Dodge City [Kansas] *Times*, 1878.

Ford County [Kansas] *Globe*, 1878, 1883.

Fort Worth Gazette and *Fort Worth Daily Gazette*, 1885–1890.

Fort Worth Democrat (weekly and daily) 1873–1882.

Fort Worth Democrat-Advance, 1882.

Fort Worth Morning Register, 1897–1901.

Fort Worth News-Tribune, 1976–1977 and 1986–1988.

Fort Worth Press, 1927.

Fort Worth Record, 1906, 1921.

Fort Worth Record and Register, 1905–1908.

Fort Worth Standard, 1876.

Fort Worth Star-Telegram, 1915–1990.

Geuda Springs [Kansas] *Herald*, 1893.

Jacksboro [Texas] *Echo*, 1877.

Junction City [Kansas] *Union*, 1871.

Knoxville [Tennessee] *News-Sentinel*, 1930.

Knoxville [Tennessee] *Sentinel*, 1901.

Las Vegas [New Mexico Territory] *Optic*, 1879.

Leavenworth [Kansas] *Daily Times*, 1861.

National Tombstone Epitaph, December, 1988–August, 1989.

New Orleans Daily Picayune, 1892.

Pecan Press (College Station: Texas Pecan Growers Association), 1983.

San Francisco Globe-Democrat, 1881.

Texas Baptist Herald (Houston), 1883.

Topeka [Kansas] *Daily Commonwealth*, 1872.

Wichita [Kansas] *Eagle*, 1873.

Periodicals

Bailey, Tom. "King of Cards." *New Magazine for Men*. May, 1958.

Berk, Lee. "Butch Cassidy Didn't Do It — Winnemucca." *Old West*. Vol. 20, No. 1/Whole No. 77, Fall, 1983.

Bradford, Louis C. "Among the Cow-boys." *Lippincott Magazine*. June, 1881.

Breihan, Carl. "How Well Do You Know These Western Badmen?" *Frontier Times*. New Series No. 17, Winter, 1961.

Chapman, Art. "Butch Cassidy." *The Elks Magazine*. April, 1930.

Conner, Ruth. "Charlie Sam and the Sojourners." *Journal of Arizona History*. Vol. 14, No. 4, Winter, 1973, pp. 303–16.

Cormack, George. "Shootout at Round Rock." *San Antonio Express-News*. May 8, 1976.

Cunningham, Eugene. "Courtright the Longhaired," *True West*. No. 21, May–June, 1957, pp. 12–13 ff.

Dobie, J. Frank. "The Robinhooding of Sam Bass." *Montana: The Magazine of Western History*. October, 1955.

Field and Farm Journal (Denver), December 7, 1889.

Foy, Eddie and Alvin F. Harlow. "Clowning through Life," *Collier's, The National Weekly*. January 8, 1927, pp. 25–27.

Gardener, Helen B. "A Battle for Sound Morality," *The Arena* Magazine. Vol. 14, No. 3, November, 1895, pp. 408–11 ff. (Part of a series edited by B. O. Flower).

Holden, W. C. "Law and Lawlessness on the Texas Frontier, 1875–1890." *Southwestern Historical Quarterly*, Vol. 44, No. 2. October, 1940, pp. 188–203.

Humphrey, David C. "Prostitution and Public Policy in Austin, Texas, 1870–1915," *Southwestern Historical Quarterly*. Vol. 26, No. 4, April, 1983, pp. 473–516.

Kildare, Maurice. "American Valley Went Up In Smoke," *Frontier Times*. New Series, No. 98, October–November, 1975, pp. 8–11 ff.

Lacy, Steve and Jim Dullenty. "Revealing Letters of Outlaw Butch Cassidy." *Old West* Magazine. Winter, 1984.

Lewis, Alfred Henry. "The King of the Gun-Players, William Barclay Masterson." *Human Life* Magazine. November, 1907.

MacTosh, P. J. R. "Fort Worth's Centennial." *Texas Weekly*. August 15, 1936.

Masterson, W. B. (Bat) "Famous Gunfighters of the Western Frontier." Series of articles in *Human Life* Magazine, January–April, 1907, on Wyatt Earp, Ben Thompson, Luke Short, et al.

McLain, John. "Robbery Recalled." *Grit* Magazine. October 22, 1972.

Orme, Nicholas. "The Reformation and the Red Light." *History Today*. Vol. 37, March, 1987, pp. 36–41.

Pendleton, Albert S., Jr., and Susan McKey Thomas, "Doc Holliday's Georgia Background," *Journal of Arizona History*. Vol. 14, No. 3, Autumn, 1973, pp. 185–204.

Peterson, Thomas. "Cash Up or Nor Go." *Journal of Arizona History*. Vol. 14, No. 3, Autumn, 1973, pp. 205–222.

Reynolds, Franklin. "The Winnemucca Bank Robbery." *Frontier Times*. December, 1938.

Riegel, Robert E. "Changing American Attitudes Toward Prostitution (1800–1920)." *Journal of Historic Ideas*. Vol. 29, June, 1968, pp. 437–52.

"Rugged Marshal in Fort Worth History." no author. *The Pecan Press* (College Station: Texas Pecan Growers Association), July, 1983 ("Hell's Half Acre" file, Fort Worth Public Library).

Roberts, Gary L. "The West's Gunmen: The Historiography of the Frontier Heroes." *The American West*, Vol. 8, No. 1, January, 1971, pp. 10–15 ff.

Schuessler, Raymond. "Bawdy Houses of the Old West," *True West*. May, 1984.

Scott, Jay. "Marshal of Fort Worth." *True Western Adventure*. December, 1959.

Sharpe, J. A. "The Criminal Past: The Face of Crime in Later Medieval England." *History Today*. January, 1988.

Shrake, Bud. "Old Days on a Mule Cart." *Fort Worth Press*. September 1, 1957.

Upchurch, J. T. "The Lawless Liquor Traffic and the Infamous Traffic in Girls." *The Purity Journal*. March, 1906.

Walker, Wayne T. "Killer in Fancy Pants." *True West*. September-October, 1956.

West, Elliott. "Wicked Dodge City." *American History Illustrated*. Special Edition, Vol. 17, No. 4, no date.

Westermeier, Clifford P. "Cowboy Sexuality, A Historical No- No?" *Red River Valley Historical Review*. Vol. 2, No. 1, Spring, 1975, pp. 92–113.

White, June. "Recollections of Fort Worth: 'We Still Wonder How They Built It, Paid for It.'" *Fort Worth News-Tribune*. September 30, 1988.

Williams, Mack. "In Old Fort Worth: A Series on the Life of Jim Courtright." *Fort Worth News-Tribune*. Six-part series, October 3, 1986–November 7, 1986.

Willis, Delbert. "Woman Dies in Fire in Small E. 15th Hotel." *Fort Worth Press*. January 26, 1962.

Wukovitz, John F. "Gunfighters and Lawmen." *Wild West*. August, 1988.

Yowell, Gordon. "Money of the Merchants." *Frontier Times*. February–March, 1966.

Interviews and Correspondence

Correspondence with author and western historian Ed Bartholomew of Fort Davis, Texas, 1988–1989.

Correspondence with author, editor and western historian Jim Dullenty of Hamilton, Montana, 1988–1989.

Interview with Mrs. Octavia Bennett, June 6, 1952, Fort Worth, Texas. Tarrant County Historical Society.

Interview with Mrs. Lenore Conway of Sacramento, California, February, 1986.

Interview with Frank DeBuque, "The Underworld of Fort Worth, Texas, or Hell's Half Acre." Tarrant County Historical Society (no date).

Interviews with Bill Jary (deceased Fort Worth author and historian), June 1983.

Interviews with Mrs. Ruby Schmidt (former president of the Tarrant County Historical Society), 1983–1989.

Public Records, Unpublished Works, and Manuscript Collections

Baker, Brookes. "Map of Fort Worth, Texas, Centennial Edition, Compiled from Deed Records and Actual Surveys." 2 vols. Fort Worth: Brookes Baker, 1949.

Copeland, David R. "Hell's Half Acre: Fort Worth's First Amusement Center, 1873–1889." Unpublished research paper in Master of Arts history program, Texas Christian University, 1969. Copy on file with Fort Worth Public Library.

Census Records for Tarrant County, 1880 and 1900. On microfilm in Fort Worth Public Library: Genealogy and Local History Department.

Fort Worth City Directories, 1877–1901. On microfiche in Fort Worth Public Library: Genealogy and Local History Department.

Fort Worth City Ordinances. Book A, Nos. 1–298, 1873–1882. City Secretary's Office, Fort Worth City Hall.

Mary Daggett Lake Papers. 5 Series. 18 boxes. In Fort Worth Public Library: Genealogy and Local History Department.

Minutes of the City Council of Fort Worth, 1873–1878. Book A. Fort Worth City Hall, City Secretary's Office.

Paddock, B. B. "Account Book, 1889–1891." Barker History Center, University of Texas at Austin.

Sanborn Fire Maps of Fort Worth. New York: Sanborn Map and Publishing Company, Ltd. Barker History Center, University of Texas at Austin.

Tarrant County Criminal Docket (Criminal Minutes), County Court, 1878–1881, 1886–87. Special Collections, University of Texas at Arlington.

Tarrant County Index to Criminal Minutes, 1893–1897. Special Collections, University of Texas at Arlington.

Tarrant County Deed Records. Tarrant County Administrative Building, Tax Research/Refund Office, Fort Worth.

Texas Baptist Historical Collection. Southwestern Baptist Theological Seminary, Fort Worth.

"Texas Writers' Project. Research Data: Fort Worth and Tarrant County, Texas." Seventy-seven bound typescript volumes plus eight volumes of indices. Fort Worth: Fort Worth Public Library Unit, 1941. Copies on file at the Fort Worth Public Library.

Tidwell, Donovan Duncan. "A History of the West Fork Baptist Association (Texas)," Th.D. dissertation for Southwestern Baptist Theological Seminary, 1940.

Appendix I

Fort Worth City Marshals and Police Chiefs, 1873–1909*
(Source: Fort Worth Police Department)

NAME	TENURE
E. S. Terrell	Apr.–Nov., 1873**
T. M. Ewing	Apr.–Nov., 1874
H. P. Shiel	1874–1875
T. P. Redding	1875–Feb., 1876
John Stocker	Feb.–Apr., 1876
T. I. Courtright	1876–1879
S. M. Farmer	1879–1883
W. M. Rea	1883–1887
S. M. Farmer	1887–1891
J. H. Maddox	1891–1897
W. M. Rea	1897–1905***
J. H. Maddox	1905–1909

*The city marshal and police chief were one and the same person, with one important distinction: the marshal was elected by popular vote in a yearly election; the chief of police was a position appointed by the City Council every year after the municipal elections. In practice the Council merely confirmed the will of the electorate when it made the marshal the chief of the city's police force, but in theory the Council always reserved the right to appoint someone else, a right which it never exercised. The threat alone was sufficient to remind the marshal that he was beholden to the City Council as well as to the voters. Until 1887, the men who held the office of marshal/police chief preferred the title "Marshal." W. M. Rea, however, preferred the more modern-sounding title "Chief." Both the newspapers and the public at large continued to refer to him as "Marshal Rea," however.

**Elections were always held at the beginning of April.

***Beginning in 1898 terms of office for city officials were extended to two years. Rea was the first marshal to be covered by this law.

Appendix II

Fort Worth Mayors, 1873–1906*
(Source: *Fort Worth Star-Telegram,* February 10, 1915)

NAME	TENURE
W. P. Burts	Feb. 17, 1873–Nov. 9, 1874
G. H. Day	1874–1876
R. E. Beckham	1876–1880
John T. Brown	1880–1882
J. Peter Smith	1882–1885
H. S. Broiles	1886–1890
W. S. Pendleton	Apr. 1890–Aug. 4, 1890 (resigned)
J. Peter Smith	1890 (special election)–1891
B. B. Paddock**	1892–1900
J. T. Powell	1900–1906

*Elected in annual elections held in April of every year. Fort Worth held its first municipal elections as an incorporated city in April, 1873.

**Second longest tenure of any Fort Worth mayor to date.

Appendix III

Tarrant County Sheriffs, 1873–1902 *
(From, Oliver Knight, *Fort Worth: Outpost on the Trinity*, pp. 249–52.)

NAME	TENURE
M. T. Morgan	???? – 1876 **
John M. Henderson	1876–1880
W. T. Maddox	1880–1886
B. H. Shipp	1886–1888
J. S. Richardson	1888–1892
E. A. Euless	1892–1896
S. P. Clark	1896–1902

* Following the Civil War and lasting until 1873, all county officials were appointed by military authorities in Texas. Starting in 1873, local elections were held without federal interference.

** Morgan, although appointed under the Reconstruction regime, continued to serve when popular elections resumed in 1873. County elections were held every two years, unlike city elections, which were annual affairs.

Appendix IV

City and County Attorneys for Fort Worth and Tarrant County, 1873–1900
(From, *Oliver Knight, Fort Worth: Outpost on the Trinity,*
pp. 275–76 and 249–51.)

CITY ATTORNEY	TENURE	COUNTY ATTORNEY	TENURE
Frank W. Bell	1873–1874	Sam Furman	1876–1878*
J. S. Chapman	1874–1877	W. S. Pendleton	1878–1884
Henry Field	1877–1881	N. R. Bowlin	1884–1886
Robert McCart	1881–1883	R. L. Carlock	1886–1890
J. W. Swayne	1883–1885	O. W. Gillespie	1890–1894
Wm. Capps	1885–1887	Burt M. Terrell	1894–1896
Ed F. Warren	1887–1889	James W. Swayne	1896–1900
J. T. Powell	1889–1893		
C. M. Templeton	1893–1897		
W. D. Williams	1897–1903		

*In 1876 Sam Furman became the first county attorney to fill that office, which did not exist before that date.

Appendix V

Fort Worth had a number of newspapers in its early years, although most were small-circulation, limited-interest farm, labor and religious journals that tended to disappear quickly. The major newspapers covering 1871 to 1903, which are of greatest importance as sources for this volume, are a special boon for the researcher trying to piece together daily events in the city. The existence of two rival papers at the same period clarifies the picture even more. Unfortunately, even the major newspapers constitute an incomplete source. There are gaps in what has been preserved on microfilm; there is no index or comprehensive guide to help the modern researcher; and of the microfilmed newspapers which do exist, some are practically unreadable due to the poor condition of the originals when they were photographed and/or the normal limitations of the photocopying process.

The major papers published between 1871 and 1903 (the *Democrat*, the *Standard* and the *Gazette*) went through a number of name changes. This tends to confuse the issue rather than clarify it because of the use of compound names and titles, the publishers adding words like "Weekly" and "Daily" to their mastheads. To clear up any confusion created by the citations used in this book, the following list of newspapers shows the evolution of titles and the years of publication, as well as the earliest year the familiar name first appeared, followed by its various permutations.

For the availability and location of specific issues, consult the Library of Congress' *Newspapers in Microform* (1984) or the older *Union List* (1937).

Fort Worth Democrat, 1871–1882 (weekly and daily).
Fort Worth Weekly Democrat, 1871–1881.
Fort Worth Daily Democrat, July 4, 1876–1882.

Fort Worth Advance, 1880–1881 (daily).
Fort Worth Democrat-Advance, 1883–1885 (daily, after combining with the *Democrat*).

Fort Worth Gazette, 1886–1898.
Fort Worth Weekly Gazette (and semi-weekly), 1886–1892.
Fort Worth Daily Gazette, 1886–March 13, 1891.
Fort Worth Gazette, 1891–1898 (daily).

Fort Worth Standard, 1873–1878(?) (weekly and daily).
Fort Worth Weekly Standard, 1873–?
Daily Fort Worth Standard, September 3, 1876–March 21, 1878.
Fort Worth Daily Standard, 1878–?

Fort Worth Morning Register, 1896–1902 (daily).

Fort Worth Record, 1903–1925 (daily).

Appendix VI

The Ballad of Hell's Half Acre

In old Fort Worth town,
Between Jones and Main,
From Tenth through Twelfth streets,
Stood a district of sin and shame,
Where once a Preacher found the Devil,
Before he met his maker,
Looking for a little heaven,
Down in "HELL'S HALF ACRE."

Inside the Passion Parlors,
And card cheat Saloons
The smell of stale cigar smoke,
Once mixed with cheap perfume.
Where Harlots were known to hustle,
A gentleman taker,
Looking for a little heaven,
Down in "HELL'S HALF ACRE."

There scarlet painted ladies
Wore red rouge on their faces,
And stood at raised windows,
In all their fallen grace.
Whores who'd tempt a man
To be one of the takers,
Looking for a little heaven,
Down in "HELL'S HALF ACRE."

Where cowboys in ten gallon hats,
Came lusting for women and sin,
And shook the trail dust off,
Their high heel boots, in the city
Where the West begins.
Where dancehall girls used blackjacks,

To roll a rowdy taker,
Looking for a little heaven,
Down in "HELL'S HALF ACRE."

It was a hangout for outlaws,
With a price on their head,
Like the Wild Bunch Gang,
Butch Cassidy and the
Sundance Kid.
Where Luke Short sent Jim Courtright,
To the undertaker,
Looking up to heaven,
Down in "HELL'S HALF ACRE."
Looking up to heaven,
FACE DOWN IN "HELL'S HALF ACRE."

Index